SharePoint 2010
Workflows in Action

SharePoint 2010
Workflows in Action

PHIL WICKLUND

MANNING

Greenwich
(74° w. long.)

For online information and ordering of this and other Manning books, please visit
www.manning.com. The publisher offers discounts on this book when ordered in quantity.
For more information, please contact

> Special Sales Department
> Manning Publications Co.
> 180 Broad Street
> Suite 1323
> Stamford, CT 06901
> Email: orders@manning.com

	Development editor:	Susan Harkins
Manning Publications Co.	Copyeditor:	Betsey Henkels
180 Broad Street, Suite 1323	Cover designer:	Marija Tudor
Stamford, CT 06901	Typesetter:	Gordan Salinovic

ISBN 9781935182719
Printed in the United States of America
1 2 3 4 5 6 7 8 9 10 – MAL – 15 14 13 12 11

brief contents

contents

vii

preface

I can't believe I'm sitting here writing the preface to my book! After the most intense six months of my career, it feels good to be at the finish line. Working on this book, I learned that I still enjoy technical writing and I still love SharePoint—and now that I'm finished, I'm remembering how much I love sleep!

What prompted me to write a book?

This book started in 2004, when I first began working with SharePoint 2003. I had been hired as a SharePoint Instructor for Mindsharp, where I was mentored by Todd Bleeker, MVP. It was Todd who inspired me to write this book. No one has a greater passion for technology and SharePoint than Todd, and watching him write several books motivated me to write my own.

The other motivating factor was my love of research. That's what I enjoy most about my career choice—taking a problem and researching the solution. SharePoint is a gargantuan product: there's an incredible amount to learn, which has made my career and writing this book fulfilling. Digging into the depths of SharePoint workflows was a boatload of fun.

After working at Mindsharp, I moved into consulting. I first dived into SharePoint workflows on a project with RBA Consulting, implementing a Visual Studio workflow solution that managed the company's business projects and initiatives. The trifecta of Visual Studio workflows, SharePoint, and InfoPath sparked my excitement for this technology.

SharePoint workflows are one of the most prevalent ROI-generating features in the SharePoint project stack. After this first round of workflow experiences, I began to see the applicability of workflows in almost every company where I consulted. And most companies have manual business processes that can stand to benefit from SharePoint workflows.

After taking this passion from company to company and building countless workflows, I realized that my experiences were source material for a book. With SharePoint 2010 on the horizon, the timing was perfect; and in May 2009, I submitted my proposal to Manning. Now, all I can say is, "The rest is history!"

acknowledgments

Many people contributed to this project during the many months I worked on it. Sincere thanks to Todd Bleeker, MVP, for inspiring me to write the book in the first place, and to Paul Grafelman and Eric Hanes, contributing authors, for sharing their expertise. Paul wrote chapters 3 and 5 about SharePoint Designer, and Eric contributed chapters 2 and 6 about out-of-the-box workflows and Office Visio.

At Manning Publications, I'd like to thank Marjan Bace; Mike Stephens; development editor Susan Harkins; and the production team of Betsey Henkels, Nermina Miller, Mary Piergies, and Gordan Salinovic. Special thanks to Wayne Ewington, MCM, for his careful technical review of the final manuscript during production.

The following reviewers offered valuable feedback after reading the manuscript several times during its development and made this a much better book as a result: Kunal Mittal, Jonas Bandi, Raymond Mitchell, Brandon Kobel, Andrew Grothe, Margriet Bruggeman, Nikander Bruggeman, Monty Grusendorf, Darren Neimke, and Berndt Hamboeck.

I'd also like to thank the readers of Manning's Early Access Program (MEAP) for their contributions and corrections posted in the online forum.

I also want to extend my thanks to my employer, RBA Consulting. It has been an honor for me to work with such a great group of people, and my family is very thankful for the employment and provision we receive through them. This book wouldn't have been possible without RBA Consulting's support as its foundation.

But most of all, I'd like to thank my wife Sarah and my three kids Adalyn, Noah, and Molly. There's no doubt in my mind that their sacrifice was greater than mine, because of the many evenings and weekends without their husband and father. To Sarah I give more credit for this book than I take for myself. Without her encouragement and cheerleading spirit, there's no doubt that I would've failed to go the distance and finish this race. Thanks, babe. I love you.

about this book

Workflows are one of the highest ROI-generating features of SharePoint. Many corporations waste millions of dollars each year on faulty and inefficient business processes. This is often because these processes are manual and, therefore, time-consuming and undependable. If you adopt SharePoint as your collaboration platform, you are likely to bring your business processes into SharePoint as well (even if you do so unintentionally). The workflow features in SharePoint are a powerhouse that you should tap into. With the help of this book, you can bring your business processes to life.

The primary goal of this book is to teach you how to build custom workflows on the SharePoint 2010 platform. To do this, you need to be comfortable with a host of tools and methodologies such as using out-of-the-box workflows, modeling workflows in Office Visio, building custom forms with InfoPath, building custom workflows with SharePoint Designer, and building custom workflows with Visual Studio. This book covers these workflow-building tools and options. The book also responds to more complicated business requirements with such solutions as state machine workflows, custom activities, workflow modifications, and external communication.

How to use this book, and who should read it

Both IT professionals (nondevelopers) and developers will find this book helpful in building SharePoint workflows. The first seven chapters cover the playing field of IT pros. This book takes no-code workflows to a much deeper level than other books attempt to do in a single chapter.

The first seven chapters are also relevant for developers. Some things that are easy and quick in SharePoint Designer would require considerable time in Visual Studio.

Making the jump to Visual Studio happens only after you determine that SharePoint Designer won't be sufficient. Then, chapters 8 through 12 focus on how to build the most advanced solutions with Visual Studio.

Roadmap

This book is divided into three parts.

Part 1, "Introduction to SharePoint workflows," introduces workflows, discusses where SharePoint comes into play, and explains which tools to use and how to configure one of the out-of-the-box workflows:

- Chapter 1 gets you started with workflows by introducing you to the types of SharePoint workflows and their architecture. It also introduces tools you can use to build custom workflows and provides a list of workflow features that are new with the release of SharePoint 2010.
- Chapter 2 leads you through the workflow basics by helping you use an out-of-the-box workflow, the Three State workflow. You'll see how to add and remove workflows, start and stop workflows, and view a workflow's history.

In part 2, "No-code SharePoint workflows," the book transitions into how to build custom workflows without writing code. Chapters 5 to 7 will be right up the alley of folks who aren't programmers, although programmers shouldn't skip these chapters. As a seasoned programmer, I use no-code workflow techniques more frequently than coding techniques:

- Chapter 3 takes you through your first custom workflow, using a tool called SharePoint Designer. This tool provides an intuitive user interface to create custom workflows; the chapter leads you through this interface and the core actions that your workflow can perform.
- Chapter 4 takes a SharePoint Designer workflow to the next level by discussing task processing within workflows. Almost all workflows revolve around human interaction, which you can accomplish by issuing tasks.
- Chapter 5 extends SharePoint Designer workflows further by covering techniques such as templates and workflows involved in document sets and security. The chapter also covers workflow interactions with external data via Business Continuity Services.
- Chapter 6 digs into business analyses connected with workflows by introducing Office Visio workflows. The chapter covers the technique of diagramming a workflow in Visio and subsequently importing that workflow into SharePoint Designer.
- Chapter 7 discusses using custom forms with InfoPath. SharePoint workflows and InfoPath are coupled together. For an InfoPath and SharePoint newbie, this is a great introduction. You'll learn how to customize the out-of-the-box forms, publish custom forms to content types, and map form data to columns.

In part 3, "Custom-coded SharePoint workflows," you'll put on your development hat and learn how to build the most complex workflows:

- Chapter 8 is the first chapter in which you use Visual Studio to build a custom workflow. The chapter covers how workflows are packaged and deployed into SharePoint. Then, we discuss sequential workflows and state-machine workflows.
- Chapter 9 takes the Visual Studio workflow discussion further by demonstrating how to introduce custom forms into your workflows. The chapter covers both Info-Path and ASP.NET forms, as well as association, initiation, and modification forms.
- Chapter 10 covers task-edit forms. The chapter is dedicated to task processing in custom Visual Studio SharePoint workflows.
- Chapter 11 is focused on how to build custom activities for your Visual Studio workflows. The chapter leads you through how to publish those custom activities into SharePoint Designer as actions. We also cover custom conditions for SharePoint Designer.
- Chapter 12 is a compilation of shorter but valuable workflow developer techniques. These include how to debug and handle errors in your workflows. We discuss versioning workflows, as well as workflow events. The chapter ends with a brief discussion of the workflow object model.

Code conventions and downloads

All code in the book is presented in a `fixed-width font like this` to separate it from ordinary text. Code annotations accompany many of the listings, highlighting important concepts. In some cases, numbered bullets link to explanations that follow the listing.

In longer code examples, only the important code segments are included in the book. You will find the full code for all the examples in the book available for download from the publisher's website at www.manning.com/wicklund or www.manning.com/SharePoint2010WorkflowsinAction.

Software requirements

Because this is a SharePoint 2010 workflow book, you'll obviously need Share-Point 2010. If you're a programmer, this will include a SharePoint development workstation where you have your own local instance of SharePoint 2010. For nondevelopers, browser access to a SharePoint site is sufficient. Workflow in SharePoint 2010 is a feature of SharePoint Foundation, which means SharePoint Server isn't required. But if your workflow will use server features such as InfoPath Forms Server, you may need SharePoint Server, Microsoft Office Visio 2010, SharePoint Designer 2010, and Visual Studio 2010 (for developers).

Author Online

The purchase of *SharePoint 2010 Workflows in Action* includes free access to the private online forum hosted by Manning Publications. There comments can be made, questions can be asked, and help can be given, all on a voluntary basis by the authors and other forum geeks. You can access the forum for this book at www.manning.com/SharePoint2010WorkflowsinAction.

About the author

PHIL WICKLUND has worked with SharePoint since 2004. He started in the SharePoint space as a developer and trainer for Mindsharp, a SharePoint training company. Today, as a SharePoint consultant at RBA Consulting, Phil shares real-world insights and in-depth best practices with clients on a wide range of projects, including architecting a SharePoint solution for a 100K user partner portal, a 70K user intranet, and a 60K heavily customized MySite implementation. Phil maintains an active SharePoint blog at http://philwicklund.com.

Phil lives in Minnesota with his wife Sarah and three children, Adalyn, Noah, and Molly. His hobbies include reading, hunting, home remodeling, and admittedly, mowing the lawn.

About the contributing authors

PAUL GRAFELMAN (chapters 3 and 5) has been in the IT industry for the past 10 years, after earning his bachelor's degree at Bemidji State University in Northern Minnesota. Paul has been a SharePoint consultant since 2006 when MOSS 2007 was first released. His focus is on infrastructure and out-of-the-box capabilities, with occasional forays into custom development. In addition to consulting, Paul participates in community events and teaches other consultants at RBA Consulting about SharePoint and its capabilities. Paul lives in the Minneapolis area with his wife Lani and two children, Danica and Milaina.

ERIC HANES (chapters 2 and 6) has worked in the IT industry for more than 15 years and has been heavily involved with SharePoint for the last 7. Eric is an information architect and a business analyst, a combination that gives him a unique perspective and the ability to craft solutions based on Business Process Management (BPM) and User Experience Design. Additionally, Eric has experience in dealing with leadership in both the business and technical domains. At this intersection of business acumen and technical depth, Eric is a high-powered liaison within customer organizations who can problem-solve while dealing with technical design.

About the technical reviewer

WAYNE EWINGTON is a principal consultant for Microsoft Consulting Services based in Auckland, New Zealand. He focuses primarily on technologies such as SharePoint (MSS, MSF, MOSS, and WSS), as well as development tools such as Visual Studio Team System (VSTS) and Team Foundation Server (TFS). Wayne is a Microsoft Certified Master on SharePoint 2010 and was one of the first to obtain this certification in Australasia. As a principal consultant, Wayne works with clients and partners, assisting them with the successful deployment and use of Microsoft technologies. During his spare time, he enjoys renovating his 104-year-old house and spending time with his wife and two daughters.

about the title

By combining introductions, overviews, and how-to examples, the *In Action* books are designed to help learning and remembering. According to research in cognitive science, the things people remember are things they discover during self-motivated exploration.

Although no one at Manning is a cognitive scientist, we are convinced that for learning to become permanent it must pass through stages of exploration, play, and, interestingly, retelling of what is being learned. People understand and remember new things, which is to say they master them, only after actively exploring them. Humans learn in action. An essential part of an *In Action* book is that it's example-driven. It encourages the reader to try things out, to play with new code, and explore new ideas.

There is another, more mundane, reason for the title of this book: our readers are busy. They use books to do a job or solve a problem. They need books that allow them to jump in and jump out easily and learn just what they want just when they want it. They need books that aid them in action. The books in this series are designed for such readers.

about the cover illustration

The figure on the cover of *SharePoint 2010 Workflows in Action* is captioned "A man from Draganić, near Karlovac, Croatia." The illustration is taken from a reproduction of an album of traditional Croatian costumes from the mid-nineteenth century by Nikola Arsenovic, published by the Ethnographic Museum in Split, Croatia, in 2003. The illustrations were obtained from a helpful librarian at the Ethnographic Museum in Split, itself situated in the Roman core of the medieval center of the town: the ruins of Emperor Diocletian's retirement palace from around AD 304. The book includes finely colored illustrations of figures from different regions of Croatia, accompanied by descriptions of the costumes and of everyday life.

Draganić is a small town in Karlovac County located in central Croatia. The man on the cover is wearing a costume typical to this region. Over a white shirt, he dons a waistcoat with double buttons. His jacket and pants are made of white wool with blue embroidered edges. He tops the outfit with a black hat and a tie around his neck. He also carries a red woolen bag over his shoulder and is wearing high black boots.

Dress codes and lifestyles have changed over the last 200 years, and the diversity by region, so rich at the time, has faded away. It is now hard to tell apart the inhabitants of different continents, let alone of different hamlets or towns separated by only a few miles. Perhaps we have traded cultural diversity for a more varied personal life—certainly for a more varied and fast-paced technological life.

Manning celebrates the inventiveness and initiative of the computer business with book covers based on the rich diversity of regional life of two centuries ago, brought back to life by illustrations from old books and collections like this one.

Part 1

Introduction to SharePoint workflows

This book is divided into three parts. With part 1, my goal is really just to introduce you to SharePoint workflows. Chapter 1 kicks this off by informing you of the types of workflows as well as what SharePoint objects on top of which you can run workflows. You'll also see an overview of the various tools used in the building of custom workflows, as well as the new workflow features that are a part of the 2010 release of SharePoint.

Chapter 1 also takes you through the process of analyzing and diagramming a workflow. This process is important to go through because different types of workflows won't work well for some tooling choices.

Chapter 2 puts workflows into practices. You'll be lead through the process of creating your first workflow utilizing one of the out-of-the-box workflows in Share-Point. In addition, you'll get familiar with how to configure and administer workflows. This includes learning how to add and remove workflows, start and stop workflows, and view a workflow's status and history. At the end of the chapter, you'll find high-level business cases for the rest of the out-of-the-box workflows.

SharePoint workflows for your business processes

1

This chapter covers
- Introducing SharePoint workflows
- Adding workflows on SharePoint objects
- Building a custom workflow
- New workflow features in SharePoint 2010

Business processes surround us and affect the typical employee daily. Whether you like it or not, the company you work for depends heavily on processes to get things done and be profitable. Someone who makes burgers at a fast food outlet, for example, has to follow a specific process that will transform raw materials into a finished burger.

Workflows are systems that manage the execution of a business process. They solve many of the most troubling problems that workers face. The burger outlet process is simple, but there's no doubt that large companies have complicated business processes, and it can be difficult to determine how far a process has progressed and what is delaying it.

Consider how often business processes are hindered because of poor communication. Does your business process live or die entirely by email? Email has become the default communication method for everything from conversations and decisions to tasks and documents. Consider a process that runs when a new person is hired into your company. That employee needs a new account, email, badge, phone number, benefits, direct deposit, and contract. In many cases, getting all that accomplished involves many people who communicate through email. Inevitably, things get lost. Email works for small companies, but what happens if you onboard 50 people per day? You need a system that will manage all of these activities; otherwise, you'll have confusion and inefficiencies. You need a workflow.

This chapter defines a workflow and shows how it relates to your business processes. We'll talk about how workflows function within the Microsoft® SharePoint platform and the architecture of a SharePoint workflow. After you've learned those basics, we'll take a closer look at all the tools and applications that go into building workflows in SharePoint and you'll discover numerous options. Beyond this introductory chapter is a world where your business processes come to life. The rest of the book is about building your company's workflows on the SharePoint platform. So, let's make sure we're all speaking the same language.

1.1   What is a workflow?

A workflow is primarily described as a process that manages the flow of work among individuals, offices, departments, or entire companies. Some work depends on numerous people or systems for completion. As these recurring dependencies are identified in a company, a business process emerges. Business processes run throughout a company and are often similar even in companies of different types.

Take, for instance, a business process that manages expense reports. Most companies need a defined business process to manage the submission and approval of employees' monthly expenses. The flow of work in figure 1.1 shows an employee tracking his expenses and then submitting them electronically to a manager.

The flow is based on a business logic that determines who needs to approve the expenses and how the individual is reimbursed. A workflow helps to negotiate the execution of the steps in a process like this.

Business processes run regardless of whether a workflow manages them. Some

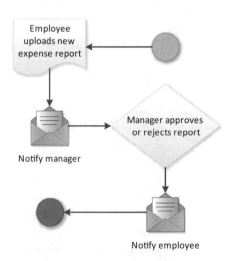

Figure 1.1   A workflow is generically described as a business process. This example shows a common workflow that manages an expense-reporting business process.

business processes are self-contained and easy for people to manage. Others are much more complicated and difficult for people to comprehend.

It's with these more complicated business processes that workflows show their value to a company.

Workflows can bring value to a company by highlighting where in the business process the flow of work is currently executing. Workflows can also help a company automate their business processes. Consider again the expense report example. If your business process allows for all food expenses less than $100 to be automatically approved and sent to accounts payable for reimbursement, the workflow could manage this business logic and automatically approve the expense, without having to directly involve your manager.

Workflows are also good at managing parallel processes or multiple instances of work running at the same time, for example, in a manufacturing company. A car manufacturer could have a workflow for the engine construction, and another for the frame, and another for the interior. Then a parent workflow could manage all of the *child* workflows and start another process as soon as a dependent workflow finishes.

It's easy to see that your investing in workflows would help to manage and automate your company's business processes. Minimizing human dependencies in business processes always saves a company's money. Because human costs are always the most expensive investment a company makes, let's make the people in our organizations work as efficiently and effectively as possible. That's what makes workflows such a great investment.

1.2   How does SharePoint help?

A SharePoint workflow is an automated flow of objects through a sequence of operations that are related to a business process. An object in SharePoint is a document or an item in a list like an announcement or a task. For example, one of the workflows that you get when you install SharePoint is the Approval workflow. You can attach this workflow to a document in a document library and specify individuals who need to approve the document for use before another action can occur.

> ### SharePoint document libraries
> SharePoint, in addition to being a collaboration platform (teammates sharing information), is a document management system. A document library in SharePoint is the tool you can use to upload documents into SharePoint.

The expense report system (figure 1.1) is a common example of document library use. Within SharePoint, users can upload their expense reports into a document library. The upload action will initiate the Approval workflow on the document, and a series of individuals will receive an email stating they need to approve the expense report. When all those individuals have approved the expense report, the document can be routed to the payroll team site where a payroll officer processes the expense report.

A SharePoint workflow, like the document Approval workflow, could be set up to manage the business process from start to finish. The workflow will handle all user interaction within the system. It will also manage the point of execution in the workflow. Additionally, SharePoint will provide an out-of–the-box user interface that reports on the status of the workflow, or, more specifically, who must act on the workflow before it can continue, or if it has finished executing.

This out-of-the-box experience is a compelling reason to manage your business processes within SharePoint, because it provides a user interface and other workflow fundamentals like security, reporting, and logging. These features make SharePoint workflows and your business processes a powerful combination.

Another great strength of SharePoint workflows is that individuals who are not technically savvy can configure their workflows directly through the browser window. Consider the expense report system again. If a company built this system from scratch, it would cost much more time and money because they would not have all the fundamental components that SharePoint provides out of the box. Rather, you can empower your end users to build these business processes and, at the most basic level, all they need is a browser and possibly a few minutes. That's cost effective!

In figure 1.2, notice that you can manage the settings of the document library that contains expense reports.

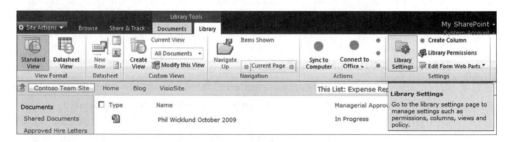

Figure 1.2 **To manage workflows on a list or library, go to that list or library's Settings page.**

In Library Settings, there's a Workflow Settings link under the Permissions and Management heading. On the Workflow Settings page (figure 1.3), you can add a workflow to a library. Select Add a workflow and choose the one you want. It's that easy!

After adding the workflow to the library and initiating the workflow process, a new column (figure 1.4) will display in the document on which the workflow process is running.

This column will track the execution point of the workflow. The workflow

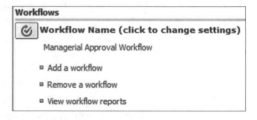

Figure 1.3 **Within the Settings page of a list or a library, you can add a workflow.**

Figure 1.4
After a workflow is started on a list item or document, an autogenerated column appears, showing the workflow status.

might be halfway through the process, waiting for user interaction. A manager might need to approve the expense before it can continue. This status would show up in the new column such as Pending Manager Approval. After the workflow has finished, Completed will show in this column.

1.3 SharePoint as a technology platform

We've been discussing a workflow from a business perspective and its execution within SharePoint. This only scratches the surface of SharePoint workflow foundations. SharePoint workflows leverage a separate platform called Windows Workflow Foundation (WF), which is part of the .NET 3.0 application development framework. This foundation has many applications totally unrelated to SharePoint—in fact, you can use WF to build all sorts of workflow-enabled business applications that never touch or interact with SharePoint. SharePoint benefits an application developer by providing a robust user interface and implementing the necessary persistence services required to run WF workflows. This means that SharePoint will manage the persistence of a workflow if it becomes idle and provide a user interface that end users can employ to start and stop workflows and determine where the workflow is executing. For example, the expense report workflow needs to be persisted as it awaits a manager's approval.

SharePoint also has out-of-the-box workflows built on top of the programming layer (figure 1.5) and, with tools like SharePoint Designer, you can customize those workflows if they don't meet your requirements. If you determine that a custom workflow is necessary, it's important to consider what type of workflow your custom workflow would need. The WF architecture and SharePoint support two types of workflows—sequential and state machine. Each type supports a unique type of business processes. Before we dig into the differences between these two types, let's take a look at the architecture of the foundation we're building on.

1.3.1 Windows Workflow Foundation architecture

The WF architecture is built upon three main tiers of services: the hosting layer (first tier), the runtime layer (second tier), and the programming layer (third tier) as seen in figure 1.5. You could say that SharePoint workflows sit on top of the third tier's services as its foundation. Out-of-the-box workflows, SharePoint Designer workflows, Visual Studio workflows, and our expense report example would build on top of this foundation.

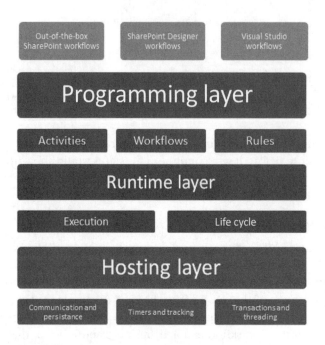

Figure 1.5   **SharePoint workflows build on three layers of the Windows Workflow Foundation architecture. The programming layer is the interface between SharePoint and WF and resides on top of the core layers that manage the runtime and hosting.**

HOSTING LAYER

A workflow is not an application and needs a host process in which to run. Similarly, if you install the .NET framework on a server, you don't have a line of business applications when you click Finish on the install wizard. WF acts as a platform you build on. From a hosting perspective, the WF requires the application to implement a few things to keep the lights on.

As previously mentioned, part of what is required of the application is the host process. The application must also provide persistence capabilities. A workflow is typically long running, meaning that it may start and then suspend for a while, possibly even many months. The *state* of the workflow needs to be persisted while the workflow is waiting for an action to occur and, when that action occurs, the workflow should resume where it left off.

Another area of responsibility for the hosting layer is to provide timer and tracking capabilities. As previously mentioned, a workflow may be suspended as it waits for an external action to occur or it may be time bound. For example, maybe the expense report workflow assigns a task to the manager to approve the report, but that task is not completed for seven days. At that point, the workflow wakes up and reassigns the task to someone in payroll. This also relates to tracking, in that you'll want to know, or track, where in the process the workflow is currently executing. In a nutshell, this is part of the responsibility of the timer and the tracking aspect of the host process. Transactions are another important aspect of the hosting framework, in that you can leverage transactions to roll a workflow back to a previous state if an error occurs, for example.

RUNTIME LAYER

This layer represents all the core services that come with WF. For instance, at runtime, the tracking, scheduling, and persistence services are all performing WF-critical activities that negotiate the workflow's execution and life cycle. This layer has interfaces that the hosting layer uses to connect the outside world to the WF engine.

PROGRAMMING LAYER

The programming layer is the SharePoint developers' favorite layer and is typically the only layer they need to worry about. This layer has out-of-the-box activities (actions for SharePoint Designer workflows) that can perform various functions in the workflow, and it allows for custom activities and rules that workflows interact with. Activities are the building blocks of a workflow. Activities do the work. A workflow is a structure that contains the activities and manages the choice and the timing of activities' execution. Rules allow the developer to declaratively create business logic that the Visual Studio workflow can use to structure its activities. For example, rather than hard-coding logic into the workflow, you can create a rule for that logic. Then, subsequent changes to the rule won't require an update to the workflow's dynamic-link library (DLL). Conditions in SharePoint Designer are loosely similar to rules in Visual Studio workflows.

1.3.2 *Types of workflows*

Workflows execute from one to another step in the process in two ways. A workflow is either sequential—in that the steps within the workflow execute sequentially, one after another—or a workflow is a state machine, whereby it executes in no particular order. A sequential workflow always progresses forward, never going back to a previous step (figure 1.6).

A state machine, on the other hand, has no such constraint but moves from one state to another until the logic concludes the workflow has completed. A good example of a state machine is a bug tracking workflow that tracks bugs in a computer program (figure 1.7).

When the workflow starts, the bug may be placed in a pending state, where it waits for a developer to be assigned to the bug and begin working on the bug. Thereafter, the developer starts working on the bug and fixes it, putting the bug into a fixed state. When a bug is fixed, a tester tries to confirm the resolution of the bug. If they find that it was not fixed, they place the bug back into a pending state. This ability to go back in time or to a previous state is only available with state machine workflows.

Figure 1.6   A sample sequential workflow that, in the process, always advances forward, never backward

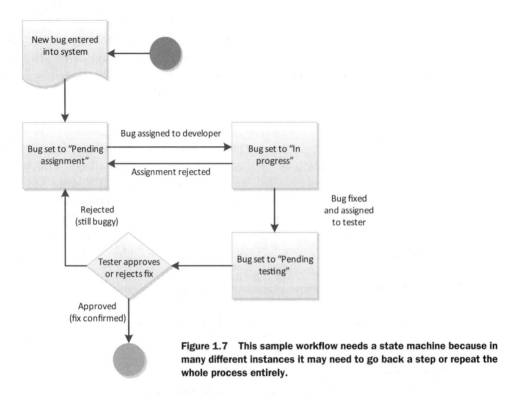

Figure 1.7   This sample workflow needs a state machine because in many different instances it may need to go back a step or repeat the whole process entirely.

Some business processes will require a state machine and others won't. It's important to think through the requirements of your business processes before you begin building a custom workflow because it's difficult to change a workflow from being a sequential workflow to a state machine workflow and vice versa. As you progress through this book, you'll notice that some workflow tools can do only sequential workflows (as with SharePoint Designer), whereas other tools can do both types (as with Visual Studio). If you start building a workflow with a tool, and that tool doesn't support state machines, you may find yourself starting over when you realize you need to change course. The bottom line is—understand the business requirements to determine which type of workflow is required before you start.

1.4   *Workflow-enabled SharePoint objects*

Now that you have an understanding of what a workflow is, you might be wondering how a workflow displays and shares information with users. For that task, SharePoint workflows depend on many different types of objects, such as lists, list items, libraries, documents, forms, content types, site columns, views, web parts, sites, and site collections. Going back to our expense report example, the workflow runs on a document that was uploaded in the document library. In addition to documents, there are several other types of SharePoint objects that workflows can execute on.

1.4.1   *List items*

As with documents, workflows can run on generic SharePoint list items. For instance, you could set up an approval process on an announcement list. With this setup, announcements won't be displayed to end users until they're approved. Another effective use of list items is on task lists and issues lists (both are out-of-the-box SharePoint list types). When a task or issue is assigned to someone, and that individual resolves the task or issue, a workflow might forward the task to another individual who is responsible for verifying its completion before it can be finalized. If that individual finds an error, the Workflow could reassign the list item back to the original user. Figure 1.8 shows the workflows menu item on a list item.

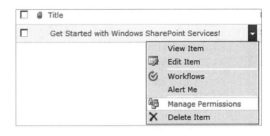

Figure 1.8   To start a workflow on a list item or document, click the dropdown on that item, and then select the Workflows menu item to take you to a page where you can initiate a new workflow instance.

Through this menu item, you can start a new workflow instance on the item.

1.4.2   *InfoPath forms*

When an InfoPath form has its data stored in a form library (figure 1.9), it's considered a document and it falls under the document library category of SharePoint objects.

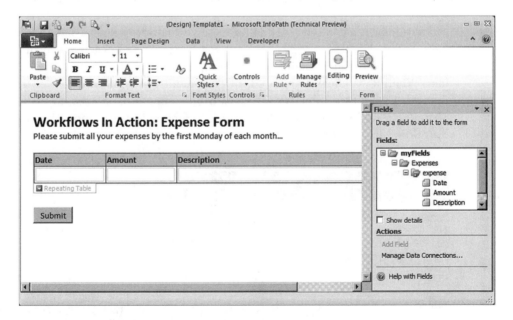

Figure 1.9   InfoPath forms are excellent tools for developing custom forms for your workflows. This example shows the InfoPath Office client in design mode.

It's commonplace to attach a workflow to a form. Take, for instance, the expense report system. Often, a company requires their employees to use a standard expense report template. Such template usually has special requirements and a look unique to that company. The Microsoft Office InfoPath 2010 client application is an effective tool for building forms that your users can fill out.

The strength of InfoPath is its ability to make form creation easy even for novice users. If you're familiar with Microsoft Word, you'll catch on to InfoPath quickly. Info-Path gives you the flexibility to control the look and feel of a form. You have far more user interface flexibility with InfoPath than with an Excel document. As with Microsoft Office documents, workflows can be bound to an InfoPath form and, when the user fills out all the appropriate areas in the form, the workflow can manage the business process behind it and get that form approved or denied. We discuss other form options in section 1.6.4 of this chapter and in greater detail in chapters 7 and 9.

1.4.3   *Content types*

Content types in SharePoint are an important concept; however, they are already highly documented elsewhere and won't be covered in great detail in this book. At a basic level, content types are a way to package pieces of metadata and make metadata collections reusable. For instance, let's say you wanted three columns on every list or library in your site collection. Rather than go to each list and add each column manually, you can create a content type that has those three columns and then add the content type to the lists or libraries. This can be a significant time saver and provide substantial reuse benefits when you need to make changes to the content type.

Additionally, a content type can have one or many workflows assigned to it. If you have a complex business process with many types of workflows that all need to execute simultaneously, deploying that workflow to a content type may be a good idea. When a workflow is deployed into a content type, new instances of that workflow can be initiated wherever list items of that content type exist no matter which SharePoint list they reside in. This introduces reusability across more than one list to your workflow.

Note the new expense report dropdown (figure 1.10).

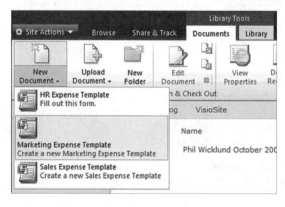

Figure 1.10   Workflows often run on a content type. As you add content types to a list or library, more options appear in the new dropdown allowing you to select a content type.

This demonstrates how you can use content types to allow several different expense report templates, for example, one for each department in the company. The form and workflow for the HR department's expense reports may be different from the workflow for the sales department, in which case using two different content types would allow users to choose a form and workflow that suites them.

1.4.4   SharePoint sites

You can also bind a workflow to a SharePoint site, which is then called a site workflow. While all of the other SharePoint object examples boil down to list items (whether it be a document, form, or content type), a workflow deployed onto a site can run actions on and react to events across all lists, document libraries, and items in that site. For example, take a site that has many document libraries and many documents in each. A workflow that would be well suited for running at the site level could check each document within that site and ensure that all the documents have been routed for approval and that none have been declined. Workflows can execute across an entire SharePoint site and are initiated from within View Site Content.

1.5   Out-of-the-box SharePoint workflows

Now that you have an idea of all the types of objects in SharePoint on which work-flows execute, we should explore further the workflows that come out of the box. In section 1.2 of this chapter, we introduced the Approval workflow. This is one of several workflows that are available in SharePoint. SharePoint provides six workflows out of the box that end users can configure on their sites. You don't need to be a programmer to introduce valuable workflows into your organization. These workflows are available for adding to various SharePoint objects right through the user interface and require little if any configuration. Figure 1.11 shows the Start a New Workflow page for an Excel document in SharePoint.

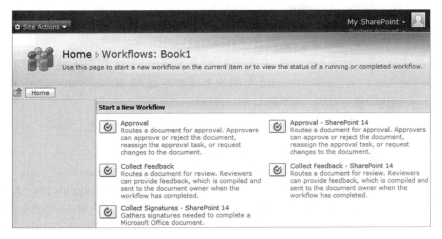

Figure 1.11   The out-of-the-box workflows that come in SharePoint. This is a list of out-of-the-box workflows that can be started on an Excel document.

It's easy to start a workflow that kicks off a wizard-like experience for end user configuration. Let's get a bird's eye view of all of the out-of-the-box workflows.

CHECK OUT CHAPTER 2 FOR MORE DETAIL   Refer to the last section in chapter 2, "Additional out-of-the-box workflows," for a more detailed overview and a flow diagram of each of the six workflows.

1.5.1   *Three-state workflow*

The Three-state workflow by default is leveraged on issue tracking lists in SharePoint. The issue tracking list tracks an issue through three states—Active, Ready for Review, and Complete. This workflow can be customized and used in other lists or in custom SharePoint lists, and the names of the three states are configurable.

SHAREPOINT FOUNDATION VERSUS SHAREPOINT SERVER   When you install SharePoint, you have at least SharePoint Foundation installed. SharePoint Server on the other hand is an add-on, which is installed on top of SharePoint Foundation. You get a few extra out-of-the-box workflows when you purchase the Server. Foundation comes with only one workflow—the Three-state workflow. Server gives an additional five out–of-the-box workflows. Regardless of which version of SharePoint you install, you have all of the functionality for building custom workflows.

1.5.2   *Approval workflow*

One of the simplest workflows, the Approval workflow is certainly the most popular. It involves routing a piece of SharePoint content to all designated approvers requesting their approval or denial of the content. The submission process can either be serial, where the order of approvers is predetermined, or parallel, where any approver can approve at any time.

1.5.3   *Collect Feedback workflow*

The Collect Feedback workflow gives submitter the ability to acquire feedback for their peers on the status of the submitted document. This workflow routes the document to the specified team members, in which case each can weigh in and contribute their feedback on the document. After it has circulated through the team, the feedback is compiled and the submitter is notified.

1.5.4   *Collect Signatures workflow*

An alternative to the Approval workflow where the approval process makes no changes to the document, the Collect Signatures workflow will require each approver to place a digital signature on the document. After those signatures have been acquired through the workflow, you can take the document off line and the approval will still be recognizable. Note that this workflow can only be initiated from the Office client, such as Microsoft Office Word. It cannot be initiated from the browser like other workflows can.

1.5.5 Disposition Approval workflow

This workflow allows you to manage document expiration and retention. This enables you to decide what will happen to documents when they expire. A possible option, instead of deleting a document, is to archive it and send email notifications.

1.5.6 Translation Management workflow

Use this workflow to help facilitate the manual process of translating office documents from one language to another. This workflow works with two list types—a Translation Management Library and a translators list. A document that needs to be translated is uploaded into the Translation Management Library, and translators in the translators list receive tasks to start translating the source document into their respective languages. When all the translation tasks are completed, the Translation Management workflow is completed.

1.6 Tools for building custom SharePoint workflows

Under the SharePoint umbrella, there are many layers of tools for a variety of audiences to use when building your SharePoint workflows. Some of them are entirely optional, and others are not. An end user might love digging into SharePoint Designer but be daunted by Visual Studio, yet Visual Studio may be necessary for what they're trying to do. It's critical to know about all the available tools, how they can be helpful, and what purpose each serves.

1.6.1 SharePoint Designer 2010

SharePoint Designer is a powerful tool that can be used to customize SharePoint sites. Many of its unique capabilities are used to change the look and feel (brand) of a site, create, add, and move web parts, and bring list data and external data onto SharePoint pages. You can do a great deal in SharePoint Designer including building workflows.

Building workflows with SharePoint Designer is a popular and widely used approach. The tool is easy to use because it provides the user with a wizard-like experience (figure 1.12) that is more familiar than the Visual Studio's code editor.

SharePoint Designer isn't a tool for the average end user, however. Microsoft would categorize the tool in the power users group—people who are not programmers but who are savvy enough to be proficient with other Microsoft Office tools like Excel and Access. Using SharePoint Designer is unlike using the browser, where things are simpler and more intuitive. This book will cover SharePoint Designer workflows in much greater depth in chapters 3, 4, and 5.

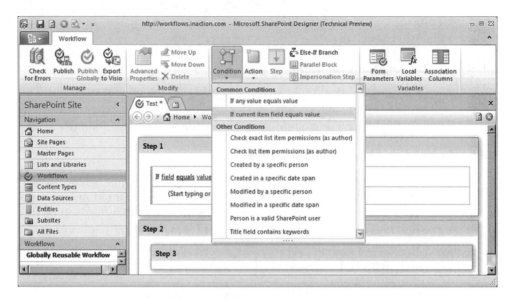

Figure 1.12   The SharePoint Designer workflow engine provides a rich suite of customizations for workflows, allowing you to easily meet unique and sometimes complex workflow requirements

1.6.2   Visual Studio.NET 2010

Although SharePoint Designer is a highly usable and robust workflow tool, your business requirements might require more than SharePoint Designer can deliver. This is where building custom workflows within Visual Studio comes into play. Visual Studio adds flexibility in terms of the types of activities your workflow can perform. This is because Visual Studio provides a full fidelity development experience, whereas Share-Point Designer is wizard based.

Visual Studio gives you a designer interface into which you can drop activities. Also, each workflow and activity will have its own code that you can call into or extend. Workflows built in Visual Studio leverage the .NET 3.5 Framework, and the Windows Workflow Foundation platform. Windows Workflow Foundation workflows can be packaged and deployed into SharePoint. This will allow you to meet even the most complicated business requirements.

Figure 1.13 shows what a workflow looks like within Visual Studio. The various activities are laid out on the workflow designer surface. By looking at the activity names and how they're associated with one another, you can see what the workflow is doing.

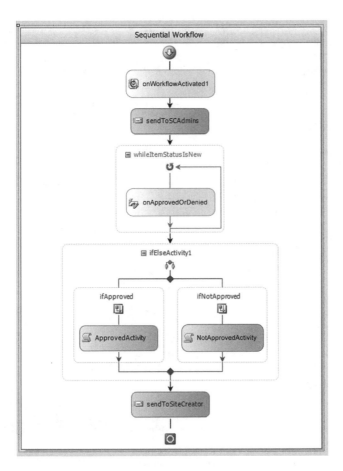

Figure 1.13   Visual Studio is the utmost in workflow customization flexibility. This is a view of the workflow designer surface within Visual Studio.

1.6.3   *Visio 2010*

Microsoft Office Visio 2010 comes with an excellent new feature for SharePoint workflow implementers—a new template called Microsoft SharePoint Workflow. This template (figure 1.14) allows business analysts to model custom workflows that need to be built out by power users (in SharePoint Designer) or developers (in Visual Studio).

In earlier versions of Visio, you could do this using a generic flowchart template and adding shapes and connectors onto the Visio designer surface to model out the basic flow of events. With the new SharePoint Workflow template, power end users or developers can take the work you have done in Visio and import it into SharePoint Designer and then into Visual Studio. This reuse saves time and benefits the requirements integrity because of the connectedness among tools. Details on how to implement a Visio 2010 SharePoint workflow will be discussed in chapter 6.

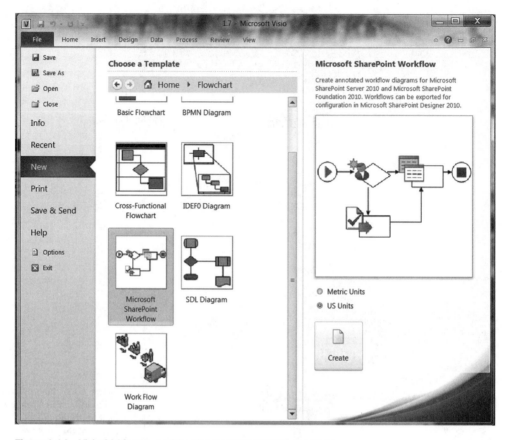

**Figure 1.14   Visio 2010 comes with a SharePoint workflow template
that can be used to model your business process before you build it.**

1.6.4   *Forms*

Forms and SharePoint workflows make a powerful combination. Much of the data in a business process is captured within a form and, thereafter, the business process reacts to the values specified in the form. For an expense reporting workflow, employees typically fill out a form and enter their expenses. Submitting the form will initiate a business process to retrieve approval for that expense. Countless other form and workflow combinations can be found in an average business. Common form examples include forms for gathering personal information (health insurance benefits), purchase order requests, invoices, paid-time-off requests, new SharePoint site requests, and helpdesk tickets. This strong relationship between a business process and a form makes SharePoint workflows and forms a powerful combination. The retention and digital availability of form data, paired with the automation of these business critical processes, realizes substantial return on investment to an organization. Paper is the past, and workflows are the future!

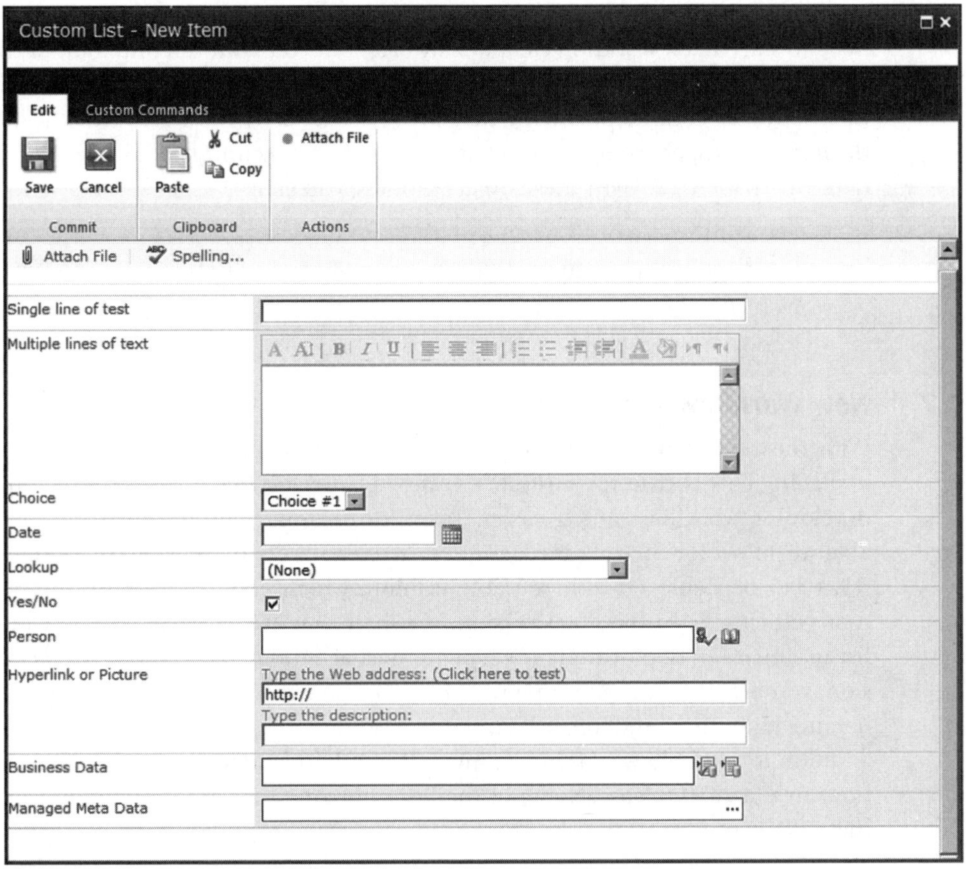

Figure 1.15 An example of a form where a user can enter and submit data. Forms and workflows are powerful combinations. A workflow often reacts to a user's submitting information in a form.

In SharePoint, three main tools are used in the building forms that workflows can execute on. You can use the out-of-the-box forms that SharePoint allows you to build by adding metadata to lists and libraries. For more complicated forms, you can use Office InfoPath 2010 and ASP.NET forms. InfoPath is an excellent nonprogrammer form design tool for end users, while ASP.NET tries to resolve the most demanding requirements developers face. Figure 1.15 shows a sample out-of-the-box form in SharePoint that can be used to gather information from a user and kick off a workflow.

Chapter 7 offers detailed instructions on form fundamentals such as building custom InfoPath forms and using forms in SharePoint Designer workflows. For Visual Studio workflow form, refer to chapter 9.

1.6.5 Object models

At times, you may need to programmatically interact with workflows through custom code. An example is when there's a custom report that shows the statuses of various business-critical workflows on a manager's dashboard. Another example is when you need to start a new workflow on a weekly basis but you want the initiation of that workflow to be automatic and independent of human interaction. Both of these cases lend themselves to code deployment that programmatically interacts with the workflows through the respective object models. Object model techniques will also be covered in detail in chapter 12. With these object models, you can:

- Start or stop a workflow on a SharePoint object.
- Get a list of the running workflows on a SharePoint object.
- Detect and delete orphaned workflows.
- Report on the state of a workflow.

1.7 New workflow functions

With the release of SharePoint 2010, a host of new functionalities for workflows is available. This is true for custom workflows, where a few of the new features make developing workflows much easier. Take, for example, the introduction of the reusable workflow for SharePoint Designer 2010. With 2010, SharePoint Designer workflows can be deployed in a reusable fashion, which enables Designer users to work more efficiently. In the 2007 version, you had to recreate each workflow onto every list instance for deployment (except for Visual Studio workflows). In the 2010 version, you create and maintain a workflow in a single place. Moreover, you can install it onto many lists and receive updates if someone edits the original workflow. In addition to reusable workflows, many useful enhancements have been made to workflows in the 2010 release. Some of the key improvements are outlined in the sections that follow.

1.7.1 Visio 2010 SharePoint workflows

The new functionality in Office Visio 2010 will delight SharePoint business analysts. With Visio 2010, you can model your SharePoint workflows and leverage that model to help elicit business approval. The best part is that, after you've solidified the high-level flow, you can export the workflow as a template and import it into SharePoint Designer and start building all the steps! This will greatly improve the efficiency of requirements gathering and translation for developers. See chapter 6 for more information.

1.7.2 Customizing the out-of-the-box workflows

Have you ever used an out-of-the-box workflow in SharePoint 2007 but realized that it didn't do exactly what you required it to do? If so, you'll be pleased to hear that these out-of-the-box workflows can be customized in SharePoint Designer 2010 (figure 1.16). See chapter 5 for more information.

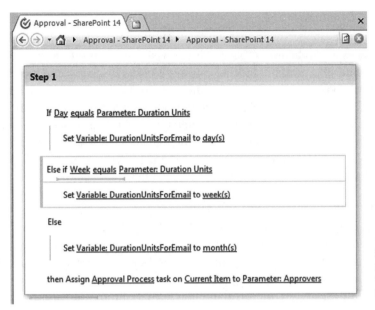

Figure 1.16   Editing the out-of-the-box Approval workflow in SharePoint Designer 2010

1.7.3   *New actions and conditions in SharePoint Designer*

SharePoint Designer 2010 offers a host of new out-of-the-box conditions and actions. For example, you can now manage permissions in a workflow, which you couldn't do before (think of the possibilities). Additionally, you can interface with a Records Center to satisfy your retention policies.

1.7.4   *Reusable workflows*

As mentioned in the introduction to this section, you can now create reusable workflows and deploy them to the site or site collection level to be consumed by various objects within that scope. The major benefit is that you no longer need to maintain more than one copy of the same workflow. Chapter 3 shows you how to build a reusable workflow in SharePoint Designer.

1.7.5   *Site workflows*

Site workflows take the concept of reusable workflows a step further. In addition to being capable of running on a list, library, or list item within a site, a site workflow can run on the site. A good business example of this is a workflow that ensures that the entire site's documents, regardless of the list in which they reside, are approved. A site workflow could iterate through all of the libraries and check each document to see whether it has been approved or not. There is a host of other applications for deploying a workflow. See chapter 3 for more information.

1.7.6   Task processing customization

Most workflows delegate tasks to certain individuals. When a task is assigned, the workflow typically waits for an action to occur on that task and then the workflow resumes processing. In SharePoint 2007, task processing was static—you could not alter the way the out-of-the-box workflows handled the tasks and events associated with them. In SharePoint 2010, you can fully customize the actions that follow task events. Events can react when a task is assigned, expires, is deleted, and is completed. When each of these events occurs, you can inject your custom activities to change the way the task processing flows. Task customization for SharePoint Designer workflows is discussed in detail in chapter 4. For tasks in Visual Studio workflows, see chapter 10.

1.7.7   Workflow templates in SharePoint Designer

In SharePoint 2007, you couldn't move a SharePoint Designer workflow from one farm to another. So, if you had a development, test, and product series of farms, you couldn't prototype a workflow in, say, development and then promote it to production. The 2010 version enables you to save a workflow as a SharePoint solution package (WSP) file and export and import that SharePoint Solution into another farm!

1.7.8   Viewing workflow status with Visio web access

A useful new reporting feature available in SharePoint Server Enterprise edition is the ability to view a workflow's status through a Visio diagram. If you first build your workflow in Visio 2010, and then import that workflow into SharePoint Designer, you can enable Visio web access on that workflow. Throughout the workflow's lifecycle, the Visio diagram will dynamically update to reflect where the workflow is currently executing. Notice the checkboxes in figure 1.17.

You can see the path that the workflow has taken and where it's executing. In this case, it has finished executing. For more information on how to set this up, see chapter 6.

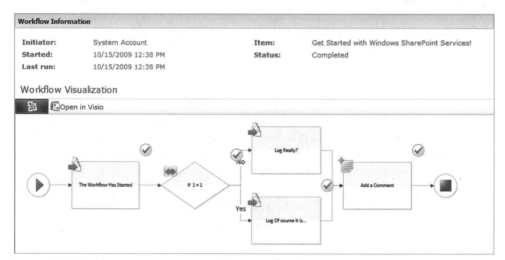

Figure 1.17   Workflow status can now be observed through a dynamic Visio 2010 diagram.

1.7.9 Importing SharePoint Designer workflows into Visual Studio

A stunning new feature that comes with the 2010 version is the ability to export a SharePoint Designer workflow into Visual Studio (figure 1.18).

You would typically first create a workflow in SharePoint Designer because it's such an easy tool to use. After a year, you might realize that your business requirements have become more complicated, necessitating a Visual Studio workflow. In Share-Point 2007, you would have had to recreate the SharePoint Designer workflow from scratch within Visual Studio. Now, thanks to the new export and import functionality, you won't lose the valuable man-hours it took to build the Designer workflow in the first place.

1.7.10 Visual Studio 2010 environment improvements

Clearly, building custom workflows within Visual Studio has become dramatically easier with the 2010 releases of SharePoint and Visual Studio. Many would agree that most of the effort to build Visual Studio 2008 workflows in SharePoint 2007 was for the packaging and deployment of the workflow itself. You had to build all of the features, Diamond Directive Files (DDFs), manifests, keys, tokens, globally unique identifiers (GUIDs), and everything else by hand! This is no longer true with Visual Studio 2010—all of the necessary features and solution packages necessary to deploy a workflow into SharePoint are generated for you automatically. Right-click and deploy! For the steps in detail, see chapter 8.

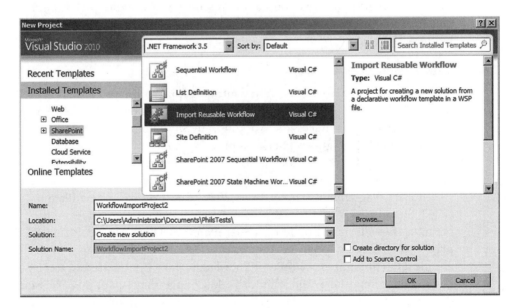

Figure 1.18 Visual Studio 2010 comes with a new ability to import a workflow created in SharePoint Designer.

1.7.11 Pluggable workflows

SharePoint 2007 offered no easy way of running workflows to receive updates from the outside world such as a payroll system, for example. With the new pluggable capabilities, SharePoint 2010 workflows can execute up to a certain point and then wait for information from an external process. The developer needs to implement an event handler or web service to handle the request of the external process and then respond by calling into a method within the workflow itself, informing it to continue processing. For more on this topic, see chapter 12.

1.7.12 New event handlers

SharePoint 2010 supplies a couple of new event handlers, including the ability to react to a workflow's initialization or completion. These handlers may be external to a workflow or embedded within a workflow. For instance, you may want to fire some code that logs in a centralized repository every time a workflow of a certain type has been started and completed. With the new event handlers, this is easy. See chapter 12 for more information about event handlers.

1.8   Building custom workflow solutions

Before you jump into the later chapters and start building workflows, it's important to consider how a workflow is born and progresses to completion. We've already discussed the many tools you can use to build custom workflows, but you could also use a careful comparison of these tools and a discussion of workflow diagramming. In this section, you'll diagram, design, scope, and choose the authoring tools for a generic business process.

1.8.1 Diagramming business processes

When gathering requirements for any software application, you usually work from the top down. First, you determine the high-level requirements, and then you get more and more detailed, as necessary. Working with SharePoint workflows is no exception. You first model the high-level business process. In effect, determine what you need to build. After you've received the approval from business stakeholders for *what* you're going to build, you can consider *how* you're going to build it.

To start diagramming, open Visio 2010. You'll notice a new diagram template called SharePoint Workflow. You may feel compelled to start with this template because, after all, you *are* building a SharePoint workflow. The problem with this template is that it's easy to get into the *how* prematurely. Many shapes in the template assume a fair amount of SharePoint knowledge. Take the Create List Item, Send Document Set to Repository, and Wait for Field Change shapes. For a SharePoint person, this may not be confusing. However, you probably wouldn't want to use that diagram in front of nontechnical stakeholders.

Instead of the SharePoint Workflow template, start with a standard flowchart template. With the flowchart template, focus on the *what* to specifically meet the business need. With the first diagram you should focus on identifying the various states the workflow may use. A state defines the time a workflow waits for something to happen before proceeding to the next step. Figure 1.19 shows a flowchart model of a shopping cart workflow for an internet business that sells golf equipment. At a high level, there are only four states in this business process:

1 *Pending payment*—When an order is submitted, the workflow waits for the payment to be processed.
2 *Pending manufacturing*—In this example, a buyer may order golf clubs fitted to a custom length, which causes the workflow to wait for the manufacturing department.
3 *Pending shipping*—Before the order is fulfilled, the workflow must wait for it to be shipped. This may involve the assembling, packaging, and delivering of the ordered equipment to a shipper.
4 *Fulfilled*—After the order is shipped, the order is complete.

The corresponding workflow will certainly be more complex than this diagram shows, but it's a good start. Someone viewing this diagram can quickly see what the workflow will do. With this high-level diagram accepted by business stakeholders, you can move to a lower level.

Taking it to a lower level doesn't mean going to a SharePoint Workflow template in Visio just yet. First, let's expand on each of the four states. Figure 1.20 shows how you would drill down through the Pending payment state.

The Pending payment state first checks the payment type. If payment is by credit card, the card is processed. If it's by check, the workflow waits for the check to arrive in the mail and clear the bank. In both the credit card or the check methods, if the payment clears the Pending payment state, the workflow completes. Otherwise, a different workflow that handles bad payments is started, and the current workflow terminates.

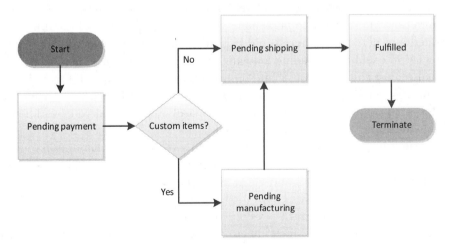

Figure 1.19 Start molding your business process by showing how the workflow will move from one state to another. Agree on the high-level requirements before getting too technical.

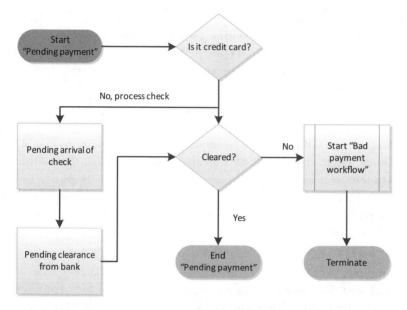

Figure 1.20   Take your high-level model and drill down through each of the states by creating a new diagram for each state. This will provide valuable detail but remain nontechnical for easy consumption.

Figure 1.20 is still fairly high level. It would be easy to get into the weeds of *how* to do this but, again, this early in the process it's more important to focus on *what.* Create diagrams for the other three states and run the flowchart past stakeholders. If, at this point you get a green light to go forward, you're probably ready to start using the SharePoint workflow template.

1.8.2   *Identifying human interaction and SharePoint objects*

Now that you know what the high-level business process is, it's time to turn your attention to how you're going to implement it. The first step is to take the flowcharts you created and determine where you'd expect human interaction. Examples of human interaction could be uploading a document or perhaps submitting a form with data. You also must consider what SharePoint objects your workflow will touch. In the case of the golf equipment e-business, the workflow starts when a buyer submits their order. That order could be logged into a SharePoint list, and your workflow would automatically fire when a new item is added.

From a human interaction perspective, let's consider the Pending payment state again. Notice that, if the payment is in the check form, the workflow waits for the check to arrive in the mail and clear the bank. Both of these points are examples where human interaction can help the workflow progress. For instance, mail department personnel who log into SharePoint after they receive checks could tell the workflow that the check for which the workflow is waiting has arrived. Similarly, an Accounts Receivable employee may monitor bank deposits and notify the workflow when the check clears.

One way to accomplish this is through tasks. Before the workflow waits for the check to arrive, it could create a task assigned to an individual in the mail department. When the mail clerk processes the check, he would edit this task in SharePoint, informing the workflow that the task has been received. You could similarly assign a task to someone in the Accounts Receivable department. That person could edit the task when they see the check has cleared.

Both of these examples of human interaction illustrate a workflow waiting for an event to occur before proceeding. You'll need to think through these points of interaction and how to inform the workflow to proceed.

This is where the SharePoint diagram template in Visio Premium can help. This template definitely lends itself to designing the workflow. With the task example, there's a shape called Assign a To-do Item. By dropping this shape onto the diagram, you specify that the workflow will create a task assigned to someone. This is shown in figure 1.21, where our original high-level flowchart has been created with the SharePoint workflow template.

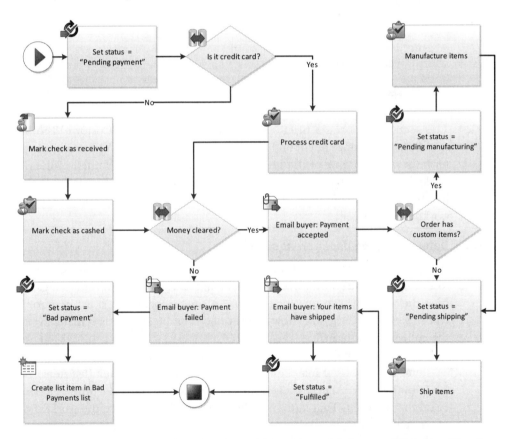

Figure 1.21 The SharePoint Workflow template in Visio produces detail at a much lower level than the standard flowchart diagram. The advantage is the design is more clearly seen, but the disadvantage is it may be harder for nontechnical people to read.

You'll notice the two boxes for check processing have been replaced with the Collect Data From a User shape and the Assign a To-do Item shape. You'll also notice the diagram is considerably more granular. Notice the shapes signifying that an email is sent, which you can see if the payment was bad. First, the workflow sends an email to the buyer when they submit a bad payment. Then the Create List Item follows, signifying that the workflow will create a new list item in a separate list. This, in effect, starts the Bad payment workflow, which is defined elsewhere. After the secondary workflow is started, the current workflow sets its status to Bad payment and then terminates. The other three states (Pending manufacturing, Pending shipment, and Fulfilled) have slightly been developed further.

What type of person uses the SharePoint Workflow Visio template?

Each shape in the Visio workflow template corresponds to an action in a SharePoint Designer workflow. Because of this, the Visio diagram developer needs to know quite a bit about SharePoint Designer workflows to model the workflow using the Visio workflow template. That's why I recommend that nontechnical people use the flowchart template and those with more technical experience use the SharePoint workflow template. My recommendation is to let the nontechnical business analyst focus on the high-level business process and to let someone with experience building workflows do the design work in the SharePoint workflow template.

This section has been a brief introduction for chapter 6, "Custom Visio SharePoint workflows." For more detail on how to diagram workflows in Visio, take a look at chapter 6. In addition, one of the best features of workflows diagramed in the SharePoint workflow template is that the diagram can be imported into SharePoint Designer. This is a big timesaver because all of the actions and conditions are precreated for the workflow developer.

1.8.3   *Determining the deployment scope*

With the design of the workflow now at a fairly low level, it's time to turn our attention to the scope of the workflow. Scope encompasses a few different things. First, what does the workflow run on (for example, a site, a document, a list item, or a content type)? Secondly, if the workflow needs to be reusable, where is it made available (site, site collection, or farm)?

For our golf equipment example, it's easy to see that the workflow runs on top of a list item. This list itself may be called Orders, and every order (list item) has its own workflow instance. Alternatively, a workflow could run on a document, a content type, or on the site itself. That latter is called a site workflow, where the workflow runs on a site, not an item.

Reusable means that you want users to be able to add the workflow onto multiple lists or sites. For example, all the out of the box workflows are reusable; they can be used more than once. Our golf e-business example would not need to be reusable because it meets a one-time business need. If it needed to be reusable, you'd decide which scope the workflow should be deployed at. This involves four possible options: site, site collection, web application, and farm.

Workflows targeted to either site or site collection can be created with either SharePoint Designer or Visual Studio. In SharePoint Designer, you would create a *reusable workflow* to make a workflow available across a single site. If you want that workflow to be available across an entire site collection (multiple sites), you'd promote the workflow to be a *globally reusable workflow*. Alternatively, if you want the workflow to be available across an entire web application or the entire farm, you'll need a Visual Studio workflow.

1.8.4 *Choosing appropriate workflow authoring tools*

There are a few tools you can use to build custom workflows, but SharePoint Designer stands out for many reasons including its ease of use and speed. SharePoint Designer has some downsides where tools such as Visual Studio are needed to fill the gap, and it's important to know which tool is right for the job.

SHAREPOINT DESIGNER

SharePoint Designer is the first of the two authoring options. SharePoint Designer workflows are what's called *declarative*, meaning the workflow is based on Extensible Object Markup Language (XOML), rather than compiled code (as is the case with Visual Studio workflows). The following are six compelling reasons to use SharePoint Designer for your custom workflows:

- *It's easy to learn*—The language and terminology within the workflow components is easy to understand because it's written in plain English. Wizards and familiar interfaces are also used. For example, when composing a workflow-based email message, the dialog box is structured to look like an email message in an email client.

- *It's fast*—Writing software, which is essentially what a workflow is, typically requires a complex programming language such as .NET or C#. A workflow that might take all day to develop with .NET could be written in a few minutes with SharePoint Designer (although there are many limitations when compared to .NET workflows). This speed is due in large part to SharePoint Designer's point and click interface.

- *It's more powerful than previous versions*—SharePoint Designer 2007 allowed users to create workflows, but the new version includes many more features and has refined the development process significantly. It's now easier to work with and move workflow steps. Also, there are many more actions available than before, such as the utility workflows that allow you to manipulate text strings. It's also possible to access the users' profile data, such as their phone numbers and the managers' names through the workflow. Also, some complex tools have been introduced, such as parallel blocks, which allow multiple activities to happen simultaneously. All of these concepts and many others make SharePoint Designer 2010 more powerful than previous versions.

- *Its workflows can be moderately complex*—It's easy to configure your workflows to make decisions using components called conditions. Large selections of actions allow the workflows to modify data and send notifications to users.

- *It doesn't require Visual Studio .NET coding or expertise*—As powerful as Visual Studio .NET is, it takes time to become proficient with it. SharePoint Designer 2010 requires no code but still allows for the user of common programming tools such as variables, which store data temporarily, and functions (in this case, called actions), which perform a variety of tasks. The learning curve for Share-Point Designer is much shorter than for its Visual Studio counterpart.

- *It uses a familiar interface*—SharePoint Designer uses the same interface as the rest of Office 2010, allowing business users to adopt it more quickly. In addition, the hyperlink-based configuration process will be accessible to anyone familiar with web browsing.

Anyone who needs to create SharePoint workflows will find value in SharePoint Designer 2010. In the past, business people did not have a role in the development of new software functionality. SharePoint and SharePoint Designer have changed that, allowing people who do not write code to create functionality that can be shared with other users.

.NET developers will be impressed with how quickly a complex workflow can be created compared to starting from scratch with a code-based solution. They may even find that creating a new workflow in Designer initially, then using Visual Studio .NET to add more functionality yields results faster than using Visual Studio .NET alone. This process is aided by the fact that workflows created with SharePoint Designer can be imported directly into Visual Studio.

Most businesses have a group of people who know the businesses processes well but are not developers by trade. These users will appreciate how easy it is to translate existing processes into SharePoint workflows using SharePoint Designer.

Finally, SharePoint administrators and power users will likely find the most value from SharePoint Designer 2010 workflows. This is because they are often asked to quickly translate business requirements into SharePoint solutions.

VISUAL STUDIO WORKFLOWS

When you realize you need a workflow, and you're considering using SharePoint Designer because of its apparent ease of use, it's important to stop and compare the process with Visual Studio workflows. There are some key pros and cons that ought to be considered before moving forward with one or the other. Visual Studio workflows are covered in detail in chapter 8.

The foremost thing to consider is how technically skilled the developer of the work-flow is. SharePoint Designer is primarily for power users and site administrators. Visual

Studio is primarily for .NET developers with a programming background. If you don't have any resources available that have a .NET programming background, it's easy to conclude that a SharePoint Designer workflow is your best choice. Be aware that SharePoint Designer comes with some out-of-the-box functionality and, although it's rather extensive, it may not be able to accommodate the most complicated of business requirements. This may necessitate going outside of your organization for a .NET developer.

Beyond these high-level deciding factors, there are several other comparisons that should be made between SharePoint Designer and Visual Studio workflows. Table 1.1 highlights the main differences between the two tools. The ordering of the table brings to attention the most common deal breakers that necessitate Visual Studio or SharePoint Designer at the top, followed by differences that are not quite as critical.

Table 1.1 Comparison of the main differences between SharePoint Designer and Visual Studio workflows

SharePoint Designer	Visual Studio
Code-free development (limited to safe, predeployed activities).	Code-centric development (anything goes).
Sequential workflows only.	Supports both sequential and state machines.
Deployable across a site collection but not beyond.	Deployable across entire farm via a feature.
Automatically deployed into SharePoint.	Must be packaged within a feature and deployed by a farm administrator or in a sandbox.
Visio can be used to model workflow logic.	No support for Visio.
No debugging available to step through a workflow at runtime.	Full debugging experience available.
Intuitive support for forms customization.	Less intuitive InfoPath integration. Availability for ASP.NET custom forms.
Workflows cannot be modified at runtime.	Workflows can be modified while running (see chapter 9).
Compiled just-in-time.	Compiled at design time.

The first differentiator was already mentioned—SharePoint Designer is a code-free environment, whereas Visual Studio is a code-centric environment intended for programmers. This has obvious implications.

The second differentiator is that SharePoint Designer supports only sequential workflows. This can be a problem because many business processes don't take place sequentially but go from state to state without any foreknowledge. For instance, consider a bug tracking system for a computer program. A bug may be placed into a *Pending* state, waiting for a developer to start working on the bug. That developer starts working on the bug and fixes it, putting the bug into a *Fixed* state. Thereafter, a tester confirms that the bug was fixed and finds that it was not and must place the bug back in a *Pending* state. This ability to go back in time or to a previous state is only available with state machine workflows and not present with sequential workflows—ruling out SharePoint Designer as a viable option.

Although several other differentiators are mentioned in the table, the third in the list is the last of the most common deal breakers, necessitating Visual Studio. SharePoint Designer supports deploying workflows globally. This global deployment means deploying the workflow across one particular site collection. You may have a requirement that a workflow can be instantiated from anywhere, on every site, across the entire farm. This true global deployment is only achievable with a Visual Studio workflow deployed via a feature. You will find more on Visual Studio and features in chapter 8.

WHAT'S RIGHT FOR THE GOLF EXAMPLE?

The golf equipment online sales workflow example lends itself to a Visual Studio workflow. The most apparent reason is the bad payment requirement. If someone makes an order online, and they type their credit card number incorrectly, you don't want the workflow to stop. The example shows it starts a new workflow instance, but wouldn't it be better if the workflow set its state back to pending payment and requested from the buyer resubmission of information? This would require a state machine to go back in time. Because you can build state machines only in Visual Studio, it remains the best option. If starting and terminating a new workflow is acceptable, you could still use SharePoint Designer.

1.9   *Real-world examples*

The examples found throughout this book can easily be applied to real-world business needs. Rather than make you search through the pages to find all of the examples, this section will serve as your table of contents for the examples you can take to your company. Table 1.2 briefly describes each example and what it does.

Table 1.2   Examples in this book

Chapter	Example name	Description
1	Purchase order and fulfillment workflow	At the end of chapter 1. This workflow is conceptually architected from start to finish. You'll get a good idea of the decisions and techniques used to plan and design your own custom business process.
2	Requirements document workflow	This simple example uses the Three-state workflow to compile and get the approval for a requirements document for a software application.
3	PTO request workflow	This SharePoint Designer workflow allows for a user to submit a request for paid time off (PTO) and get the manager's approval for the request.
4	Capital expenditure request workflow	We build a form that allows users to submit a capital expenditure request when they need funds for a new company initiative. A custom task process is used to get the approval for the request.

Table 1.2 Examples in this book *(continued)*

Chapter	Example name	Description
5	Document sets, security and expense reports, and sales order external data workflow	This chapter has three examples. The first includes a walk-through of how to send a document set containing sales presentation materials to a records center for retention. The second involves an expense report workflow that manages security. Users can upload their expense reports, and the SharePoint Designer workflow alters the security on the reports so only their managers can see and approve or reject the expenses. The final example is a SharePoint Designer workflow that tracks sales orders stored in an external SQL database. The workflow uses Business Connectivity Services (BCS) and external content types to connect to the external data.
6	Training request workflow	Visio 2010 is used to model a training request workflow. After the workflow is built in Visio, it's imported into SharePoint Designer and then published to SharePoint.
7	Expense report InfoPath form	InfoPath is used to create a custom expense report form in which users can enter and publish their expenses. This is a great primer for anyone new to InfoPath. Advanced InfoPath topics like creating dynamic dropdowns from SharePoint Data, customizing the out-of-the-box forms, as well as working with initiation forms in SharePoint Designer workflows are also covered in this chapter.
8	Maintenance order fulfillment workflow	A workflow is created with Visual Studio to manage the submission and fulfillment of a maintenance request for a college dormitory.
9	Service request workflow	A Visual Studio workflow is created for the fulfillment of service requests for a technical helpdesk. The example relies heavily on custom InfoPath and ASP.NET forms for the submission and fulfillment of the requests.
10	Capital expenditure request workflow	A workflow is created similarly to the one in chapter 4, except this time it's created in Visual Studio rather than SharePoint Designer. This is a good comparison between the two authoring tools.
11	Create custom subsite action and subsite exists custom condition	A custom Visual Studio workflow activity and condition is created and later published to SharePoint Designer for power end users. The action provisions subsites from within SharePoint Designer workflows.
12	Pluggable workflow	A local service workflow is created to send and receive messages from the outside world. The example shows an event handler communicating with a running workflow instance.

1.10   *Summary*

SharePoint workflows are excellent tools for automating, tracking, and organizing your company's business processes. Automating many of your most common business processes including expense reporting systems, paid time-off requests, and capital expenditure requests is easily feasible within SharePoint, and you can see how this automation can substantially benefit your organization.

SharePoint workflows can execute on list items, documents, forms, content types, and even across an entire site or site collection within SharePoint. The boundaries of this technology and platform are almost limitless. Without much effort, you can put to use several compelling out-of-the-box SharePoint workflows and introduce immediate value into your SharePoint sites. If those workflows don't meet your business's unique needs, there's a host of workflow customization tools available like Visio diagramming, SharePoint Designer, InfoPath forms, and Visual Studio.

The 2010 release of SharePoint has introduced a slew of new functionality that greatly improves how workflows are architected in SharePoint. Tools like Visio will allow a nontechnical business analyst to model a workflow and hand that diagram to a SharePoint designer or programmer to import and use—saving time, energy, and miscommunication problems. Another useful improvement in 2010 is the ability to create reusable workflows. With SharePoint Designer 2007, you had to recreate a workflow on every list in the entire farm where you needed that workflow to execute. This was inefficient and costly. With the 2010 version, you can publish workflows globally, which saves time and drives consistency.

Next, we'll take what you've seen at a high level in this chapter and walk through the details and specifics on how to set up your first out-of-the-box workflow. In later chapters, you'll see a detailed walkthrough of all the out-of-the-box workflows and how to implement them in your company. Much care will be given to describing specifically how to build custom workflows from scratch.

Your first workflow

Workflows that track features for in-development software are highly desired. Clients often have software requirements written in a SharePoint-hosted document. A workflow is helpful in this scenario because it tracks the progress of the requirements document from start to finish. Additionally, the workflow enforces the final approval of that document before it's given to the team. An example demonstrated in this chapter facilitates the development of this requirements document by automatically assigning tasks, tracking versions, and centralizing the document management. We accomplish this using one of the out-of-the-box workflows called the Three-state workflow.

This chapter will take you through the planning process for developing your first workflow and preparing a document library for a workflow in SharePoint. After we lay the foundation, we'll walk through the steps for implementing and then maintaining the Three-state workflow. This establishes the foundation that other chapters will build on. We will demonstrate much of the basic nomenclature and many of the SharePoint workflow concepts. The Three-state workflow used in the requirements document example will serve as an excellent starting point for a developer new to workflows.

The Three-state workflow belongs to a suite of out-of-the-box workflows such as the Approval workflow, Disposition Approval workflow, and Collect Feedback workflow. The remaining out-of-the-box workflows in SharePoint will be covered at a high level toward the end of this chapter.

2.1   *Planning and preparing for your workflow*

As you may have surmised by now, the first workflow we're going to look at is the Three-state workflow. The implementation of this workflow is straightforward. The Three-state workflow is available across all versions of SharePoint 2010, making it an excellent place to start for both beginners and experienced users. The first step in setting up any workflow is to figure out the business process you're trying to solve and map that process. Most out-of-the-box workflows, including the Three-state workflow, have a defined set of steps and parameters; it's important to make sure they will meet your needs before starting. Additionally, you'll need to configure columns before using the workflow.

2.1.1   *Identifying your business process*

A new requirements document, which is often created by an analyst, contains a number of steps. The analyst's manager would be required to approve the document. Table 2.1 details the tracking of tasks and the need for a task list and describes the corresponding document library.

Table 2.1   Steps for managing a requirements document

Step	Detail
Create document	Create a requirements document. A document is added to a library, and the workflow is started on that document.
Assign task to analyst	Assign the document to an analyst. The task needs to be tracked to enable the manager to see the status and find out when it's completed.
Update document	The analyst works on the document in a SharePoint library, where versioning, check-in, and check-out features can be used to manage the document creation.
	When the analyst marks the task as complete, that will trigger the workflow to move to the review stage where it will go to the manager.
Assign task to reviewer	The document will now be assigned to the reviewers who will receive a task informing them to review the document. The reviewers can track the review process in the task by setting the percent complete field.
Update document	When the review process is done, the reviewer will mark the task as complete and the workflow will move into the final state.
	After the workflow moves into the final state, the workflow will end, and the document status will now be Approved.

Task lists

A task list is a feature in SharePoint that allows you to assign tasks to members in your team. Those tasks are stored in a SharePoint list and the assignee can navigate into that list and edit or complete the task. Examples of how task lists can be used include tracking bugs in software or handling maintenance requests for a facilities management department.

To get this set up, you'll need to enlist the help of one of the Three-state workflows. There are a number of workflows that can be used when managing documents and tasks, and each has its own advantages. Because you are going to be assigning tasks and tracking status for the development of the requirements document, the Three-state workflow is the best fit for this job. Other options would include the Approval workflow or even turning on the Content Approval option for the library. But, because you want to track issues, you'll benefit from the Three-state workflow.

2.1.2 *Introducing the Three-state workflow*

By default, the Three-state workflow is designed to track the status of a list or library item through three states. This workflow is typically used for managing business processes that require your organization to track multiple tasks assigned to a document or other type of content. It's also used to track items such as customer support issues and sales leads.

The three different states occur sequentially. They can be named whatever you like, but there's always an initial state, a middle state, and a final state. Each state represents a different phase in the workflow, and between each phase is a transition state. With each transition between states, the workflow assigns a customized task to a person and sends that person a customized email that refers to the task they need to complete. Figure 2.1 shows how this may look.

When this task is completed, the workflow updates the status of the item (in this scenario, a requirements document) and sends it to the next state. You'll use the Three-state workflow with a document library but it can be used with any list that is set up with a Choice column with three or more values. The values in this Choice column serve as the states that the workflow tracks.

Now, let's apply these technical details to a simple example. A team of developers might use the Three-state workflow to track service requests from clients wanting updates to a custom application. In this case, the team process has three states: In Development, Testing, and Complete. All three states apply to the same update, and

Figure 2.1 The Three-state workflow's states, with transitions between each state

there can be many updates in development at the same time. First, the team manager assigns each update request to an individual developer and marks the items as In Development. Doing so creates a task for the developer. After making the necessary changes, the developer flips the status to Testing, which creates a task for someone in testing. After testing is finished, the tester marks the status as Complete. This is a simplistic look at a complex process, which is easily managed by the Three-state workflow.

> ## Issue tracking and the Three-state workflow
> The Three-state workflow is designed to work primarily with the issue tracking list. You can also use it with any custom list that has been configured to contain a Choice column with three or more values.

A more formalized visualization of how the workflow operates when using the Three-state workflow is shown in figure 2.2.

The workflow automatically manages the creation of each task as well as the final state, and the tasks are updated and completed by the individual they are assigned to.

2.1.3   Preparing a document library for the Three-state workflow

Before you can use a Three-state workflow, you must set up a list or a library to use in conjunction with the workflow. This library must contain the items that you plan to track or manage through the workflow. For our requirements document example, we need to set up a document library that will hold our requirements documents, as well as a couple columns on that library that the Three-state workflow requires.

When you create a custom library in a team site to use with the Three-state workflow, you must make sure the library contains at least one column of type Choice. This column, in turn, must include three or more choice values that the workflow needs to track.

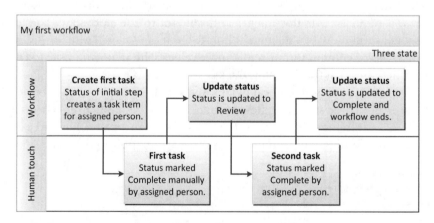

Figure 2.2   Human interaction as it occurs in the lifecycle of a workflow

Figure 2.3 The new Ribbon look and feel make SharePoint 2010 familiar to Microsoft Office users. Use the Workflow Settings button on the far right to add and configure workflows.

To get started, you first need to create a document library where documents can be created, uploaded, shared, and tracked. This library is where the workflow will be assigned and can automatically start when a new document is created or added. In this scenario, you should be using the Shared Documents folder that is provided by default with a new team site.

First, you need to know how to get to the Workflow Settings screen. As with many features of SharePoint, there are a number of ways you can do that. As you have probably noticed by now, the menus in SharePoint 2010 have adopted the look, feel, and functionality of the Ribbon style (figure 2.3) that most Microsoft Office products have been using for the last few years.

Figure 2.3 shows the Ribbon style layout displaying the Library Tools menu. Specifically, it's on the submenu item of Library. On this menu, you'll find most of your library settings and features like Views, Create Column, RSS Feed, E-mail a Link, and Edit Library. With SharePoint 2010, the introduction of the Ribbon has dramatically reduced the number of clicks it takes to operate many of the administrative features.

Click on the Workflow Settings button on the far right of the Ribbon. You'll be taken to the Workflow Settings screen (figure 2.4).

If you click on the context arrow for this button, you'll see all the options available. The first option is Workflow Settings, because this is the first option displayed on the

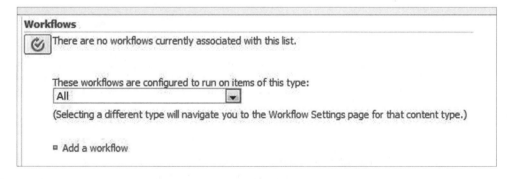

Figure 2.4 The Workflow Settings screen shows which workflows are available for adding to a list or library. You can also remove a workflow from this screen.

menu and is the default setting for the button. When you click on the arrow, it takes you to the Workflow Settings screen.

The next option is Add a Workflow; you can use this to skip the extra screen if you want to get straight to adding a workflow. The last two options Create a Workflow in SharePoint Designer and Create a Reusable Workflow in SharePoint Designer are also present but you'll not be using these in this chapter. Refer to chapter 3 to learn how to create custom workflows in SharePoint Designer.

The Workflows screen for this library should now be displayed; the library shouldn't have any workflows associated with it in this example. As you can see in figure 2.4, the message "There are no workflows currently associated with this list" should be present. Otherwise, the names of workflows associated with this library would be displayed.

Now you need to add two new columns to this library. The first will be a column type of choice and you'll call it Status, and the second will be a column type of Person or Group and you call it Assigned To. The workflow will use these two columns to track both the status and the people assigned to the documents. You'll use the column type of Person or Group, also known as the People Picker, because the information that is pulled from SharePoint will allow you to send this person emails or assign tasks. If you use a text field, you will not be able to assign tasks or send emails. Table 2.2 shows the steps for creating these columns.

Table 2.2 **Adding two custom columns to the document library used by a workflow**

Action	Steps	Result
Create a Status column.	From the Library Tools menu in the Ribbon, click on the Create Column button. Add a column called Status. This field should be a Choice field type and should have three options: Create, Review, and Approved. Make sure you type each choice on a separate line.	Column name: Status The type of information in this column is: ○ Single line of text ○ Multiple lines of text ● Choice (menu to choose from) ○ Number (1, 1.0, 100) ... Type each choice on a separate line: Create Review Approved
Create an Assigned To column.	Create a new Person or Group column called Assigned To. This field will be used to assign the work of the workflow to a specific individual. Accept the rest of the settings as default. Click OK.	Created a new column that tracks the persons to whom the requirements document is assigned.

The default view of this Shared Documents library should look like the document library in figure 2.5. You should see the default columns Type, Name, Modified, and Modified By and the new columns you've just added—Status and Assigned To. Your

Figure 2.5   After the columns have been set up, you should see an empty document library with the new columns.

default library template might differ from the templates out of the box; some organizations change the default settings to include customized default configurations.

You now have a customized document library with two columns that will be used by the workflow that we will create in the next section. The order of the columns does not matter to the workflow, so you can order them however you want.

2.2   *Implementing a workflow*

There are three main steps to implementing an out the out-of-the-box workflow in SharePoint. First, you must add the workflow to the list or library. Then, start the workflow on one of the list items or documents in that list or library. Lastly, you must test the workflow to ensure everything is behaving as you expect it.

You add the workflow to a list through the list's settings page or the Ribbon when you're on that list in the browser. When you select to add a workflow to that list, you'll see a list of all of the currently installed workflows. Some workflows have other dependencies. This was the case with our Three-state workflow; it necessitated the two custom columns we added in the previous section.

After you've added the workflow, it can start either automatically or manually. In both cases, the workflow should be tested from start to finish. For our requirements document example, we'll add the Three-state workflow to the library we worked with earlier and, to test the workflow, we'll create a new Microsoft Office Word document that will start the workflow after it's saved into the library. This will generate tasks and, as those tasks are completed, the workflow will progress from start to finish.

2.2.1   *Adding the Three-state workflow to a document library*

Now that the document library is set up, it's time to set up the workflow. As mentioned previously, a number of out-of-the-box workflows come with SharePoint Server 2010. For our requirements document example, we'll be using the Three-state workflow. You may be inclined to start with the Approval workflow because the name sounds exactly like what you want to do, but you'd discover that it's not robust enough. This workflow also happens to be the only out-of-the-box workflow that comes with SharePoint Foundation. (Even someone with the free version of SharePoint can follow along with this part of the book.)

When you add a Three-state workflow to a library or a list, you must specify which column in the list contains the state values that you want the workflow to track. In this

Foundation vs. Server out-of-the-box workflows

SharePoint Foundation includes only one out-of-the-box workflow, and that is the Three-state workflow. With SharePoint Server, you also get the Approval, Collect Signatures, Collect Feedback, Disposition Approval, and Translation workflows. Please check out chapter 3 for more information on these out-of-the-box workflows.

scenario, you'll be using the Status column that you added to your document library in the previous section. Because there is only one column, the workflow template will automatically choose it by default.

Site collection feature activation dependency

The Three-state workflow site collection feature must be activated on the site collection before the workflow will show up in available workflows. To do this, navigate to Site Collection Features under Site Settings at the root site in the site collection.

You also will specify information about what happens at each stage of the workflow. For example, you'll be specifying the individuals to whom tasks should be assigned and the details of the email alerts that the task recipients receive. Follow the steps in table 2.3 to add the Three-state workflow to a document library.

Table 2.3   Adding two custom columns to the document library used by the workflow

Action	Steps	Result
Navigate to the document library's workflow settings page.	1 Open the Shared Documents document library from your Team Site where you'll add the workflow. 2 On the Library Tools menu in the Ribbon, click Workflow Settings.	You're on the Workflow Settings page and ready to add a workflow to the library.
Add a workflow and choose a workflow template.	1 On the Workflow Settings dropdown, click Add a Workflow. 2 On the Add a Workflow page in the Workflow section, select Three-state under Select a workflow template. 3 In the Name section, type a unique name for the workflow. In this scenario, you'll call this workflow My First Workflow.	Select a workflow template: Three-state Collect Feedback - SharePoint 2010 Collect Signatures - SharePoint 2010 Approval - SharePoint 2010 **NOTE:** If you're running only SharePoint Foundation, you'll have fewer options in the list of workflows than if you were running SharePoint Server. You may also see custom workflows, if applicable. Type a unique name for this workflow: My First Workflow

Table 2.3   Adding two custom columns to the document library used by the workflow *(continued)*

Action	Steps	Result
Associate the work-flow with a task and history list.	**1** In the Task List section, specify a task list to use with the workflow. **2** In the History List section, select a history list to use with this workflow. The history list displays all of the events that occur during each instance of the work-flow. Use the default of Workflow History for this scenario. **NOTE:** You can use the default history list or you can create a new one. Much like previous tasks, if you plan on having numerous workflows, you might want to create a separate history list for each workflow.	**Document Sets** Provides the content types required for creating and using document sets. Create a document set when you want to manage multiple documents as a single work product.
Specify start options.	In the Start Options section, check Allow this workflow to be manually started by an authenticated user with Edit Permissions, if unchecked. All other check-boxes should be blank or unchecked.	☑ Allow this workflow to be manually starte ☐ Require Manage Lists Permissions ☐ Start this workflow to approve publishing ☐ Start this workflow when a new item is c ☐ Start this workflow when an item is chan
Specify workflow states.	**1** Click Next to continue to the second stage of the workflow's configuration. **2** In the Workflow states section, under Select a Choice field, you should see the Status column you created earlier selected by default; if not, select the Status column manually. **3** Select the column values that you want for the Initial state, Middle state, and Final state of the workflow. This is where you'll refer back to the Status column you created earlier, which had the choices of Create, Review, and Approved.	The states should be configured similarly to figure 2.6: Initial state = Create Middle state = Review Final state = Approved

Workflow states:

Select a 'Choice' field, and then select a value for the initial, middle, and final states. For an Issues list, the states for an item are specified by the Status field, where:
Initial State = Active
Middle State = Resolved
Final State = Closed
As the item moves through the various stages of the workflow, the item is updated automatically.

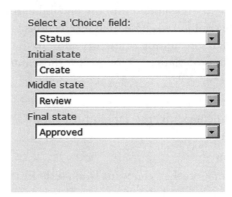

Select a 'Choice' field:
> **Status**

Initial state
> **Create**

Middle state
> **Review**

Final state
> **Approved**

Figure 2.6
When setting up the Three-state workflow, you must specify the three states to be used from the custom column that was created earlier.

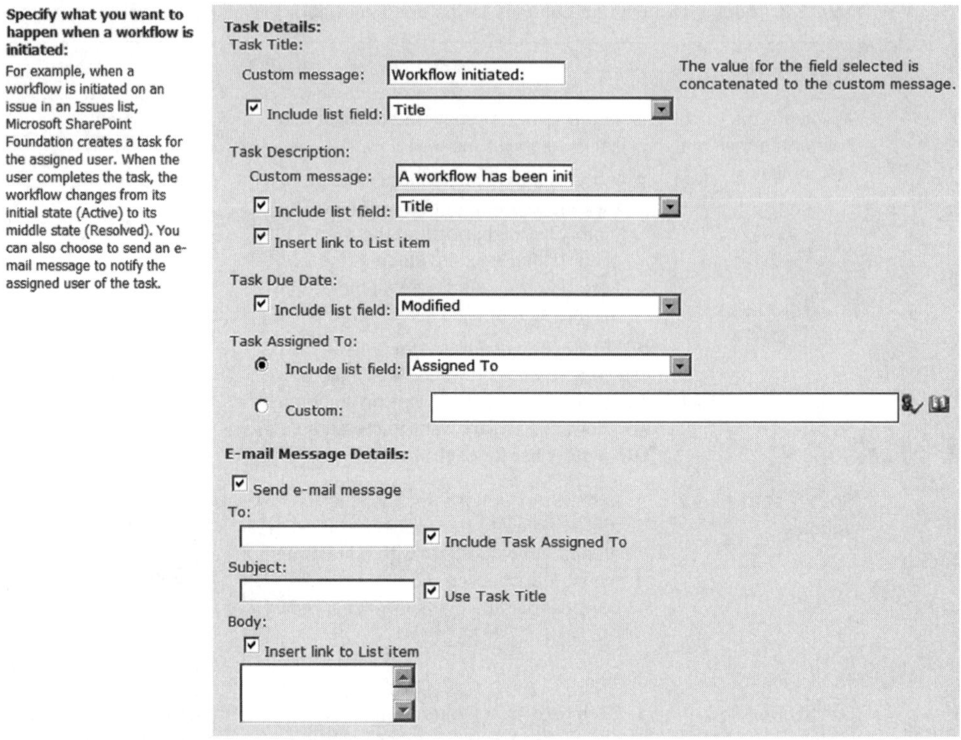

Specify what you want to happen when a workflow is initiated:

For example, when a workflow is initiated on an issue in an Issues list, Microsoft SharePoint Foundation creates a task for the assigned user. When the user completes the task, the workflow changes from its initial state (Active) to its middle state (Resolved). You can also choose to send an e-mail message to notify the assigned user of the task.

Task Details:
Task Title:

Custom message: [Workflow initiated:]

☑ Include list field: [Title ▾]

The value for the field selected is concatenated to the custom message.

Task Description:

Custom message: [A workflow has been init]

☑ Include list field: [Title ▾]

☑ Insert link to List item

Task Due Date:

☑ Include list field: [Modified ▾]

Task Assigned To:

● Include list field: [Assigned To ▾]

○ Custom: [   ] 📖

E-mail Message Details:

☑ Send e-mail message

To:

[   ] ☑ Include Task Assigned To

Subject:

[   ] ☑ Use Task Title

Body:

☑ Insert link to List item

[   ]

Figure 2.7   You can configure the look and behavior of the tasks that are created by the Three-state workflow. For example, you can specify who should be assigned to the tasks and provide a custom email message to the assignee.

Most of the time, you'll leave the defaults for the next two sections in this second configuration screen. The basic premise is how you want your tasks to function. If you remember, the Three-state workflow issues tasks between states. After the issued task is completed, the workflow moves to the next state. In figure 2.7, you'll notice our Assigned To column is already set in the Task Assigned To field. This is enough to continue in the example, but note there are other handy settings. For instance, you can specify unique text to be added into the email that the task's assignee receives.

After you've configured these final two sections to your liking, click the OK button. This will complete the adding of the workflow to the library. A more detailed description of the settings on figure 2.7 follows for those interested in further customization.

TASK TITLE

Type the information that you want to include in the task title. If you select the Include list field checkbox, the Title information for the list item will be added to the custom message.

TASK DESCRIPTION

Type any information that you want to include in the description of the task. If you select the Include list field checkbox, the Title information for the list item is added to the custom message. If you select the Insert link to List item checkbox, a link to the list item will be included in the description.

TASK DUE DATE

If you want to specify a due date for the task, select the Include list field checkbox, and then select the date column from the list that contains the due date information that you want to use. If you want, you could make this a calculated date; for example, the due date could be set 30 days after the created date. You would create a date column with a calculated value in the document library and you would use that as your choice in this field.

TASK ASSIGNED TO

To assign the task to a person who is specified in the list, click Include list field, and then select the column from the list that contains the user information that you want to use. When this workflow is started, the first task is assigned to the person whose name appears in this column for the workflow item. To assign this task in all instances of this workflow to a person or group you specify, click Custom and then type or select the name of the person or group to whom you want to assign the task.

If you want to send an email message to notify the assigned user that they have a task assigned to them, you can check the Send e-mail message box. Or, if you do not want to send email alerts, uncheck the Send e-mail message box.

TO

Type the name of the person to whom you want to send an email alert about the workflow task. Select the Include Task Assigned To checkbox if you want to send the email alert to the task owner.

SUBJECT

Type the subject line that you want to use for the email alert. Select the Use Task Title checkbox if you want to add the Task title to the subject line of the email message.

BODY

Type the information that you want in the message body of the e-mail alert. Select the Insert link to List item checkbox if you want to include a link to the list item in the message.

> ### Emails not working in SharePoint?
> If you or other workflow participants are not receiving email messages, you need to check with your system administrator to ensure that email messaging is configured for your environment.
> Sometimes email messages are also referred to as email alerts.

2.2.2   *Starting a workflow*

With the workflow added to the library, it's time to start the workflow on a document. To start the Three-state workflow in this library, you'll need to upload a document to your library and initiate the workflow on that document. You can either upload a document manually or you can create a new document from the Word client and save it to the library. Since you'll be able to set the column data created in the previous section from within the Word client, you'll create a new document from Word and start the workflow manually off that new document.

First, navigate to your Shared Documents document library to which you added the workflow in the beginning of section 2.1.3. You need to add a new document in this library and set metadata on that document. Follow the steps shown in table 2.4 to create and assign metadata to a new document.

Table 2.4   Adding a new document into a document library

Action	Steps	Result
Create a new document	In Shared Documents, click on the New Document icon.	A new Word document will open. You'll notice that the columns you added earlier are present at the top of the document in the Document Properties section (figure 2.8.). If the properties are not immediately noticeable, click on File > Info > Properties and select Show Document Panel from the dropdown.
Set Assigned to and Status columns	Enter Create in the Status column, add a user into the Assigned To column, and enter text in the body of the document.	The columns should be set similarly to those in figure 2.8.
Save the document and provide a unique document file name	1 In the Save dialog popup, change the filename to My First Workflow. 2 Click the Save button. **NOTE:** When you save the document, you'll see a save window that has been updated for SharePoint and Office 2010. This window shows the location to which the file will be saved. This location will be defaulted to the document library from which you clicked the New Document link. You also have many other options, like Adding Tags, Thumbnails, and Map a Network Drive.	After saving the document, you should be taken back to your SharePoint library, where you'll see your new document (figure 2.9).

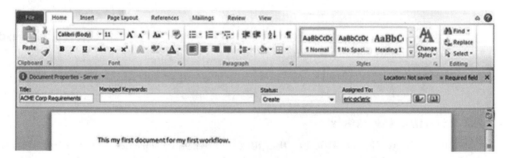

Figure 2.8   A workflow can be started on a document in a document library. From the Word client, you can publish a document into a library along with metadata that is needed by the workflow (Assigned To column).

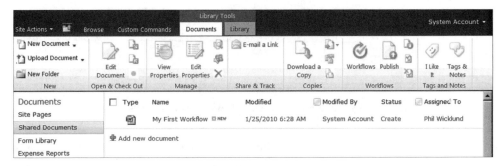

Figure 2.9   After the document is saved, it will appear in the browser showing the columns specified from the Word client.

Notice that the status of the document is set to Create and the value of the Assigned To column also is set. Now that you have your document, you need to initiate the workflow because you indicated that this workflow should be started manually. If you had set it to start automatically, it would have started as soon as you saved the document to this library.

Click on the arrow next to the name of the file and a context menu will drop down (figure 2.10). These are all of the actions available for this document but, for this scenario, you are only interested in the Workflows option. Click on Workflows.

After you click on Workflows, you'll see a screen with all of the available workflows that can be chosen for this library. Figure 2.11 shows the three defaults that come with SharePoint as well as the one you created earlier, My First Workflow.

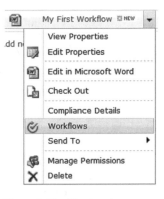

Figure 2.10   The dropdown context menu gives the user quick access to all of the actions that can be performed on this document including starting a workflow on the document.

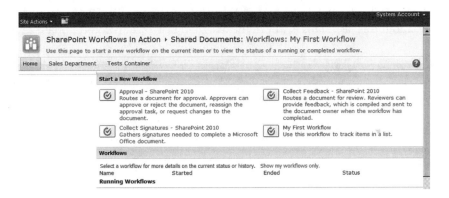

Figure 2.11   Having clicked on Workflows, you'll notice you can start a workflow or view any running or completed workflows.

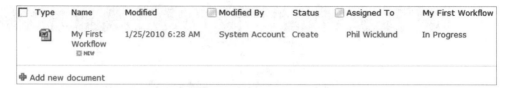

	Type	Name	Modified		Modified By	Status		Assigned To	My First Workflow
☐		My First Workflow 🗅 NEW	1/25/2010 6:28 AM		System Account	Create		Phil Wicklund	In Progress

➕ Add new document

Figure 2.12   The My First Workflow column shows the status of this workflow.

Click on the My First Workflow link. You'll briefly see a processing screen as the workflow starts. Then, SharePoint will return to your document library where you'll see a new column called My First Workflow (figure 2.12).

This column will hold the status of the workflow. Because it started, it's In Progress. You'll also notice that the Status field in figure 2.12 has been grayed out indicating a workflow has updated this field.

2.2.3   *Testing the workflow*

Now that you have created and saved a document and kicked off the workflow successfully, you need to test the moving parts that create the tasks and move the document through the workflow. First, you'll look at the first assigned task and make sure the task looks right and that it works. You'll then close the task and verify that the next phase of the workflow is kicked off properly. Then, you'll test the second task in the same manner and, afterward, the workflow should be completed successfully.

To get started, navigate to the task list with which you associated the workflow. Because this task list is used only for this scenario, you see only one task on your screen (figure 2.13). This is the task that was created and assigned to an analyst based on the parameters you set in the workflow earlier. You'll see the name of the task that has been assigned to the analyst and when it is due.

Click on the Title of the task to get to the next screen. In figure 2.14, you'll see the task details. This is where you can read about or edit the task. There is also a link to the document with which this task is associated.

Here, you'll find the Title, Status, Due Date, Assigned To, Description, and other details about this task. This is where the assigned task owner would update their status

Figure 2.13   The Three-state workflow created a task that the analyst needs to complete before the workflow can proceed.

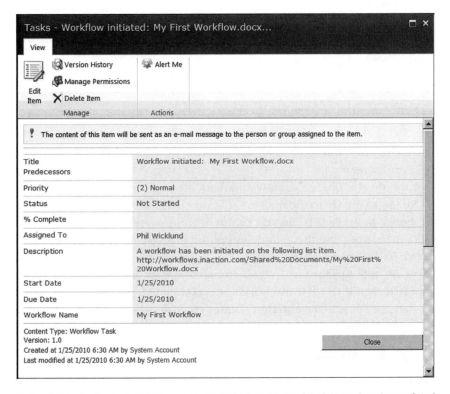

Figure 2.14 On the task details screen, you'll find all the details of the task and associated content. When the task is completed, the workflow will move to the next state.

as they work on this task. Click on the Edit Item button to change the status of the task. You are going to change only the Status field. Change the Status to Completed, and click on the Save button.

You'll be taken back to your task list, where you should see two tasks, one Completed and one Not Started (figure 2.15). Following the requirements document example, this second task would be assigned to your manager (or to whomever you

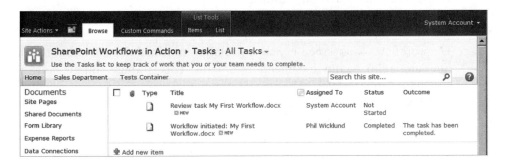

Figure 2.15 After the first task is completed, a second task will be created and assigned to the reviewer of the document.

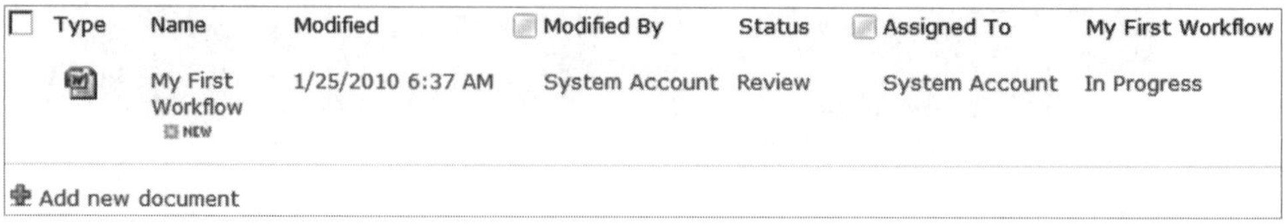

	Type	Name	Modified	Modified By	Status	Assigned To	My First Workflow
☐	📄	My First Workflow ⚡ NEW	1/25/2010 6:37 AM	System Account	Review	System Account	In Progress

➕ Add new document

Figure 2.16   Notice that, when the task is complete, the workflow's status column is updated to Review.

assigned this when you configured the workflow in section 2.1.2). If you don't see two, refresh your screen.

Before you edit this second task and mark it complete, let's take a look at the document library again. Go to the document library from which you initiated the workflow. You'll notice in figure 2.16 that the Status of this document is now Review. The workflow is working because the completion of the first task moved the workflow from the first state to the second state.

Now, go back to your task list and complete the second task. After completing the second task, you'll see that the workflow is completed, and the Status field is in the third state, *Approved*. The workflow's status column, which in this example is named My First Workflow, is now showing Completed as its value.

2.3   *Maintaining workflow instances*

After creating and testing workflows come management and cleanup that have to happen from time to time. It's important to have a thorough understanding of all the information on the workflow status screen and know how to terminate and delete workflows. The workflow status screen shows you where in the process the workflow is currently executing. Terminating a workflow may be necessary if it fails on starting or if an error occurs and the workflow gets hung up. If a workflow is no longer useful, you may have to delete that workflow from the list or library to avoid creating new instances. Beyond specific workflow instances, you can apply certain settings across all workflows in a given web application. A few of these settings are managed in Central Administration and include notifications, disabling SharePoint Designer, and the auto-deletion of a workflow's history.

2.3.1   *Working with the workflow status screen*

The workflow status screen contains workflow information such as Started date, Last run date, a link to the document, and Status. This is where you get your high-level overview of the workflow. The screen also contains a list of tasks associated with the workflow and links to direct users to those tasks.

This screen is useful when dealing with multiple documents and many different workflows. Most people use it to track down the document's progress in the workflow lifecycle or to get more details on where the document has been. This screen allows certain users to terminate workflows, if needed.

Workflow Information

Initiator: System Account   **Document:** My First Workflow

Started: 1/25/2010 6:30 AM   **Status:** In Progress

Last run: 1/25/2010 6:37 AM

If an error occurs or this workflow stops responding, it can be terminated. Terminating the workflow will set its status to
▫ Terminate this workflow now.

Tasks

The following tasks have been assigned to the participants in this workflow. Click a task to edit it. You can also view these tasks in the list Tasks.

☐	☐ Assigned To	Title	Due Date	Status	Related Content	Outcome
	Phil Wicklund	Workflow initiated: My First Workflow.docx ☐ NEW	1/25/2010	Completed	My First Workflow	The task has been completed.
	System Account	Review task My First Workflow.docx ☐ NEW	1/25/2010	Not Started	My First Workflow	

Workflow History

▫ View workflow reports

The following events have occurred in this workflow.

☐	Date Occurred	Event Type	☐ User ID	Description	Outcome
	1/25/2010 6:30 AM	Error	System Account	The e-mail message cannot be sent. Make sure the e-mail has a valid recipient.	
	1/25/2010 6:30 AM	Workflow Initiated	System Account	Three-state workflow started on http://workflows.inaction.com/Shared%20Documents/My%20First%20Workflow.docx.	
	1/25/2010 6:37 AM	Task Completed	System Account	Three-state workflow state change on http://workflows.inaction.com/Shared%20Documents/My%20First%20Workflow.docx. Shared Documents.Status is now Review.	The task has been completed.
	1/25/2010 6:37 AM	Error	System Account	The e-mail message cannot be sent. Make sure the e-mail has a valid recipient.	

Figure 2.17 On the workflow status page, you'll find all the associated details and history for a particular instance of a workflow. This includes tasks associated with the workflow and a log of the workflow's progress.

Most importantly, the last section on the workflow status page contains the workflow history.

To get additional details on a workflow, click on the workflow's Status column. For our example, click the Completed or In Progress link for this item in the My First Workflow column. You'll now see the screen in figure 2.17 with all of the associated information for this workflow, including tasks, basic information, and history. This screen can be used to help track the workflow and all of the associated events.

2.3.2 *Terminating workflows*

Sometimes it's necessary to terminate or cancel a workflow. It might have been started by accident or data may have changed in the initial library or list item. Or, the workflow might have failed for some reason, as in the case shown in figure 2.18.

Figure 2.18   The workflow status shows that this document has a workflow that failed on start. It may be a good idea to terminate this workflow to clean up the orphaned tasks.

Whatever the reason, it's not difficult to cancel one if you have the right permission level in SharePoint.

Locate the item whose workflow you want to cancel. The example in figure 2.18 shows an item with a workflow that failed on start (note the status of the workflow). If you click on the status of the workflow for the item, you'll be taken to the Workflow Status screen. Here, you'll find the link for Terminate this workflow now. You'll find it at the bottom of the Workflow Information section shown in figure 2.19.

Terminating deleted associated tasks

Terminating a workflow will also delete any tasks related to that workflow. Make sure this is what you want to do because you'll not be able to get them back.

When you terminate your workflow, the Workflow Status screen will update accordingly, as shown in figure 2.20. All tasks will disappear and only the events will display on the screen.

When terminating a workflow, you terminate only one instance. Note that you can have the same workflow running multiple times simultaneously on the same document. If you want to remove all instances across all documents, you'll need to delete the workflow from the library.

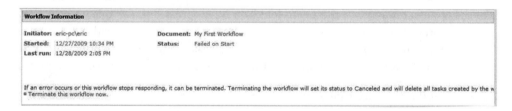

Figure 2.19   The Workflow Information screen will have the Terminate this workflow now link you can use to cancel the workflow.

Workflow Information

Initiator: eric-pc\eric	Document: My First Workflow
Started: 12/27/2009 10:34 PM	Status: Canceled
Last run: 12/28/2009 2:05 PM	

Tasks

The following tasks have been assigned to the participants in this workflow. Click a task to edit it. You can also view these tasks in the list Tasks.

☐ ☑ Assigned To	Title	Due Date	Status	Related Content	Outcome

There are no items to show in this view of the "Tasks" list. To add a new item, click "New".

Workflow History

◌ View workflow reports
The following events have occurred in this workflow.

☐ Date Occurred	Event Type	☐ User ID	Description	Outcome
12/27/2009 10:34 PM	Workflow Initiated	eric-pc\eric	Three-state workflow started on http://eric-pc/Shared%20Documents/My%20First%20Workflow.docx.	
12/27/2009 10:34 PM	Error	System Account	The e-mail message cannot be sent. Make sure the outgoing e-mail settings for the server are configured correctly.	
12/27/2009 10:34 PM	Task Completed	eric-pc\eric	Three-state workflow state change on http://eric-pc/Shared%20Documents/My%20First%20Workflow.docx. Shared Documents.Phase is now Review.	The task has been completed.
12/27/2009 10:34 PM	Error	System Account	The e-mail message cannot be sent. Make sure the outgoing e-mail settings for the server are configured correctly.	
12/28/2009 2:05 PM	Error	System Account	An error has occurred in My First Workflow.	
12/28/2009 4:19 PM	Workflow Cancelled	eric-pc\eric	Workflow My First Workflow was canceled by eric-pc\eric.	

Figure 2.20 After a workflow has been terminated, the workflow status page will show that the status of this workflow instance is canceled.

2.3.3 Deleting workflows

You may want to delete a workflow because it isn't used any longer or you have created a bigger and better replacement. Be careful when making the decision to delete a workflow. There is no going back and this can cause serious issues if other workflows or instances rely on this workflow.

You would delete a workflow from the same Workflow Settings screen where you manage and add workflows. When you click on the Remove Workflow link, you'll be prompted to select the workflow you want to remove (figure 2.21).

The options are straightforward. By default, the Allow option is checked, which permits new instances of the workflow to be initiated. Instead of removing the workflow outright, it's recommended that you choose the No New Instances option. Deleting (removing) workflows instead of disallowing new instances can cause data loss.

Workflows

	Workflow	Instances	Allow	No New Instances	Remove
Specify workflows to remove from this document library. You can optionally let currently running workflows finish.	My First Workflow	1	⦿	○	○

OK	Cancel

Figure 2.21 You can specify whether a workflow should accept new instances, not accept new instances, or be removed from the list or library entirely.

Deleting can also cause other workflows that rely on this particular workflow to get stuck in weird states from which it is difficult to recover. The No New Instances option will save you headaches down the road. Use it.

2.3.4   *Unauthorized access to workflows*

Until this point, we've assumed that the persons participating in the workflow are users that have been granted access to the site in which the workflow is running. If a workflow in the current site assigns a task to a user that doesn't have access, we may or may not want to send an email to that person. For internal users, the default is to send an email letting them know they have a task. For external users, the default is not to send an email. To toggle this behavior, navigate to SharePoint Central Administration and, under Application Management, click Manage web application. Choose the application you want to configure, click the dropdown below General Settings in the Ribbon, and select Workflow. Figure 2.22 shows the defaults set in the Workflow Task Notifications section.

Global workflow settings

The settings found in sections 2.3.4, 2.3.5, and 2.3.6 are global settings. The settings we've discussed so far are for a given workflow instance. Global settings apply across the entire web application.

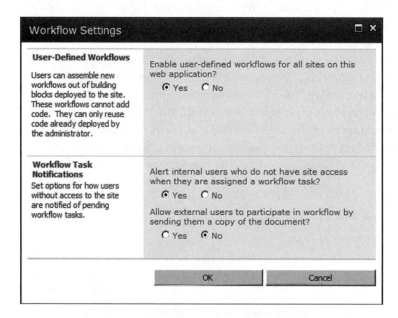

Figure 2.22   In Central Administration, you can disable SharePoint Designer workflows and specify notification rules for workflows.

2.3.5 *Enabling or disabling SharePoint Designer workflows*

Now that we have the first workflow under our belts, we'll be transitioning to custom workflows. Not all companies want end users to create custom workflows with SharePoint Designer. Just as we managed anonymous access and history, we can disable SharePoint Designer workflows.

This functionality is configured in the same dialog menu as displayed in figure 2.22. Navigate to SharePoint Central administration and, under Application Management, click Manage web application. Choose the application you want to configure, and click the dropdown below General Settings in the Ribbon. In the Workflow Settings dialog box, select No under the Enable user-defined workflows for all sites on this web application? option.

2.3.6 *Preserving workflow history*

Earlier, we discussed the workflow history log associated with each workflow. What is not well known about this log is that the events in the log are deleted 60 days after the workflow completes, and you might not want that to happen. To change this setting for a web application, go to Central Administration, click Monitoring on the left navigation, and then click Review Job Definitions. Click the Workflow Auto Cleanup job for the web application you want to configure. Note that there are several hundred jobs and only the first hundred are shown. You may need to go through a few pages before you find the right job. After you've found the job, click the Disable button to disable the auto-cleanup feature.

> **Caveat on disabling the auto cleanup**
>
> If you disable the cleanup, you may experience performance issues with the history lists used by your workflows. Browsing the workflow history may slow down when there are thousands of items in the list. If you want audit functionality for your workflows, it may be better to have a history list for each workflow or write to an external database such as SQL, which can scale better.

2.4 *Additional out-of-the-box workflows*

Anything labeled *out of the box* conjures up these characteristics: inflexible, overly simple, irrelevant, and difficult to use. SharePoint has overcome these assumptions by developing six powerful out-of-the-box workflows to help you be more efficient, organized, and productive with your daily tasks. You can look at these workflows as templates or they can quickly become a foundation for creativity. The important thing is that they can be used by individuals without a high level of technological knowledge. Regular users are now equipped with highly powerful tools to make them more successful in their daily activities.

> **Extension of chapter 1**
>
> In chapter 1, each of these remaining out-of-the-box workflows was introduced. Only their business case was discussed. This section will take them to a deeper level to show their flow of work involving human interaction and include an extended discussion of their business case.

In the previous sections, we walked through the first of six out-of-the-box workflows in great detail. Fortunately for you, the other five workflows are configured in a similar way. In most cases, you'll use the same pages, configurations, and settings for all of the six out-of-the-box workflows. Therefore, this section focuses on the business behind the workflow. What's the purpose of the workflow, and what business problems does it solve?

> **SharePoint Server license required**
>
> All of the workflows in this section require a SharePoint Server license (Standard or Enterprise). The Three-state workflow is the only out-of-the-box workflow that comes with SharePoint Foundation.

2.4.1   Approval workflow

The Approval workflow (figure 2.23) is similar to the Three-state workflow previously described, except that a name of Two-state workflow would be better fitting. This workflow is used to approve or reject documents. When the workflow is started, the state of the workflow is Pending. A task is assigned to the approver(s) and, after the task is approved or rejected, the workflow goes into its second state of Completed. The Three-state workflow has a beginning, middle, and an end state, whereas the Approval workflow only has a beginning and an end.

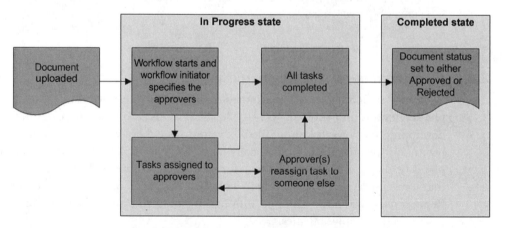

Figure 2.23   The approval workflow uses tasks to track the approval of a document or list item.

Another difference is that, with the Three-state, workflow you can define the states however you wish. With the Approval workflow, the states are not configurable. The Approval workflow is a trimmed down version of the Three-state workflow, used only for the approval of documents or items.

You may be thinking, "Why not use the readily available out-of-the-box content approval features?" The nice thing with the Approval workflow is that it creates tasks assigned to people to manage the approval, whereas, with content approval, you update the document or list item directly. With content approval, the document may be waiting to be approved but no one is notified that it's waiting. With the Approval workflow, the approver gets the notification via email.

Another important thing that the Approval workflow brings to the table is the use of Assignment stages. Assignment stages are discussed in greater detail in chapter 4. They give your users the ability to specify more than one individual that needs to approve the document. You can also specify the order in which the approvals will take place or if the approvals can happen in parallel. Assignment stages also let the person starting the workflow specify all the approvers and settings at runtime. This is convenient because you don't have to know who the approvers are ahead of time like you would in the Three-state workflow.

Finally, the Approval workflow has the advantage of allowing the tasks assigned to the approvers to be reassigned. This may happen if the designated approver doesn't feel qualified to make the approval. They can then reassign the task of approving the document to someone else, in which case the workflow will no longer be waiting for the original individual but rather for the one to whom the document was reassigned.

2.4.2 *Collect Feedback workflow*

The Collect Feedback workflow (figure 2.24) is a highly efficient and manageable way for individuals to have their items reviewed by their team members. When the workflow starts, the initiator of the workflow first needs to specify who will provide the feedback. They enter the names of those individuals and select if they want the feedback to be gathered at the same time (in parallel) or one after another (sequentially). If they choose parallel, for example, a task is created for each reviewer and assigned to that reviewer. The reviewer can than edit the task and, from within the task, they can type in their feedback. As feedback comes in, it is logged into the workflow's history log and the requestor of the feedback can then go to the log to see the reviewers' comments.

Just as with the Approval workflow, the reviewers can reassign the review to another person if they don't want to provide the feedback. The task will then be reassigned to that person and the workflow will no longer be waiting for the original reviewer to leave feedback.

The reviewers can request a change be made to that document. When the reviewers start the change request, they need to specify the individual who will do the work and make the update. This individual will get a separate task stating the work that needs to be done. After it's completed, the requestor will get a new task to review the

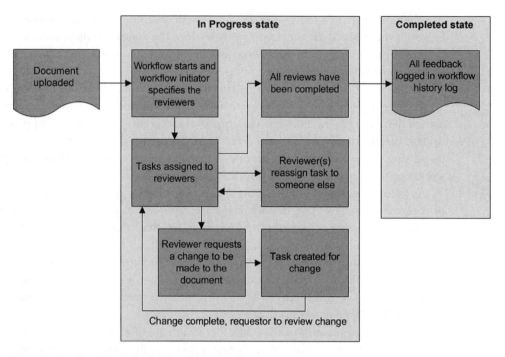

Figure 2.24　The Collect Feedback workflow assigns tasks to people who are requested to provide feedback on a document or list item. The person leaves his feedback in the task, which the workflow then compiles for the requestor to read over.

change. If they agrees with the work, they can then complete that task and leave the feedback in the original workflow. Figure 2.24 shows the full feedback request process, along with these alternate paths. After all the feedback has been received from the reviewers, the workflow will be completed.

2.4.3　Collect Signatures workflow

The Collect Signatures workflow (figure 2.25) facilitates the gathering of digital signatures on Word documents. Consider a contract document that needs to be signed by four individuals. Rather than emailing the document around and having each person add their signature manually, this workflow will add the signature to the document through a task.

This workflow can be started only from within Word, and not from the SharePoint UI. When the workflow is started, the initiator will specify which individuals need to sign the document. Each signer gets a task and an email informing them that they need to sign the document. When they open the task, they click on the Sign button to add their digital signature to the document. After all signatures have been placed on the document, the workflow completes.

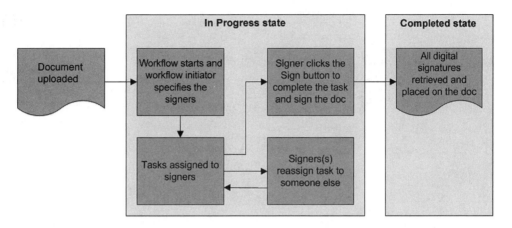

Figure 2.25   The Collect Signatures workflow facilitates the gathering of digital signatures for a document. The workflow assigns tasks to the signers, who then sign the document by clicking the Sign button within the task.

2.4.4 Disposition Approval workflow

The Disposition Approval workflow (figure 2.26) facilitates the deletion of expiring documents. Often, this workflow operates in conjunction with the records management features of SharePoint, such as the Records Center site template. These features help a company manage their records and compliance needs. Depending on the requirements, a document may need to expire after a specified amount of time and, when that document expires, this disposition workflow can be used to verify the document's deletion.

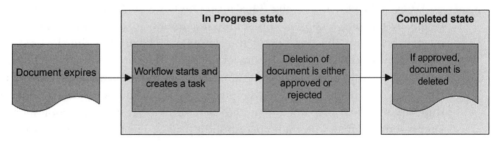

Figure 2.26   Documents can be set to automatically expire, and the Disposition Approval workflow helps facilitate the approval to delete these expiring documents.

After the workflow starts, it will add a task to the task list. A user can accept or reject the request to delete the document by clicking either the Delete this Document or Do not Delete this Document link, respectively. If the document is deleted, the approver can retain the document's metadata in the workflow's history log.

2.4.5 Translation Management workflow

The Translation Management workflow (figure 2.27) is less known and used less frequently than the others. Organizations, in particular those with a global presence, can

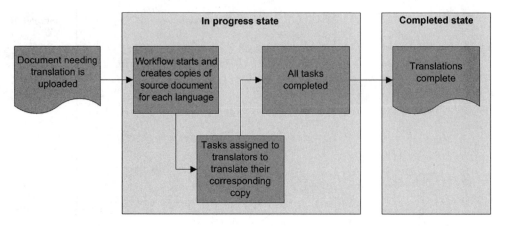

Figure 2.27   The Translation Management workflow helps with the translation of a document from one language to another. Tasks are assigned to the translators and, after the translators translate their copy of the document, the workflow completes.

immediately see the benefit of instituting this type of workflow to help facilitate the translation of documents from one language to another.

In this workflow, two major components need to be created prior to enabling the workflow. The documents requiring translation must be stored in a Translation Management Library. Also, as a complement to the Translation Management Library, a Translation List is used for storing the names of people who translate the documents. These two items are always present with the Translation Management workflow.

When a document needing translation enters the document library, the workflow begins by creating a copy of this source document. It will create as many copies as needed based on the number of translators associated with the document. (Each translator will receive their own copy of the source document that must be translated into their corresponding language.) The workflow then sets the appropriate language type to the document (based on the specific translator) and creates a unique relationship between the source document and each of the corresponding copies. Each translator is sent an email with their corresponding tasks. The workflow is completed when all translators have marked their tasks complete (signifying they have finished translating the document) or if the source document is changed in any way.

2.5   *Summary*

With SharePoint, you can configure and set up robust workflows without involving anyone from the technology or support group. SharePoint has done an excellent job of putting the power of the platform into the end users' hands, allowing the IT department to focus on other areas instead of having to be involved with day-to-day processes like simple workflows.

This chapter introduced the concept of using a workflow to automate an everyday business process. We set up a workflow through the out-of-the-box features provided in SharePoint. A business user can take a napkin sketch and turn it into a full-blown workflow within SharePoint much more easily than ever before.

The Three-state workflow is one of the easiest out-of-the-box workflows to set up. Setting up this workflow involves creating a few columns on a list or library, adding the Three-state workflow to that library, and starting the workflow on a list item or document. After the workflow has been started, you can do interesting things like viewing the workflow's status page, which contains information such as tasks that are associated with the workflow and the workflow's history. You can also terminate the workflow from this page.

The Three-state workflow is the first of many out-of-the-box workflows available in SharePoint 2010. There are five others available to those with a SharePoint Server license. Of the five, the Approval workflow and the Collect Feedback workflow are very popular. The Approval workflow can route a document to one or more people to obtain approval before it is published or marked as approved. The collect feedback workflow is similar, in that it routes a document to one or more people. However, this workflow allows reviewers to add their comments to the document, and those comments are then tabulated and saved into the workflow's history.

Part 2

No-code
SharePoint workflows

In part 1 of this book, we looked at adding workflow functionality to Share-Point using one of the out-of-the-box workflows. Well, it is often the case that these out-of-the-box workflows do not meet your company's unique business requirements and, when this happens, custom workflows are what's needed to bridge the gap. Parts 2 and 3 focus on custom workflows.

In this part of the book, you'll see that no-code workflows in SharePoint 2010 are very powerful and that you can meet very complex business requirements with them. Chapter 3 opens the custom workflow discussion by leading you through custom workflows with SharePoint Designer. Even developers may find that they use tools like SharePoint Designer for workflows more often than Visual Studio (covered in part 3). This discussion is continued in chapters 4 and 5. Chapter 4 focuses on task processing within workflows, and chapter 5 focuses on advanced techniques such as working with external data in workflows.

Once SharePoint Designer is well understood, we transition to diagramming workflows with Office Visio in chapter 6. You'll learn how to take a Visio diagram and import it into SharePoint Designer. Chapter 7 focuses on custom forms. Workflows frequently revolve around human interaction, and you can get humans to interact with a workflow by having them enter data into a custom form. InfoPath is the tool of choice to build custom forms.

3

Custom
Designer workflows

This chapter covers

- Comparing different types of SharePoint Designer workflows
- Building blocks of SharePoint Designer workflows
- Implementing and testing your first SharePoint Designer workflow

SharePoint Designer (SPD) is a powerful tool you can use to help extend the out-of-the-box features in SharePoint. You may want to use SPD for unique business needs such as implementing a custom look and feel with your company's logos, colors, and fonts on your SharePoint sites. Branding is a common use for SPD and it performs many other functions such as building custom web parts, modifying page layouts and, you guessed it, building custom workflows.

SPD has a strong capacity to build custom workflows that can meet complex business needs and processes. SPD leverages the workflow architecture that SharePoint is built on by generating XOML, the declarative workflow markup language we briefly mentioned in chapter 1. SPD publishes this XOML into SharePoint, which is then interpreted by the Windows Workflow Foundation architecture, and your business processes start coming to life! SharePoint Designer workflows are often called declarative workflows, whereas Visual Studio workflows are called compiled workflows.

SPD's greatest benefit is that nontechnical people can *design* workflows that are then translated into what the platform needs in order to run them. Ease of use and speed are two of the excellent benefits of SPD workflows.

SPD workflows are made up of several types of components, including *steps, actions,* and *conditions.* These components are the building blocks of all SPD workflows. Steps organize the flow of the workflow from one *step* to another. Within steps you can have conditions that check values before proceeding, for example. And actions do some *work* like sending an email or creating a list item. This chapter will feature an example that puts all of these components to use by managing the approval process of paid time off (PTO) requests from employees.

3.1   Introduction to SharePoint Designer workflows

As mentioned in the brief introduction, SPD is an excellent tool for customizing your SharePoint sites. In particular, SPD has a powerful workflow engine that you can use to model, add logic to, and publish workflows into SharePoint for user interaction.

SharePoint Designer 2007 supplied only one type of workflow, a list workflow. In SharePoint Designer 2010, we have many more options and greater flexibility. This chapter will cover only the list workflow in detail. Regardless of the type of workflow you are creating, the production process and the toolset remain the same. Following are the summaries of all of the different types of workflows that are available in SharePoint Designer 2010.

3.1.1   List workflows

List workflows are similar to the workflows that were available in SharePoint Designer 2007. They are created to work with the data in a specific SharePoint list and are commonly used for one-off scenarios where you need to run a specific set of actions against a single list. List workflows can also access data in other lists, as you'll see in the example at the end of the chapter. List workflows cannot be easily copied and used with other SharePoint lists, but they are easy to create.

3.1.2   Site workflows

Site workflows are not tied to a single list; instead, they are created at the site level and can perform operations on data from any list within the site. Site workflows are useful when you need to run processes that involve multiple lists. For example, a site workflow could analyze all of the data created in a site within a date range regardless of the lists on which the data was created. Because they are not tied to a specific list, site workflows cannot be started automatically when a list item is created or modified as other workflows can be. Instead, they must be started manually by a site administrator from within View All Content.

3.1.3 Reusable workflows

Reusable workflows are not associated with a specific list but a site. When created, they can be added to any type of list using the List Settings screen, in the same way that the default Approval and Collect signatures workflows are added to a list. Because they are reusable, they can be added to as many lists as necessary within the site. If the default workflow, such as Approval and Collect Signatures, does not meet your needs, you could create your own versions of these reusable workflows and tailor them to your needs.

3.1.4 Globally reusable workflows

Globally reusable workflows are similar to reusable workflows, except that they are available to the entire site collection, not only to a single site. They can be added to any list within the site collection, whereas a regular reusable workflow is available only to lists within the site for which it was created. Globally reusable workflows would be handy if you needed to implement a corporate-wide process and needed all sites in your site collection to use the same workflow to complete this process.

3.1.5 Workflow templates

After creating a workflow, you can save it as a template, which is actually a SharePoint .wsp file. The workflow can then be deployed to another SharePoint site or farm. Previously, this was only possible when working with Visual Studio workflows. For a walk-through on how to work with templates, see section 5.1.

3.1.6 SPD's user interface

Anyone who has worked with the previous version of SPD will notice changes to the interface as soon as they open SharePoint Designer 2010. Microsoft has now adopted the same interface across all its Office 2010 products. This interface includes the new File tab, which replaces the Office Orb and is used to connect to and open sites. It also includes the Ribbon User Interface, which is used to access most of the tool commands. Finally, tabs are used to access open files and display their contents.

The first thing you see when you open SharePoint Designer 2010 is the File tab. The File tab, shown in figure 3.1, includes tools for opening and creating SharePoint sites.

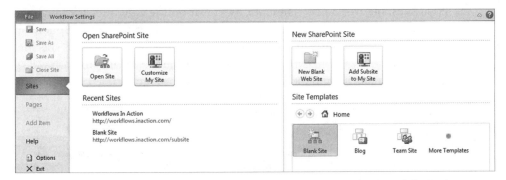

Figure 3.1 The same interface is used in all Office 2010 products, including SharePoint Designer 2010. The new interface is designed to make it easier to find the available tools and options.

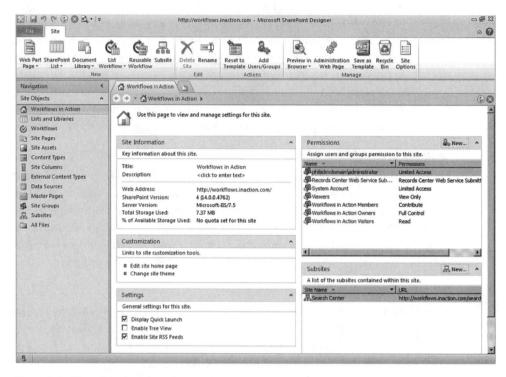

Figure 3.2   The editing interface changes based on the area of Designer in which you are working. When creating workflows, for example, the interface will show you information relative only to workflows.

The editing interface, which is displayed after connecting to a SharePoint site, includes three major areas: the Ribbon, site objects on the left, and the Home tab. See figure 3.2 for an example of the editing interface. The Ribbon provides access to the functions needed to work with SharePoint sites and, for the purposes of this book, SharePoint workflows. The site objects area is used to access the different areas of a SharePoint site. Finally, the Home tab is where you will create and edit lists and workflows.

The Ribbon (figure 3.3) is used to access tools and functions that make up SharePoint sites and workflows. The options shown on the Ribbon will change depending on what you are working on. For example, if you are editing a list, options specific to lists will be show. If, instead, you are editing a workflow, only options specific to workflows will be shown. The dynamic nature of the Ribbon means that you will spend less time looking for the options and tools you need and more time creating functionality.

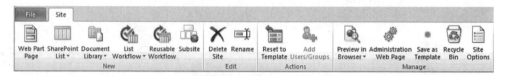

Figure 3.3   The Office Ribbon changes depending on what you are editing. The buttons and, in some cases, the tabs, adjust to show you only the relevant options.

The Site Objects panel (figure 3.4) allows you to access all of the different components of a SharePoint 2010 site. This is where you will go to create new pages, lists, and content types. It is also how you access existing workflows and create new ones. Clicking the different object types under Site Objects will allow you to work with the different object types. As you click the different object types, notice how the Ribbon and Home tab change to show you relevant options.

On the panel of the Home tab and other tabs, you can make settings changes and edit SharePoint objects. Figure 3.5 shows the Home tab, which is displayed when you first open a SharePoint site. The content of this tab changes depending on the Site Objects section you have opened and the type of objects you are editing. For example, when you first connect to a site, you can change the name of the site and modify security on the Home tab.

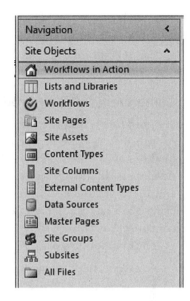

Figure 3.4   The Site Objects panel lists all components that make up a SharePoint 2010 site. For this book, we are primarily interested in the Workflows object but will also look at the Lists and Libraries objects.

Figure 3.5   The Home tab is displayed when you first connect to a site with SharePoint Designer. It allows you to view and adjust the settings that affect the entire SharePoint site.

When editing a workflow, you can adjust how the workflow is started and develop the workflow—all within the same tab. As you open and work with objects, they will appear as additional tabs at the top of the content area, allowing you to quickly switch between them.

3.2 Components of a SharePoint Designer workflow

SPD workflows comprise many components including steps, conditions, and actions. As with writing code in a traditional programming language, these components are used to control the workflow, the actions it takes, and its results. Fortunately for non-developers, all the components are easy to add and configure with the built-in wizards and the point-and-click interface. In addition, all of these components are written using plain English statements like "Calculate 100 plus 50," which makes them easy to configure. You will see some at work in the examples at the end of the chapter.

The components of a workflow fall into six functional categories:

- *Steps*—Help you organize the workflow process.
- *Conditions*—Add decision-making logic into the workflow.
- *Actions*—Make the workflow do something.
- *Variables*—Store data temporarily.
- *Else-if conditions*—Add additional decision making.
- *Forms*—Allow the user to provide data to the workflow.

3.2.1 Steps

Steps are the foundation of any workflow and allow you to organize it into logical sections. The first step typically includes the preparation of data that will be needed later on in the workflow. This could include preparing variables, which are used to store data temporarily while the workflow is running or collecting data from a user. Subsequent steps are used to work with the data and process commands. This is where the bulk of the work is done in the workflow, such as performing calculations and waiting for users to make changes to data. The last step is usually used to record the results of the workflow and send notifications to the user or administrators if required. This might include sending an email to indicate the conclusion of the workflow or logging an error message for troubleshooting.

Although it is possible to create a large workflow with only one step, breaking it into multiple steps can make it easier to understand and modify. This is important when someone other than the original author is making modifications.

It is also important to name your steps to improve the readability of the workflow. Steps can be named and renamed by clicking on the existing titles. In addition, steps can be moved around within the workflow or deleted using the Move Up, Move Down, and Delete keys, shown in figure 3.6.

Figure 3.6   The Move Up and Down Ribbon keys are used to move workflow steps, actions, and other components, whereas the Delete key deletes the currently selected item. Note that there is no Undo when working with Designer workflows, so use Delete carefully.

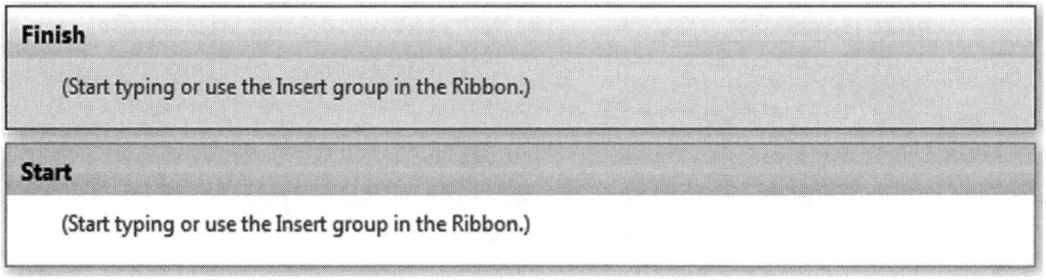

Finish

(Start typing or use the Insert group in the Ribbon.)

Start

(Start typing or use the Insert group in the Ribbon.)

Figure 3.7   Steps can be moved into any order using the Move Up and Move Down Ribbon keys. In this image the Finish step has been illogically moved before the Start step.

In figure 3.7, the Finish step has been placed before the Start step using this method. Although illogical, it demonstrates how you can rearrange the steps in your workflows at any time in the development process.

Similarly, if you need to delete a step, click on the step's header to select it and click the Delete key on the Ribbon or the Delete key on your keyboard. Figure 3.6 shows the Delete button. Keep in mind that there is no Undo option, so make sure that you indeed want to delete the step.

Nested steps are shown in figure 3.8. These allow you to organize your workflows into major steps and minor substeps. As your workflows become more complex, nested steps will allow you to move entire sets of commands at one time, making the development and modification of your workflows easier.

Parallel blocks are another layer on top of steps. Parallel blocks are similar to steps, except they allow you to run multiple actions consecutively. For a complex workflow with many steps that don't necessarily depend on each other, parallel blocks will allow

Figure 3.8   Steps can be nested or placed within other steps. In this example, you can see that Steps 4, 5, and 6 are all nested within Step 1. This allows you to organize complex workflows into logical sections.

Parallel blocks

> **Step 1**
>
> The following actions will run in parallel:
>
> > **Step 2**
> >
> > The following actions will run in sequence:
> >
> > **Step 3**
> >
> > The following actions will run in sequence:

Figure 3.9   **With parallel blocks, your steps can run in parallel, rather than in sequence.**

you to complete the workflow or at least progress to the next nonparallel actions much faster. Note that parallel blocks can be created only within, and not outside, workflow steps. You can place steps within a parallel block to run entire sets of actions in parallel (figure 3.9).

3.2.2   *Conditions*

Conditions allow the workflow to make decisions and respond differently based on the data that is provided by SharePoint lists or end user entries. The example at the end of this chapter shows you how to perform a process if a manager approves an item and take an entirely different set of actions if the item is rejected. Multiple steps can be included within the condition when you need to perform a series of commands.

The following conditions are available in SPD 2010. Some are only available on certain types of workflows. Site workflows, for example, are missing some conditions because they are not tied to a specific list.

COMMON CONDITIONS

These conditions will likely be the ones you use most:

- *If any value equals value*—Allows you to compare a value from any data source to a value from any other data source, as shown in figure 3.10. These data sources can include the data from SharePoint lists, variables, or static values.

If <u>Current Item:Modified</u> equals <u>Today</u>

Figure 3.10   **This condition is checking to see if an item was modified today.** Today **always indicates the current date. If the item is modified today, the actions below the If will be executed.**

- *If field equals value*—Allows you to compare the value of a field on the current item with the value from any other data source. This condition is not as flexible as the previous condition, because it must compare the data from the item on which the workflow was started. Because it must be used with a list item, this condition is not available when creating a site workflow.

OTHER CONDITIONS

Many of the comparisons allowed by the following conditions can be created using the two previous conditions:

- *Created by a specific person*—Checks to see if the current item was created by a specific person.
- *Created in a specific date span*—Checks to see if the current item was created within a specific data range.
- *Modified by a specific person*—Checks to see if the current item was modified by a specific person.
- *Modified in a specific data span*—Checks to see if the current item was modified within a specific data range.
- *Person is a valid SharePoint user*—Checks to see if a specified user is recognized by SharePoint.
- *Title field contains keywords*—Checks for a specified string within the Title field of the current item.

Because these are configured for a specific purpose, they are generally faster and easier to configure. But, because they are fairly specific, you're not likely to use them as often.

Conditions can be configured to examine workflow data, which is any type of data usable by the workflow, including data from list items, variables, or other data sources. This workflow data can be compared with the static information entered when the workflow is written or other pieces of workflow data.

For some conditions, the type of comparison, also known as the operator (figure 3.10), can be changed to allow for other types of comparisons. By default, the operator is set to `equals`, but you can change this to a variety of options by clicking on the currently used operator and selecting a different operator.

The list of available operators changes based on the type of data you are comparing. For example, when comparing a value to a Date or Time field, the `begins with` and `ends with` operators are not available. The following operators are available in SPD workflows:

- *Equals*—Checks if two values are exactly equal; works all data types. The condition is case sensitive:
    - `Summer equals Summer` = True
    - `Summer equals summer` = False (Note the lowercase s.)
- *Not equals*—Checks if two values are not equal; works with all data types:
    - `Summer not equals Winter` = True
- *Is empty*—Checks if the referenced field is blank.
- *Is not empty*—Checks if the referenced field is not blank.
- *Begins with*—Checks if the referenced field starts with a value:
    - `Summer begins with Sum` = True

- *Does not begin with*—Checks if the first characters of a string match another string:
  - Summer begins with Wint = False
- *Ends with*—Similar to begins with but checks the end of the value instead of the beginning:
  - Summer ends with er = True
- *Does not end with*—Checks that the string does not end with the characters from another string:
  - Summer does not end with ter = True
- *Contains*—Checks to see if a string contains a second string:
  - Summer contains int = False
- *Does not contain*—Checks if a string does not exist within another string:
  - Summer does not contain int = True
- *Matches regular expression*—Checks to see if a string matches a defined format. The format to match is defined using character sequences to match letters and numbers.
- *Equals (ignoring case)*—Same as equals but does not compare the case of the characters in the strings:
  - Summer equals (ignoring case) summer = True
- *Contains (ignoring case)*—Same as contains but does not compare the case of the characters in the strings:
  - Summer contains (ignoring case) MME = True

When in doubt, use the any value equals value comparison because it provides the most flexibility and allows you to compare the largest variety of data.

3.2.3 Actions

So far, we have looked only at telling a workflow how to make decisions. A workflow that only makes decisions and doesn't perform any actions is not useful. To make our workflows useful, we need to add actions. Many workflow actions available in Share-Point Designer 2010, and each is designed to perform a different function. The available actions are categorized into six groups, plus a seventh group that includes the recently used actions. To add actions to a workflow use the Action Ribbon button, shown in figure 3.11.

Most of these actions are self-explanatory. A few of the more complex actions are covered in the examples further in this chapter. Here is list of the most popular actions:

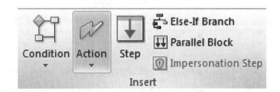

Figure 3.11   The insert action Ribbon button is a dropdown menu. After clicking it, you can select from all of the available actions.

Core actions	List actions	Utility actions
▪ Add a Comment	▪ Check In Item	▪ Extract Substring from End of String
▪ Do Calculation	▪ Check Out Item	▪ Extract Substring from Index of String
▪ Log to History List	▪ Copy List Item	▪ Extract Substring from Start of String
▪ Pause for Duration	▪ Create List Item	▪ Find Interval Between Dates
▪ Pause until Date	▪ Delete Item	▪ Extract Substring from Index of String
▪ Send an Email	▪ Discard Check Out Item	with Length
▪ Set Workflow Variable	▪ Set Field in Current Item	
▪ Stop Workflow	▪ Update List Item	
	▪ Task actions	
	▪ Assign a To-do Item	
	▪ Collect Data from a User	
	▪ Start Approval Process	

SharePoint Designer 2010 allows you to perform many more types of actions by default than SharePoint Designer 2007. The core and list actions will be used more often than most because they allow you to interact with SharePoint data in a manner similar to end user interaction. The Set Workflow Variable action is the most important because it must be used to capture the data from external sources before you can perform more complex actions, such as Do Calculation.

3.2.4   *Variables*

As mentioned earlier, variables are used to store and manipulate data while the workflow is running. Each time a new workflow instance runs, a new set of variables is used, even if multiple copies of the workflow have been initiated by multiple users. When a workflow is finished, the data in the variables is lost unless you first store that data to a field in a SharePoint list item or preserve the data in some other way, such as including it in an email message.

When you first create a workflow, it does not have any variables. In some cases, adding actions to your workflow will automatically create a new variable or variables. For example, adding a Do Calculation action will automatically create a `calc` variable. Adding a second Do Calculation action will create a `calc1` variable. All variables must have unique names, so SharePoint Designer appends a number to the end of automatically created variables to keep them unique. You can rename any variable, whether it was manually or automatically created, to suit your needs.

Variables are set to allow only certain types of data, called data types. Some actions require certain data typesto function correctly. The following data types are available when creating workflow variables:

- *String*—A text string of any length, `ABC`.
- *Boolean*—`Yes` or `No`.

- *Date.Time*—1/1/2010 12:00:00 AM.
- *Integer*—A number without any decimal value, 100.
- *List Item Id*—A unique reference to a list item, 1.
- *Number*—A number with or without a decimal value, 1.5.

These are self-explanatory, with the exception of List Item Id. This data type allows you to store the unique identifier of a list item. This can be useful if you need to refer to a specific list item later in the workflow.

The actions in your workflow are used to assign values to variables. Some actions do this automatically and with others you need to assign the values yourself using the Set Workflow Variable action. When the action itself assigns the value, you only need to choose the variable to which to assign the output. Only compatible variables are shown, preventing you from selecting a variable with an incompatible data type.

When using the Set Workflow Value action, all available variables are shown, even if they are not directly compatible. In some cases, it is possible to assign an incompatible value to a variable by converting it; this is called *coercion*. To use coercion when assigning a value to a variable, adjust the Return String As dropdown on the Lookup dialog, as shown in figure 3.12.

The options available in the Return field as dropdown depend on the data type of the variable and the data type of the field you have selected in the Field from source dropdown. For some Field from source and variable data type combinations, coercion is not possible and the Return field as dropdown will be set to the only possible type and disabled. When coercion is possible, the dropdown will be populated with possible coercion types. In figure 3.12, the variable has a String data type, and the Field from source has a User ID variable type. You can see that it's possible to apply several different user profile properties to the variable. Due to the number of possible combinations, the best way to see what coercion options are available in your workflows is to experiment.

Not all data types can be coerced into all other data types even when those data types are listed in the Return field as dropdown. You cannot coerce a String into a

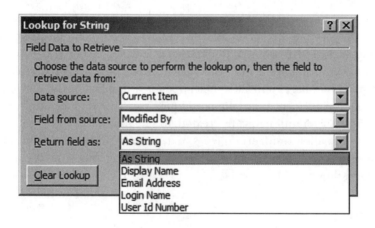

Figure 3.12
Using coercion allows you to return the value of a field as a different type of data. In this example, the Modified By field is returned as a String data type. By default, it would be returned as a Person data type.

Error	System Account	Coercion Failed: Unable to transform the input lookup data into the requested type.

Figure 3.13 A coercion error logged in the workflow history indicates an invalid coercion selection was attempted. If this happens, you'll need to adjust to coercion to return a valid type.

`List Item Id`, for example. The Set Workflow Value action does not prevent you from attempting an invalid coercion but, when you run the workflow, you will receive an error in the workflow history, as shown in figure 3.13.

If this occurs, you will need to adjust either the type of coercion you are performing or the data type of the input assigned to the variable.

3.2.5   *Else-if branches*

Else-if branches work directly with conditions for more advanced decision making. They can be set to execute whenever the preceding condition is False (similar to an else statement). To do this, place the cursor inside the existing condition and click the Else-If Branch key on the Ribbon. No additional configuration is necessary to use the else-if in its simplest form. Figure 3.14 shows an else-if added to a condition.

If an additional comparison is needed within the else-if branch, you can add another condition, again using the Condition button on the Ribbon. Your choice of any type of available condition does not need to be the same as the initial condition. Figure 3.15 shows an else-if with an additional condition.

Finally, you can compare multiple pieces of data within a single condition using and conditions and or operators. This is done by adding another condition immediately after the existing conditions and changing the operator as necessary. SharePoint Designer 2010 will combine these into a single statement automatically. And operators and or operators can be added to the primary if statement or to any else-if branches, as shown in figure 3.16.

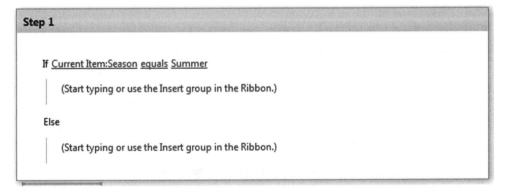

Figure 3.14 An else-if branch added to a condition allows the workflow to perform specific processes whether the result of the condition is True or False. An else without an additional condition will always be executed if the preceding if is False.

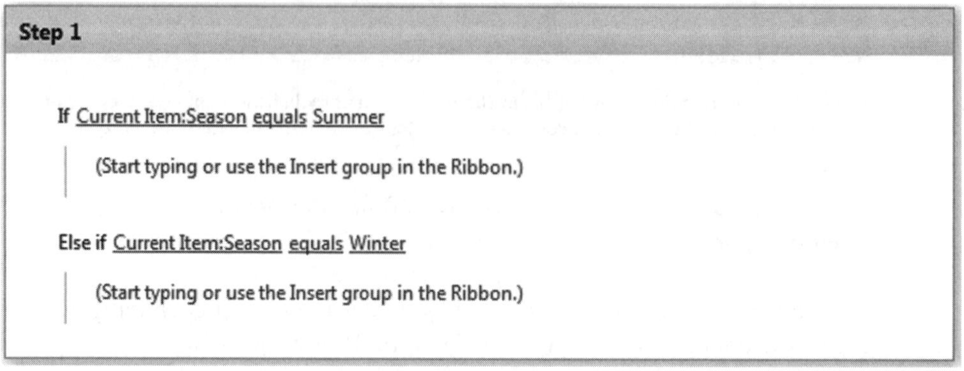

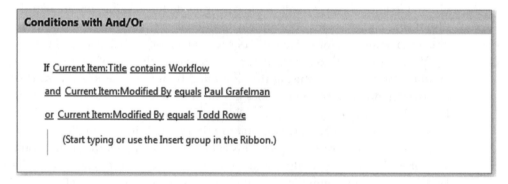

Figure 3.15   An else-if branch with a second condition allows multiple values to be compared or the same value to be compared in multiple ways. In this example, a Season value of Spring would mean that neither the if actions nor the else-if actions would execute.

Figure 3.16   And and or statements permit multiple comparisons within one condition. This will allow you to create a single complex if statement instead of several simple if statements.

3.2.6   *Workflow forms*

Users can interact with workflows through *forms*. Forms are pages viewed through the browser that allow the user to supply additional data to a workflow. The easiest way to use forms is to add initiation parameters to your workflow. Initiation parameters are similar to variables, except that they are displayed to the user when the workflow is started manually. The user can then choose the data to enter into the parameters. Variables, on the other hand, use data from the lists and do not allow users to directly interact with them. Forms are covered in detail in chapters 7 and 10.

3.3   *Creating your first SharePoint Designer workflow*

Now that you have learned about the core components of an SPD workflow, it's time to get some hands-on experience. We're going to create a PTO request system using SharePoint lists and workflows. The example is divided into several sections, with each section focusing on different workflow components. Also, each section builds on the previous sections, so make sure to go through the example in order.

The first section will concentrate on building the lists necessary to support the PTO workflow. In the second section, we'll create a simple logging workflow. Then, we'll add basic functionality that handles notifications when a PTO request is submitted and, lastly, we'll add advanced functionality that tracks the available hours of PTO.

3.3.1 *Configuring a PTO calendar*

The sample PTO request calendar will allow employees to go to a calendar and create a new item that spans the length of their requested PTO. The workflow that will be built in the next section will route that request to the employee's manager. But, before we build that workflow, we first need to create the calendar and set up content approval. Follow the steps in table 3.1 to create this PTO Calendar list.

Table 3.1 Setting up your PTO Request Calendar list

Action	Steps	Result
Create a new Calendar list in SharePoint Designer.	**1** Open SharePoint Designer from the desktop or Start menu and connect to your SharePoint site using the Open Site button. **2** Click the Lists and Libraries under Site Objects. Click the SharePoint List Ribbon button (see figure) and select the Calendar list. **3** Name the new calendar PTO Calendar and click OK.	A new calendar is created.
Set up content approval on the PTO Request Calendar.	**1** Click the PTO Calendar link under Lists. 	

Table 3.1   Setting up your PTO Request Calendar list *(continued)*

Action	Steps	Result
	NOTE: After creating a new list, it will appear on the Lists and Libraries tab. Opening the list from here does not give you access to the data within the list but allows you to adjust the lists settings. 2 Under Settings, check the box for Require content approval for submitted items, and then save your work by clicking on the Save button.	After opening the list, you can adjust a variety of list aspects. The Settings section allows you to enable content approval, which is needed for the PTO workflow.

With our PTO calendar set up, employees can start submitting their PTO requests. Now, we build the workflow that helps facilitate their approval!

3.3.2   *Creating a custom workflow that logs to the History List*

Having set up our calendar, we can now build the PTO request workflow. Before adding logic to the workflow, let's build a simple workflow that performs logging and publish that workflow to the calendar to make sure everything is deploying properly. Follow the steps in table 3.2 to create a basic SPD workflow and publish that workflow to the PTO Calendar.

Table 3.2   Creating a new workflow that logs to the workflow history list

Action	Steps	Result
Create a new list workflow off the PTO Calendar.	1 Connect to your SharePoint site with SPD and click on the workflow's Site Objects button on the left. 2 Click the List Workflow button on the Ribbon and choose the PTO Calendar. 3 Name the new workflow PTO Workflow and click OK.	A new list workflow is bound to the PTO Calendar after it's published. At this point, the workflow is empty.

Table 3.2   Creating a new workflow that logs to the workflow history list *(continued)*

Action	Steps	Result
Set up a dedicated History List that you can use to log workflow information.	**1** In the breadcrumb (figure 3.17), click on the PTO Workflow link to access the workflow settings. **2** Select New History List... for History List. Click OK on any pop-up dialogs. After you click OK, a new history list called PTO History List will be created automatically. **NOTE:** Instead of creating a new history list, we could use the predefined history list. In some cases, this is OK, but, in other cases, it's helpful to log each workflow's history to a dedicated list. This is true for complex workflows that are generating numerous log messages. Having the history logged to a dedicated history list can make troubleshooting easier because you will not be sifting through the log messages of multiple workflows. For simple workflows or workflows that do not have many log messages, a shared history list is fine.	A new list to which the workflow can log is created.

Figure 3.17   As you dig deeper into the workflow settings and editor, you will need to use the breadcrumbs displayed beneath the tabs. The breadcrumbs not only show you exactly where you are, but they allow you to move to different levels of the workflow editing process.

Table 3.2   Creating a new workflow that logs to the workflow history list *(continued)*

Action	Steps	Result
Specify that the workflow should start automatically when a new PTO request is created.	While you are still in the PTO Workflow tab via the breadcrumb (figure 3.17), under Start Options, check Start workflow automatically when a new item is created.	**Start Options** Change the start options for this workflow. ☑ Allow this workflow to be manually started ☐ Require Manage List permissions ☑ Start workflow automatically when an item is created ☐ Start workflow automatically when an item is changed

Table 3.2   Creating a new workflow that logs to the workflow history list *(continued)*

Action	Steps	Result
Add a logging action to log that the workflow has started.	1 Under Customization, click on the Edit Workflow link. 2 Click the title of Step 1 and rename the step PTO Workflow Initiation. 3 Click inside the step and then click on the action dropdown (in the Ribbon) to show the list of actions. Click Log to History List action and change the message to PTO Workflow Started.	A single action will be in the workflow that logs to the history list. After the publishing, the workflow is bound to the PTO Calendar and will fire when new requests are created. **PTO Workflow Initiation** Log PTO Workflow Started to the workflow history list
Click the Publish button in the Ribbon and test the workflow.	1 Click the Publish button, open the SharePoint site using Internet Explorer, and browse to the PTO Calendar. 2 Create a new calendar item. Then, verify the workflow ran successfully. 3 Navigate to the workflow status page by clicking the Completed text in the status column and verify the workflow's history was populated from your logging action.	**Workflow History** View workflow reports The following events have occurred in this workflow. Date Occurred / Event Type / User ID / Description 12/28/2009 7:22 PM Comment System Account PTO Workflow Started If the workflow ran successfully and the PTO Workflow Started message was logged to the history list, you're ready to move on to the second example. If not, recheck your steps.

We now have a simple workflow deployed onto our PTO calendar. The workflow isn't powerful yet. In fact, it only logs to the history log. Now, it's time to start sending emails when PTO requests are submitted.

3.3.3   *Adding notifications to the custom PTO Request workflow*

Now that the workflow is running automatically and logging successfully, it's time to add more advanced functionality. We'll add conditions and actions to notify the user's manager that a PTO request was submitted. We'll also add logic and actions to notify the user whether or not their request was approved or rejected. Finally, we'll add error handling in case something goes wrong with the approval. The approval of the PTO Request will be done through the out-of-the-box content approval features. Follow the steps in table 3.3 to add this managerial approval to the PTO Request workflow.

Table 3.3   Adding managerial approval notifications to the PTO Request workflow

Action	Steps	Result
Add a manager lookup action to the workflow.	1 Add a step after the PTO Workflow Initiation step and name it PTO Workflow Approval. 2 Within this new step, add a Lookup Manager of a User action using the Actions button on the Ribbon. **NOTE:** The lookup manager action is under the Relational Actions category.	**PTO Workflow Initiation** Log PTO Workflow Started to the workflow history list **PTO Workflow Approval** Find Manager of Current Item:Created By (output to Variable: manager)

Table 3.3 Adding managerial approval notifications to the PTO Request workflow *(continued)*

Action	Steps	Result
	3 Set the action to look up the manager of the user who created the PTO Calendar item by clicking the This User link, and then click OK. NOTE: The Select Users dialog box allows you to select a dynamic user, such as the User who created the current item, or a specific user. You can also perform a lookup based on workflow data.	
Add a Send an Email action.	**NOTE:** If your environment does not have outgoing email configured or you cannot use email for any reason, use a Log to History action instead of the Send an Email Action. Be sure to configure the Log message to include references to the same data, such as Manager and Created By, to ensure that these components are working. **1** Add a Send an Email action to the step after the Manager Lookup action.	**PTO Workflow Approval** Find Manager of <u>Current Item:Cr</u> then Email <u>these users</u>
Specify sending the email to the manager.	**1** Click the These Users link on the email action to open the email configuration dialog. **2** Click the address book icon next to the To: field to select a user to be emailed. **3** Select Workflow Lookup for a User... and click the Add button in the center of the dialog. **4** Change the Data source to Workflow variables and Parameters in order to select the manager variable. **5** Select Variable: manager for the Field from source. Then, change the Return field as dropdown to Email Address and click OK twice.	The email is now configured for sending to the requestor's manager.

Table 3.3   Adding managerial approval notifications to the PTO Request workflow *(continued)*

Action	Steps	Result
Configure the contents of the email message, including the subject and the body of the email.	**1** In the email configuration dialog box, click the ellipsis after the Subject field to add subject line text. **2** Add text and a lookup for the Created By field to the subject line using the Add or Change lookup button: Subject: PTO Request Submitted for [%Current Item:Created By%] **NOTE:** The Subject line of the email action can include workflow data. In this case, the Created By field has been added to the subject line along with some static text. **3** Add text and a lookup to the body, including a link to the PTO Calendar item, again using the Add or Change lookup button. [%Variable: manager%], [%Current Item:Created By%] has requested PTO for the following: [%Current Item:Start Time%] to [%Current Item:End Time%] Please review this request and approve or reject as required. [%Current Item:Server Relative URL%] **NOTE:** Like the Subject line, the email body can include static text and workflow data. Including all relevant data in the email will allow the end user to take action or make a decision without necessarily having to open the SharePoint item in question. **4** Click OK to close the email action editor and save your changes.	The email subject and body are defined.

At this point, we want to pause the workflow until the user's manager either approves or rejects the PTO request. We will also need to check the Approval Status field on the item to determine how the manager responded to the request. Note that the values in the Approval Status field contain special characters along with the text; these are required for an `equals` comparison. You could use a `contains` comparison instead, but the `equals` comparison is more efficient because it does not need to examine the string characters one by one.

Again, if email is not available, use a Log to History instead of the Send an Email action. Include all of the referenced fields in the log message to ensure that everything is working as designed.

Table 3.3 Adding managerial approval notifications to the PTO Request workflow *(continued)*

Action	Steps	Result
Add a pause action to wait for the request to be approved or rejected.	1 Add a Wait for field change in the current item to the PTO Workflow Approval step. 2 Set the field to Approval Status, the operator to not equal, and the value to 2#;Pending.	then Wait for <u>Approval Status</u> <u>to not equal</u> <u>2;#Pending</u> Pausing a workflow: The Wait for field change in the Current Item action allows you to suspend the operation of the workflow until certain criteria are met. In this case, the workflow will pause until the PTO request is either approved or rejected.
Add an if condition to check if the PTO Request was approved.	1 Add another step to the workflow and name it PTO Workflow Notification. 2 Add an If current item field equals value condition to the new step. 3 Set the field parameter to Approval Status and the value to 0;#Approved. 4 Add a Send an Email action to the if condition and configure it to notify the creating user that his request is approved.	**PTO Workflow Notification** If <u>Current Item:Approval Status</u> <u>equals</u> <u>0:#Approved</u> Inside the if condition will be a Send an Email action notifying the requestor that their request has been approved.

We now need to add an email notification that will go to the user that created the PTO request when the request is approved. We also need to create an else-if condition to check for a rejected request and send an email accordingly.

Table 3.3 Adding managerial approval notifications to the PTO Request workflow *(continued)*

Action	Steps	Result
Add an else-if branch to check if the PTO request was rejected.	1 Add an else-if branch to the condition using the Else-If button on the Ribbon. 2 Add an If current item field equals value condition to the else-if branch. 3 Set the field parameter to Approval Status and the value to 1;#Rejected. 4 Add a Send an Email action to the condition and configure it to notify the creating user that their request was rejected.	Else if <u>Current Item:Approval Status</u> <u>equals</u> <u>1:#Rejected</u> Also, the else-if condition will contain a Send an Email action notifying the requestor that their request has been rejected.

If the Approval Status field is not equal to Approved or Rejected at this point, something went wrong with the workflow. Instead of stopping the workflow, it's important to let the users know. In the real world, it would also be beneficial to notify whoever is responsible for maintaining the workflow that an error occurred. These notifications can be done by adding another else-if with no conditions.

Publish the workflow and create two test items on the PTO calendar as your test user. The manager of the test user will receive two emails, one for each PTO calendar

Table 3.3   Adding managerial approval notifications to the PTO Request workflow *(continued)*

Action	Steps	Result

Add another else-if to notify both the manager and the requestor that an error occurred.	1 Add another else-if branch to the end of the step.
	
	2 Add a Send an Email action to the final else-if branch.
	
	3 Configure it to notify both the user and the manager that an error occurred.
		PTO Workflow Notification
		
		If <u>Current Item:Approval Status</u> <u>equals</u> <u>0;#Approved</u>
		
		    Email <u>Current Item:Created By</u>
		
		Else if <u>Current Item:Approval Status</u> <u>equals</u> <u>1;#Rejected</u>
		
		    Email <u>Current Item:Created By</u>
		
		Else
		
		    Email <u>Current Item:Created By; Variable: manager</u>

item. As the manager, approve one request and reject the other. The test user will receive two email notifications, one for each PTO request.

> **More options for managing approvals**
>
> There are multiple approaches to getting approval within workflows. This example uses the built-in content approval functionality, but instead we could have used the out-of-the-box Approval workflow. In this scenario, the manager would be assigned a new task in the task list instead of being sent an email. The manager could then use this task to approve or reject the PTO request.

3.3.4   *Adding calculation logic to the workflow*

The last step will be to configure a second list to track how many remaining PTO hours each employee has. This list will help the manager to decide whether to approve or reject the request because it tracks the cumulative and the remaining PTO hours for each user. If the PTO request is approved, this new list will be updated to reflect the number of remaining and used PTO hours for the requestor.

To get started, let's first set up this PTO tracker list. In SharePoint Designer, click on the Lists and Libraries site object menu. Click on the Custom List Ribbon button to create a new custom list named PTO Tracker. After the list is created, add a column of type Person or Group and name the column Employee.

Click OK to save the changes to the Employee column. Switch back to SharePoint Designer and add two Number columns to the PTO Tracker list. One list should be named Available Hours, and the other column should be named Used Hours (figure 3.18).

Column Name ▼	Type
Title	Single line of text
Employee	Person or Group
Available Hours	Number (1, 1.0, 100)
Used Hours	Number (1, 1.0, 100)

Figure 3.18   List columns can be added to a list in SharePoint Designer. It's much easier to add numerous columns to a list with Designer because you do not need to wait for page refreshes that occur when adding columns using the browser-based settings page.

Changes to lists made in SharePoint Designer do not take effect until you press the Save button. The result is that any workflows you are editing will not be aware of the newly added columns until the changes to the list have been saved. When making changes to lists directly in SharePoint, those changes take effect immediately and clicking on a Save button is not required. These different behaviors can be confusing when switching back and forth from SharePoint Designer to SharePoint, so make it a habit to always save list changes when working in SharePoint Designer.

Click on the Save button to save the changes to the list. Open the PTO Tracker list in SharePoint and add an item for your test user. For the test user, set Available Hours to 80 and the used hours to 0 and save the item (figure 3.19).

To use and modify the data from the PTO Tracker list in your workflow, you need to capture the data using variables. These variables can then be modified as required and eventually applied back to the PTO Tracker list. You can also add these variables into the email message body, so the manager will be able to see in the email if the PTO requestor has a positive PTO balance. Follow the steps in table 3.4 to set up these variables pointing to the PTO Tracker list and to reference them in the email body.

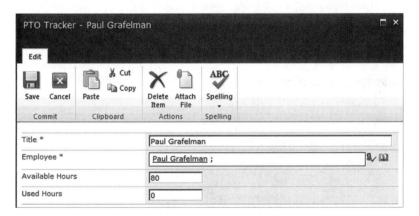

Figure 3.19   Add a new item to the list using the SharePoint interface to mimic how the end users will interact with the system. This test item will allow you to test the calculation of Available and Used hours.

Table 3.4   Updating Request Notification to include available and used hours

Action	Steps	Result
Add a Set Workflow Variable action and reference a new variable titled Available Hours.	1 Switch back to SharePoint Designer and add a Set Workflow Variable action as the first action in the PTO Workflow Approval step. 2 Click the Workflow Variable link in the action and choose Create New Variable at the bottom of the dropdown. 3 Name this variable Available Hours and give it the type Number.	The Set Workflow variable action will be added to the workflow and will be configured to assign data to a new variable titled Available Hours.

To find the correct item on the PTO Tracker list, you need to tell the workflow which item you are looking for. Setting the Ensure Unique Values option earlier will prevent duplicate entries, which would confuse the workflow.

Table 3.4   Updating Request Notification to include available hours and used hours *(continued)*

Action	Steps	Result
Set the value of the Available Hours variable with the requestor's available hours from the PTO Tracker list.	1 Click the Value link on the action. Click the f_x button in the popup. Set the Data source to the PTO Tracker list. **NOTE:** The Lookup dialog allows you to use the data from one list to find a specific record in another list. In this case, you are looking for a specific row in the PTO Tracker list, identified by the data in the Created By field of the current list. 2 Set the Field from source to Available Hours to capture the PTO hours remaining for the specified user. 3 Set the Field to Employee and the value to the Current Item:Created By (f_x button), then click OK. 	You'll have two new variables, one called Available Hours and one called Used Hours. These variables are referenced in an email to the manager so they can make an informed decision.

Table 3.4   Updating Request Notification to include available hours and used hours *(continued)*

Action	Steps	Result
	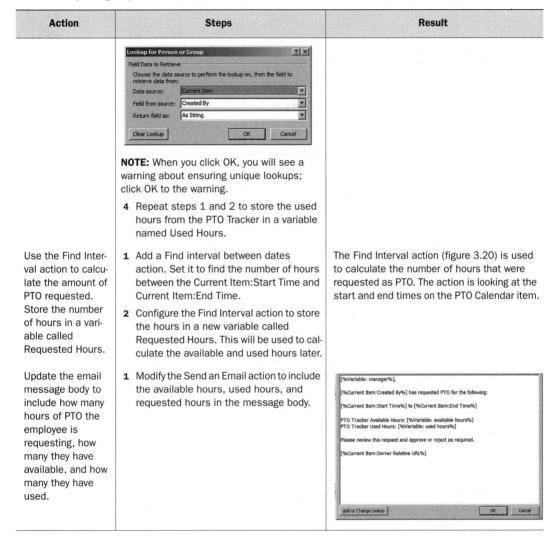 **NOTE:** When you click OK, you will see a warning about ensuring unique lookups; click OK to the warning. 4 Repeat steps 1 and 2 to store the used hours from the PTO Tracker in a variable named Used Hours.	
Use the Find Interval action to calculate the amount of PTO requested. Store the number of hours in a variable called Requested Hours.	1 Add a Find interval between dates action. Set it to find the number of hours between the Current Item:Start Time and Current Item:End Time. 2 Configure the Find Interval action to store the hours in a new variable called Requested Hours. This will be used to calculate the available and used hours later.	The Find Interval action (figure 3.20) is used to calculate the number of hours that were requested as PTO. The action is looking at the start and end times on the PTO Calendar item.
Update the email message body to include how many hours of PTO the employee is requesting, how many they have available, and how many they have used.	1 Modify the Send an Email action to include the available hours, used hours, and requested hours in the message body.	

then Find <u>hours</u> between <u>Current Item:Start Time</u> and <u>Current Item:End Time</u> (Output to <u>Variable: Requested Hours</u>)

Figure 3.20   The Find Interval action is used to find the days, hours, and minutes between two Date and Time fields. In this example, you are calculating the hours between the PTO request's start and end time to determine how many hours to subtract from the employee's available hours.

With the email message going to the manager now updated and showing the data, you need to obtain the manager's response. If the manager approves the request, the requested PTO hours need to be deducted from the PTO Tracker list. Follow the steps in table 3.5 to accomplish this action.

Table 3.5   Updating the employee's available hours when the request is approved

Action	Steps	Result
Add a Do Calculation action that subtracts the Requested Hours variable from the Available Hours variable.	1 Add a Do Calculation action to the PTO Workflow Notification step. 2 Click on the First Value link and set it to the variable Available Hours. Set the Operator to Minus to subtract the available hours from the requested hours. **NOTE:** To select a workflow variable, change the Data Source to Workflow Variables and Parameters. 3 Set the Second Value link to the Requested Hours variable. 4 Set the Output to field to the Available Hours variable.	The Available Hours variable will be updated by subtracting the Requested Hours.
Add another Do Calculation that adds the Requested Hours variable and the Used Hours variable.	1 Add another Do Calculation action to the PTO Workflow Notification step. 2 Click the First Value link and set it to the Used Hours variable. Set the Operator to Plus in order to add the requested hours to the used hours. 3 Set the Second Value link to the variable Requested Hours. 4 Set the Output to field to the Used Hours variable.	The Used Hours variable will be updated by adding itself to the Requested Hours.

Now that you have updated the data within the variables, you need to write this data back to the PTO Tracker list to store it permanently. Remember that, when the workflow finishes, the data in the variables is lost. Using the Update List Item action, you can set the values of multiple fields of an item with a single action. You only want to save the data back to the PTO Tracker list if the PTO request is approved. If it is rejected, you don't need to save the data. Perform the following steps to save the data back into the PTO Tracker list.

Table 3.5   Updating the employee's available hours when the request is approved *(continued)*

Action	Steps	Result
Within the Notification Step and inside the Approved if-else condition, add an Update List Item action to update the PTO hours data.	1 Add an Update List Item action. Click the This List link. Change the list dropdown to PTO Tracker. 2 Click on the Add button. Set the dropdown to Available Hours. Set the value to the Available Hours variable. Click OK. 3 Click on the Add button again. Set the dropdown to Used Hours. Set the value to the Used Hours variable. 4 Click OK.	The Update List Item action writes back to the PTO Tracker list, updating the requestor's available PTO.

Table 3.5   Updating the employee's available hours when the request is approved *(continued)*

Action	Steps	Result
In the Update List Item action's This List popup, use a lookup to find the correct item in the PTO Tracker list.	1 In the Find the List Item section, set the Field drop-down to Employee. 2 Set the Value field to Current Item:Created By using the f_X button. 3 Click OK on the This List pop-up. **NOTE:** You will again see the message about ensuring unique values. Click Yes because you are enforcing unique items on the list. 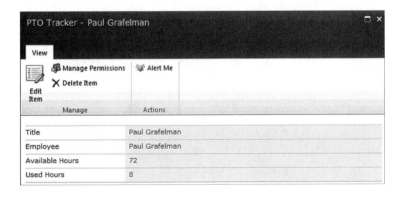	The Update List Item action will be configured and, when PTO requests are approved, the data stored in the variables will be written back to the PTO Tracker list.

Publish the workflow and create a new item on the PTO Calendar as a test user. Approve this item as the test user's manager. On the PTO Tracker list, you should notice that the available and used hours were updated correctly (figure 3.21).

PTO Tracker - Paul Grafelman

View

Edit Item   Manage Permissions   Alert Me
              Delete Item

Manage   Actions

Title	Paul Grafelman
Employee	Paul Grafelman
Available Hours	72
Used Hours	8

Figure 3.21 After running the workflow with the advanced functionality, the PTO Tracker list will be updated to show how many PTO hours each employee has used and how many are still available.

3.4 *Summary*

This chapter has given you an introduction to SharePoint Designer 2010 workflows. You have learned how Designer workflows are beneficial and how easy it is to create them without the knowledge of complex programming languages like Visual Studio .NET. Because of this, SharePoint Designer workflows are intended to be created and used by both information workers and traditional developers.

You have also learned about the components of a Designer workflow and how these components are used in workflow development. Steps and conditions can be used to organize your workflows and make them easier to read and maintain. Actions allow you to build workflows that do a variety of tasks, including creating and updating list items and sending notifications to users. In addition, if and else-if statements are available to add logic to your workflows, allowing them to make decisions. Variables can be used to store data, which can later be referenced throughout your workflow such as within an if-else condition. All of these components can combine to build powerful workflows, including the example described in this chapter, a PTO request system.

Now you are at a point where you are comfortable thinking about and discussing how workflows can benefit your organization. We go from here back to a higher level of workflow planning and diagramming by discussing workflows with Office Visio 2010.

Task processing
in SharePoint
Designer workflows
4

This chapter covers
- Using task actions in SPD workflows
- Building custom task processes in SPD
- Customizing the task edit form
- Responding to task outcomes

By introducing task processes into your workflows, you can greatly increase the efficiency of the interaction between users and workflows. This is because task processes can issue tasks assigned to a user, and the workflow can go idle while it waits for that task to be completed. It's easy for users to forget they have workflows waiting for their input. By using task lists, you can provide a location that users can easily reference to find their outstanding tasks.

SharePoint Designer has three main task-related actions that help facilitate this process. The Assign a To-do Item action does exactly this; it assigns a task to a user and waits for that task to be completed. If the workflow needs to gather information from the user rather than wait for a task to be completed, the Assign a Form to a Group and Collect Data From a User actions can help take this task processing to the next level.

For more complicated workflow requirements, SharePoint Designer provides another action called the Start a Task Process action. This action creates what Designer calls a task process whereby, instead of basic task processing, you can add actions that respond to all sorts of task-related events, such as task expiration, deletion, and completion.

This chapter explores task processing for SharePoint Designer workflows. You'll cover the core task-related actions. You'll also cover how to customize the overall task process through the Start a Task Process action.

4.1   SharePoint Designer task actions

SharePoint Designer workflows have several actions that add task processing functionality. You can use these actions to create tasks and assign them to users, wait for those tasks to be completed, and respond to tasks when they have been completed. The Assign a To-do Item action gives you this functionality. Other actions like the Collect Data from a User action can facilitate the gathering of information from users. Most of these actions take only a few minutes to configure. Let's take a look at the three main out-of-the-box SharePoint Designer workflow task actions: Assign a To-do Item, Assign a Form to a Group, and Collect Data from a User (figure 4.1).

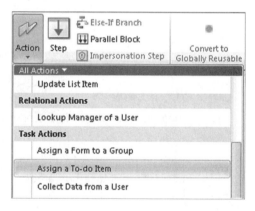

Figure 4.1   **By default, your workflows will interact with three main task actions.**

4.1.1   Assigning To-do items

The Assign a To-do Item action is the most straightforward task action in SharePoint Designer. All you do is create a task that's assigned to one or more people, and the workflow goes idle and waits for each person to complete their task before continuing. This action allows for two parameters, the task itself and the person or group assigned to the task (figure 4.2).

Assign A To-Do Item

Assign <u>a to-do item</u> to <u>these users</u>

Figure 4.2   **The Assign a To-do action is the simplest of task-related actions. The workflow creates a task and waits for that task to be completed.**

When you click on a to-do item, a wizard box appears and prompts you for the task title and description values (figure 4.3).

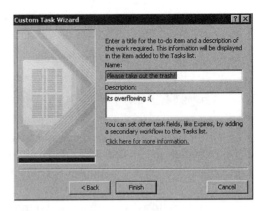

You can set the title and description of the task, but no other fields. The title and description can't be dynamically based on other workflow data, so this action is only for the simplest of tasks because these values must be entered statically at design time. After you publish the workflow containing this action, the workflow will create a task in the task list assigned to the user. At that point, the assignee won't be able to edit

Figure 4.3 When you are assigned a to-do action, you see a screen with a wizard prompting you for the task name and description.

the task; they can only complete the tasks. When users click the task item in the task list, they get a pop-up form with a button to complete the task (figure 4.4).

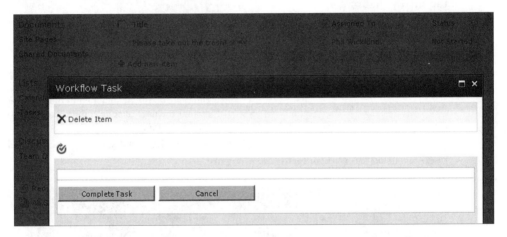

Figure 4.4 When the person assigned the tasks clicks the task, they see two buttons. The first completes the task, and the second cancels the operation.

After clicking the Complete Task button for each task, the workflow continues.

4.1.2 Using the Assign a Form to a Group action for a survey

The Assign a Form to a Group action is similar to the Assign a To-do Item action in that it assigns tasks to one or more people. The difference is that, when the user clicks on their task with the Assign a Form to a Group action, they are asked a defined list of questions. This differs from the previous action where users saw only a Complete button and a Cancel button.

Figure 4.5   Assign a Form to a Group will use tasks to facilitate the gathering of responses to a survey.

The Assign a Form to a Group action behaves like a survey. The difference between using this action and the default SharePoint Survey functionality is that the workflow will wait for all the survey responses to come in before it continues. The answers to these questions are stored in the task list with each answer stored in a separate column as part of a new content type. The action accepts two parameters: the first defines what questions to ask; and the second specifies which users to assign the task to. They will be required to respond to the survey (figure 4.5).

When you click on a custom form, another wizard pop-up appears in a manner similar to the Assign a To-do Item action. This time the difference is that you'll be prompted to enter the values in the form that the task assignee needs to fill out (figure 4.6).

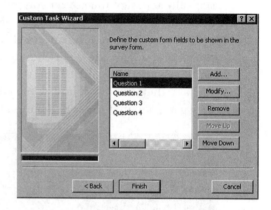

Figure 4.6   The Assign a Form to a User action will prompt the user to specify data that will be saved in the task itself.

After you publish the form and the users open their tasks, they'll see the fields they need to fill out to complete the task (figure 4.7).

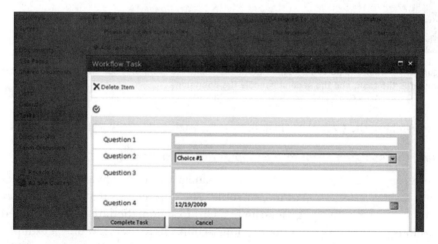

Figure 4.7   When users click the task, they'll see all the data elements and questions that where specified in the action pop-up.

4.1.3 *Using tasks to collect data from a user*

The Collect Data From a User action is similar to the Assign a Form to a Group action with the exception that it allows the data entered in the form to be accessed by the workflow. The data entered in the form is saved in task columns through a new content type; the data is also stored in a workflow variable (see figure 4.8).

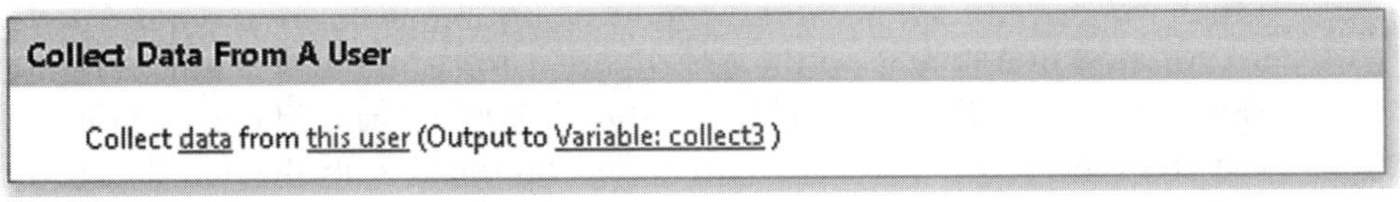

Collect Data From A User

Collect <u>data</u> from <u>this user</u> (Output to <u>Variable: collect3</u>)

Figure 4.8   Unlike the Assign a Form to a Group action, the Collect Data From a User action can save the values entered by the user into a workflow variable.

The workflow can then react to the submission of the form by looking at the values entered in this variable.

4.2 *Custom task processes in SharePoint Designer workflows*

We've finished discussing simple tasks, where a task is assigned to a user and the workflow waits for the task to be completed. The trouble with these tasks is that they don't support complex requirements. For example, what if your workflow needs to allow a task to be reassigned to someone else? Or, what if you need to set an expiration date on a task, and then react when the task expires? In these situations, custom task processes are valuable. A custom task process works from a single task assigned to one or more people. The main difference is the dozen or so events you can respond to during that task's lifecycle including task updates, expirations, and reassignments.

A custom task process can be created from within a SharePoint Designer workflow through the Start Custom Task Process action. The action requires three parameters: the task process instance, the item to start the task on, and the users to assign the task to (figure 4.9).

When that task instance is clicked (first parameter), a new custom task process is created. You'll also notice that, when you click the instance, you'll be navigated to the Settings tab of a new custom task process (figure 4.10), where the task process is named Task X. It's through this Settings tab that you can add functionality to the task process. We'll cover three main boxes on this Settings tab: the Customizations box, the Task Form Fields box, and the Task Outcomes box.

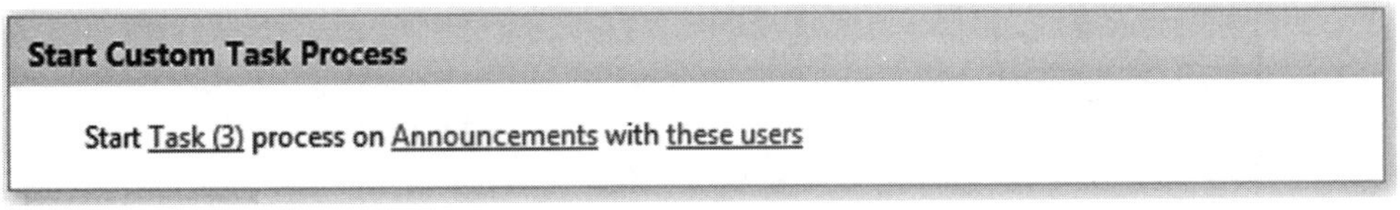

Start Custom Task Process

Start <u>Task (3)</u> process on <u>Announcements</u> with <u>these users</u>

Figure 4.9   A custom task process is used when requirements necessitate responding to events beyond the completion of a task.

Notice the Customization box (figure 4.10) in this tab. In the box, you can click into three areas where you can add conditions and actions into the task process. You can modify the overall task process by responding to events like process cancellation or completion. Secondly, you can respond to task events like task assignment, expiration, deletion, or completion. And, lastly, you can set up conditions that must be met for task completion. All three of these sections contain the shell for all the events to which you can add actions to incorporate your unique business requirements.

Another useful item on the tab (figure 4.10) is the Task Form Fields box, which can be used to add custom fields to the Task Edit form. The Task Edit form is presented to the task assignee when they click on the task. By default, they'll see the normal task fields and the custom fields you've added.

You can use the Task Outcomes section to specify custom task outcomes for your tasks. A task outcome is the state of a task when it is completed. For example, Approved and Rejected are default outcomes. You may want a custom task outcome called Deferred. If you add a Deferred task outcome, users will see a third button called Defer on the task edit form next to Approve and Reject. Having clicked on the button, your workflow will flag the task with that outcome when the task completes.

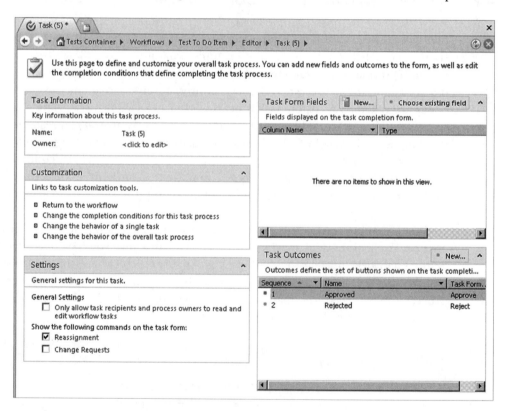

Figure 4.10   When you add a Start Custom Task Process action, you are taken to the custom task process settings tab where you can start to build a custom task process.

The rest of this section will walk you through each of the three boxes in the custom task processes settings tab. We'll also discuss the subject of *assignment stages* where we'll give the end user the ability to choose who should be assigned the tasks through an association form when the workflow first starts. This is useful when, while you're building the workflow, you don't know who the appropriate assignees should be and would rather let the user decide.

To explain the settings for a custom task process, I will use an example that deals with capital expenditure requests. A capital expenditure request is used by a company when a department or person needs to use some of the company's capital to fund a project or initiative. For example, a capital expenditure request might be submitted to purchase and set up a new branch office. A capital expenditure request is rarely simple. This is where the custom task process can help, because you'll be able to add your unique business logic into the approval of the expenditure request that will guide the approval from start to finish.

To set up the example, first create a new generic list called Capital Expenditure Requests. Add two new columns to the list, Request Description as a multiline text field and Dollar Amount as a currency type. Then, within SharePoint Designer, create a new List workflow called Expenditure Request Approval and select the Capital Expenditure Requests list. You need to add only one activity onto the workflow—the Start Custom Task Process activity. Leave the second parameter as Current Item and assign a user as the approver for the expenditure requests. Note that, when you assign a user, you'll be prompted to fill out an email template. The user will receive an email when the task process starts. At this stage, you can also set up a due date for the task process if you wish. When completed, your workflow surface should look something like figure 4.11. After you set up your workflow to this point, click the first parameter of the action—the task process instance. This will load the task process's settings tab, and the sections that follow will walk you through these settings.

The example will cover the three boxes on the custom task process setting tab in an alternating order. First, we discuss how to change the overall task process from the Customization box. Then, we customize a task edit form and return to the Customization box on the settings tab to discuss how to change the behavior of a single task. Last, we complete the example by setting up custom task outcome and assignment stages.

Step 1

Start <u>Task</u> process on <u>Current Item</u> with <u>PHILSDEVDOMAIN\pwicklund</u>

Figure 4.11 The Start Custom Task Process action has three parameters: the process instance, the item that on which to start the task, and the user(s) to which to assign the task.

4.2.1   Customizations box: changing the overall task process

With the Capital Expenditure Requests list created, the Expenditure Requests Approval workflow set up, and the Start Custom Task Process activity added, it's time to bring the business logic into the custom task process. First, look at the events surrounding the overall task process. In the Customizations section in the custom task process's settings page, click on the link titled Change the behavior of the overall task process.

When you click on this link, you go to a tab that contains four events to which you can add actions (figure 4.12). With these events, you'll be able to respond when the task process first starts, when it's running, when it's been cancelled, and after it completes.

Let's first focus on task process completion. For the capital expenditure request system, you want the approver to be able to Approve, Defer, or Reject the request. In the When the Task Process Completes event, you want to identify the approver's action and email the requestor the outcome. The email should be context sensitive, in that the language is specific to whether it was approved or not. Also, you want to set the workflow's status to Approved, Deferred, or Rejected; otherwise, the status default will be set to Completed, which isn't helpful if someone wants to report on the rejected requests. Follow the steps in table 4.1 to set up this event.

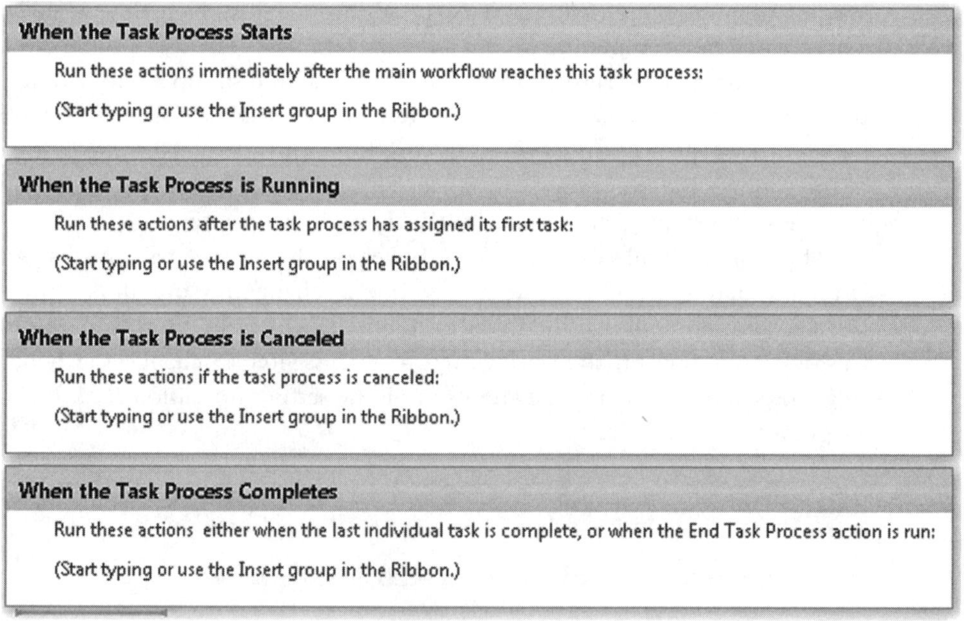

When the Task Process Starts

Run these actions immediately after the main workflow reaches this task process:

(Start typing or use the Insert group in the Ribbon.)

When the Task Process is Running

Run these actions after the task process has assigned its first task:

(Start typing or use the Insert group in the Ribbon.)

When the Task Process is Canceled

Run these actions if the task process is canceled:

(Start typing or use the Insert group in the Ribbon.)

When the Task Process Completes

Run these actions either when the last individual task is complete, or when the End Task Process action is run:

(Start typing or use the Insert group in the Ribbon.)

Figure 4.12   Editing the overall task process, you can add actions that respond to events such as task process start, running, cancellation, and completion.

Table 4.1   Email requestor and setting the workflow's status when the task process completes

Action	Steps	Result
Create a new variable to hold the status of the approval.	1 Click Local Variables in the Ribbon, and create a new workflow variable called ApprovalStatus and select the String option as the variable's data type. **NOTE:** The actual value of the variable will be set later in the section 4.2.3 example.	A new variable that will store the approval status of the capital expenditure request is added.
Add an If any value equals value condition.	1 Add the If any value equals value condition into the When the Task Process Completes event. 2 Add an else-if condition by clicking the Else-If Branch button. The condition branch will be labeled Else. To add the second condition, add another If any value equals value condition into the Else branch, and it'll be retitled Else-If… 3 Add an else condition again by clicking the Else-If Branch button a second time.	An if/ else if/ else series of conditions will be added to the event.
Complete the if conditions, checking to see if the ApprovalStatus variable is either Approved or Deferred.	1 For the first if statement, check to see if the ApprovalStatus variable is equal to Approved. 2 For the second if statement, check to see if the ApprovalStatus variable is equal to Deferred. **NOTE:** For the last Else block, you're assuming that, because the request was neither approved nor deferred, it's been rejected.	The first if condition will meet the condition if the status is Approved, and the else-if condition will likewise meet if the status Is Deferred.
In each If-Else-Else block, add an email action to email the requestor of the status and add the Set Workflow Status action to set the workflow's status.	1 Drop the Send an Email action into each if and else-if conditions. 2 Fill out the email properties appropriately, like specifying a body for the email with language specific to the approver's response. 3 Use the Set Workflow Status activity to set the status of the workflow for each approval response.	Your When the Task Process Completes event should now look like figure 4.13.

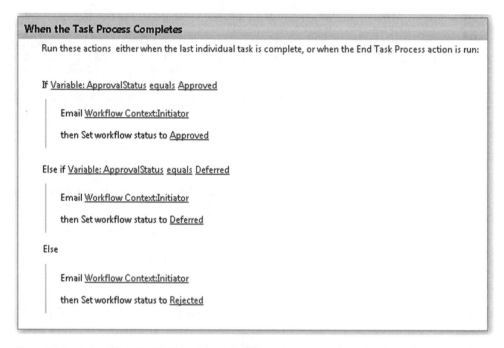

Figure 4.13   In the When the Task Process Completes event, you add actions that determine if the approver approved the request or not and whether an email should be sent to the requestor accordingly.

The final task you complete in this section is to add to the approval notification email a determination of when the requested funds will become available. We'll set this up later but, for now, create a new variable called DateFundsAvailable that is of the Date-Time type. In the approval email, refer to this variable. For instance, your approval notification email may look something like figure 4.14.

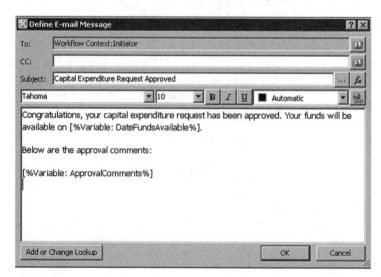

**Figure 4.14
In the approval notification email, add a reference to the DateFundsAvailable variable, informing requestors when their funds will be available.**

Next, you react when the expenditure request list item changes. You don't want the user submitting the request to be able to change the amount after the request has been approved. If the request is changed or deleted, you want the requestor and approver to be notified that the request has been canceled.

To set this up, drop a parallel block (click on Parallel Block in the Ribbon) inside the When the Task Process is Running event. Next, add two steps into this parallel block and an event into each step: the Wait for Change in Task Process Item action and the Wait for Deletion of Task Process Item action. The When the Task Process is Running event is helpful because, if the request is edited anywhere in the task process, the workflow will react and execute the Wait for Change and Wait for Deletion actions. The parallel block is handy because you can listen for multiple events simultaneously. Because you want to listen for two events (edit and change), you need this parallel block.

After you add the parallel block, the steps, and the wait actions, follow them up with an email to the requestor and the approver. Also, end the task process so the workflow will complete and, for the changed action, set the workflow's status to canceled. Afterwards, your When the Task Process is Running action should look like the one in figure 4.15.

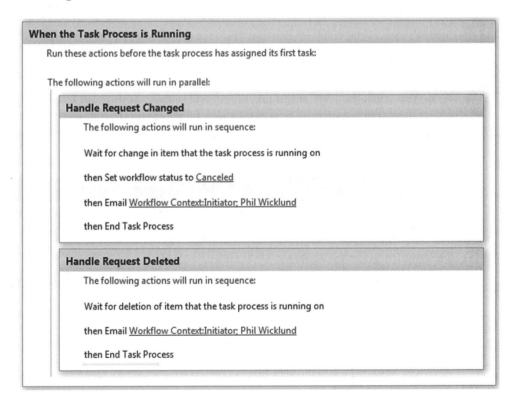

Figure 4.15 At the When the Task Process in Running event, you can effectively listen for changes made to the workflow's item, such as its editing or deletion.

4.2.2   *Task Form Fields box: customizing the task edit form*

Before you continue modifying the task process through the Customizations box, you need to configure the task edit form. You need this form to prompt the user to enter the Date Funds Available field that the approval notification email is using. In the next section, you'll take this date and assign it to the DateFundsAvailable variable that was set up in the previous section. But, before you can assign the variable, you need to prompt the approvers to enter it because they are approving the task. On the custom task process settings tab, there's a section called Task Form Fields (figure 4.16) where you can add new fields onto the task edit form.

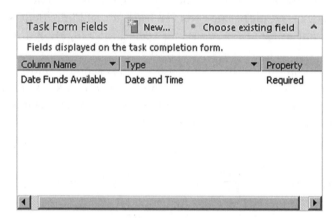

Figure 4.16   You can add more fields to the task edit form by entering them into the Task Form Fields section on the custom task process settings tab.

To do this, click the New button. A pop-up will appear, asking you to specify the field name, description, and data type. Add a new field called Date Funds Available and set it as a DateTime type. Don't publish yet; when you do, the approvers will notice a new field at the top of the task edit form (figure 4.17).

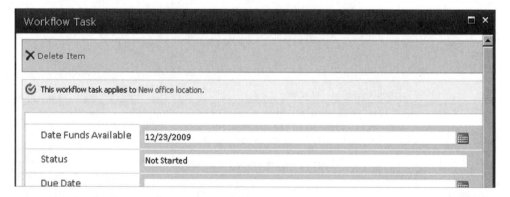

Figure 4.17   After the workflow is published, the fields entered in the Task Form Fields section will display on the task edit form.

4.2.3   *Customizations box: changing the behavior of a single Task*

With the task form fields in place, you can now resume configuring the task process through the Customizations box. You add actions that respond to the approver of the task. To do this, you add actions into the Change the Behavior of a Single Task tab. To get to this tab, click the Change the Behavior of a Single Task link in the Customization box. In this tab, you'll see five events to which you can add business logic when the task is first assigned, goes into a pending state, expires, is deleted, and is completed (figure 4.18).

For the capital expenditure request workflow, let's drop actions into three of these events. For the first event, you want to react when the request expires. If the approver doesn't approve or rejects the request in an allotted amount of time, you escalate the request to the approver's manager. Drop the Escalate Task action into the When a Task Expires event (figure 4.19). This action automatically figures out the person to whom the approver reports and reassigns the task to that person.

It is also important to respond if the task is deleted. There's nothing stopping a user with full control of the tasks list from deleting tasks, and the workflow should

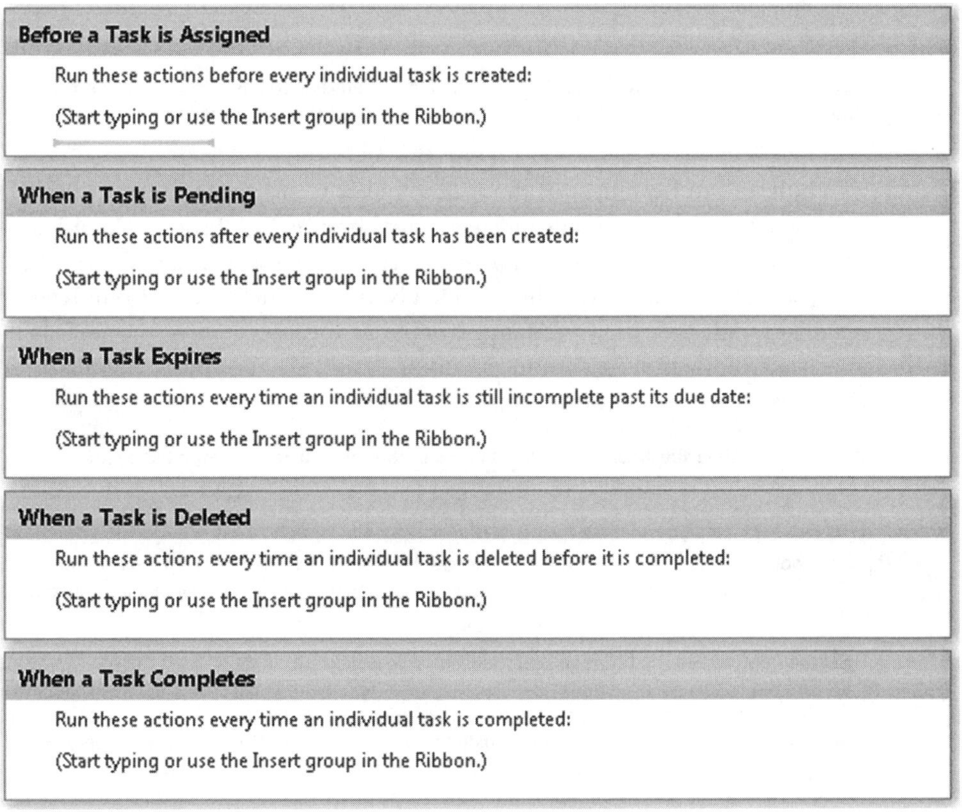

Before a Task is Assigned

Run these actions before every individual task is created:

(Start typing or use the Insert group in the Ribbon.)

When a Task is Pending

Run these actions after every individual task has been created:

(Start typing or use the Insert group in the Ribbon.)

When a Task Expires

Run these actions every time an individual task is still incomplete past its due date:

(Start typing or use the Insert group in the Ribbon.)

When a Task is Deleted

Run these actions every time an individual task is deleted before it is completed:

(Start typing or use the Insert group in the Ribbon.)

When a Task Completes

Run these actions every time an individual task is completed:

(Start typing or use the Insert group in the Ribbon.)

Figure 4.18   By changing the behavior of a single task, you can respond to events such as task assignment, set to pending, expiration, deletion, and completion.

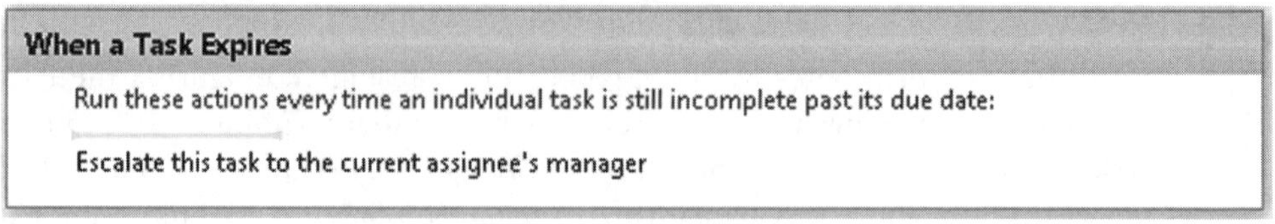

When a Task Expires

Run these actions every time an individual task is still incomplete past its due date:

Escalate this task to the current assignee's manager

Figure 4.19   At the When a Task Expires event, you can escalate the task to the assignee's manager.

have logic that appropriately responds to a deletion. Inside the When a Task is Deleted event, add the Set Workflow Variable action and choose the ApprovalStatus variable to assign it a new status. Set the variable to Canceled. Last, add the End Task Process action to cancel the task process and stop the workflow (figure 4.20).

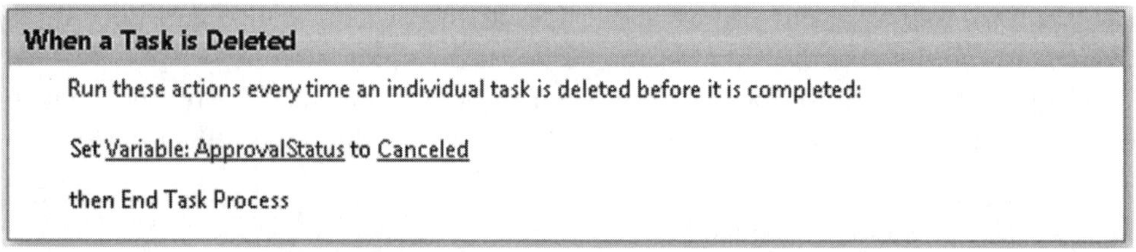

When a Task is Deleted

Run these actions every time an individual task is deleted before it is completed:

Set Variable: ApprovalStatus to Canceled

then End Task Process

Figure 4.20   If a task that a workflow depends on is deleted, ensure a clean exit for the workflow. In this case, you're setting the workflow's status and ending the task process.

The bulk of the logic lives in the When a Task Completes action. In the overall task process set of events, you customized the When the Task Process Completes event. In that event, you looked at a variable called ApprovalStatus and, depending on how the status was set, you sent out different emails. In the When a Task Completes event, you need to assign the ApprovalStatus variable to the outcome of the task. If the task is approved, the capital expenditure request should also be approved, and so on. Follow the steps in table 4.2 to set this up.

Table 4.2   Setting the ApprovalStatus variable in the When a Task Completes event

Action	Steps	Result
Add another if/else/ if-else condition.	Follow the same steps as in the When the Task Process Completes example.	An if /else-if /else series of conditions will be added to the event.
Set the ApprovalSta- tus and the DateFund- sAvailable variables in the first if condition.	1 In the first If condition, check whether the current task's outcome is Approved, and If so, assign the ApprovalStatus variable to Approved by using the Set a Workflow Vari- able action.	Both the ApprovalStatus and DateFundsAvailable variables will be set to values when the status is approved.

Table 4.2 Setting the ApprovalStatus variable in the When a Task Completes event *(continued)*

Action	Steps	Result
	NOTE: To get the current task's outcome, click the *fx* box in the If condition and change the Data Source to be Current Task: Task; then change the Field from source to be Outcome. **1** Add a second Set a Workflow Variable action in the first if condition and assign the DateFundsAvailable variable to the current task's Date Funds Available field that you created when you edited the task's edit form.	
Configure the else-if condition to check if the task was deferred	**1** In the else-if statement, check if the current task's outcome is set to Deferred by using another If any value equal value condition. **2** Assign the ApprovalStatus variable to Deferred.	The else-if condition will now be set to check whether the task was deferred. If so, the ApprovalStatus variable is set to Deferred.
In the Else block, set the ApprovalStatus variable to Rejected.		The ApprovalStatus variable is set to Rejected in the Else block.
End the task process by adding the End Task Process action below the If-Else action.		After completing these steps, your When a Task Completes event should look something like figure 4.21.

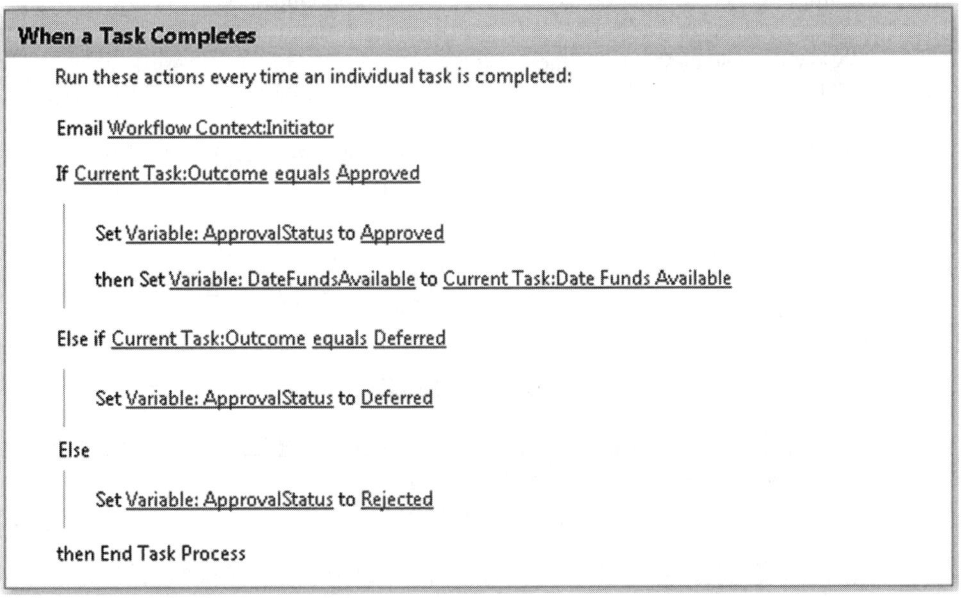

When a Task Completes

Run these actions every time an individual task is completed:

Email Workflow Context:Initiator

If Current Task:Outcome equals Approved

  Set Variable: ApprovalStatus to Approved

  then Set Variable: DateFundsAvailable to Current Task:Date Funds Available

Else if Current Task:Outcome equals Deferred

  Set Variable: ApprovalStatus to Deferred

Else

  Set Variable: ApprovalStatus to Rejected

then End Task Process

Figure 4.21 In the When a Task Completes event, you're assigning the ApprovalStatus variable to its corresponding task outcome.

4.2.4   *Task Outcomes box: defining custom task outcomes*

The last step in the capital expenditure request's journey is to set up a custom task outcome for request deferrals. As mentioned, there are two default outcomes—Approved and Rejected. A task outcome is the state at which a task is set after it is completed. In the case of the capital expenditure request, after the approver completes the task, its outcome will either be Approved, Deferred, or Rejected.

Notice the Task Outcomes section in the custom task process's settings tab (figure 4.22). By default, the first two outcomes are present. To add the third, click the New button and name the outcome Deferred and name the button Defer.

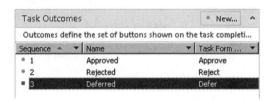

Figure 4.22   **You can add custom outcomes, such as Deferred, to the Approved and Rejected outcomes.**

When this third outcome is selected by the approver, the name Deferred will be stored in the task's Outcome variable. Defer refers to the name of the button on the task edit form. Notice that, when the user approves the task, a new option becomes available on the task edit form (figure 4.23). The user can now defer the request until a later date, when the workflow will be re-initiated.

Request Change and Reassign Tasks buttons

You may wonder where the Request Change and Reassign Task buttons are coming from in figure 4.23. These are called *workflow modifications*, whereby you can modify the behavior of a workflow after it has started. Refer to chapter 9 for information on how to build custom modifications.

When the user clicks the Defer button, the task's Status will be set to Completed, and the task's Outcome will be set to Deferred (figure 4.24). Click the Publish button and test your custom task process.

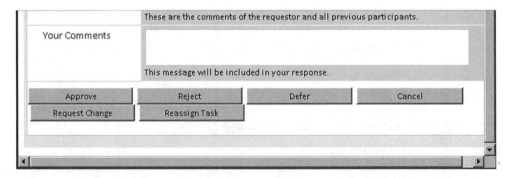

Figure 4.23   After the workflow is published, your custom task outcomes will appear as buttons on the task edit form.

Figure 4.24   After a task is completed, whichever task outcome is selected on the task edit form will be populated in the task's Outcome column.

Because the custom task process is waiting for the task to be completed, it will respond to this button click as well. In the When Task is Completed event, the if/else-if/else branch will determine that the approver deferred the request and it will set the ApprovalStatus to Deferred. Then, back in the overall task process events, the When the Task Process Completes event will look at the ApprovalStatus variable and send an email to the requestor notifying them that their request has been deferred. After that, the workflow will complete and the workflow's status will be set to Deferred (figure 4.25).

Figure 4.25   For the Expenditure Request workflow, after the task is completed, the outcome is stored in the workflow's Status column.

4.2.5   *Assignment stages*

When you first set up the custom task process, you assign the task process to a specific person. What if more than one person needs to approve the expenditure request? What if you don't know who the approvers should be at design time and you want your user to specify the approver? For instance, you might have several teams using the same workflow. Most likely, each team has a different manager. In this case, you'd want the person initiating the workflow to determine which manager should approve the process.

Assignment stages are an effective way to give the user the ability to determine who should receive the tasks that are assigned. Rather than entering someone's name directly into the workflow, you can assign custom task process to an assignment stage. Then, that assignment stage will appear on the workflow's initiation form and the user can edit the stage and specify all the users they think should be assigned the tasks.

Figure 4.26 shows what this association form may look like when assignment stages are enabled. The figure shows two stages configured, where the first stage has two users assigned the task in tandem, and the second stage has a single user.

With this assignment stage, the capital expenditure request will be executed three times, the first two times in tandem. Notice in figure 4.26 that two users are assigned in the first stage. After these two users have approved their requests, the requests will

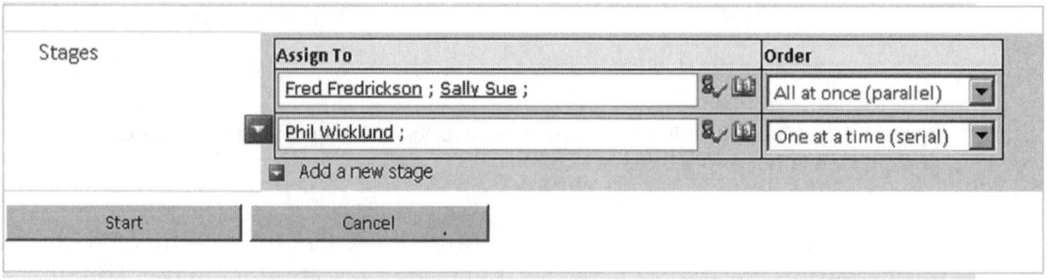

Figure 4.26   By enabling assignment stages, you can give your end users the ability to choose the persons to whom to assign the tasks. The assignment stage appears on the workflow's initiation form when it's first started.

go into the section stage, directed toward a third user for approval. The user can specify that the requests occur in parallel or sequentially. In the Start Custom Task Process action, instead of assigning the task process to a specify individual, you can assign it to an assignment stage instead (figures 4.27 and 4.28).

To make an assignment stage appear on the workflow's association form, click the Initiation Form Parameters button on the Ribbon within SharePoint Designer. Add a new parameter by clicking the Add button on the pop-up window that appears. Give the parameter a name and change the Information Type to be Assignment Stage (figure 4.29). Click OK and, after you publish the workflow, the assignment stages will appear on the workflow's association form.

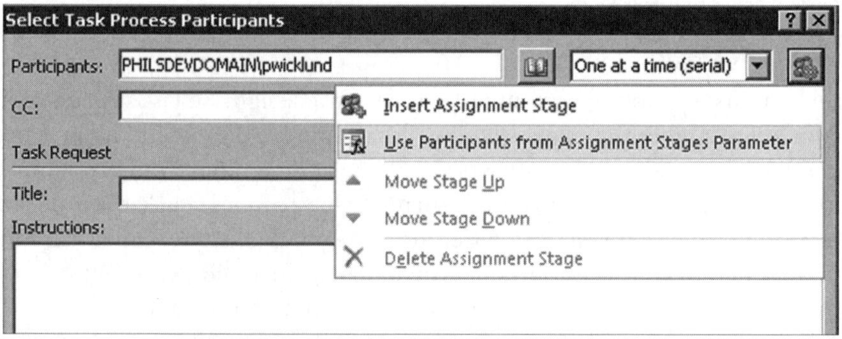

Figure 4.27   Instead of entering the name of an individual, you can set the task to be assigned to an Assignment Stage.

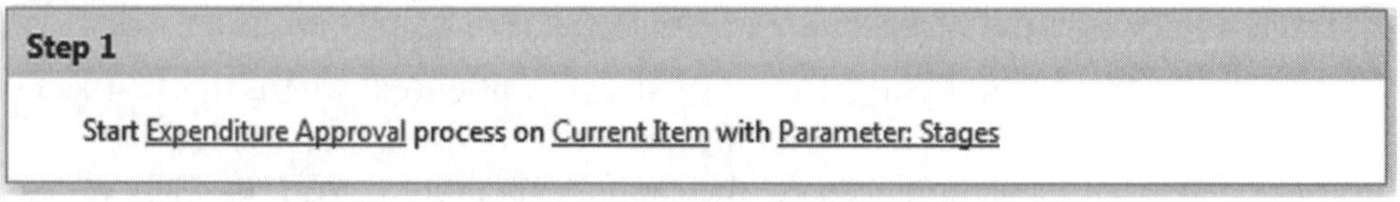

Figure 4.28   The third parameter is set to an assignment stage rather than to a specific user.

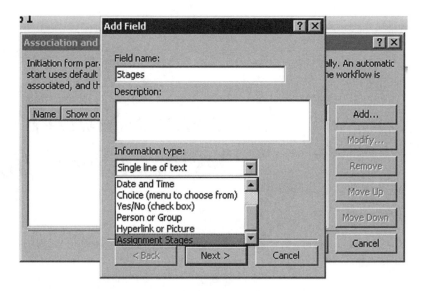

Figure 4.29 To enable assignment stages, add a new initiation parameter through the Initiation Parameters button in the Ribbon.

4.3 *Summary*

Workflows and task processes are like peas and carrots; they complement one another. Because most workflows require substantial human interaction, they often depend heavily on tasks to help manage that human interaction. Tasks can be used to help a workflow facilitate the gathering of information that the workflow needs in order to proceed. An approval workflow, for example, issues tasks to the approvers, and the approver can approve the item directly from that task. After the task is completed, the workflow can then proceed.

There are several ways to develop a task process for a SharePoint workflow. Share-Point Designer has several actions right out of the box that can be used for task management. You can create one-off tasks, like a generic task the workflow waits for it to be complete. There are also actions that help the workflow gather data if there's something the workflow needs before it can proceed. For the most complex task processing needs, you can create a custom task process in SharePoint designer using the Start Custom Task Process action. With a custom task process, you can change the overall behavior of the process. For example, you can drop actions that fire when the process first starts or is completed. You can also modify the behavior of a single task by adding actions that respond to a task's assignment, completion, or expiration.

Even custom task outcomes and custom task edit forms with InfoPath are possible through SharePoint Designer workflows. We cover these more advanced, form-related topics near the end of chapter 7.

Advanced SharePoint Designer workflows

5

This chapter covers

- Saving a workflow as a template
- Managing security within workflows
- Declaring records within workflows
- Leveraging Business Connectivity Services within workflows
- Customizing the out-of-the-box workflows
- Working with document sets within workflows

In chapter 4, we looked at the basics of creating workflows, including how to use the fundamental components of a workflow and how to use the workflow editing interface. Although that was a good start, there's much more to it.

In SPD 2010, you can save a workflow as a template. This template can be deployed across the entire farm, rather than the site or site collection. Even more valuable is the ability to deploy this workflow template to an entirely separate farm. This gives you the ability to test your SPD workflows in a nonproduction environment without the risk of causing unforeseeable production issues.

Another important technique that didn't fit into the previous SPD chapter involves customizing the out-of-the-box workflows. SharePoint 2010 offers several powerful out-of-the-box workflows, but they often are too generic to meet specific business needs. Rather than starting from scratch, you can extend the out-of-the-box workflows with custom functionality.

In addition to those two techniques, SPD 2010 has a host of new actions and conditions of particular interest. The two most exciting groups include actions and conditions that manage document sets and security permissions. Document sets are groups of documents. Workflows can run on top of these sets and do interesting things such as routing them for retention within the Records Center. This may be desirable for compliance or legal considerations. The second group includes actions and conditions concerning SharePoint security. With SPD 2010, your workflows can manage security by adding and removing user permissions on documents, for example.

Lastly, SPD workflows can interact easily with external data through Business Connectivity Services (BCS). By creating an External Content Type and an External List, your workflows can generate the BCS plumbing on your behalf to connect and work with external data such as SQL. Each of these functions will allow your workflows to provide additional value to your organization, either by further improving and automating processes or by leveraging the existing business data to make decisions.

5.1 SharePoint Designer workflow templates

You can save an SPD workflow as a template. The workflow can then be deployed to another SharePoint web application or even another farm. Previously this was only possible when working with Visual Studio workflows, which usually require significant amounts of time to be expended by experienced .NET developers. Using SPD 2010, it can be done quickly and without any .NET experience. The main benefit to these templates is the ability to test your workflows in a nonproduction environment, such as a development or test environment. After you thoroughly test the workflow, import it into production and make it available to your users. This reduces the risk of having users experience issues with your workflow because it's currently in use.

To save a workflow as a template, open the workflow in SharePoint Designer and click on the Save as Template Ribbon button. The template is saved with a .wsp extension in the Site Assets library within that site. It can then be downloaded and deployed to the entire farm or to a different farm. Follow the steps in table 5.1 to save a workflow as a template and deploy it to the entire farm.

NOTE Only reusable workflows can be saved as workflow templates.

Table 5.1 Deploying an SPD workflow across the entire farm

Action	Steps	Result
Open SPD and save a workflow as a template.	1 Open SPD and connect to your SharePoint site. 2 Open a reusable workflow or create a new one. Save the workflow as a template by clicking the Save as Template Ribbon button: 	The .wsp file (the solution file) is saved to the Site Assets library. You will see a prompt to indicate that it was successfully saved, and the .wsp file will appear under Site Assets, as in figure 5.1.

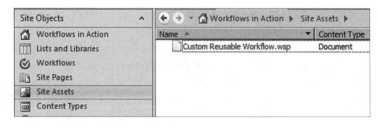

Figure 5.1   After you save an SPD workflow as a template, the workflow is packaged and saved into the Site Assets library within that site.

Table 5.1   Deploying an SPD workflow across the entire farm *(continued)*

Action	Steps	Result
Download the .wsp file to the server's file system.	**1** Browse to the Site Assets library and click Send To > Download a Copy: **2** Save the file to the root of the C drive on one of the servers in the farm.	The .wsp template file is downloaded to the root of the C drive on onc of the servers in the farm.

The next step is to add this template into the SharePoint farm. Some operations in SharePoint cannot be done using the Central Administration or Site Settings interfaces and can only be done using the command-line prompt. SharePoint 2010 includes a PowerShell commandlet called Add-SPSolution that allows these otherwise hidden operations to be performed. In this case, we are trying to add code to the server in the form of a .wsp file, also called a solution. The only way to add a solution to a SharePoint farm is through PowerShell. Because it is a command-line tool and must be run directly on the server, you may not have access to it within your organization. If you do not have access to the server or permissions to run a command-line operation, you'll need to coordinate with your SharePoint server administrator to issue the command described in the steps that follow.

Table 5.1   Deploying an SPD workflow across the entire farm *(continued)*

Action	Steps	Result

Log onto the server where you downloaded the .wsp and execute the PowerShell command to add the solution.	**1** Log on to the server and open the SharePoint 2010 Management Shell through the start menu.
	
	2 Run the following command:
	
	`Add-SPSolution`
	`c:\Custom_Reusable_Workflow.wsp`
	
	NOTE: The command is similar to this, but be sure to adjust the name and path of the .wsp file as required.
		The .wsp template solution is added into the SharePoint farm through stsadm.

Although a .wsp can be added to the farm only by using stsadm, it can be deployed using the Central Administration web interface. Continue with the steps to deploy the solution.

Table 5.1 Deploying an SPD workflow across the entire farm *(continued)*

Action	Steps	Result
Deploy the solution (.wsp template) through Central Administration.	1 In the target farm's central administration, click System Settings on the left of the screen and, under Farm Management, click Manage farm solutions. 2 Find the .wsp you added to the farm. It should be listed with a status of Not Deployed. Click the name of the solution to open the Solution Properties screen. 3 Click Deploy Solution at the top of the screen and then leave all settings at their default and click OK.	You are returned to the Solution Management screen where you should see that your solution is deployed to the farm (figure 5.2).

Central Administration ▸ Solution Management
This page has a list of the Solutions in the farm.   I Like

Name	Status	Deployed To
custom_reusable_workflow.wsp	Deployed	Globally deployed.

Figure 5.2 By using the stsadm command-line tool on the Solution Management screen, you can easily deploy solutions to the farm after they have been added.

After the Solution is deployed to the farm, it must be activated in order to take effect or become visible to end users. This allows you to activate it only in the specific areas where it is needed. Workflow templates are activated at the site level. Continue on to activate the template in a site.

Table 5.1 Deploying an SPD workflow across the entire farm *(continued)*

Action	Steps	Result
Activate the workflow's feature on a SharePoint site.	1 In a site different from where the workflow was created, activate the feature using the Manage Site Features screen under Site Settings: Workflow template "Custom Reusable Workflow" from web template "Workflows In Action" [Activate] 2 Add the workflow to a list using the Add Workflow option: Select a workflow template: Custom Reusable Workflow Approval - SharePoint 2010 Collect Signatures - SharePoint 2 Collect Feedback - SharePoint 20	The workflow's feature is activated on a site, and the workflow is ready for use on that site.

5.2   *Customizing the out-of-the-box workflows*

SharePoint 2010 includes several workflows out of the box, including List workflows and Site workflows such as the Approval workflows, the Collect Signatures workflows, and the Collect Feedback workflow. The default workflows are powerful and fairly complex. As powerful as they are, Microsoft had to make them generic in order to apply to numerous situations. For example, the Approval workflow can be applied to any list in SharePoint 2010. In some cases, the default workflows will come close to meeting your needs but may fall short. For instance, you may want the Approval workflow to log all approvals and rejections to a common list, a function that is not done with the default Approval workflow. By modifying the default workflows, you can add functionality to the built-in processes. This provides value to you as an SPD workflow developer because, rather than start from scratch, you can extend the default workflows and save considerable time.

SharePoint 2007 workflows cannot be modified

Out-of-the-box 2007 workflows could not be modified, but that's not the case with 2010 workflows. This means that, if, for instance, you used a 2007 Approval workflow and you decide to upgrade from 2007 to 2010, you won't be able to take that workflow instance and modify it. You'll need to start over with a 2010 Approval workflow and modify that one.

A "- SharePoint 2010" suffix is added to the workflow names to differentiate the workflows from the 2007 versions, which are also included in a SharePoint 2010. This allows for easier migration and backwards compatibility, but they are not activated by default. Even if their features are activated, they cannot be modified and will not appear in SharePoint Designer.

To modify an out-of-the-box workflow, open your site using SharePoint Designer 2010 and open the Workflows site object from the left-hand menu. You'll see the three workflows listed and any custom workflows that may exist (figure 5.3).

Clicking on the name of any of the workflows will open the workflow editing interface. From here, you can click the Edit Workflow link to see the steps and actions associated with the workflow. If you edit the *Approval - SharePoint 2010* workflow and view the workflow steps, it will at first appear to be a simple workflow with only one step (see figure 5.4).

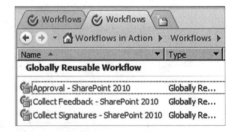

Figure 5.3   **SharePoint includes several workflows by default, all of which are now editable in SharePoint Designer.**

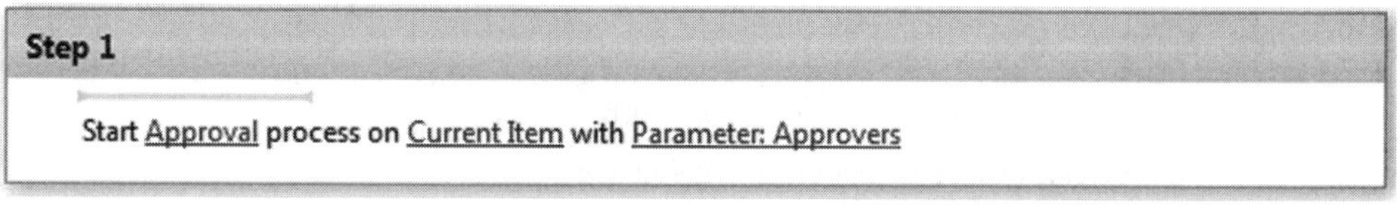

Step 1

　Start <u>Approval</u> process on <u>Current Item</u> with <u>Parameter: Approvers</u>

Figure 5.4　At first glance, the Approval workflow looks simple. The Approval action contains its true functionality including multiple Completion conditions and task behaviors.

Clicking on the Approval task will reveal the true logic, which includes completion conditions, single item behaviors, and overall behaviors (figures 5.5 and 5.6), all of which can be modified using the workflow editing interface.

　Because of the complexity of the out-of-the-box workflows, I recommend that you not modify the originals. Instead, copy the original and make changes to the copy. To do this, right-click on the workflow you want to copy and choose Copy and Modify. You can also use the Copy and Modify Ribbon button to copy an out-of-the-box workflow.

　After using a Copy and Modify option, you will see a dialog that will allow you to give your workflow a unique name. Enter a name for your new copy. Optionally, you can bind the new workflow to a content type and limit the scope of where that workflow is available to a particular content type. After making your content type selection, click OK.

　When you click OK, you will be taken directly to the Workflow editor screen. You may notice that the action names are modified slightly due to the copy process. The text (en-US) Copy has been added to the Approval action name in figure 5.7. You can leave these as is or adjust the names. At this point, you can save and publish the workflow, with or without making any changes, and you'll be left with an exact copy of the original default workflow, except now with a different name.

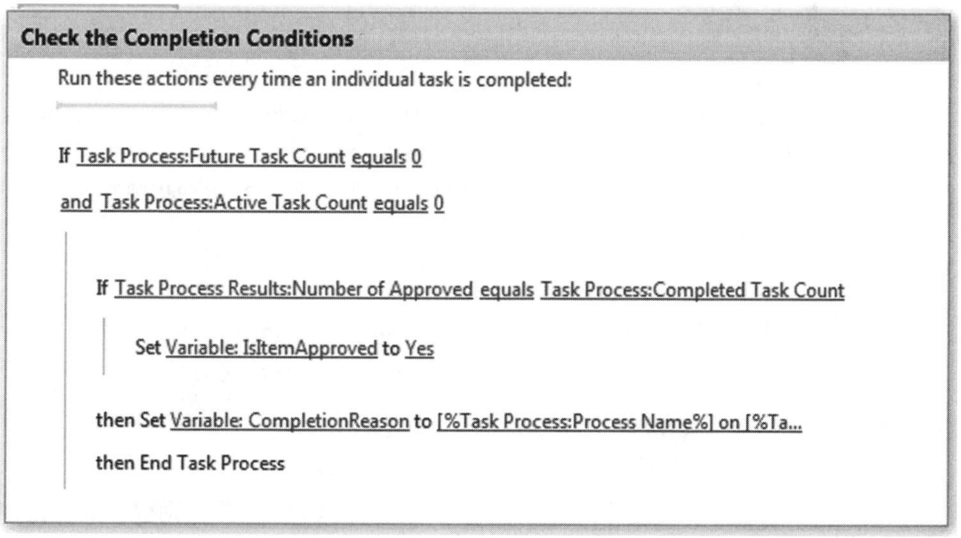

Check the Completion Conditions

　Run these actions every time an individual task is completed:

　If <u>Task Process:Future Task Count</u> <u>equals</u> <u>0</u>

　and <u>Task Process:Active Task Count</u> <u>equals</u> <u>0</u>

　　　If <u>Task Process Results:Number of Approved</u> <u>equals</u> <u>Task Process:Completed Task Count</u>

　　　　Set <u>Variable: IsItemApproved</u> to <u>Yes</u>

　　　then Set <u>Variable: CompletionReason</u> to <u>[%Task Process:Process Name%] on [%Ta...</u>

　　　then End Task Process

Figure 5.5　The completion conditions determine when the Approval task is complete.

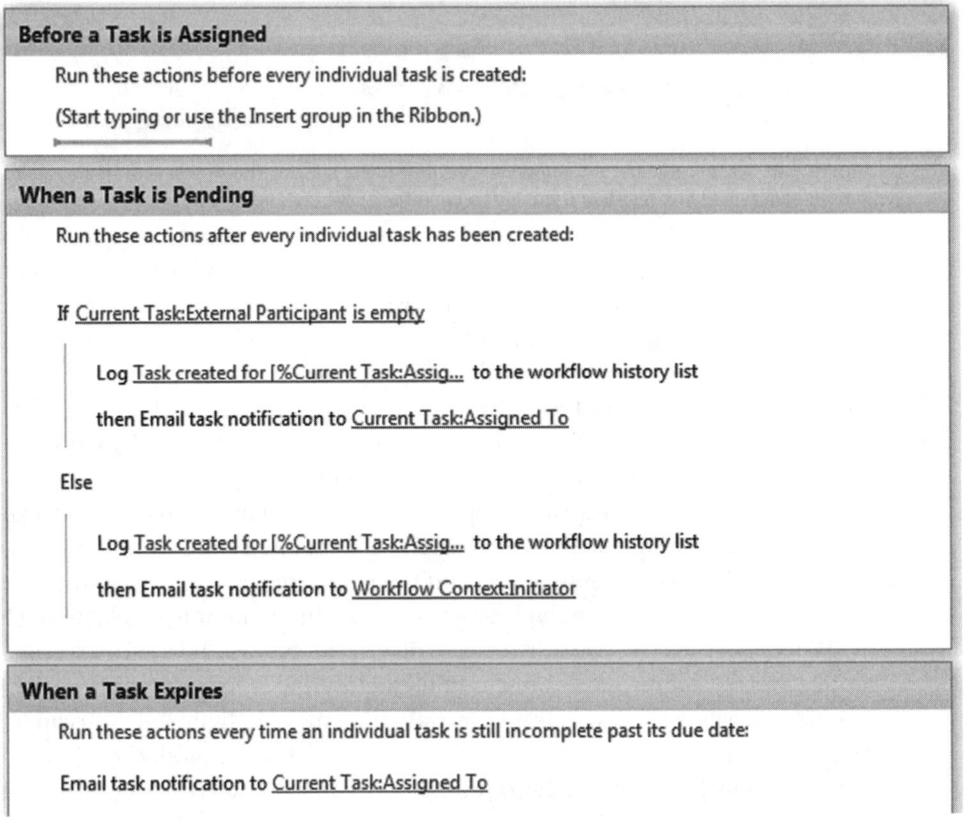

Before a Task is Assigned
Run these actions before every individual task is created:
(Start typing or use the Insert group in the Ribbon.)
When a Task is Pending
Run these actions after every individual task has been created:
If Current Task:External Participant is empty
Log Task created for [%Current Task:Assig... to the workflow history list
then Email task notification to Current Task:Assigned To
Else
Log Task created for [%Current Task:Assig... to the workflow history list
then Email task notification to Workflow Context:Initiator
When a Task Expires
Run these actions every time an individual task is still incomplete past its due date:
Email task notification to Current Task:Assigned To

Figure 5.6 The behaviors determine what happens at different stages of the task process.

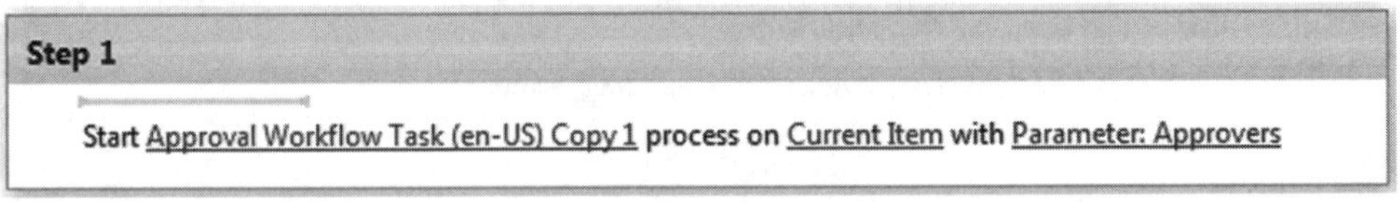

Step 1
Start Approval Workflow Task (en-US) Copy 1 process on Current Item with Parameter: Approvers

Figure 5.7 The action names may be automatically adjusted when you copy a reusable workflow.

Adjust the workflow settings, conditions, and actions as required and then save and publish the workflow as usual. The workflow will now be listed under Reusable Workflows along with the default global workflows (figure 5.8).

Globally Reusable Workflow
Approval - SharePoint 2010
Collect Feedback - SharePoint 2010
Collect Signatures - SharePoint 2010
Reusable Workflow
Approval - SharePoint 2010 - Customized

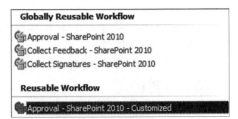

Figure 5.8 Copying a globally reusable workflow results in a new reusable workflow.

Remember that reusable workflows are available only to the site in which they were created and not to the entire site collection, whereas globally reusable workflows can be used

throughout the site collection. To promote the copied and customized workflow to a globally reusable workflow, open the customized workflow and return to the workflow editor. Then, click the Publish Globally Ribbon button seen in figure 5.9.

Figure 5.9   The Publish Globally Ribbon button will promote a reusable to a globally reusable workflow and make it available across the entire site collection.

When publishing a reusable workflow globally, you will always get a warning about making it available to all lists in the site collection and visible to all users. Click OK on this warning. Thereafter, the workflow will be copied again and published, but this second copy will be published as a globally reusable workflow. The reusable workflow will not be deleted by this process, and you will likely want to manually delete it to avoid confusion.

Using this process, you can modify the out-of-the-box workflows to meet your organization's needs. This may mean that you make a single customized version for your entire organization or several versions for different purposes. In either case, starting with the out-of-the-box workflows may significantly reduce development time because much of the work has been completed already.

5.3   *Workflow actions for document sets*

Document sets are a new concept in SharePoint 2010. They represent a collection of documents, similar to folders, except that they allow for additional functionality. For example, it is possible to secure all of the documents in a document set at one time. If the security is applied to a folder, documents within that folder could break inheritance and would not be affected by the change. It is also possible to run workflows against document sets; you couldn't do that with simple folders. Before we dig into document sets and workflows, we need to learn how to create a document set. That will help set the stage for what the new actions bring to the table and will give an example of document sets in use.

5.3.1   *Creating document sets*

Before you can interact with document sets in a workflow, you must activate the Document Set feature and apply the content type to a document library. Follow the steps in table 5.2 to enable document sets in your site. Note that you must be a site collection administrator to activate the document set feature.

Table 5.2   Creating a document set in SharePoint 2010

Action	Steps	Result
Activate the Document Sets feature in your Share-Point site.	1 In the root collection site, browse to Site Settings under the Site Actions menu. 2 Click the Site collection features link under the Site Collection Administration category. 3 Click the Activate button next to the Document Sets feature.	The Document Sets feature becomes active. **Document Sets** Provides the content types required for creating and using document sets. Create a document set when you want to manage multiple documents as a single work product. Deactivate Active

Table 5.2   Creating a document set in SharePoint 2010 *(continued)*

Action	Steps	Result
Add the Document Set content type to a Document Library.	1 In a document library such as Shared Documents, browse to Library Settings using the Ribbon. 2 Click the Advanced settings link under General Settings. 3 Set Allow management of content types to Yes and click OK. 4 At the Library Settings screen, under Content Types, click the Add from existing site content types link. 5 Highlight Document Set in the available content types list and click the Add button, then click OK.	Document sets can be created in the library by clicking the New Document menu item and choosing Document Set (figure 5.10).

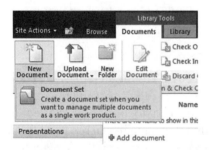

Figure 5.10   Document sets are created using the New Document menu in the same way that new documents are created, as long as they have been added as a content type to the list.

Table 5.2   Creating a document set in SharePoint 2010 *(continued)*

Action	Steps	Result
Create a new Document Set.	1 Click the New Document dropdown and select the Document Set content type (figure 5.11). 2 In the New Document Set dialog, give the document set a name such as Sales Presentation and give it a description. Then click OK.	The Document Set is shown with no documents. To upload documents into the document set, use the Upload Document Ribbon button.

5.3.2   *Document set workflow actions*

With a document set in place, it's time to transition to how the SPD workflows interact with it. In order to interact specifically with document sets, four new workflow actions have been created.

- *Capture a Version of the Document Set*—Captures a snapshot of the document set and saves it in the version history.
- *Send Document Set to Repository*—Moves or copies the document set to a Share-Point 2010 Records Center, which is used to permanently store documents for archiving purposes.

- *Set Content Approval Status for the Document Set*—Approves or rejects the set from within the workflow.
- *Start Document Set Approval Process*—allows the user to approve or reject the set.

CAPTURE A VERSION OF THE DOCUMENT SET

The Capture a Version of the Document Set action captures the current state of either the major or minor versions of all documents in a document set and saves them to the document set's version history. This allows you to take a snapshot of the document set as a whole, instead of relying on the major and minor versions of the individual documents. The action accepts two parameters, type and comment (figure 5.11). The type parameter determines the versions that will be captured. The choices include capturing the latest minor versions or the last major version. The comment parameter allows you to add a comment that will be stored with the captured document set version.

After using this action on a document set, you can view the document set's version history using its context menu in the SharePoint interface. You'll see the latest major or minor versions, along with the comment that was captured with the action. From here, it's possible to restore the previous version of a document within the set or the entire document set.

The Capture a Version of the Document Set action could be useful when creating a presentation that includes several documents containing related information. As the presentation is developed and its documents are modified, saving a snapshot of all related documents will allow you to more easily track the progress of the presentation. You can still manage the documents individually, including their version history, if required. After capturing a version of the document set, you can view it by opening the document set from within a document library. You'll notice that the Ribbon will include a new tab called Document Set. Opening this tab will reveal the Capture Version button, which is similar to the workflow action but is used manually. There is also the Version History button, which will show you the captured document set versions (figure 5.12).

Clicking the Version History button for a document set will show you a version screen similar to the one used for documents, except that documents within the document set are also shown, with their respective versions (figure 5.13). Note that modifying the document set's properties such as the title still generates a new version of the set. The documents will not be captured or shown in the history unless you use the Capture a Version workflow action or Ribbon button again.

Step 1

Capture a version of this Document Set that includes the <u>type</u> versions of the contents with comment: <u>comment</u>

Figure 5.11   The Capture a Version of the Document Set action takes a snapshot of all the documents in the document set and saves the set to the version history with a comment.

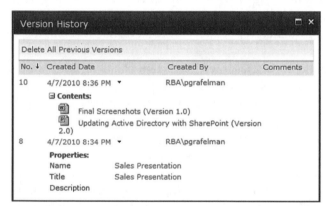

Figure 5.12   A Document Set's version history shows all the related documents at a point in time.

Figure 5.13   A Document Set's version history shows all of its related documents at a point in time, with individual document versions.

SEND DOCUMENT SET TO REPOSITORY

The Send Document Set to Repository action is used to send a document set to a Records Center for permanent storage of important documents. The action requires three parameters—the action, destination content organizer, and explanation (figure 5.14). The this action parameter determines if the document set will be copied, moved, or moved with a link (a link to the final destination of the original document is left in place). The destination content organizer is the address of the Records Center Router that you will use to process the document set. A Records Center Router is configured within the Records Center to allow for the management and storage of

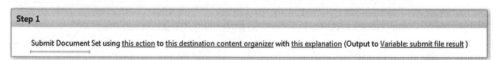

Figure 5.14   The Send Document Set to Repository action sends a document set to a Records Center using data supplied in several parameters.

multiple types of documents. See the example at the end of this section to learn how to configure a Records Center and a Records Center Router. Finally, this explanation is text that is associated with the record when it is placed in the Records Center.

> ## Brief introduction to the Records Center in SharePoint
>
> A SharePoint Records Center is used for permanent storage of important documents. Records Centers are usually used when a company has documents that are sensitive for compliance or legal reasons. Such a company can use a Records Center to house those documents in a noneditable fashion. Those documents can also have a retention policy, such as seven years, after which they are deleted.
>
> The Records Center can be configured to manage multiple types of documents by creating rules. These rules allow documents to be sent to one common location by a workflow or by a manual process. After they are in Records Center, they can then be routed to the correct library based on the document type or other metadata.

As we hinted earlier, a document set can be copied, moved, or moved with a remaining link. The first two options are self-explanatory, but note that a document set is converted to a zip file when it is placed in a Records Center (figure 5.15). Converting the document set to a zip saves storage space and allows all of the documents to be downloaded at once. The Move and Leave a Link option will store the document set in the

Figure 5.15   Document sets that are saved to a Records Center are automatically converted to zip files, allowing them to be downloaded as a set to save storage space.

Records Center but will leave behind a link in the list allowing users to find the document set easily. The results of the action are stored to a variable, allowing you to take further action if the action fails or succeeds.

SET CONTENT APPROVAL STATUS FOR THE DOCUMENT SET

Document sets, like documents, can require approval if their library is configured to require it. The Set Content Approval Status for a Document Set action is used to set the approval status of a document set. This process is usually done manually using the SharePoint interface, but this action allows it to be automated when required. The action only has two parameters, the status to apply and comments to include (figure 5.16). The action can be run only against the current item and cannot be used to define the status of a document set in a different library.

This action would be useful to automatically approve or reject a document set after a given amount of time. It is also wise to include logic that stops the workflow if a user manually adjusts the approval status before the automatic approval is started.

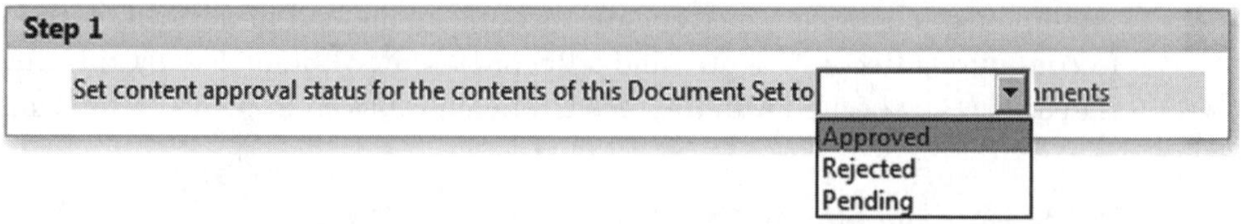

Figure 5.16   Document Set Approval status can be adjusted using the Set Content Approval Status for the Document Set workflow action.

START DOCUMENT SET APPROVAL PROCESS

The Start Document Set Approval Process action is related to the Set Document Set Approval Status action, but it is used differently. Instead of performing the approval or rejection, this action is used to start an instance of the Approval workflow on the set, prompting a user or users to review and approve or reject the document set. The Approval link is not related to a parameter; instead, it opens a new instance of the default Approval workflow as a child to the original workflow.

5.3.3   *Document set and Records Center workflow example*

The following example will illustrate using a workflow to send a document set to a Records Center. The scenario is that a document set is used to create and collect data required for a sales proposal. After the proposal is complete, it must be approved by a manager. Finally, after the client accepts the proposal, the document set must be sent to a Records Center to prevent changes for compliance and legal reasons. For instance, a signed proposal might stipulate that you provide seven employees for a total of 280 work hours per week, with no unapproved overtime. The proposal might further stipulate the salaries for each of those seven employees. Most likely, the proposal includes a completion date. All of these details that you can't change can be saved by the workflow. The first set of steps involves configuring a Records Center to which you can route document sets from your workflow. Follow the steps in table 5.3 to configure a Records Center in SharePoint.

Table 5.3   Provisioning a new Records Center in SharePoint 2010

Action	Steps	Result
Create a new site collection using the Records Center site template.	From within Central Administration > Application Management, create a new site collection using the Records Center site template: 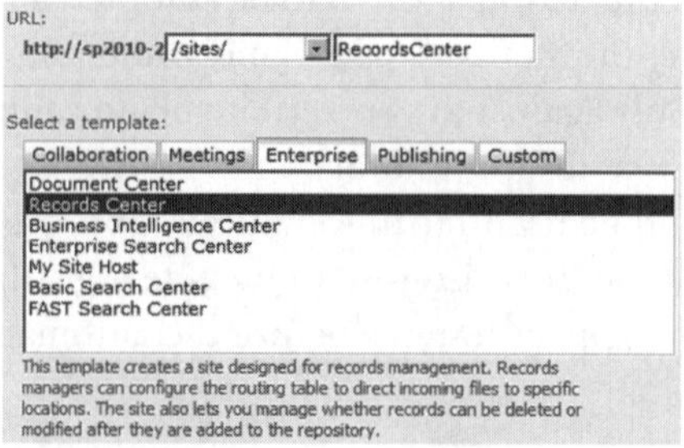	A new site collection is created using the Records Center template.

Table 5.3 Provisioning a new Records Center in SharePoint 2010 *(continued)*

Action	Steps	Result
Create a new library in the Records Center to store your sales proposal document sets.	1 Browse to the newly created Records Center and select Manage Records Center under Site Actions. 2 Click Create a new Records Library and then click Record Library to create a new library to store document sets. 3 Name the library Document Set Records. 4 Add the document set content type to this new library using the Content Types settings on the Library Settings page, as you did in the second action in table 5.2.	A new document library that will receive the routed document sets is created in Records Center.
Set up the set's content organizer rules.	1 Click Manage Records Center under Site Actions again and click Create Content Organizer Rules. 2 Click Add New Item and Fill in the Rule properties to match figures 5.17 and 5.18. **NOTE:** The Content Type must be set to Document Set and the target location must point to the Document Set Records library that you previously created.	After saving the rule, documents sent to the Records Center's Drop Off Library is automatically moved to the Document Set Records library, created in the previous action, if they have the document set content type.

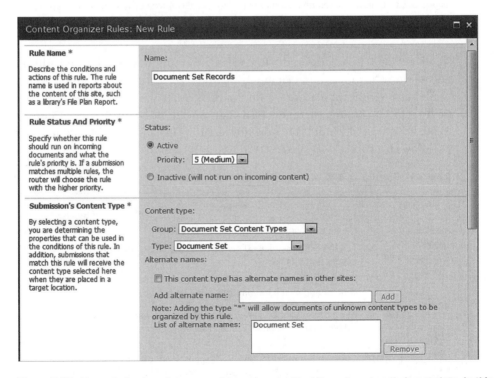

Figure 5.17 Records Center rules are used to route submitted items based on their metadata. In this case, you're going to route all document sets into a specific record library by examining the content type.

Conditions

In order to match this rule, a submission's properties must match all the specified property conditions (e.g. "If Date Created is before 1/1/2000").

Property-based conditions:

Property: Content Type ▾   X

Operator: is equal to ▾

Value:

(Add another condition)

Target Location *

Specify where to place content that matches this rule.

When sending to another site, the available sites are taken from the list of other sites with content organizers, as defined by the system administrator.

Check the "Automatically create a folder for each unique value of a property" box to force the organizer to group similar documents together. For instance, if you have a property that lists all the teams in your organization, you can force the organizer to create a separate folder for each team.

Destination:

/sites/RecordsCenter/Document Set Records   Browse...

Example: /sites/DocumentCenter/Documents/

☐ Automatically create a folder for each unique value of a property:

Select a property (must be a required, single value property): ▾

Specify the format for the folder name: %1 - %2

When the folder is created:
  %1 will be replaced by the name of the property
  %2 will be replaced with the unique value for the property

OK   Cancel

Figure 5.18   Conditions can be added (but are not required) using the Conditions settings. It is required to indicate where the submitted items need to be stored. Note that this target location must be configured to allow the document set content type or you will not be allowed to save the new rule.

Now that you have configured a Records Center and have configured a library to use document sets, you can use the new document-set-specific workflow actions. Records Center is a significant feature within SharePoint 2010 but, for the scope of this book, we'll focus on routing documents through workflows. With Records Center all ready to go, we can finally build our workflow. Follow the steps in table 5.4 to build an SPD workflow that routes document sets to Records Center.

Table 5.4   Creating an SPD workflow that routes document sets to Records Center

Action	Steps	Result
Create a new document library to hold the proposals.	1 Create a document library called Proposals. 2 Add the document set content type to the library using the Library Settings menu. 3 Under the library's Versioning settings option, set Require content approval for submitted items to Yes.	A new document library is created to store customer proposals.
Create a new List workflow called Approve Proposal.	1 Using SharePoint Designer, create a new List workflow called Approve Proposal in the Proposals library. 2 Add a Set Content Approval Status for the Document Set action to the workflow and configure it to set the status to Approved and add a comment, as shown in figure 5.19. 3 Save and publish the workflow.	A new workflow called Approve Proposal that will handle the approval or rejection of the document set is created.

Step 1

Set content approval status for the contents of this Document Set to <u>Approved</u> with <u>Proposal Approved</u>

Figure 5.19   The Set Content Approval Status action can be used to set the status to Approved, Pending, or Rejected.

Table 5.4   Creating an SPD workflow that routes document sets to Records Center *(continued)*

Action	Steps	Result
Create another workflow called Send Proposal to Records Center.	1 Create another List workflow on the Proposals library called Send Proposal to Records Center. 2 Add a Send Document Set to Repository action to the workflow and configure it with the URL to the Records Center's Drop Off Library (figure 5.20). 3 Save and publish the second workflow.	A second workflow titled Send Proposal to Records Center is created. This workflow will route the document set to Records Center.

Step 1

Submit Document Set using <u>Move and Leave a Link</u> to <u>http://sp2010-2/sites/RecordsCenter/D...</u> with <u>this explanation</u> (Output to <u>Variable: submit file result</u>)

Figure 5.20   The Send Document Set to Repository action can Copy, Move, or Move and Leave a Link. In this case, it is set to Move and Leave a Link to allow users to find the proposals easily after they are sent to the Records Center.

Table 5.4   Creating an SPD workflow that routes document sets to Records Center *(continued)*

Action	Steps	Result
Create a new document set called Acme Proposal.	1 Within the Proposals document libraries, create a new Document Set named Acme Proposal by using the New Document Set option under the New Document Ribbon button. 2 Add some documents by opening the document set and using the Upload Document Ribbon button.	A new document set on which your two workflows will execute is created.
Run the Approve Proposal workflow.	3 Switch to the Manage tab and click the Workflows Ribbon button. 4 Run the Approve Proposal workflow.	The status of the document set changes to Approved.
Run the Send Proposal to Records Center workflow.		The document set is moved to the Records Center and the original set changes to a Document Link in the Proposals library after the Content Organizer Processing timer job executes, which by default is 11:30 pm daily.

5.4   *Workflow actions and conditions for security*

Sites, libraries, and even documents can be managed with different permissions. Additionally, multiple levels of permissions are available right out of the box, such as Full Control, Designer, Contributor, and Reader. Custom permission levels can also be created to suit your needs. New to SharePoint Designer 2010 is the ability to manipulate the permissions on list items within workflows. Previously, this could only be done manually within SharePoint or by using custom .NET code. It is now also possible to run workflow actions as a different user, taking advantage or their permissions. All this is done using impersonation steps and a slew of new security-related actions and conditions within SharePoint Designer.

5.4.1   *Impersonation steps*

When a user starts a workflow, most of the actions taken by the workflow will be attributed to that user. In some cases, the user running the workflow may not have the permission required to execute the required action. For example, you may want to prevent users from deleting list items directly, but you still want to allow a workflow to delete the items. If you remove the user's delete permission level, they will not be able to run a workflow that deletes an item. If this is not the desired behavior, you can use impersonation steps to allow the user to run the delete action as another user who has the necessary permissions to delete items. There are a few limitations to impersonation steps that you need to be aware of:

- The impersonation step can be run only as the user who is authoring the workflow. You cannot set the step to run as a different user.
- Messages logged to the workflow history as part of an impersonation step will still be logged as a system account and not a workflow author.
- You cannot create an impersonation step within another step; they can only be created as top-level steps.

The following figures show the creation of two new list items in the Sample List. The first list item is created as part of a standard step, and the user who started the workflow will be listed in the Created By and Modified By fields. The second item is created as part of an impersonation step and the workflow author, Paul Grafelman, will be listed in the Created By and Modified By fields. Figure 5.21 shows the two steps and their Create List Item actions.

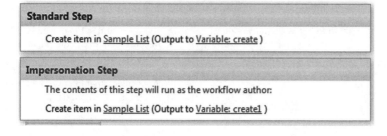

Figure 5.21
Although the actions within the steps are nearly identical, the author will be different for each item.

Although Todd Rowe ran the workflow that created the list items in figure 5.22, the second created item (the first item shown) was created as part of the impersonation step and is shown as created by Paul Grafelman, the author of the workflow.

Title↓	☐ Created By	☐ Modified By
List Item from Impersonation Step ☐ NEW	Paul Grafelman	Paul Grafelman
Item from Standard Step ☐ NEW	Todd Rowe	Todd Rowe

Figure 5.22   Although the two items were created by a single workflow, only the item created by the Standard Step is attributed to the end user.

5.4.2   *Security-related conditions and actions*

In addition to the impersonation, several new security-related conditions and actions are available in SharePoint Designer workflows. These allow a workflow to inspect and modify a user's permissions for an item or document. Note that these additional conditions and actions are available only within an impersonation step and cannot be added to a conventional step.

CHECK LIST ITEM PERMISSION LEVELS CONDITION

The Check List Item Permission Levels condition checks to see if the specified user has been given explicit permissions on the specified list. The first parameter indicates which user's permissions should be checked. The second parameter shows which permission level is being checked. The third parameter indicates which list item is being examined. The list item can be set to Current Item or to an item in any other accessible list. Table 5.5 shows the results of different condition configurations.

Table 5.5   Comparing user permission levels in an impersonation step

User's item permission level	Condition checks for	Condition result
Contribute, Approve	Approve	True
Contribute, Approve	Full Control	False
Full Control	Contribute, Approve	False

Inherited vs explicit permissions

The two security related conditions look only at explicit permissions; inherited permissions are not taken into account. Explicit permissions are when a user is given direct, or explicit, permissions to the item in question. An inherited permission is when that an item is inheriting its permissions from its parent, and does not define any of its own unique permissions.

Note this interesting feature in table 5.5: if the user has full control on the item but the condition is checking for Contribute, the condition will return false. This is interesting because you're typically given contribute rights when you receive full control to an item. If this is problematic for your workflow, use the next condition, Check List Item Permissions.

CHECK LIST ITEM PERMISSIONS CONDITION

The Check List Item Permissions condition checks to see if the specified user has the specified permissions on the specified list item. It is configured the same way as the previous condition, but the results are potentially different. This is because it is not looking for the exact specified permission. Instead, it is checking to see if the user has at least the specified permission. Table 5.6 shows some examples.

Table 5.6   How user permissions are compared in an impersonation step

User's item permissions	Condition checks for	Condition result
Full Control	Contribute	True
Contribute	Read	True
Read	Contribute	False

ADD LIST ITEM PERMISSIONS ACTION

The Add List Item Permissions action is used to give a user explicit permissions for a list item. This will also break inheritance on the item's permissions. The specified permissions are then added to the existing permissions. The Add List Item Permissions action can also be used to give multiple users permissions for the list item at one time (figure 5.23).

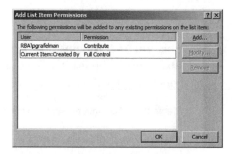

INHERIT LIST ITEM PERMISSIONS ACTION

The Inherit List Item Permissions action removes all explicit permissions for the item and sets them to inherit permissions from its

Figure 5.23   Multiple users can be given a variety of permissions with one Add List Item Permissions action.

parent. An example of this is a workflow that sets explicit permissions on a list item while the workflow is running in order to prevent anyone from editing the item. After the workflow is complete, users need to be able to edit the list item again. Using the Inherit List Item Permissions action would allow anyone with contribute or edit permissions on the list to re-edit the list item.

REMOVE LIST ITEM PERMISSIONS ACTION

The Remove List Item Permissions action removes the specified explicit permissions from the list item. Other explicit permissions will not be removed. Note that, if the item has inherited permissions, this action will break the inheritance.

REPLACE LIST ITEM PERMISSIONS ACTION

The Replace List Item Permissions action removes all existing explicit permissions and applies the permission specified in the action instead. When the action starts, it will also break inheritance if it is in place. A Workflow Users SharePoint group will be added to the list item automatically. This group will allow users who do not have access to the parent list to be added to the list item permissions through workflows.

5.4.3 *Working with permissions and security in a workflow*

This workflow example will demonstrate the use of the previously described conditions and actions to allow a user without permissions to a list to approve an item. The scenario is an expense report approval system in which employees need to be able to submit expense reports to a document library but they should not have access to view other employees' reports. In addition, the employee's manager must be given the ability to approve expense reports submitted by her employees only. Managers should not be able to read the reports submitted by other employees. To accomplish this, the workflow will include actions that will break inherited permissions and give the submitting user read access only. In addition, the user's manager will be given approve permissions on the item. This will all happen automatically when the item is uploaded. To do this, follow the steps in table 5.7.

Table 5.7 Working with security-related Actions and Conditions in an SPD workflow

Action	Steps	Result
Create a document library called Expense Reports and configure security on that library.	**1** Create a new document library called Expense Reports and navigate to the library's Library Settings page. Then choose Permissions for this document library. **2** Click the Stop Inheriting Permissions Ribbon button: **3** Delete all permissions from the library by selecting all users and groups and clicking the Remove User Permissions Ribbon button. **4** Click the Grant Permissions Ribbon Button and type NT AUTHORITY\AUTHENTICATED USERS in the Users and Groups field and then click the check box next to Contribute. Click OK.	A new document library is created for users to upload their expense reports. The library is set to not inherit permissions for its parent site and all authenticated users have the ability to upload documents.
Create a new SharePoint Designer list workflow to manage the approval of expense reports.	**1** Create a new List Workflow titled Submit Expense Report for Approval on the Expense Reports library. **NOTE:** On the new list, be sure you are logged in as a user with full control, such as a site collection administrator. **2** Add an Impersonation Step to the workflow: 	A new SPD workflow is created that will break inheritance on the expense report and add the submitter as a reader on the report and also add the submitter's manager as an approver.

Table 5.7   Working with security-related Actions and Conditions in an SPD workflow *(continued)*

Action	Steps	Result
	3 In the Impersonation Step, add a Lookup Manager for a User action and set it to look up the manager of the user who created the current item: Find Manager of <u>Current Item:Created By</u> (output to <u>Variable: manager</u>) **4** Add a Replace List Item Permissions action and set it to give the user who created the item read permission and that same user's manager approve permissions: 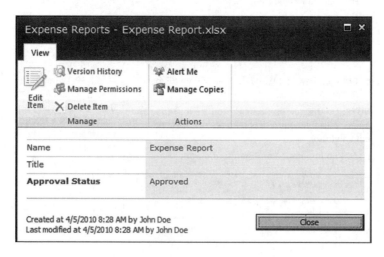 **NOTE:** The user who created the item has contribute permission on the list item but, to prevent them from changing a submitted report, they are given read permission. The user's manager is then given approve permissions.	
Publish the workflow.	**1** Set the workflow to run automatically when an item is created. **2** Click Publish.	The workflow is set to automatically start and is published to the Expense Reports library.

Notice in figure 5.24 that, after the workflow runs, you are no longer able to edit the document, but you are still able to view it. This is apparent because the delete and edit

Figure 5.24   The Edit Item and Delete Item links are now disabled because John Doe's permissions have been removed by the workflow.

item options are disabled. Also notice that the manager of the submitting user now has approval rights on the document and neither user has access to other documents in the library. Sign in as the user's manager to verify that Approve is available when viewing the item.

These new conditions and actions will allow you to dynamically and automatically give access to otherwise nonprivileged users. This workflow could be extended to re-establish edit rights for the user if the manager rejects the item (allowing the user to make changes again).

5.5 *External data in a SharePoint Designer workflow*

So far, all of the workflows you have seen in this book have referenced and modified SharePoint list data. It is also possible to use SharePoint workflows to interact with external data, such as SQL databases. Using a new concept called External Content Types it's possible to display and create external data using the SharePoint environment. By extension, it is also possible to write workflows that leverage this external data.

> **Workflows and external data—a workaround**
>
> It's not possible to create SharePoint Designer workflows that interact directly with external data. Also, workflows cannot be assigned to lists that use External Content Types. Despite these limitations there is a workaround for writing workflows that interact with External Content Types and even create data in lists that contain external data.
>
> This is accomplished by using a secondary list or a site workflow. The workflow can use lookups to read data out of the external list. By using the Create List Item action you could write data into the list, for example.

In order to display external data and create workflows that use this data, External Content Types must be created. The most important thing to know when creating External Content Types to use with workflows is that they must be configured to use the Secure Store Service when authenticating, if you want to provide credentials, or to Revert to self, which means to use the app pool's identity. Revert to self requires that the service account have read or write access to the external data in question.

Each of these topics is moderately complex and beyond the scope of this book so, instead of describing them in detail, a specific example is shown to explain one path to complete configuration. This example is broken into sections for each major topic. The example uses the AdventureWorks database, which is included as a test database with SQL server to display and edit sample purchase order data.

5.5.1 *Configuring a Secure Store Service*

The Secure Store Service is used to store credentials that will be used when accessing other systems. This can be useful when individual users do not have credentials to access the backend system, which is the case in this example. See table 5.8 for the steps to take to configure a Secure Store Service.

Table 5.8   Configuring Secure Store Service application

Action	Steps	Result
Create a new target application in the default Secure Store Service application.	**1** In Central Administration, click Manage Service Applications, scroll down and click Secure Store Service, and then click on Manage. **2** Click the New button on the Ribbon to create a new target application. **3** Enter the values shown in figure 5.25 for the ID, Name, and E-mail. Be sure to select the Group type, which indicates that this Application will use shared credentials for all users, and then click Next. **4** Add your account as an administrator and All authenticated Users in the Members box shown in figure 5.26, and then click OK.	A new target application is configured half way with the general settings configured and the administrator and members configured.

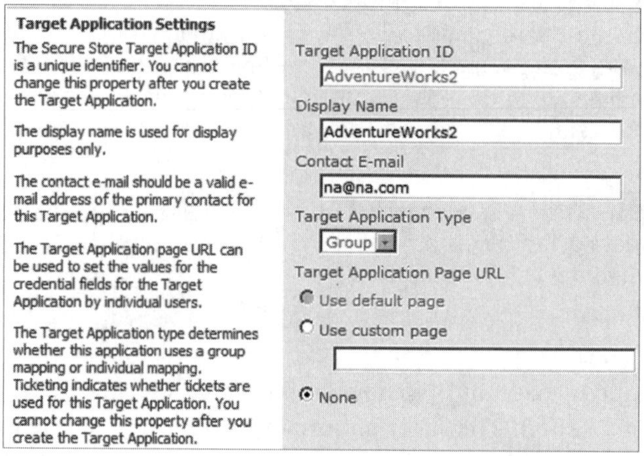

Figure 5.25   Enter a name and an email address for the application, along with the Group Application Type.

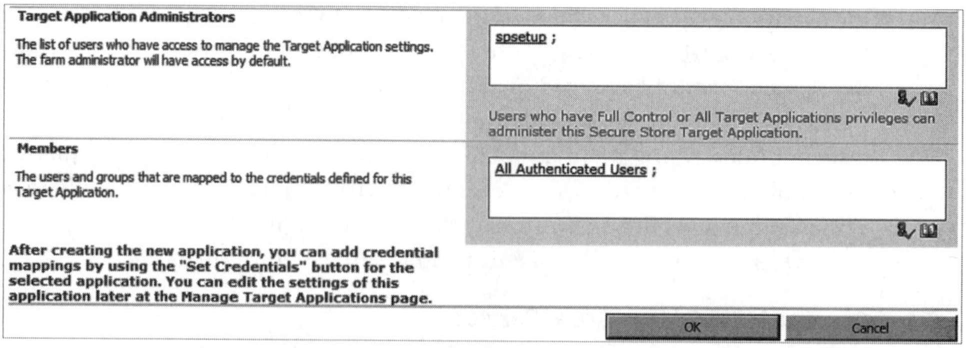

Figure 5.26   Adding All Authenticated Users to the Members field will allow anyone to use this Secure Store Application and BCS applications associated with it.

Table 5.8   Configuring Secure Store Service application *(continued)*

Action	Steps	Result
Continue configuring the new target application.	**1** Leave the default values, which define the stored credential fields, as shown in figure 5.27, and click Next. **NOTE:** In most cases, the default User Name and Password fields are the only fields that need to be stored in order to access a backend system. The Secure Store Service can also be configured to store additional credential values, such as a PIN number or a Key. If the Masked setting is enabled for a field, the typed text will not be displayed when entered by the user. This is commonly used on password entry fields to prevent anyone from reading the user's password. **2** To allow all system users to authenticate using this application, add yourself or an applicable account in the Administrator field and add All Authenticated Users to the Members field and then click OK. **NOTE:** This may not be appropriate for your production environment!	The target application named AventureWorks2 is created and all authenticated users are able to leverage the credentials to connect to remote data.

Figure 5.27   The standard username and password are stored by default but other fields can be stored, if needed. For this example, use the default username and password only.

Table 5.8   Configuring Secure Store Service application *(continued)*

Action	Steps	Result
Set the credentials of the new target application.	**1** Select the Application you created by clicking the check box and click the Set Credentials button in the Ribbon: **2** Enter the credentials for an account that has permissions to read the external database. **NOTE:** In figure 5.28 the spsvc account has read and write permissions. You may need to check with your SQL DBA to confirm that the correct permissions are in place. **3** Click OK to save the Credentials for the Secure Store Application.	The credentials are stored in the newly created target application.

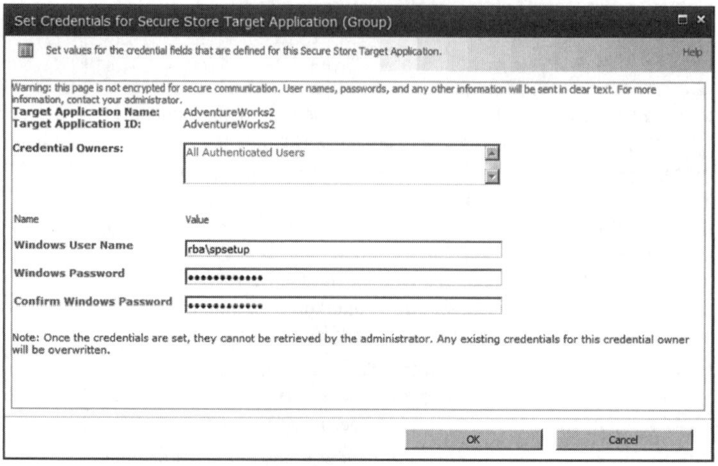

Figure 5.28   After setting permissions, which determine who can use the Secure Store Application, the Credentials that are used to connect to SQL must be set. This is done using the Set Credentials button.

5.5.2   *Creating an External Content Type*

The Secure Store Service has now been configured, and it is time to create an External Content Type. Remember that the Secure Store Service defines what credentials you will use to connect to the external data source. The External Content Type will do the work of retrieving, updating, and deleting data within SharePoint. Follow the steps in table 5.9 to create a new External Content type.

> **EXAMPLE DEPENDENCY**   The following example is dependent upon having Microsoft's Adventure Works sample database installed. Before executing these steps, proceed to Microsoft.com to download and find instructions to install the Adventure Works samples.

Table 5.9   Creating a new External Content Type

Action		Result
Open Share-Point Designer and create a new External Content Type within your SharePoint site.	**1** Click the External Content Types link under Site Objects on the left navigation panel: 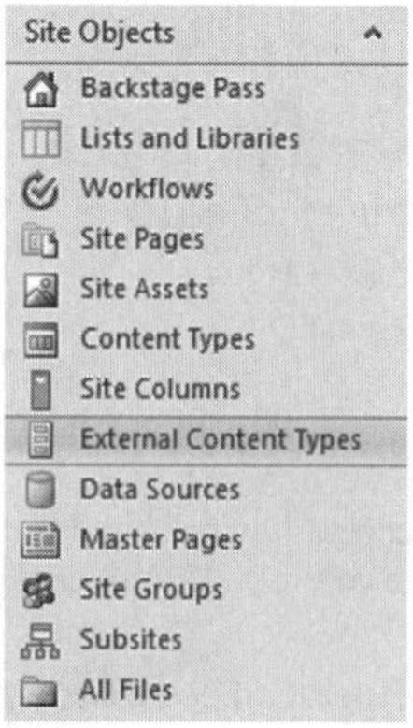 Site Objects Backstage Pass Lists and Libraries Workflows Site Pages Site Assets Content Types Site Columns External Content Types Data Sources Master Pages Site Groups Subsites All Files	An External Content Type that points to a SQL database is created.

Table 5.9 Creating a new External Content Type *(continued)*

Action		Result
	2 Click the External Content Type link in the Ribbon, which will create a new External Content Type.	
	3 Give the new content type a Name and Display Name and click the link next to External System.	
	4 Click the Add Connection button and choose SQL Server from the dropdown. Click OK.	
	5 Fill out the form as follows and then click OK:	
	NOTE: Be sure to specify the appropriate SQL Server name, which may or may not the local host. Be sure to select Impersonated Windows Identity and enter the name of the Secure Store Application that you created earlier.	
Configure the new External Content Type to pull Sales Order information out of the database.	**1** Expand the Database that you added and open the Tables folder. Scroll down until you find the SalesOrderHeader table. **2** Right-click the SalesOrderHeader table and choose Create All Operations, which will create all of the necessary connection settings to read, create, update, and delete data from the SQL database:	The content type is specifically pulling records out of the SalesOrderHeader table.
Complete the All Operations wizard.	**3** Click Next on the first two screens of the All Operations wizard. **4** On the Filter parameters screen, click the Add Filter Parameter button. **5** Select the Click to Add link next to the Filter definition and set the filter to match figure 5.29. Click OK. **6** In the Default Value dropdown, type 100, click OK, and then click Finish. **NOTE:** By specifying a default value of 100, only 100 records are returned by the database. Returning all records can cause timeout errors in some situations, and setting a limit in this manner can prevent these errors.	After the wizard completes, all the necessary Business Connectivity Services that the content type will use to retrieve the external data are created.

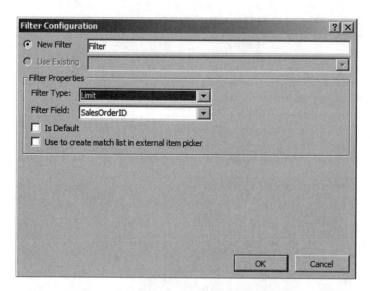

Figure 5.29   Adding a Limit filter will ensure that your application does not return so many records that a time-out is caused.

Table 5.9   Creating a new External Content Type *(continued)*

Action	Steps	Result
Create a new external list of the newly created External Content Type.	1 Click the Create Lists and Form button on the Ribbon and, if you see a popup message about saving the content type, click OK. 2 Give the list a name of SalesOrders and click OK: 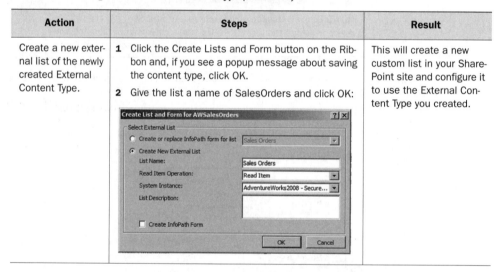	This will create a new custom list in your SharePoint site and configure it to use the External Content Type you created.

You have now configured an External Content Type and created an external list that uses that content type. When you browse to the new list in SharePoint, you should see data from the AdventureWorks SalesOrderHeader table similar to that shown in figure 5.30.

Sales Orders › AWSalesOrders Read List ▾							I Like It Tags & Notes

SalesOrderID	RevisionNumber	OrderDate	DueDate	ShipDate	Status	OnlineOrderFlag	SalesOrderNumber
43659	2	6/30/2001 7:00 PM	7/12/2001 7:00 PM	3/20/2010 12:00 AM	5	Yes	SO43659
43660	1	6/30/2001 7:00 PM	7/12/2001 7:00 PM	3/20/2010 12:00 AM	5	No	SO43660
43661	1	6/30/2001 7:00 PM	7/12/2001 7:00 PM	7/7/2001 7:00 PM	5	No	SO43661
43662	1	6/30/2001 7:00 PM	7/12/2001 7:00 PM	7/7/2001 7:00 PM	5	No	SO43662
43663	2	6/30/2001 7:00 PM	7/12/2001 7:00 PM	7/7/2001 7:00 PM	5	No	SO43663
43664	1	6/30/2001 7:00 PM	7/12/2001 7:00 PM	7/7/2001 7:00 PM	5	No	SO43664

Figure 5.30 An External List displaying sales order data from the AdventureWorks SQL database in SharePoint.

5.5.3 Creating a workflow using the External Content Type

Now that you have created a Secure Store Application, External Content Type, and a List that uses that content type, you can create a workflow that leverages the external data. See table 5.10 for the steps. In this example, you will create an Order Status Request system. This will allow a user to request the status of an AdventureWorks order by entering an order ID. The workflow will look up the order using this ID and email the results to the supplied email address.

Table 5.10   Creating a new workflow that leverages external data

Action	Steps	Result
Create a new list to store sales order requests.	1 Create a new custom list called list Sales Order Status Requests. 2 Create two columns on this list, one called E-mail address that's a Single line of text column, and the other called Sales Order Lookup, which you should configure as a Lookup type column. 3 While configuring the lookup in the *Get Information From* dropdown, choose the Sales Orders list and check the box next to SalesOrderID. **NOTE:** This will instruct the lookup to get items from the Sales Orders external list and will show users all of the available Sales Order IDs when they use the field. 4 Leave all the rest of the defaults on the create lookup column screen and click OK.	A new list is created that users can use to request the status of an order. The list should look similar to that in figure 5.31.

Notice the two icons next to the lookup column in figure 5.31. The first icon allows users to validate a value that they typed in. The second button shows a popup where they can select from all available Sales Orders (figure 5.32). This will help ensure that invalid Sales Order IDs are not passed to the workflow and it also allows users to see additional data to help them select the correct item.

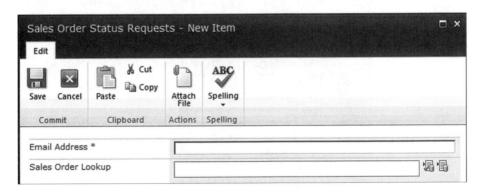

Figure 5.31   The user can validate a lookup value using the Validate link to the right of the field.

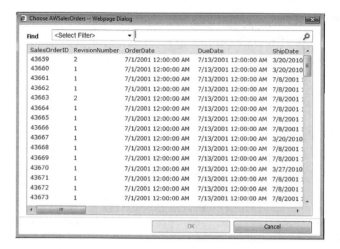

Figure 5.32   This dialog will allow users to see additional data, helping them to select the item they want.

Table 5.10   Creating a new workflow that leverages external data *(continued)*

Action	Steps	Result
Create a new workflow named Sales Order Status Request.	**1** In SharePoint Designer, create a new List Workflow using the Sales Order Status Requests List and name it Sales Order Status Request. **2** Edit the workflow and add a single Send an Email action. **3** Configure the mail action to send using the Email Address from the status request in the To: field. Add a descriptive subject line. **4** In the body of the email, add information about the order the requestor is requiring using the Add or Change Lookup button and looking up information in the Sales Orders external list. **NOTE:** You can add references to any field that was included in the External Content Type created earlier. Be sure to configure the Data Source to reference the Sales Order list that was created as part of the External Content Type configuration. To find the correct sales order item, use the Current Item:Order ID field and the SalesOrderID from the Sales Order list. You will need to configure this lookup for each field that you want to return. If you see a warning about returning unique items, click OK. You will always see this warning when working with external data. The following figure shows a configured lookup that's getting the order's order date: **5** Publish the workflow.	A new workflow that when run will email the requestor the sales order status is created.

To test the workflow, create a new list item in the Sales Order Requests list and enter a Sales Order ID manually or use the popup to select one and save the Request item. Manually initiate the workflow. You should again receive an email message with the relevant Order Date and Ship Date, or whatever external order information you entered for lookup into the body of the email.

5.6   *Summary*

This chapter walked you through five advanced techniques with SharePoint Designer 2010 workflows. The first of the five involved creating workflow templates. You can save a workflow as a template, and then deploy that template across the entire farm or to a separate farm entirely. The template is saved as a .wsp file, and deployed using the stsadm command-line utility.

Another advanced trick is to customize the out-of-the-box workflows. With SharePoint Designer 2010, you can extend the default workflows if they don't meet your needs. Rather than start from scratch, you can make the necessary tweaks to save time.

SharePoint Designer 2010 also comes with a bunch of new workflow actions and conditions related to working with document sets and security. You can use workflows to route document sets to Records Center and to manage security with tools such as the breaking permission inheritance or adding and removing user permissions.

Last, we took a look at how to leverage external data in your SharePoint Designer workflows through the Business Connectivity Services suite. With SharePoint 2010, you gain the ability to quickly configure access to external data and to read and modify that external data through SharePoint and SharePoint workflows.

Custom Visio SharePoint workflows

6

This chapter covers

- Introducing Visio workflows
- Building a Visio workflow
- Importing a Visio workflow into SharePoint Designer
- Using Visio Graphics Services

Designing and developing SharePoint workflows quite often requires strong communication and collaboration skills to clearly define and document what the stakeholders require and what the developer needs to build. Sometimes, a business analyst is the best choice for gathering these workflow requirements. With Visio 2010, a nontechnical person can create what's called a Visio SharePoint workflow. They can then hand this Visio workflow off to someone more technical for importing into SharePoint Designer and filling in all the details. This act of importing can be an excellent time and cost saver. Rather than starting from scratch, the developer can start where the business analyst left off.

Visio 2010 is a diagramming application and part of the Microsoft Office product stack. It can be used to create:

- Diagrams showing an organizational hierarchy (reporting structure).
- Floor plans for office buildings.
- Network diagrams showing server and firewalls.
- Gantt charts and timelines.
- Flowcharts (also known as workflows).

A flowchart is the foundation of every workflow. In chapter 2, we discussed using a napkin drawing to capture the flow of work for the first time. This *flow of work* represents the business requirements and the workflow's purpose. Visio is an excellent tool for documenting requirements because a picture can often tell a story better than words.

In this chapter, you'll learn the steps for building a workflow using Visio. Unfortunately, you can't create a fully functional workflow in Visio, but you can certainly use it as a starting point. New features in Visio 2010 make all of this possible through a new diagram template called the SharePoint Workflow template. Inside this template are connectors and actions that can be used to model your workflows.

After you have your diagram built out, you can import it into SharePoint Designer and publish it to SharePoint. Another great new feature is the ability to use this diagram as a status indicator of the workflow. After the workflow starts, the diagram will show where in the process the workflow is currently executing.

6.1   *Introducing Visio workflows*

Before we get into Visio SharePoint workflows, let's take a brief look at what is new in the latest version of Visio. Visio 2010 focuses on three major areas of investment:

- *Ease of use*—Visio 2010 incorporates the Office Fluent User Interface and design philosophy, more commonly called the Ribbon.

    The improved organization and presentation of Visio's capabilities helps you to complete tasks and create better looking diagrams with greater efficiency. The Shapes Window gets a new look and new capabilities to make organizing shapes and adding them to the drawing even easier. Within the drawing window, Microsoft added productivity improvements like shape insertion and automatic alignment and spacing to speed up initial diagram creation and assist with editing and maintaining diagrams over time. You'll find that these improvements save you time. Because it's been some time since Visio has had a major enhancement, they may be confusing at first.

- *Process management*—Visio 2010 delivers an excellent new experience when you're working with process diagrams.

    Microsoft has redesigned the cross-functional flowcharts to be simple, scalable, and reliable. Also, new diagram types are added for the Business Process Modeling Notation standard and for designing SharePoint workflows, which can be configured and deployed with SharePoint Designer 2010. Subprocesses and containers break up a diagram into understandable pieces, and the Validation feature can analyze a diagram to ensure it is properly constructed. Visio integrates with SharePoint to provide a process diagram library for centralized storage of process documents.

- *Visio Services*—Visio 2010 can take data-refreshable diagrams and publish them to SharePoint for broad distribution to anyone with a web browser.

  Visio Services performs data refresh and rendering on the server and delivers up-to-date diagrams in the browser. The diagram author no longer needs to repost the diagram every time the data changes, and diagram viewers no longer need the Visio client to see the diagram. This is much the same as Excel Services in SharePoint 2007 and even easier to get set up and running.

In Visio Premium 2010, Microsoft introduced many new high quality drawing templates. One of these is a new template called the Microsoft SharePoint Workflow template plate (figure 6.1). The first thing you'll notice when you create your first Visio SharePoint workflow diagram is the improved menu navigation (figure 6.2).

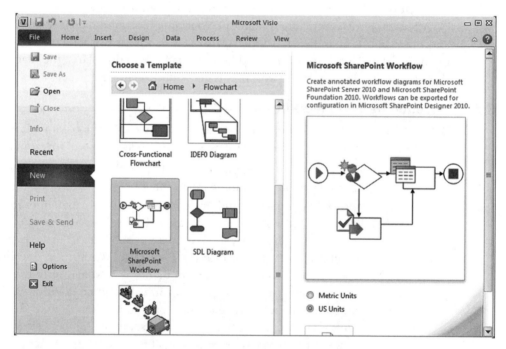

Figure 6.1   Visio 2010 brings a new diagram template called Microsoft SharePoint Workflow. This template can be used to model workflows that can then be imported into SharePoint Designer.

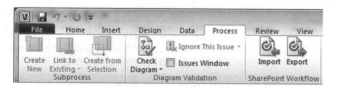

Figure 6.2   The Ribbon in Visio 2010 features a Check Diagram button for validating the configuration as well as Import and Export buttons to move between Visio and SharePoint Designer.

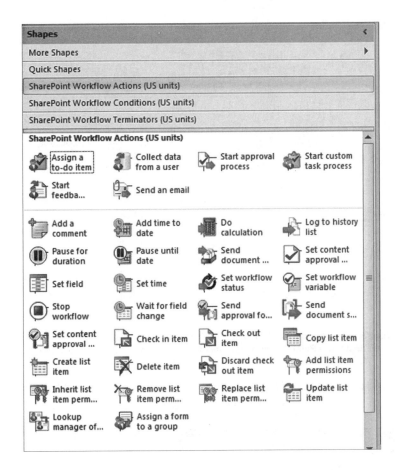

Figure 6.3 A host of actions and conditions can be used in a Visio workflow to model your business processes. Each action and condition maps to an action and condition in SharePoint Designer.

Next, you'll notice the improved shapes navigation window on the left side of the screen (figure 6.3). You'll notice new content that is specific to the SharePoint Workflow template and includes SharePoint-specific actions, conditions, and terminators. These are the shapes needed to model the workflow functionality in a way that SharePoint Designer understands and can import.

By default, the Quick Shapes item displays a combination of actions, conditions, and terminators that Visio thinks you'll want to use. You can change your view to see more actions by clicking SharePoint Workflow Actions (figure 6.3).To start authoring a SharePoint workflow, drop these shapes onto the canvas and connect them.

Notice how in figure 6.4 you can drag and drop these action and conditions onto the canvas surface. The figure looks similar to any ordinary diagram you'd find yourself building in Visio. The biggest difference between the standard flowchart template and the SharePoint Workflow template is that SharePoint Designer understands how to import the SharePoint Workflow template but cannot import the flowchart template.

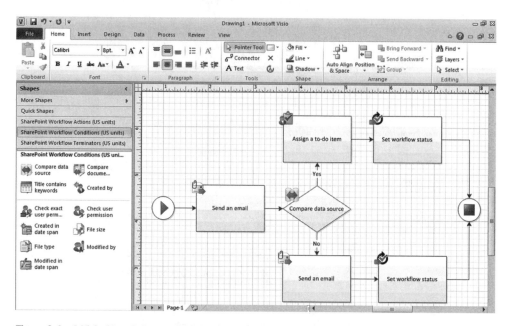

Figure 6.4   A Visio SharePoint workflow is similar to a flowchart diagram in the previous version of Visio. The big difference is that SharePoint Designer now understands how to import Visio SharePoint workflow diagrams.

A workflow in Visio 2010, like the one shown in figure 6.4, looks very different when it is imported into SharePoint Designer (figure 6.5). In SharePoint Designer, it is given a

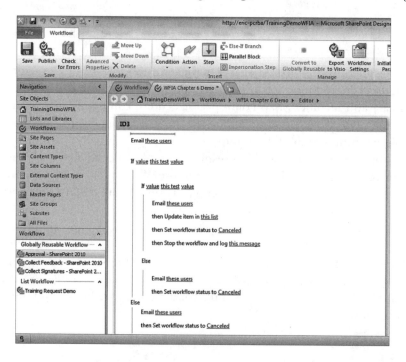

Figure 6.5
When the Visio diagram is imported into SharePoint Designer, it looks quite different. Instead of seeing shapes show the flow of work, you have a textual representation.

much more detailed and scripted look and feel. The diagram is now ready to be configured for SharePoint.

Also notice in SharePoint Designer a link in the Ribbon titled Export to Visio. You can use this link to resume editing the workflow diagram in Visio. This may be helpful if, after you've imported into SharePoint Designer, you made changes to the workflow that you'd like to represent in the diagram. It's important to note, however, that, after you export to Visio and subsequently import back into SharePoint Designer, you'll be creating a new workflow instance. There's no way to export and import back and forth and continue expanding the same instance.

6.2 Building a Visio workflow

SharePoint workflows can represent an infinite number of different business processes such as on-boarding, approvals, and purchase orders. For this chapter, we'll use the example of a training request system. We'll start by modeling the training request workflow in Visio. Then, we'll import that workflow into SharePoint Designer and publish it to SharePoint.

Authoring a Visio workflow for SharePoint requires configuring shapes correctly and validating that they are connected properly. The two terminator shapes are Start and Terminate and these are required to start and end the workflow (figure 6.6). If you don't use these terminators, you won't be able to export the Visio file to the Visio Workflow Interchange (VWI) format. This format is required for importing the workflow into SharePoint Designer. To use these shapes, drag and drop them onto the blank Visio canvas (figure 6.6).

You have begun to author a SharePoint workflow. The next step is to add an action to the workflow. There are 36 actions to choose from and 11 different conditions. For this scenario, you'll add a few to simulate a training request process.

The workflow will be added to a list called ACME Training Attendance containing a column called Training Class. When users add new items to the list, they specify the training class they are registering for. After they submit the request, the workflow needs to ensure that the user has already attended the prerequisite class, *Introduction to SharePoint*. If the user has taken the class, the user's manager needs to be assigned a task to complete the registration. If the user hasn't attended the prerequisite, the workflow needs to send an email notifying the user of the dependency.

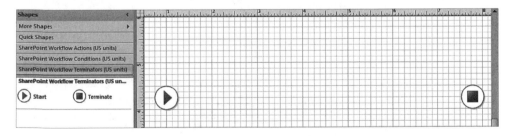

Figure 6.6   To begin modeling a SharePoint workflow in Visio, drag and drop the start and end terminators.

As a business analyst, you can easily diagram this workflow in Visio. Follow these steps to create a new Visio SharePoint Workflow and add the necessary actions and conditions for the training request system:

1. Add a Send an email action to the right of the Start terminator. This action will be used to send an email to the requestor, notifying them that the process is in progress.
2. Use the Compare data source to add a condition for this workflow and validate a prerequisite training class has already been taken. This shape will be configured later in SharePoint Designer to validate against another list in SharePoint.
3. Add another Send an email action below the Compare data source condition. This will be used in case the initiator does not meet the prerequisite and if the request is rejected.
4. Add a Set workflow status action to the right of the second Send an Email action. This will be used to change the workflow's status column to Cancelled.
5. Add the Assign a to-do Item action above the Compare data source condition. This will represent the second path for use when requests meet the prerequisites.
6. To the right of the Assign a to-do item action, add the Set workflow status action. We'll use this to change the workflow's status column to Approved.
7. Finally, add a Stop workflow action to the diagram. This may seem redundant but, for larger diagrams, you may not want dozens of lines all connecting back to a single terminator.

When these steps are complete, your diagram should look something like figure 6.7.

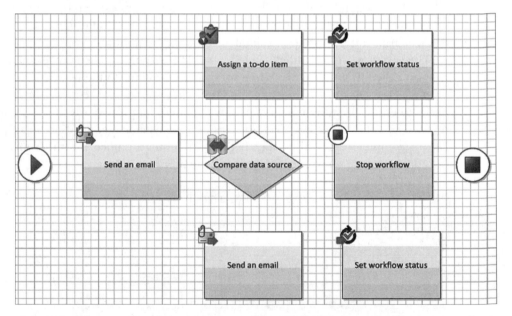

Figure 6.7 Continue by dropping the necessary actions and conditions onto the canvas. These actions and conditions have counterparts in SharePoint Designer that the developer will need to fill in.

Now that all the shapes are laid out, the next step is to connect the shapes using connectors. In Visio 2010, Microsoft has included a new shape insertion feature that provides an easier way to connect shapes. Hover your mouse over the shape you want to connect, and you'll then see four blue arrows appear. Click the arrow (figure 6.8) that points in the direction you want to connect the shape. You can also use this method to create new shapes. Notice in figure 6.8 the pop-up to the right of the right-facing blue arrow. This shows new shapes you can create. It's an easy point-and-click method of connecting all of the pieces.

> **NOTE** Another shape insertion enhancement is the ability to hold down the mouse button on the arrow you want to connect and drag the connector to another shape. This eliminates extra clicks when connecting shapes.

Connect the shapes together as in figure 6.9. After you've connected all the arrows, you'll need to do one more thing. The Compare any data source action is a bit different from the other actions. You have to identify which path represents the Yes as well as the opposite No path. To do this, right-click on the arrow you want to change. In the case of your training request process, click the arrow leaving the conditional shape and going to the Assign to-do item shape. Then select Yes or No from the menu. After you have connected all the shapes and assigned the appropriate arrows, your workflow should look like figure 6.9.

The next step is to validate the workflow by clicking the Check the Diagram icon at the top of the window located under the Process tab. This check will scan the document to inspect it against validation rules and conditions related to SharePoint workflow standards. Only if it passes the check will the diagram be successfully imported into SharePoint Designer.

After you click Check the Diagram, you should get a message saying it passed successfully. Now you need to get the diagram into a format that SharePoint Designer can use. This is done by clicking on the Export button at the top of the screen (under the

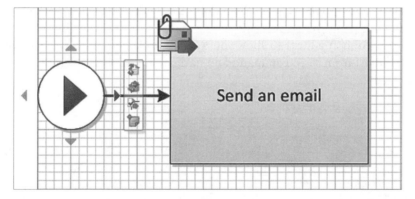

Figure 6.8 After your shapes are on the canvas, it's time to start connecting them. Hover over a shape and click the blue arrow. The nearest shape in the direction of the arrow will be connected.

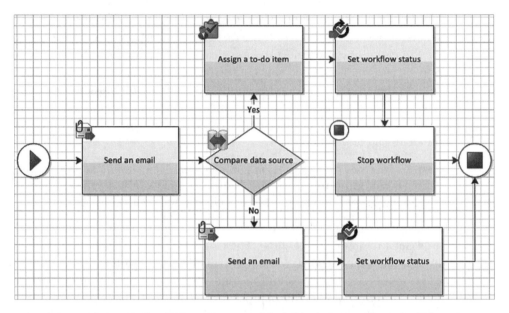

Figure 6.9   **A Visio SharePoint workflow should be validated by clicking the Check the Diagram button. All paths should lead toward the Terminate action or terminator.**

Process tab). When you click Export, accept the defaults and create a name for the workflow. Save the exported file to a place that you'll remember because in the next section you're going to import the workflow into SharePoint Designer and add it to SharePoint itself.

6.3   *Importing a Visio workflow into SharePoint Designer*

Visio is used to diagram the workflow and create placeholders of functionality. Share-Point Designer gets the workflow into SharePoint and fills in the details of the work-flow actions.

     To start, create or open a site in SharePoint Designer 2010. Click on the Workflows link on the left pane. When you switch over to the workflows section of SharePoint Designer, the Ribbon adjusts to show you workflow-related commands (figure 6.10). Click the Import from Visio command and navigate to the Visio diagram you created and exported earlier.

Figure 6.10   **The new Ribbon in SharePoint 2010 features an Import from Visio button and an Export to Visio button, so you can easily go back and forth.**

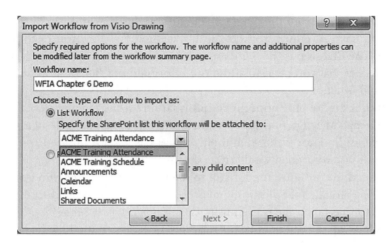

Figure 6.11   When you import a workflow, you need to designate whether it's a list workflow or a reusable workflow. If it's a list workflow, you need to choose the list to bind it to.

Remember, the Visio diagram you exported is in the new VWI format. When you import the file, you'll be prompted to choose the type of workflow you want to import. You can either choose a list workflow or a reusable workflow. For this scenario, we will choose the list view and attach it to the list from which we want the request for training to be generated (figure 6.11).

You are now looking at the Visio workflow you built earlier. It looks different in the SharePoint Designer workflow editor; instead of seeing shapes connected to one another, you see a list of actions. The list of actions still reflects the same placeholders for your training request workflow (figure 6.12).

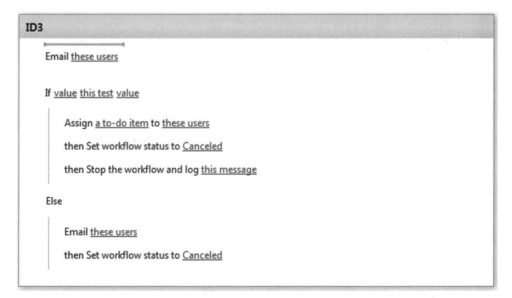

Figure 6.12   When the workflow is first imported into SharePoint Designer, you'll quickly notice that all the actions and conditions need your attention. This is indicated by the underline and occurs because importing from Visio only adds placeholders that need to be filled in.

You can see all the steps from the diagram you authored earlier in Visio in this different format. You have an empty workflow with placeholders. Now you need to finish out each step. The first step is the Send an email action you created earlier. The blue underline indicates that you need to add more information. Click on it to define how the email should function.

When you click on the blue underlined information for the email action, a window called Define E-mail Message pops up. We will configure the email to send a response back to the request initiator saying that their request has been submitted and is being processed. Configure your email similarly as shown in figure 6.13.

Next, you need to configure the lookup to see if the current user who is initiating this workflow has already taken training classes. Specifically, you need to make sure that the requestor has taken the prerequisite class, *Introduction to SharePoint*. Configure the lookup to look up the attendance list for the requestor (created by the field) and check if the Training Class field is set to Introduction to SharePoint (figure 6.14). This isn't an absolute lookup in that you could find more than result. A warning message will pop up asking if this is OK. Click Yes to continue.

After configuring the lookup, set the rest of the condition to equals, *Introduction to SharePoint* to make the workflow check that the user has already taken the prerequisite class.

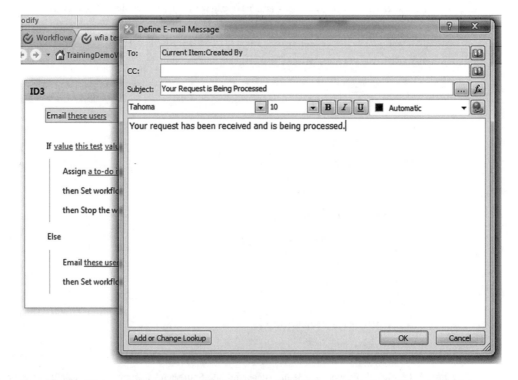

Figure 6.13   Click on the blue underscored items to provide the actions and conditions with their configurations.

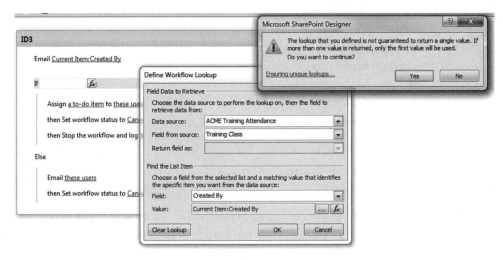

Figure 6.14   For the training request system, you confirm that the requestor has met the prerequisites.

Next we need to look up the requestor's manager and assign them a to-do item or an email. SharePoint Designer introduces the ability to use the User Profiles as a data source in workflows or almost anywhere else in SharePoint Designer. This is one of the workflow features most often requested by end users. An important point to note about Profiles is that they require a SharePoint Server license and the deployment of the User Profile Service Application.

In the Assign a new task action, click these users. You want to look up the requestor's manager (figure 6.15). In the pop-up, click Workflow Lookup for a User…. Select User

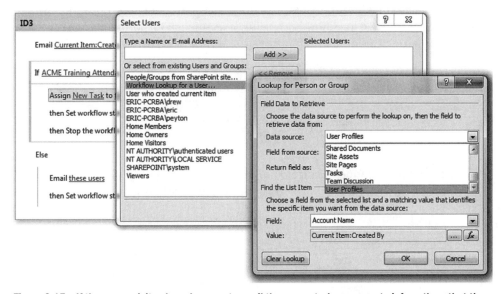

Figure 6.15   If the prerequisites have been met, email the requestor's manager to inform them that they need to finalize the registration.

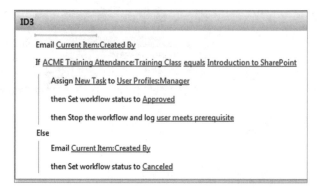

Figure 6.16   When the workflow is complete, you'll notice that all the blue underscores have been replaced by black underscores.

Profiles as the data source and Manager as the field. The workflow will now be set up to send a task to the requestor's manager. In your training request workflow, this task could be to finalize the registration through an external business process.

After you fill out the rest of the actions and conditions, the workflow should look like figure 6.16. The next step is to publish the workflow into SharePoint. You'll also enable workflow virtualization on the workflow so that your diagram shows the workflow's status pictorially.

6.4   *Publishing and Visio Graphic Services*

Before you publish the workflow, let's look at the settings on the workflow, in particular the Show workflow visualization on status page setting (figure 6.17). When this box is checked and after the workflow is published, all running or completed workflows will show the diagram on the workflow status page. More importantly, the diagram will have a green checkbox next to actions that have ended and progress symbols on the actions that the workflow is currently executing. This will give your users a visual representation of where in the process the workflow is currently executing.

> **Server dependencies required for graphics functionality**
>
> To utilize Visio Graphics Services, you must have a SharePoint Server license and the Visio Graphics Services application configured in the farm.

To enable this functionality, go to the workflow's Settings tab in SharePoint Designer. Check the box next to Show workflow visualization on status page (figure 6.17).

Settings		
General settings for this workflow.		
Task List:	Tasks	
History List:	Workflow History	
☑ Show workflow visualization on status page		

Figure 6.17   To enable the Visio diagram to display on the workflow's status page, check Show workflow visualization on status page.

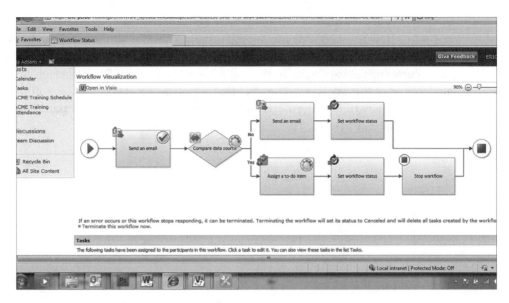

Figure 6.18 The workflow visualization features the diagram you created in Visio. This enables the user to see the status of the workflow and the path it took more quickly.

After this box is checked, click the Publish button to publish the workflow. Go to the SharePoint list to which you added the workflow and add a new item. If you specified to Start the workflow automatically when an item is created (figure 6.17), you'll find your workflow already running. Navigate to the workflow status screen by clicking the In Progress column. There's a major difference between this status screen and what you've seen in previous chapters. Now at the bottom of the screen you will see the workflow visualization (figure 6.18).

Reviewing the Workflow Visualization in figure 6.18 you can see that this workflow is on the Assign a to-do item list action. The presence of a green checkbox tells us that the first step has been completed successfully. With SharePoint 2010 and Visio Services, anyone can easily see the state of a workflow without having to decipher cryptic messages and statuses.

6.5   Summary

There was a chasm in SharePoint 2007 between the SharePoint business analyst and the SharePoint developer. In SharePoint 2010, this gap has been narrowed for SharePoint workflows. This is largely because of the new features in Visio 2010—in particular, the new SharePoint Workflow diagram template.

The new template gives nontechnical analysts the ability to diagram a high-level business process in Visio. After they've produced this diagram, the SharePoint Developer can import the diagram into SharePoint Designer to fill in the placeholders with actions and conditions. The workflow is then published in SharePoint. Developers don't have to start from scratch; they can take the product of the analyst's work and run from there.

Another great feature is the ability to show the Visio diagram on the workflow's status page. Now the end user can see pictorially where in the process the workflow is currently executing. In SharePoint 2007, your best option was to set the workflow's status column or perhaps write to the log. This left the user sifting through logs to see the course of the workflow. The visualization of the workflow's status will grant end users the ability to find the workflow's current state and execution path much more quickly than ever before.

Custom form
fundamentals

Workflows and forms are a powerful combination because most business processes revolve around forms. To have a holistic understanding of how to build custom workflows in SharePoint, you need to know how to build custom forms and the tools available for building them.

Three types of tools are available in SharePoint to build custom forms: out-of-the-box forms (auto-generated), InfoPath forms, and ASP.NET forms. It's important to know when to use each type and their pros and cons. For instance, you can accomplish a great deal with the out of the-box forms without ever needing to use a more advanced tool like InfoPath or ASP.NET. Working with the out-of-the-box forms is simple and fast, saving you time and money. Because of this, it remains a good place to start whenever considering a forms solution. However, the shortcomings of out-of-the-box forms sometimes necessitate the use of InfoPath, which will be discussed in further detail in this chapter. Because ASP.NET forms are a programming topic, they're covered in chapter 9.

With these tools, there are many fundamental ways of using the forms to build workflow solutions including customizing the out-of-the-box forms, using form libraries, and working with initiation and association forms in SharePoint Designer workflows. In this chapter, you'll go through activities such as publishing custom forms into form libraries, updating a library's default template, and making shared templates across multiple libraries.

7.1   Tools used to build custom forms

Out-of-the-box forms help users edit list items and SharePoint data and have a limited set of customizing features, whereas InfoPath forms bring a deep level of customization to the table. ASP.NET forms built in Visual Studio are used for the most technically complex forms. As you design your workflow solutions, carefully evaluate the form techniques and pros and cons. Thinking through your form requirements ahead of time may save you from having to rewrite functionality.

7.1.1   New and Edit forms

Out-of-the-box forms will be generated for you depending on what data elements you have in the list, whereas with InfoPath and ASP.NET, you'll have to build the forms from the bottom up.

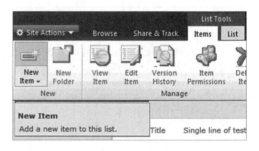

Figure 7.1   When you add a new item in SharePoint, a form will appear in which you can edit the metadata for that item. It's common to have a workflow run on an out-of-the-box item like this.

Consider for a moment the process of creating a new list or library in SharePoint and adding a workflow to that list. Most often, when you create a new custom list or library in SharePoint, you'll go back into that list or library and add custom columns. These columns make up the metadata that resides on a new list item or document when one is created or added. On a list, you have the opportunity to enter this metadata through an out-of-the-box form after you click the New button (figure 7.1).

After it has been created, you can use an Edit button (figure 7.2).

Both of these buttons take you to automatically generated forms where your users can enter information. It's natural

Figure 7.2   Similar to creating a new item, editing an item gives you a form in which you can edit that item's metadata.

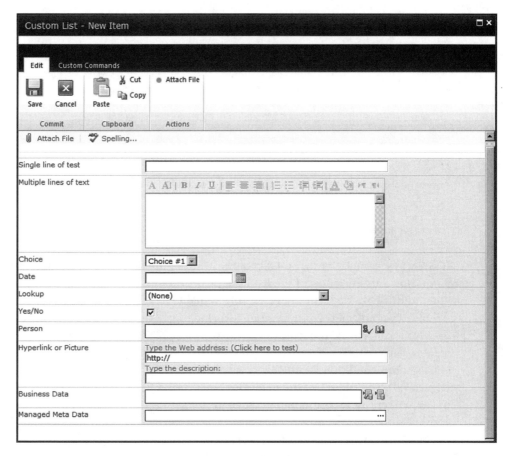

Figure 7.3   A sample out-of-the-box autogenerate new item form

to start a workflow on the item that will respond to the creation of new items or by editing the existing items.

Are the requirements for the form in your custom workflow complicated enough so that the auto-generated forms won't work? At the least it takes only a few minutes to add columns into a list or library to see if you can get by with the auto-generated functionality.

Let's take a quick look at the types of columns you can add to a list out of the box and what that translates into on an auto-generated form. Table 7.1 and figure 7.3 illustrate this.

Table 7.1   All out-of-the-box column types and how they're rendered on the form

Column type	Render style on form
Single line of text	Text box
Multiple lines of text	Text box—multiple lines

Table 7.1   All out-of-the-box column types and how they're rendered on the form *(continued)*

Column type	Render style on form
Choice	Dropdown (or left or right chooser, allow multiple)
Date	Text box with date picker
Lookup	Dropdown (or left or right chooser, allow multiple)
Yes or No	Check box
Person	Text box with people picker
Hyperlink or picture	Two text boxes—one for URL, one for description
Business data	Text box with data picker
Managed metadata	Text box with metadata picker

It's easy to see the rich functionality of these out-of-the-box forms. As stated previously, a workflow can sit on top of the list item or document, and the metadata on the item entered through the form will be readily available to act upon.

In a custom SharePoint Designer workflow, you can check the data in a custom column through the If current item field equals value condition. With this condition (figure 7.4), you can select the field you want in the current item and compare that with another value.

Similarly, in a Visual Studio workflow, the list item data entered in the form is readily available to the programmer and the workflow.

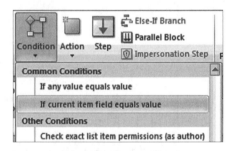

Figure 7.4   The SharePoint Designer workflow condition that compares the data in the workflow's list item

Why wouldn't you use the out-of-the-box forms all the time? Table 7.1 shows the data types that can be used, but what if you want check boxes instead of radio buttons? Or, you need more detailed instructions, logos, or graphics on the form to make it more graphically appealing? Or, the data in the dropdowns may need to come from an external line-of-business application. For these examples, out-of-the-box forms fall short. Table 7.2 shows how the pros and cons of the out-of-the-box forms stack up.

Table 7.2   The pros and cons of out-of-the-box forms

PROS	Easiest approach—all out-of-the-box functionality Fastest approach—quick to configure and add a few custom columns onto a SharePoint list
CONS	Least flexible in supporting customizations Limited ability to meet complex requirements

7.1.2   *InfoPath 2010 Forms*

InfoPath brings much to the table in its ability to offer solutions for more advanced requirements. Requirements such as pulling business data out of web services, dynamic filtering of controls, and advanced validation of form fields upon submission can all be easily accomplished with InfoPath. Another advantage is that you have much more flexibility in building a unique, branded user interface that is easier for end users to understand and work with. There's no doubt that information on Info-Path could be a book in itself, but we'll see several of the most common techniques in this chapter's InfoPath examples.

An InfoPath form may reside as a document in what's called a Form Library within a SharePoint site. Although this isn't always the case, it's the most common InfoPath scenario. Form libraries are document libraries, but they have connectors to InfoPath and are designed specifically to house forms. In this way, InfoPath supplements the out-of-the-box forms because, rather than work with the New and Edit forms, you now will edit the InfoPath form directly. When you save or submit a form in a form library, by default, the data in that form is stored in the library as XML.

Another way in which InfoPath interacts with SharePoint lists is through the customization of a list or library's New and Edit forms. When you customize the out-of-the-box forms, the data in those forms is always mapped to columns in the list or library, whereas, in the previous example, the form itself was uploaded into the form library as an attachment, and that attachment contained the data as XML.

So how do you know when to customize the out-of-the-box forms versus using a form library? Consider how much data you'll be interacting with. If you customize out-of-the-box forms, you need a column for every piece of data you want to save. If you use a form library, that data is stored as XML in the form itself, so you don't need to have any extra columns on the document. A good rule of thumb is 15. If your form needs to save more than 15 pieces of data, it's better to use a form library than create 15 columns on a list. Table 7.3 shows the pros and cons of InfoPath forms.

Table 7.3   The pros and cons of InfoPath forms

PROS	Drag-and-drop functions and wizard-based experience. You don't have to be a programmer.
	Supports advanced form customizations like connecting to external data, rules, and conditions.
CONS	Requires a SharePoint Server Enterprise license to host the form in the browser; otherwise, the InfoPath client application is needed to fill out a form.

Browser-enabled InfoPath forms and dependencies

The InfoPath client is a client application just like Microsoft Word is a client application. You can use the client to design or edit a form template, but you can also use the client to fill out and submit a form.

(continued)

The two main versions of SharePoint are SharePoint Foundation and SharePoint Server. SharePoint Server is an add-on to SharePoint Foundation. This add-on includes a feature called Form Server that enables InfoPath forms to be filled out and viewed right from within the browser window. Without SharePoint Server, your users will be forced to load the form in their InfoPath client application. Obviously, this can be problematic because not having SharePoint Foundation forces your users to have a copy of Microsoft Office installed on their workstations. To decide which avenue is best for your company, you'll have to compare the cost of buying SharePoint Server with the cost of buying copies of Microsoft Office, along with the headache of downloading the form first.

7.1.3   *ASP.NET forms built in Visual Studio*

Do you need the utmost flexibility in form customization? Do you have existing forms and code that you built long ago and want to reuse? Are you an ASP.NET developer who's not interested in learning InfoPath? If you said yes to any of these questions you'll be happy to hear that ASP.NET forms still play a role in SharePoint 2010. For example, you can replace the New and Edit out-of-the-box forms with a custom ASP.NET form. You can write a custom ASP.NET form and embed that form within a web part. When a user submits that form, you can use the SharePoint object model to add a new list item in a list and start a workflow on that item. Forms such as custom workflow initiation and association forms are commonly built in ASP.NET. For more on this topic, refer to chapter 9.

Despite the ability to support complex customizations, ASP.NET forms are growing less and less common because InfoPath is becoming such a versatile and simple tool. With ASP.NET, you literally need to start from scratch, but with InfoPath you have a host of controls and wizards that help you add the needed functionality into your form. Because of this, and because the ASP.NET form topic is rather generic to the ASP.NET platform, only the general pros and cons are described in this chapter (table 7.4).

Table 7.4   The pros and cons of ASP.NET forms

PROS	Supports customizations developed from the ground up
	Leverages legacy code
	Represents a shorter learning curve if you already have ASP.NET experience
CONS	Is the most time consuming approach because you have to build everything from scratch

7.2   *Customizing out-of-the-box forms with InfoPath*

A new feature in InfoPath 2010 is the ability to customize out-of-the-box auto-generated forms. Even if you choose the out-of-the-box approach and later decide you need more functionality, you can customize those forms with InfoPath. This section walks you through the steps involved in customizing the out-of-the-box forms.

Data storage methods differ significantly between using a form in a form library and using InfoPath to customize the out-of-the-box New and Edit forms. A form in a form library stores its data as XML that is uploaded as a document in that library. When you customize the out-of-the-box forms, that data still needs to be mapped to columns in the list item. If you have a good deal of data, you may want to go the form library route, rather than add 20 columns to the list item. You may want to change the behavior of one or two columns or possibly brand the form with a company logo or more detailed instructions. In this case, customizing the out-of-the-box forms is an excellent approach.

SharePoint Server required when customizing out-of-the-box forms
This section describes features available only to the Server edition of SharePoint 2010.

To get started, first create a SharePoint list or library and onto that list add all the columns you need to track. You can do this through the List Settings and then Add a column option. After you have all your columns set up for your data requirements, edit the forms to suit your user interface requirements. In the Ribbon's List tab, you can use the Customize List dropdown and choose Customize Form (figure 7.5) to launch InfoPath.

The example you're going to build involves a tasks list, and each task has an associated Project and Sub Project. What we want to do is change the Lookup columns for these associated projects to be dynamic so, when you select a Project, the Sub Project dropdown will change its items based on the selected Parent Project. Figure 7.6 shows what the tasks form looks like when it's first opened in InfoPath. Notice the Parent Project and Sub Project columns that you'll alter.

The Parent Project column is a lookup column for a separate list called Project Names. Sub Project is another lookup column for a second separate list called Sub Project Names. The Sub Project Names list has two columns, Title and Parent Project. Parent Project is a lookup for the Project Names list. Before continuing, set up the two

Figure 7.5   To customize the out-of-the-box forms in a list or library, click the Customize Form button in the Ribbon to launch InfoPath.

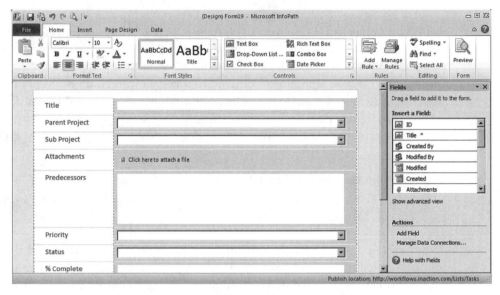

Figure 7.6   When you first select to customize the out-of-the-box New and Edit forms on a list or library, InfoPath is loaded with all the columns on that list or library, and you can start editing their behavior or appearance.

Project Names and Sub Project Names lists as previously described. Then, add a Project Name lookup column and a Sub Project Name lookup column to a task list. Last, edit the out-of-the-box form in InfoPath as shown in figure 7.5.

To make the Sub Project dropdown in your tasks form dynamically, select its items based on what is selected in the Parent Project dropdown. First, create a new data source for the Sub Project dropdown. The default data source for this dropdown only has two fields, Title and ID. Because you need to filter on the Parent Project column, add a new data source. Then, filter that data source on the selected Parent Project. And last, set up a rule on the Parent Project dropdown to ensure the data source is updated each time the dropdown is changed. The steps in table 7.5 will walk you through this process.

Table 7.5   Setting up dynamic dropdowns in an InfoPath Form

Action	Steps	Result
While customizing the out-of-the-box task edit form in InfoPath, set up a new data source for the Sub Project's dropdown menu.	1 In the Data tab in InfoPath's Ribbon, click on the Data Connections button. Click on the Add button to add a new data source. 2 Select the radio buttons to create a new data source that receives data. Click Next. 3 Choose to receive data from a SharePoint library or list. Click Next. 4 Type the URL to the SharePoint site that contains the Sub Project Names lists and then click Next and continue with the wizard.	You'll be halfway through the new data source creation wizard.

Table 7.5 Setting up dynamic dropdowns in an InfoPath Form *(continued)*

Action	Steps	Result
Specify your list and columns to be included in the data source.	1 Select the list name that contains the data for your connection (in this case, Sub Project Names) and click Next. 2 Select the columns to include in the data source (in this case, Title, Parent Project, and ID columns). Click Next twice. 3 Give the data source a name like Sub Projects Filtered by Parent Project Selection. Click Finish to complete the data source wizard, and then Close. 4 Change the Sub Project dropdown to use this data connection instead of the default connection by right-clicking on the dropdown and choosing Drop Down List Box Properties. Then, change the Data Source drop-down menu to be the data connection that was created and, finally, click OK.	A new data connection will be available, and the Sub Project dropdown will be set to use this new connection.
Filter the new data source on the selected parent project. In the Entries box directly below the Data Source selection on the Sub Project dropdown, you'll see the XPath query that points to the data. Click the Select XPath button directly to the right of the text box. (Click the ellipses image.) Follow these steps to set up the filter.	1 In the Select a Field or Group dialog box, click the Filter Data button and then click Add. 2 The first dialog box contains the fields in your custom data source. Select the Parent Project field. Leave the comparing field (middle dropdown) set to is equal to. 3 In the third dropdown, choose Select a field or group. Another dialog box will appear; change the Fields dropdown to Main to select the data that is represented on the form itself. 4 There are two sub folders: the queryFields folder will query fresh data and the dataFields folder contains the data on the form at the present time. Expand the dataFields folder. 5 Expand the sub folder containing the list item data. Select the Parent Project field. Click OK five times.	

Table 7.5   Setting up dynamic dropdowns in an InfoPath Form *(continued)*

Action	Steps	Result
Now your Sub Project dropdown is correctly filtering its data according to the Parent Project dropdown's selected value. The last thing you need to do before you publish the form into our SharePoint tasks list is to set up a rule on the Parent Project dropdown. Each time the Parent Project dropdown's value is changed, you need to tell the Sub Project dropdown to update its items.	1 Right-click the Parent Project dropdown and, under the Rules flyout, select Manage Rules. 2 Click the New dropdown in the Manage Rules toolbar and select Action. 3 Give the rule a name like Update Sub Project Dropdown. 4 Next to Run these actions, click the Add dropdown and select Query for data. 5 In the Data Connection dropdown, select the custom data connection you created earlier. In this case, select Sub Projects Filtered by Parent Project Selection and then click OK.	With the rule in place on the Parent Project dropdown, the data source for the Sub Project dropdown will update each time the parent dropdown changes.

That's it! Now all that's left is to publish the form into your tasks list. Under the File menu in the Info tab, click Quick Publish. Now, when you go to create a new task in your tasks list, the Sub Projects dropdown will be dynamically populated based on what Parent Project is selected (figure 7.7)!

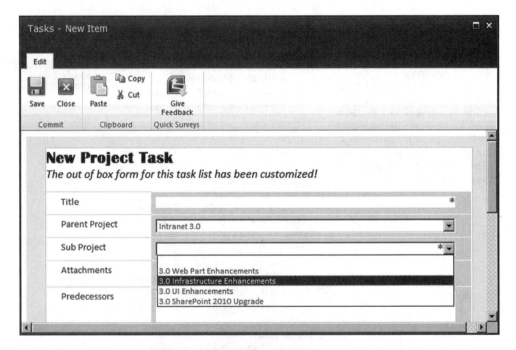

Figure 7.7   You can customize the out-of-the-box New and Edit forms to make lookup columns in your lists or libraries dynamically generate their items based on custom rules.

Only Positive Integers Allowed Error

If you get an error that says Only Positive Integers Allowed, you're trying to save a string into a column that is expecting a number. Most likely the Sub Project dropdown's value is set to a string but, because the column is a lookup, it needs to be a number instead. To fix this error, right-click on the Sub Project dropdown and choose Dropdown list properties. Then, underneath Entries, change the Value from d:Title to d:ID. After you republish the form, the form should start saving properly.

7.3 *Publishing a template to a form library*

We've wrapped up the section on how to customize the out-of-the-box forms, and now it's time to take a closer look at how forms work with form libraries. When a user fills out a form in a form library, new form (for example, an XML document) is created off a form template associated with that library. This template by default is blank and not useful. This section covers how to build a custom form template and update the default template with your custom template.

There are many ways to get an InfoPath form template into a form library. You can publish the form template straight from the InfoPath client into SharePoint. Or, from within SharePoint, you can browse through your hard drive and select the form template. Whatever you chose, you need to decide how available the form template needs to be. Do you want the form template to be only on one library or do you want your end users to be able to create a new form off a form template on any library in the entire site collection? If you need a *global* deployment of the form template, you'll need to publish the form template to a content type (see section 7.4); otherwise, updating the out-of-the-box template in a form library is sufficient.

When a form like a company's expense report only needs to be added to and edited within a single form library, updating a form library's out-of-the-box form template is the most straightforward approach. If you need a form template to be shared across several form libraries, see section 7.4 on how to do this. Before you can edit a form template on a form library, you need to create a form library as follows:

1 Navigate to your SharePoint Site.
2 Under the Site Actions menu, click More Options.
3 A pop-up will appear (figure 7.8). In the left navigation, click Library.
4 In the center navigation, choose Form Library.
5 Provide a unique name for the library and click Create.

Now that you have a form library to work with, let's take a look at how to update that library's form template. If you click on the New Document button in the Ribbon, you get an empty form. You can determine which template the library is using by navigating to that library's Advanced Settings. In the Ribbon, click Library Settings, and click Advanced Settings. Notice that the default template is stored in a Forms folder within the Form Library. This is the file you need to update (figure 7.9).

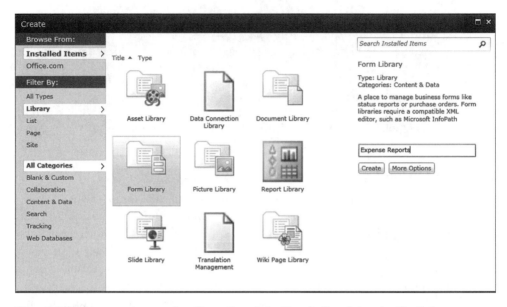

Figure 7.8   You can create a new form library through the More Options link under Site Actions on any SharePoint site.

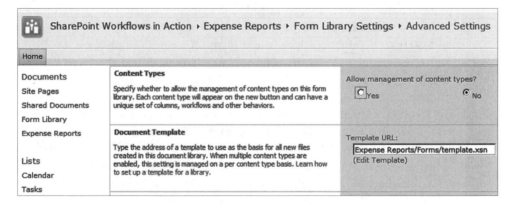

Figure 7.9   A form library has a Forms folder that contains the default template. Update this form to replace the blank form you get when you first click the New Document button on the Ribbon.

To update this form, click the Edit Template link under the Template URL. This loads the blank form in the InfoPath 2010 Designer client. The designer surface is empty and has a grey background. You'll need to build your form from the ground up. Follow these steps to set up a basic expense report template for your company:

1   By default, you get the Title only page template. Following these steps will add the Title and Body page template to this form. Click the Page Design tab in the loaded InfoPath form. Under Page Layout Templates, choose Title and Body.

2   Give your form a title, such as SP WFiA Expense Report, and a description.

3 Click below the description and add a Repeating Table by clicking into the Home tab and selecting Repeating Table from the Controls menu. I chose a table with three columns.

4 Fill out the repeating table's table column headers with column descriptions such as Date of Expense, Dollar Amount, and Description.

5 Save the template on your personal computer's hard drive by clicking the Save icon.

When you're done, your form will look something like figure 7.10.

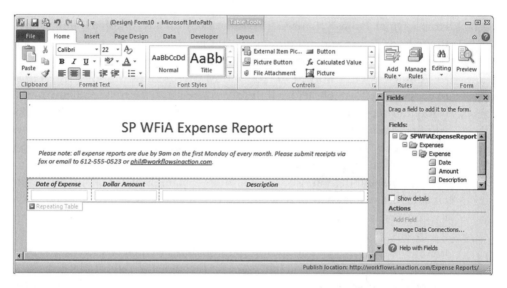

Figure 7.10   A sample form template that will replace the out-of-the-box blank template used by a new form library

InfoPath best practice: naming your underlying data fields descriptively

Figure 7.10 shows a sample form built in InfoPath. When building InfoPath forms, it's important to make sure your fields are named in a way that makes sense. By default, when you add a field into the form, the underlying data is named field1, field2, and so on. When you save the form in SharePoint, that data is stored as XML. If all your data has generic names like field1, your XML is not going to be compelling and will be difficult if not impossible to understand. You'll learn in chapter 9 how to programmatically access InfoPath form data. It's helpful when doing this to have your data named accurately. Figure 7.12 shows all the data renamed in a way that will build a solid XML structure, whereas figure 7.11 (the default) will produce unintelligible XML data.

Now that you have your form template built out to your liking, you need to publish the form into the form library. To do this within InfoPath, click the File menu and

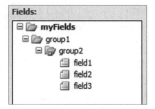

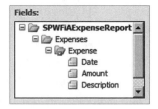

Figure 7.11   Using default data naming produces data that is difficult to understand.

Figure 7.12   It's important to have well-named data in your forms.

choose Quick Publish (figure 7.13). After the form has completed publishing, go back to the form library and test out the form. Click the New Document button in the Ribbon, and the custom expense report template will appear.

A quick publish worked for you in this case because you opened the blank template from the form library itself. InfoPath knew exactly what template in what library it should overwrite. You can also publish to a different form library if you like. When you first open the InfoPath Designer client, you can choose from several templates, one of which is called SharePoint form library. If you create a new form from this template, you'll be repeating your actions in reverse order. Rather than first creating a form library and then in Advanced Settings clicking Edit Template, you would be first creating the template from scratch and then selecting which form library to publish it to. Conversely, you can choose to create a new form library during publishing as well.

In this case, a quick publish won't be available. Instead, in the File menu, under the Publish tab, there's another option to publish to SharePoint Server (figure 7.14). This action will load a wizard to walk you through the publishing process. Click the SharePoint Server button under the Publish tab within the File menu to launch the

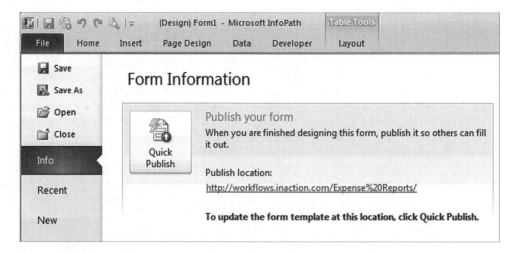

Figure 7.13   After you've finished editing the form template, click Quick Publish to save that template into SharePoint.

Figure 7.14 You can also publish to SharePoint Server, which loads a wizard that will walk you through the publishing process.

publishing wizard. Following the steps in table 7.6 to work through the wizard, you'll enable your form to be published to a different form library.

Table 7.6 Publishing your customized form

Action	Steps	Result
Update your form library's form template.	**1** Enter the URL to a SharePoint site, for example: http://workflows.inaction.com. Click Next. **NOTE:** If you have SharePoint Server, there will be a check box to make the form viewable in the browser. Leave this checked. **2** Leave the form library radio button selected. (More on content types in section 7.4.) Click Next. **3** Make selections to either create a new form library or update an existing form library if you've already created one. In this case, you'll choose to update an existing form library's template. Click Next twice, and click Publish.	Rather than publish to a content type, the form will be published to a form library. The wizard will update an existing form library's template with the newly created template.

7.4 *Publishing a template to a content type*

You've customized a form template for a single form library. What if you need that template to be available on multiple libraries in the same site collection? The best way to accomplish this is to publish the template to a content type. Wherever that content type is added to a form library, that template will also be added to the library.

Content types are useful in this type of situation: you have departmental sites in the site collection, and there is a site for sales, another for marketing, and a third for human resources. Each site needs its own expense report library because the approvers are different for each department. Each could still share a common template. In this case, you could create an expense report content type with a custom template installed on it. Then, you could add that content type onto each department's form

Flashback to chapter 1: content types

In chapter 1, you learned how content types can be used to package workflows, templates, and metadata to make them reusable across an entire site collection. Creating content types saves you time because, if you have ten form libraries that all need the same template, metadata (columns), and workflows, you can add the content type to the library. If you don't use content types, you'll need to add the template, columns, and workflows onto all 10 libraries individually, which can be time consuming and hard to maintain.

library. With this example, if you needed to update the template six months later, that change would be propagated into the libraries using the content type.

To publish to a content type, you'll use the Publish to SharePoint Server feature again. Instead of selecting a form library to publish to, you're going to create a new content type (table 7.7).

Table 7.7   Publishing a form to a content type

Action	Steps	Result
Publish the InfoPath form to a content type. Either open an existing InfoPath form template or create a new form from scratch. Click the SharePoint Server button under the Publish tab in the File menu to launch the publishing wizard.	1 Enter the URL to a SharePoint site, for example, http://workflows.inaction.com. Click Next. **NOTE:** If you have SharePoint Server, there will be a check box to enable the Form to be viewable in the browser. Leave this checked. 2 Select the Site Content Type (advanced) radio button. Click Next. Make a selection to either create a new content type or to update an existing content type if you already have one. In this case, you'll choose to create a new content type. 3 Select Create a new Content Type, select to base the content type on the Form content type, and then click Next. 4 Give your content type a name. In this example, SPWFiA Expenses was entered as the name. Click Next. 5 Enter a URL to a form library where your form template will be stored and referenced from, for example, http://workflows.inaction.com/form%20library. Click Next twice, and then click Publish.	This will publish the new content type into the site collection that was specified in the wizard. Additionally, the form template will be uploaded in the specified form library, and the content type will reference that form as its template.

Table 7.7 Publishing a form to a content type *(continued)*

Action	Steps	Result
Add this content type to all the form libraries that need to share a common template. Find the library you want to add it to, and go to the Library's Advanced Settings screen to add it.	1 Select Yes to allow the management of content types and then click OK. 2 In the Content Types section of the Library Settings page, click Add from existing site content types. 3 In the content type category dropdown, select Microsoft InfoPath. 4 Select the content type you created earlier, in this case, SPWFiA Expenses. Click Add. Click OK.	Within the New drop down on the form library you'll have your content type listed. **NOTE:** Repeat these steps for each library that needs to reuse this content type and form template.

7.5 *Mapping form data to columns*

We've finished discussing how to customize the out-of-the-box forms as well as how to use form libraries to house the custom form data. If you remember, when you customize the out-of-the-box forms, the data is saved into columns on the list item, whereas when you work with a form library, the data is stored as XML in the form itself. The trouble with keeping all the data in the form as XML is you won't be able to sort, filter, and group on the data. Perhaps you want to categorize all your expense reports by type of expenses (for example, gas mileage, lunches, and travel costs). This is done by adding a field into the InfoPath form and then mapping that field to a SharePoint list column, whereby you can sort, filter, and group on that column. In some sense, form libraries with mapped columns are the best of both worlds. You can store large amounts of data in the form and extract into the list item's columns what is interesting to your users.

To demonstrate this concept, we're returning to the SPWFiA Expense report to add a new dropdown where the user can specify the type of expense. Also, you're going to add another field that will contain the sum of all the expenses in the expense report. (The logic for calculating the sum is discussed in chapter 9, section 1). You'll then republish the form into SharePoint, this time mapping your new columns into the form library that end users can use to sort, filter, and group. Follow the steps in table 7.8 to add your two new pieces of data into the expense report form.

Table 7.8 Adding two columns to the form that will be mapped to SharePoint

Action	Steps	Result
Add a new dropdown called Expense Type.	1 In the Home tab of the Ribbon, under the Controls menu, click Drop Down List. Right-click the dropdown and choose Drop Down List Properties. 2 Within properties, give the Field name a better name, like ExpenseType, and check the Cannot be blank check box below the field name to require the user to select a value	A new piece of data will be added to the form that will track the type of expense. Later, this piece of data will be mapped to a new column on the list item.

Table 7.8   Adding two columns to the form that will be mapped to SharePoint *(continued)*

Action	Steps	Result
	3 In the List box choices section, add three choices—Gas Mileage, Lunches, and Travel Costs—and click OK.	
Add a text box called Total Amount.	1 In the Ribbon, under the Controls menu, click Text Box. Right-click the text box and choose Text Box Properties. 2 Change the Field name to be TotalAmount and, under the Display tab, make the field read only because this will be a calculated amount. Click OK. **NOTE:** Because it's a read only field, removing the border makes it look cleaner. To take the border off, right-click the text box and click Borders and Shading. To take the border off, click the None preset. Click OK.	A new piece of data will be added to the form that will track the amount of the expense. This piece of data will also be mapped to a new column on the list item.

When you are finished, your form should look something like figure 7.15.

Instead of doing a quick publish, this time publish the long way and add your ExpenseType and TotalAmount fields as mapped columns onto the list item. This will give you the ability to sort your expenses by the total amount and filter by expense type. Publish the form through the Publish > SharePoint Server in the File menu and specify the URL to the SharePoint site again. Decide whether you want to publish directly to a library or to a content type instead. In either case, you can map the data to columns. When you get to the step in the wizard stating "The fields listed below will be available as columns…," click the Add button and add the ExpenseType and Total-Amount fields (figure 7.16). Click Next and finish publishing.

In the form library that was recently updated, you'll notice two new columns. If you create a new expense report and enter several expenses, after you save and close

Figure 7.15   The Expense Type and Total Amount fields are added to the form and will be mapped to two new columns on the form's list item.

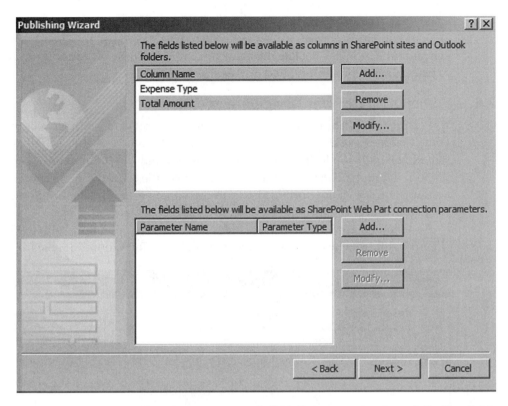

Figure 7.16 When you publish a form, you can specify fields that can map to columns in the SharePoint list item.

the form, you'll notice that the expense type and total amount fields were written to their corresponding columns (figure 7.17). With this data mapped into these columns, you can do handy things such as sorting, filtering, and grouping on that data. Additionally, you could use a SharePoint Designer workflow to respond to the submission and those fields in particular, if appropriate.

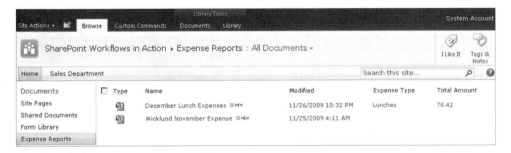

Figure 7.17 When you map fields in the InfoPath client, the corresponding columns are automatically created in the form library when you publish.

Check out section 9.1 to take this example a step further. At this point, the total amount column is not automatically calculated. In chapter 9, you'll add some .NET code into the form to calculate this value by summing all the expenses. With this code in place, the submitter won't have to calculate manually.

7.6   *Forms in SharePoint Designer workflows*

You can use InfoPath to customize initiation and association forms within a Share-Point Designer workflow. By default, when a SharePoint Designer workflow is first started, the initiation form is shown to the user, but only two buttons are showing and the form is empty. The user can confirm or cancel the start of the workflow with the buttons. The association form is shown to users when they add the workflow to a list, whereas the initiation form shows when the workflow starts.

By default, the initiation form includes Start and Cancel buttons and nothing else (figure 7.18). In some cases you may need to collect information from the user before

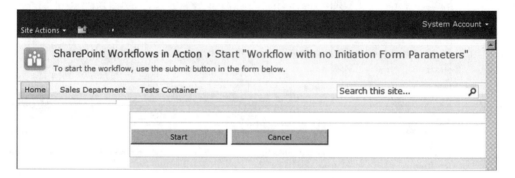

Figure 7.18   When you start a SharePoint Designer workflow, it always shows a workflow initiation form. By default this form is empty.

the workflow begins. You may also need to add information to the form to help users understand the workflow and how things work.

When you need to collect information from the user before the workflow starts, you can use initiation form parameters. These are input fields displayed on the initiation form. After the workflow starts, these parameters are available to us in the workflow. These initiation form parameters are similar to local variables. Adding parameters to the initiation form is easy; click the Initiation Form Parameters button on the Ribbon, which will open the Association and Initiation Form Parameters dialog (figure 7.19).

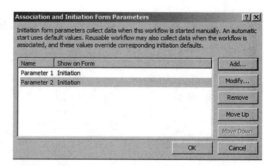

Figure 7.19   You can use the form parameters dialog to add fields to an initiation form that users will need to fill out before they can start the workflow.

Clicking the Add button will allow you to add new fields to the form using the Add Fields dialog (figure 7.20). The type of field you select will determine the available settings on the Column Settings dialogs after you click Next. For List workflows, you'll be able to create only initiation forms because SharePoint Designer will automatically associate the workflow to the list you selected. For reusable or site workflows, you'll be able to specify association parameters. Figure 7.20 shows a dropdown where you can specify which form you want the parameter to be displayed on—Initiation, Association, or both.

Figure 7.20 Use the Collect from parameter during dropdown if you want the parameter to be available on the association form or the initiation form or both.

After adding initiation parameters to a workflow, the user will be able to interact with them when they manually start the workflow from a list item. Figure 7.21 shows the initiation form after the initiation parameters are published.

To help you understand the concept of initiation forms in SharePoint Designer, you're going to walk through an example workflow that handles inventory requests for parts. A workflow like this could easily be used in an auto mechanic shop, where they manage the quantity of parts they have in stock and employ a workflow to handle their mechanics' parts order requests.

The example will work from a custom list titled Parts Inventory. The Parts Inventory list will have three columns—Part name, Quantity available, and Base cost. You want a workflow enabling your users to request additional parts when the supply is low. Then, depending on the costs and how many they want ordered, different approvers will be assigned. An initiation form will come in handy in this workflow.

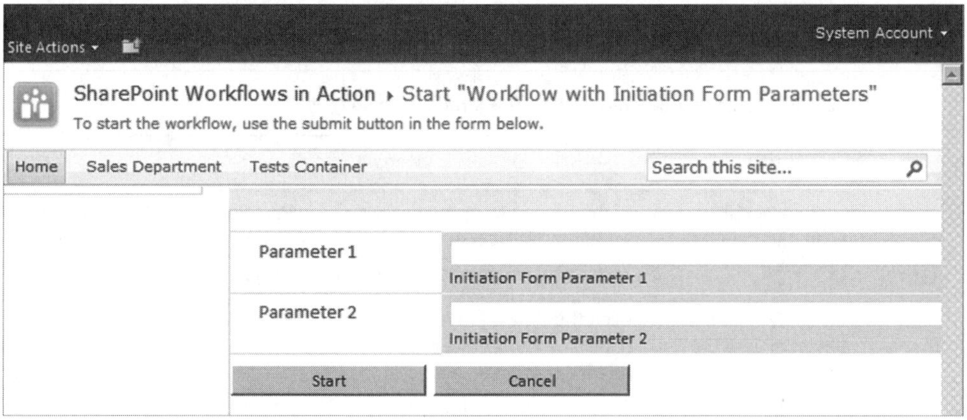

Figure 7.21 After you add initiation form parameters and publish the workflow, the initiation form will show the parameters you specified.

When the user starts the inventory request workflow, they will see a custom initiation form prompting them to enter the number of parts for order.

To set up this example, begin by creating a new SharePoint list titled Parts Inventory with the three columns. This list will store parts and host the workflow. Then, create a new List Workflow in SharePoint Designer off this list. Open SharePoint Designer to the site where you have your Parts Inventory list and, on the workflows tab, click List Workflow and select your custom list. At this point, you'll be prompted to enter the title and description of your workflow. Enter Parts Request Workflow as the title and click OK. In the workflow, start by specifying your initiation form data (table 7.9).

Table 7.9 Adding initiation data into the form

Action	Steps	Result
Add an initiation parameter into the form.	1 In the Ribbon, click Initiation Form Parameters and click Add. 2 Add a field titled Amount to Order and set its Information type to number and then click Next. Users can use this field to enter quantity needed. 3 Specify a minimum value of 0, click Finish, and then click OK to save the parameter.	

With this initiation parameter now specified, users will see a form when they start the workflow. The form will ask them to enter the quantity of the part they order. Now add business logic into your workflow to react to the submission. Let's use the Do Calculation action to calculate the cost of the request. You can then add an If-Else block to calculate if the total cost is greater than $1,000 and, if so, the inventory manager Joe Bob needs to approve the request. Otherwise Fred Fredrickson, the assistant manager, can approve it. Follow the steps continuing in table 7.9 to set up this action and condition.

Table 7.9 Adding initiation data into the form *(continued)*

Action	Steps	Result
Create a workflow variable to hold the total cost.	1 In the Ribbon from the newly created Part Request workflow, click Local Variables. 2 Add a new number variable called TotalCost.	A new variable that stores the Total Cost will be created.
Add the *Do Condition* action into the first step. Configure as follows.	1 Click the first value and specify the Base costs column under the Current Item Data Source. Select Multiply by as the operator. 2 Click the second value selection and, this time, change the DataSource dropdown to Workflow Variables and Parameters.	The final result of the calculation should look like figure 7.22.

Table 7.9   Adding initiation data into the form *(continued)*

Action	Steps	Result
	3 Select the Amount to Order variable for Field from source: **Lookup for Number** Field Data to Retrieve Choose the data source to perform the lookup on, then the field to retrieve data from: Data source: Workflow Variables and Parameters Field from source: Parameter: Amount to Order Return field as: As Double Clear Lookup OK Cancel **4** For the last setting, set the calculation result to output to the *TotalCost* variable.	

Calculate Total Cost

Calculate <u>Current Item:Base Costs</u> <u>multiply by</u> <u>Parameter: Amount to Order</u> (Output to <u>Variable: TotalCost</u>)

Figure 7.22   You can use the Do Calculation action to perform mathematical calculations. In this case, you're multiplying the cost of each part by the amount the user wants to order.

Table 7.9   Adding initiation data into the form *(continued)*

Action	Steps	Result

Add an if-any value equal value condition into a second step.	**1** For the first value, specify the TotalCost variable and set the operator to be greater than 1,000.
	
	2 If the condition is True, add an email action to email the Manager. If the condition is False, email the assistant manager.
		Email Approver
		
		If <u>Variable: TotalCost</u> <u>is greater than</u> <u>1000</u>
		
		    Email <u>Joe Bob</u>
		
		Else
		
		    Email <u>Fred Fredrickson</u>

Now that you have the basics of the workflow, publish and test the initiation form. Click the Save button in the Ribbon to save the workflow, and then click the Publish button to publish the workflow to the Parts Inventory list. On the list, select a list item and start the Parts Request Workflow. The workflow won't start immediately; you'll be prompted with a form you need to fill out. The workflow won't begin until you click the Start button. For our workflow, you'll notice a field for entry of the quantity of parts you want to order (figure 7.23).

After you click the Start button, our workflow will perform the calculation to determine who should approve the order request, and an email will be sent to the

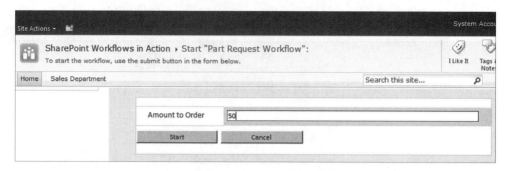

Figure 7.23   When you start a workflow that has initiation parameters set, an Initiation form will automatically load asking the user to provide values for those parameters.

corresponding approver. Now before you call this form done, you need to go back and customize it. The form has the minimum data fields you want, but it isn't intuitive to the user yet. Wouldn't it be good to show to the user descriptive text about the $1,000 milestone? Follow the steps in table 7.10 to edit this form in InfoPath.

Table 7.10   Customizing the initiation form

Action	Steps	Result
Open the Initiation Form in InfoPath.	**1** In the workflow within Share-Point Designer, click Workflow Settings in the Ribbon to navigate to the Settings page. **2** On the Settings page, you'll notice a Forms box that shows all the InfoPath forms that this workflow is using. Click on the form and the Info-Path client will appear.	Forms A list of the forms used by this workflow. File Name ▲ — Type ▼ — Modified D Part Request Workflow.xsn — Initiation — 12/11/20
In the client, make your changes, like adding more descriptive text. When your changes are complete, under *File*, click *Quick Publish*.		The form will reflect the unique appearance requirements you want.

After you publish your form, it will look something like figure 7.24. This is a rather generic example, but don't be fooled because you can do many powerful things with InfoPath in your initiation forms. People often use it to populate a dropdown with external data (covered in the chapter 6 example).

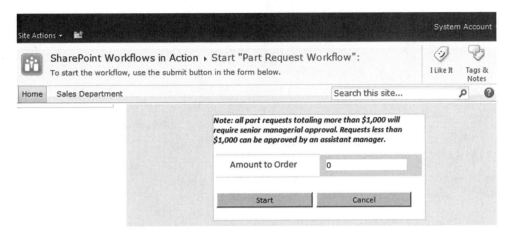

Figure 7.24 After you edit a workflow's form and publish the changes through InfoPath, those changes will show when users edit the form. In this case, the form now has informational text at the top to help guide the user through the process.

7.7 Summary

Workflows and forms are two peas in a pod. You rarely have a workflow that doesn't have any forms, because most workflows rely heavily on human interaction. Most often, human interaction takes place through a form where the user enters information into the system.

After you decide to build custom forms for these workflows, you must choose between several tooling options. Three main tools for building custom forms in SharePoint are out-of-the-box forms, InfoPath forms, and ASP.NET forms with Visual Studio (discussed in chapter 9). The out-of-the-box forms provide the easiest and fastest approach to giving your end users an interface that can accept data and information. The out-of-the-box forms have their limitations. When a more complex form is required, InfoPath is the next best choice. Be aware that SharePoint Server edition is needed to host InfoPath forms in the browser; otherwise, you'll need to have the Info-Path client installed on all your end user's workstations.

To be a good workflow solution builder, you need to understand the tools and foundation techniques related to form development. This includes knowing how form libraries work and how to build a custom form with InfoPath. After you have built a custom form, you can update the default template in your form libraries so that your end users can fill out the forms. The default template is blank and not overly useful. You can spice up your form libraries by customizing the template.

You can also display forms to those using your SharePoint Designer workflows. This includes two opportunities: when the workflow is added to a list (association form), and when the workflow first starts (initiation form). Using these forms is a good way to get data from the user before the workflow starts executing.

Custom-coded SharePoint workflows

Part 3 of this book breaks the no-code mold and digs deep into custom-coded workflows. This starts in chapter 8 with a tour of SharePoint workflows created in Visual Studio. Using Visual Studio as your authoring tool, you can build the most complex workflows possible.

Chapter 9 extends chapter 8 by introducing custom forms that run within Visual Studio SharePoint workflows. These forms include custom association, initiation, and modification forms. Custom task edit forms are covered in chapter 10.

Chapter 10 focuses on task processing with Visual Studio SharePoint workflows. Both forms and tasks are a great way to introduce human interaction into your workflows. As far as form tools are concerned, both InfoPath and ASP.NET forms are covered.

Chapter 11 brings cleanliness and reusability into your Visual Studio workflows by walking you through creating custom activities. This includes a discussion about building custom leaf activities (such as code and sendEmail activities) and composite activities (such as sequence and parallel activities). Toward the end of the chapter you'll see how to publish these custom activities as actions within Share-Point Designer workflows. Custom conditions for SharePoint Designer workflows are also covered.

The book concludes with chapter 12. Chapter 12 fills some important gaps for a SharePoint workflow developer. This includes the knowledge of debugging and handling errors in workflows. Also, it's important to learn how to properly version workflows. Events, such has how to stop a workflow and have it wait for an event to fire from the outside world, are also covered. The chapter ends with a brief introduction to the workflow object model.

Custom Visual Studio workflows

Using Visual Studio to build your custom SharePoint workflows enables you to build complex workflows. The possibilities are limitless. With Visual Studio, you write your workflows from scratch, even though you use the Windows Workflow Foundation architecture.

Visual Studio isn't a new tool for SharePoint 2010. In fact, it was first released in 1997 under the name of Visual Studio 97, well before SharePoint even existed. This was Microsoft's first attempt at having one development environment for many languages (C++, J++, and InterDev). With the arrival of SharePoint 2003, Visual Studio 2003 had SharePoint extensions, which enabled SharePoint developers to package up their development customizations and deploy them into

SharePoint more easily. Even with these extensions, you needed substantial under-the-hood knowledge, which made their value negligible.

As Visual Studio advanced, the SharePoint extensions did not. The 2005 and 2008 versions of Visual Studio did not bring much more to the table. It wasn't until the 2010 version of Visual Studio that SharePoint developers finally started to feel like first-class citizens. With that version, SharePoint developers get the famous F5 experience; they click F5 and all their customizations are automagically packaged and deployed into SharePoint. Given that the learning curve for SharePoint developers was steep in the 2003 and 2007 versions of SharePoint, Visual Studio 2010 is definitely going to bring a sigh of relief for new and experienced developers alike.

For workflow development, the same packaging and deployment benefits apply. When you create a new SharePoint workflow project, all the necessary feature and package files will be created. Click F5 and your workflow is sent to SharePoint and is ready to test!

Because Visual Studio 2010 makes it so easy, all you have to worry about is whether you want to build a sequential or a state machine workflow. If you remember from chapter 1, sequential workflows always flow in one direction—forward. State machine workflows, on the other hand, go in and out of different states until the workflow logic tells them to end. No matter which route you choose, you'll use the same techniques for dropping activities onto the Designer surface, as well as the same debugging and versioning techniques.

If you feel comfortable working with a sequential workflow, you can benefit from the new feature of Visual Studio 2010—the ability to import a SharePoint Designer workflow. This can be useful for many reasons, and here's an example. Suppose you have an existing workflow in SharePoint Designer and, after a year, your business requirements become more complex. This increase in complexity necessitates a Visual Studio workflow. Rather than start from scratch, import what you've got into Visual Studio!

8.1 *Introducing Visual Studio workflows*

A Visual Studio SharePoint workflow is made up of three basics: a template, deployment artifacts, and a type. The template is often called the Designer surface, the area to which you drag and drop workflow activities and structure the flow of work through which the workflow is navigating. Activities are reusable pieces of code that interface with this template and can be dropped onto its surface. By displaying the visual representation of what the workflow is doing, the surface increases readability and simplifies maintenance.

The deployment artifacts are one of the most exciting new aspects of Visual Studio 2010. Visual Studio workflows are deployed into SharePoint through features and solution packages. A solution package packages and deploys the workflow into SharePoint. When activated, the feature enables functionality. In SharePoint 2007, workflows were deployed in exactly the same way. You had to create these artifacts from scratch or rely on an unsupported third-party tool. With Visual Studio 2010, these artifacts are created automatically, and little knowledge of their internal workings is necessary.

A workflow always has a type. It's either a sequential or a state machine workflow. To change the workflow type, you must recreate it.

8.1.1　*Working with the workflow's template*

When you first create your Visual Studio project using one of the workflow templates, an autogenerated workflow titled Workflow1 will be in that project. When you double-click that file, the workflow template will load (figure 8.1), showing you the workflow's Designer surface. With this template, you can start dragging and dropping activities and structuring the flow of work.

At the left of the template is Toolbox (figure 8.2) that contains all the out-of-the-box activities you can drop onto the template. In general, the rule of thumb is to put all of your code in activities, and use the template only to position the activities. Placing all of your code in the template negates the visual benefit that the Designer surface offers. For example, you can right-click an activity and choose to generate handlers. This will create a method in the template's code-behind, where you can start adding code. If this code needs to be reused in other workflows, it's better to encapsulate that code in a composite activity. A composite activity is a custom activity that calls other activities. Then, instead of adding that code to the template, you can drag and drop your composite activity onto the template. Chapter 11 covers custom activities more fully.

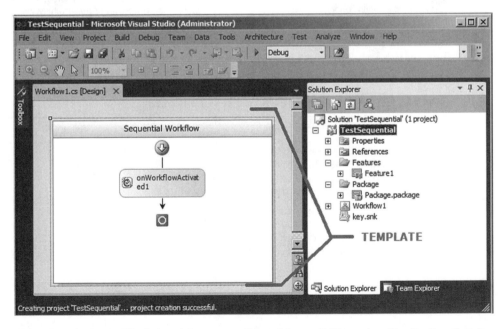

Figure 8.1　In the workflow's template, you can drag and drop activities and position the flow of work.

Figure 8.2   Dozens of out-of-the-box activities are available in your workflows. The activities are found in Toolbox's two categories, Windows Workflow and SharePoint Workflows.

Before starting to build custom activities, notice that there are dozens of out-of-the-box activities available for your use. Many are powerful, requiring little configuration. Tables 8.1 and 8.2 list the top ten fundamental activities and their uses.

Table 8.1   Windows workflow activities

Name and description	Visual
Code—The code activity allows you to drop code into the template. If you don't want to go through the process of creating a custom activity, or you don't think the code will be reused, this activity may be your best choice.	codeActivity1
If-else—You've guessed it, the if-else activity allows you to make logical decisions in the workflow. You can add additional else-if branches. Each branch requires a method that calculates whether the condition is met or not.	ifElseActivity1 — ifElseBranchActivity1 / ifElseBranchActivity2 — Drop Activities Here

Table 8.1　Windows workflow activities *(continued)*

Name and description	Visual
Parallel—The parallel activity allows you to run two or more trunks of activities in parallel. Otherwise, the activities would have to run in sequence.	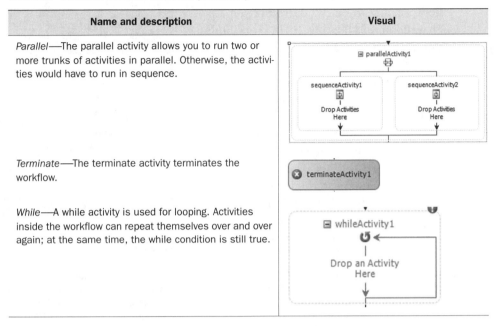
Terminate—The terminate activity terminates the workflow.	
While—A while activity is used for looping. Activities inside the workflow can repeat themselves over and over again; at the same time, the while condition is still true.	

Table 8.2　SharePoint workflow activities

Name and description	Visual
CopyItemActivity—This CopyItemActivity activity allows you to create a copy of a list item or document in another document library or list. This activity is useful for archiving or moving documents.	copyItemActivity1
CreateTask—The CreateTask activity creates tasks in task lists. See chapter 10 on task processing for more information.	createTask1
OnWorkflowModifed (and EnableWorkflowModification)—OnWorkflowModified activity responds when the workflow is modified. With Workflow Modifications, users can change the behavior of a workflow after it has already started (see chapter 9 on workflow forms for more information).	onWorkflowModified1
sendEmail—The sendEmail activity uses the exchange server specified in SharePoint Central Administration to send emails to users.	sendEmail1
SetState—The SetState activity is used to set the state of the workflow. When a workflow starts, a new column is created in the list or library. Instead of the default In-progress or Completed, you can define custom states to show in this column.	setState1

8.1.2　Workflow deployment artifacts

As mentioned before, a SharePoint workflow relies on a solution package to be deployed into SharePoint. Thereafter, it relies on the activation of a feature in a SharePoint site that enables adding the workflow to sites, libraries, and so on. When you create a new SharePoint workflow project in Visual Studio, the package and feature are automatically created and configured for you (figure 8.3).

After you have built out your workflow, click F5 (or right-click the project name and click Deploy). Your workflow's package will be deployed, and the feature will be installed. When you begin creating the project, the new project wizard will ask you to which Share-Point site you want to deploy your workflow (figure 8.4). This is how the F5 feature knows the SharePoint deployment location.

It's important to remember that the wizard is assuming a local installation of SharePoint. It doesn't support remote deployments. You should install SharePoint 2010 locally (on your personal laptop, for example) where you can do your development and unit testing.

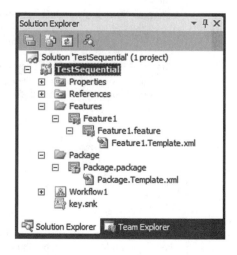

Figure 8.3   New with Visual Studio 2010, the solution package and feature files are created automatically for you. A default feature titled Feature1 is in a folder called Features, and a package titled Package.package is in the Package folder.

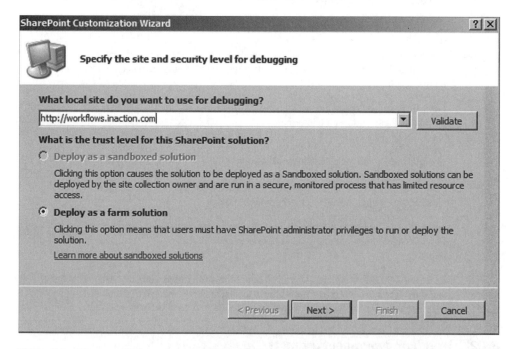

Figure 8.4   When you first create a workflow project, you'll be prompted to enter the URL of a local SharePoint site. Then, when you've built your workflow, you can click F5 to build, deploy, and start testing the workflow.

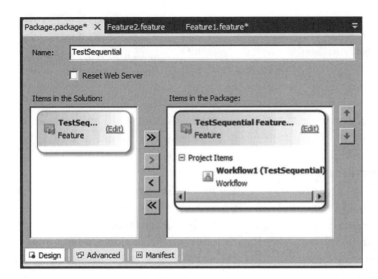

Figure 8.5   Visual Studio 2010 offers a GUI for managing your packages. Move SharePoint items in and out of the package and deploy!

After you've finished testing your workflow, you can then manually install and deploy the solution package into another environment.

Even though the solution package and feature are created and configured for you, it's important to know a little bit about how to work with them manually. Some of the more advanced techniques require under-the-hood knowledge, so let's briefly look at these files to see what they're made of and how they work.

You'll start by digging into the solution package. Technically, you don't have to use a package. A package is a deployment tool, which allows you to guarantee consistency across your servers because, instead of manually copying and deploying files, you're letting the package do the work. All a workflow needs is a dynamic-link library (DLL) and a feature that activates it. But, rather than manually copying files, let's stick with the package created for us. When you double-click on Package.package, you see a GUI that looks like figure 8.5. Notice the two main panels in figure 8.5—a left panel showing what's in the solution and a right panel showing what's in the package. The left panel shows SharePoint items in the solution that are available for adding to the package but have not yet been added. If you click on the right or left arrows, you can move objects in and out of the package. Notice that there are two features; one is in the package, and the other one is not.

You can also use the Package Explorer (figure 8.6) to drill into what's in the package. Figure 8.6 shows that the package has one feature in it. Inside that feature is a workflow. When that package is deployed and the feature is activated, the workflow is ready for use.

Figure 8.6   The Packaging Explorer gives you a hierarchical view of what's inside your package.

At the bottom of the package, you'll see three tabs (figure 8.7). The Design tab is the GUI that you first see when you double-click the package in the Solution Explorer. A package is a CAB with an XML manifest file. This GUI is generating the XML manifest on your behalf. If you still want to

Figure 8.7   If you need to make more advanced customizations to your package, switch to the Manifest tab, where you can manually edit the package's XML.

manipulate the XML manually, switch over to the Manifest tab and you can start editing the XML directly. The Advanced tab allows you to add and remove other assemblies from the package. Perhaps you have a third-party assembly that you also want to deploy with the package.

Double-click the Feature1.feature item in the Solution Explorer. You will see a different GUI (figure 8.8) that looks like the package's GUI. On the left, you'll see Share-Point customizations that are available for adding to the feature but have not yet been added. On the right are items that have already been added. Figure 8.8 shows that the feature contains a workflow named Workflow1. There is a second workflow and a web part that have not been added. Only Workflow1 will be enabled when this feature is activated in SharePoint.

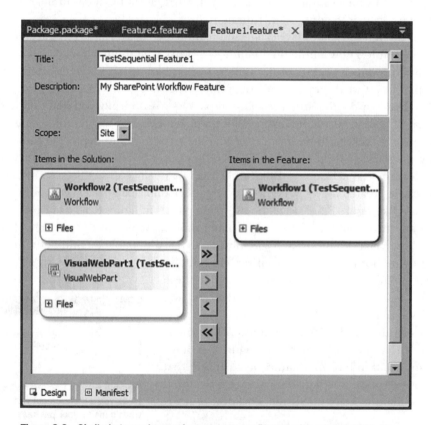

Figure 8.8   Similarly to packages, features are configured with a helpful GUI. You can move things in and out of the feature, controlling which functionality is enabled upon the feature's activation.

8.1.3   *Sequential vs state machine workflows*

A workflow executes from one step in the process to another in two ways. A workflow can be:

- Sequential, in that the steps within the workflow execute sequentially, one after another.
- State machine, where it executes in no particular order.

A sequential workflow always progresses forward and never goes back to a previous step. Figure 8.9 shows what a sequential workflow looks like on the Visual Studio workflow Designer surface.

A state machine workflow, on the other hand, has no such constraint but moves from one state to another, until the logic concludes that the workflow has completed. A good example of a state machine workflow is a bug-tracking workflow. When the workflow first starts, the bug may be placed in a Pending state, where it waits for a developer to be assigned and start working on the bug. When the developer starts working on the bug and fixes it, the bug is put into a Fixed state. When the bug is fixed, a tester confirms the resolution of the bug. If it is not fixed, he places the bug back in a Pending state. This ability to go back in time or to a previous state is only available with state machine workflows. Figure 8.10 shows what a state machine workflow looks like on the Visual Studio workflow Designer surface.

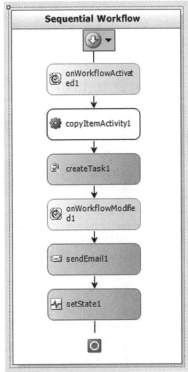

Figure 8.9   Sequential workflows move in only one direction—forward.

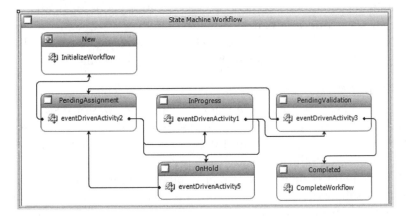

Figure 8.10   State machine workflows can go in any direction you select.

Figure 8.11   When you create a new project, you can use the sequential or state machine workflow project templates. By choosing one of these templates, the workflow, package, and feature files will be set up for you automatically.

When you create a new Visual Studio project, you'll need to decide which workflow type you're going to go with. The new project wizard (figure 8.11) will show two workflow project types. The project template you choose isn't critical because a workflow is an item inside a project, and not the project itself. If you choose the sequential project template, you can always delete the autogenerated sequential workflow and replace it with a state machine, if you so choose. Remember it's not an upgrade, so it's still important to think through your requirements first.

Obviously, some business processes will require a state machine workflow and others won't. It's important to think through your business process requirements before you start building a custom workflow because it's difficult to change course after you've already started down a path. If you start building a sequential workflow but later decide it ought to have been a state machine workflow, you're talking about starting over. The bottom line—think through your business requirements before starting!

8.2   *Building a sequential workflow*

Now comes the time to build your first SharePoint workflow in Visual Studio. Because sequential workflows are less complex than their state machine counterparts, you'll start with them. To add some real-world flavor into the mix, you'll build a workflow that tracks the progress of maintenance work orders. The scenario involves a college that needs a system for students to submit maintenance requests for their dormitories. When a student submits a work order, the order is assigned to one of the maintenance workers who then performs the work, closing out the order and completing the workflow. Figure 8.12 shows the happy path this workflow will take.

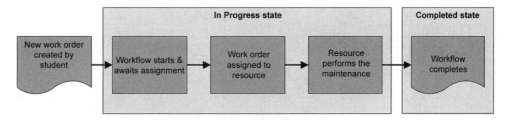

Figure 8.12 The example in this chapter features a Work Order Processing workflow. A new work order is created, assigned, and then the work is completed.

I used the phrase "happy path" because we all know that business processes are never that simple. Oftentimes, the process has alternate paths that the workflow takes depending on circumstances. Also, when you factor in the technical aspects, the flow changes.

Consider how you will complete this example in SharePoint. You'll need a list titled Work Orders to which students can add items. After an item is added, the workflow needs to wait for the status of the work order to change. You'll have four possible status conditions:

- Pending Assignment
- Pending Completion
- On Hold
- Completed

When the manager assigns the item to a maintenance worker, they'll change the status to Pending Completion at the same time. Your workflow then needs to wake up and email the worker notification of the new order. To accomplish this, you're going to leverage the OnWorkflowItemChanged activity. This activity sits and waits for the item on which the workflow is running to change. In this case, when a change happens, you want to look at the status column to see if the status changed. If the status has changed, you're going to take action. If the status hasn't changed, you resume waiting. Figure 8.13 shows a representation of the flow.

You may be wondering at this point if you are still building a sequential workflow. The answer is yes. You can use a while loop to keep looping until the status is set to either On Hold or Completed. If the status isn't set to either one of those, the workflow will loop back and use the OnWorkflowItemChanged activity again to wait. It'll keep waiting until the order is completed or put on hold. This notion of looping is important because you can't loop in SharePoint Designer workflows. This is another reason you may want to consider Visual Studio workflows over SharePoint Designer.

Figure 8.14 shows what the new work order form may look like for the student who's submitting the order. Alternatively, maintenance workers could use the same form when they change the order's status to Completed. Notice the Status column and the Assigned To column. Typically, you wouldn't want the student to see these fields. You could use a custom InfoPath form to hide these fields from students but show them to managers and the maintenance workers. Refer to chapter 7, "Custom form fundamentals," for more information on how to do this.

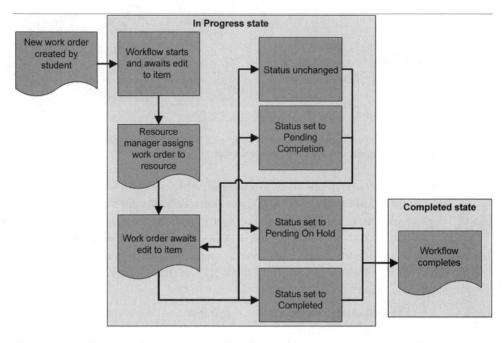

Figure 8.13   Technical challenges make the flow of work more complicated. The workflow will wait for the item to be updated, and each time it is updated, it will check the item's Status column to know what to do next.

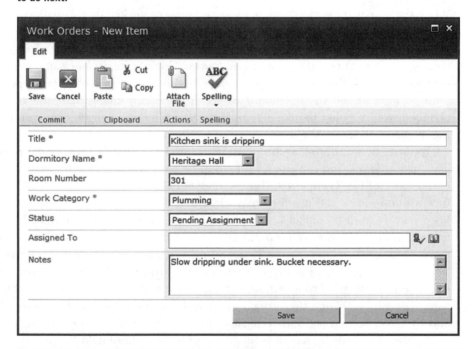

Figure 8.14   The example features a list that contains work orders. Each work order has several pieces of metadata including a title, dormitory name, and work category.

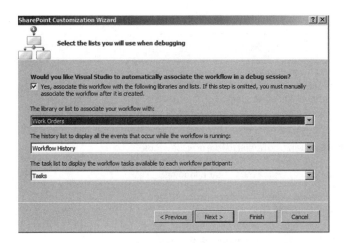

Figure 8.15 When you create a new project, set it to bind the workflow automatically to your Work Orders custom list.

With the stage set, let's start building the workflow. Open Visual Studio 2010 and create a new project by clicking File > New Project. When the project template pop-up displays, choose the Sequential Workflow template. Title the project WorkOrderProcessing. When you create the project, enter the URL to your SharePoint site and bind the workflow to your Work Orders custom list that has columns similar to the ones shown in figure 8.14. (Figure 8.15 shows the wizard screen where you bind the workflow to the list.)

> **IMPORTANT** *Debugging, Error Handling, and Versioning Workflows*—Debugging, error handling, and versioning of Visual Studio workflows are important techniques that a workflow developer ought to know. Check out chapter 12 for an extended discussion on these topics.

Double-click Workflow1 and configure the high-level activities such as the while loop, OnWorkflowItemChanged, and the If-Else branch (table 8.3).

Table 8.3 Configuring the main activities for the Work Order Processing workflow

Action	Steps	Result
Configure a while activity.	1 Drag and drop a while activity from the Toolbox onto the workflow template.	A while activity will be set up to continue looping:
	2 Right-click the activity, choose Properties, and change the name of the activity to whileNotCompleted.	
	3 Notice the red exclamation point. To resolve part of this error, under Properties again, change the Condition property to code condition.	
	4 Click the triangle next to the Condition property, and type a method name WhileOne. This is the method that the activity calls to see if it should keep looping.	**NOTE:** The while activity will have the red exclamation point until at least one child activity is added.

Table 8.3   Configuring the main activities for the Work Order Processing workflow *(continued)*

Action	Steps	Result
	5 When you type WhileOne, you'll be taken to the workflow code file and the newly created WhileOne method. Enter this one line of code: `e.Result = true;` **NOTE:** Setting the Result to True or False keeps the while activity looping or not. True means keep looping; False means stop looping.	
Add a sequence activity and an OnWorkflowItem-Changed activity.	**1** Drag and drop a sequence activity inside the while activity. **NOTE:** A While activity can only have one child activity. Because you need more than one, you'll use the sequence activity to be a container for all the rest of the needed activities. **2** Inside the sequence activity, drag and drop an OnWorkflowItemChanged activity. **3** Another red exclamation point will show on the OnWorkflowItemChanged activity. Right-click and choose Properties. Click the dropdown on the correlationToken property and select workflowToken. **NOTE:** Correlation tokens are described in greater detail in chapter 9.	

Add an if-else activity that will check the status column.	**1** Below the OnWorkflowItemChanged activity, drop an if-else activity.
	
	2 Right-click the if-else activity and choose Add Branch. Do this so there is a total of four branches.
	
	3 Change the names of each branch by right-clicking, choosing Properties, and editing the Name property. Change the names to:
	
	   ■ ifStatusHasNotChanged
	   ■ ifPendingCompletion
	   ■ ifOnHold
	   ■ ifCompleted
	
	4 On the fourth branch, change the Condition property to Code Condition. Now all four branches should show a red exclamation point.
		The resulting if-else activity will have four branches configured similarly to those shown figure 8.16.

With the while loop and the If-Else branches in place, the next step is to add activities into each If-Else branch that will handle your business requirements. You want the following to happen:

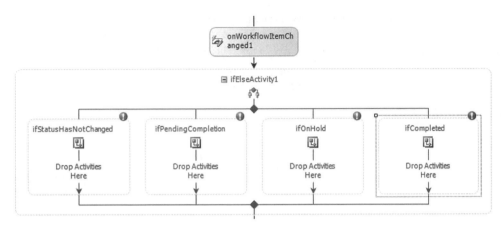

Figure 8.16   Each time the workflow item is updated, an if-else activity will check the Status column to see what the status is set to.

- If the status doesn't change, do nothing.
- If the status is set to Pending Completion, email the maintenance worker informing them they have a new work order to complete.
- If the status is set to On Hold, email the student informing them that their request is put on hold. Terminate the workflow.
- If the status is set to Completed, email the student informing them that their request has been completed. Terminate the workflow.

With the branches now configured properly, add activities into the branches to send the email and perform some logging. Follow the steps in table 8.4 to configure the branches.

Table 8.4   Adding actions into the branches

Action	Steps	Result
For the first branch, log that the workflow item did not change.	**1** Drag and drop an activity titled LogToHisto-ryListActivity from the Toolbox inside branch 1. **NOTE:** The LogToHistoryListActivity activity logs to the workflow's history list. You may want to use other logging mechanisms such as logging to the Event log on the Server. This is helpful when you have errors that you may not want end users to see. **2** Rename the action to logStatusDidNotChange. **3** Under the logger's properties, enter a message in the HistoryDescription property. This text is logged to the workflow's history log. Enter something such as "The work order was updated, but the status did not change."	ifStatusHasNotChanged logStatusDidNotChange

Table 8.4 Adding actions into the branches *(continued)*

Action	Steps	Result
Configure the isPendingCompletion branch to log and send an email to the assignee.	**1** Drop an activity titled LogToHistoryListActivity into branch 2 and change the name to be logWorkOrderAssigned and give a HistoryDescription of Status changed to Pending Completion. **2** Drop a sendEmail activity below the logWorkflowOrderAssigned activity and change the name of the sendEmail activity to be sendEmailToAssignee. **3** Click the correlation token dropdown on the sendEmail activity and choose workflowToken.	
Configure the To, Subject, and Body of the email message to the assignee.	**1** Right-click the sendEmailToAssignee activity and choose Generate Handlers. **2** Enter listing 8.1 into the newly created event handler.	The sendEmailToAssignee's To, Subject, and Body properties will be set to send the email to the assignee, informing them that a new work order has been assigned.

Listing 8.1   sendEmailToAssignee_MethodInvoking event handler

```
SPListItem wfItem = onWorkflowActivated1.WorkflowProperties.Item;
SPFieldUser assignedTo = (SPFieldUser)wfItem.Fields["Assigned To"];

SPFieldUserValue user = (SPFieldUserValue)assignedTo.GetFieldValue(
    wfItem["Assigned To"].ToString());
string assigneeEmail = user.User.Email;

sendEmailToAssignee.To = assigneeEmail;
sendEmailToAssignee.Subject = "New work order has been created.";
sendEmailToAssignee.Body = "Work order number " +
    onWorkflowActivated1.WorkflowProperties.Item.ID +
    " has just been created and assigned to you.";
```

- Get AssignedTo column ❶
- Get AssignedTo column value ❷
- Set To, Subject, and Body properties ❸

First, the code in listing 8.1 gets the AssignedTo column and casts it into a SPFieldUser object ❶. Then, the value of the field is cast into a SPFieldUserValue object ❷. From that object, you can get at the SPUser object that is the person stored in the AssignedTo column. You need this object to get that user's email address and assign it to the To property of the sendEmail activity ❸ (along with the subject and body).

Table 8.4 Adding actions into the branches *(continued)*

Action	Steps	Result
Configure the third branch to log, send an email, and terminate the workflow.	**1** Drop another activity titled LogToHistoryListActivity and change the name to logWorkOrderOnHold and provide an appropriate HistoryDescription. **2** Drop another sendEmail activity and change the correlationToken to workflowToken and the name to sendEmailToRequestorHold. **3** Right-click the sendEmail activity and choose Generate Handlers and set the To, Subject, and Body properties as follows:	

Table 8.4 Adding actions into the branches *(continued)*

Action	Steps	Result
	sendEmailToRequestorHold.To = onWorkflowActivated1.WorkflowProperties. OriginatorEmail; sendEmailToRequestorHold.Subject = "Work order put on hold"; sendEmailToRequestorHold.Body = "Work order number " + onWorkflowActivated1. WorkflowProperties.Item.ID + " has been put on hold."; **4** Drop the terminate activity below the sendEmail activity. **5** Right-click the terminate activity, and change the Error property to be a friendly message like "The work order was put on-hold." This message will display on the workflow history page.	ifOnHold logWorkOrderOnHold sendEmailToRequestorHold ⊗ terminateActivity1
Configure the fourth branch to log, send an email, and terminate the workflow.	**1** Drop another LogToHistoryListActivity activity and change the name to logWorkOrderComplete. Also provide an appropriate HistoryDescription. **2** Drop another sendEmail activity and change the correlationToken to workflowToken. Change the name to sendEmailToRequestorComp. **3** Right-click on the sendEmail activity and choose Generate Handlers. Set the To, Subject, and Body properties as follows: sendEmailToRequestorComp.To = onWorkflowActivated1. WorkflowProperties.OriginatorEmail; sendEmailToRequestorComp.Subject = "Work order has been completed"; sendEmailToRequestorComp.Body = "Work order number " + onWorkflowActivated1. WorkflowProperties.Item.ID + " has been completed."; **4** Drop the terminate activity below the sendEmail activity. **5** Right-click the terminate activity and select Properties, and then change the Error property to a friendly message like "The work order has been completed."	ifCompleted logWorkOrderComplete sendEmailToRequestorComp ⊗ terminateActivity2

With all activities in place, you're almost ready to build and test the workflow. Before you can do that, you need to resolve the red exclamation points next to each If-branch. The exclamation point tells you that the branch doesn't have a method telling the branch if the condition is met or not. Follow the steps in table 8.5 to add logic into the branches so they can determine if the condition is satisfied.

Table 8.5 Adding code condition methods for each If-Else branch

Action	Steps	Result
All the conditions depend on looking into the work order's Status column. Configure the Before and After properties of the OnWorkflowItemChanged activity so you can gain access into the Status column's data.	1 Go to the properties of the OnWorkflowItemChanged activity. 2 Double-click on the little database icon next to the AfterProperties property. 3 In the pop-up, select the Bind to a new member tab, click Create Field, and then click OK. 4 Repeat steps 1 though 3 for the BeforeProperties property.	Two new fields will be added to the workflow's template, one for After properties and one for Before properties. These fields will contain the before and after result of the Status column.
Create a condition method for the first If branch.	1 Change the Condition property of the first branch to code condition. 2 Click the triangle next to the Condition property and type the name of a method, such as HasStatusChanged. 3 Inside the newly generated HasStatusChanged method, enter the code found in listing 8.2.	The first branch will now execute a method that will determine the outcome of the condition.

Listing 8.2 HasStatusChanged method

```
string aStatus = onWorkflowItemChanged1_AfterProperties1["Status"]    ◁
    ToString();

if (onWorkflowItemChanged1_BeforeProperties1["Status"] == null)    ◁
{
    e.Result = false;                        Return if the before
    return;                                     status is null  ❷
}

string bStatus = onWorkflowItemChanged1_BeforeProperties1["Status"].
    ToString();
                                          Retrieve status after
if (bStatus == aStatus)        ◁┐  True if before and     item changed  ❶
    e.Result = true;           ❸  after are equal
else
    e.Result = false;
```

This code first retrieves the status out of the AfterProperties property ❶. This will contain the value of the status column after the change is committed to the database. A check on the BeforeProperties for null is needed ❷ because if the work item is new, it won't have a before value. Lastly, if the before and after status are equal to each other, return True because the Status column had not been updated ❸.

With these last sets of steps in place, you're now ready to deploy and test the workflow. To deploy, right-click on the solution and click Deploy Solution. This will build the project and generate the solution package. It will then add and deploy that package into SharePoint.

Navigate to your Work Orders list, create a new work order, and assign the work order to a user. This action should kick off the workflow, and the workflow should find

Table 8.5 Adding code condition methods for each If-Else branch *(continued)*

Action	Steps	Result

Create a condition method for the second If branch.	1 Change the Condition property of the second branch to code condition.
	
	2 Click the triangle next to the Condition property and type a name of a method, such as IsStatusPendingCompletion.
	
	3 Inside the newly generated IsStatusPendingCompletion method, enter the following code:
	
	``
	string astatus =
	    onWorkflowItemChanged1_AfterProperties1
	    ["Status"].ToString();
	
	if (astatus == "Pending Completion")
	    e.Result = true;
	else
	    e.Result = false;
	``
		Same as the previous step but for the second branch.

Create a condition method for the third If branch.	1 Change the Condition property of the third branch to code condition.
	
	2 Click the triangle next to the Condition property and type a name of a method, such as IsStatusOnHold.
	
	3 Inside the newly generated IsStatusOnHold method, enter the following code:
	
	``
	string astatus =
	    onWorkflowItemChanged1_AfterProperties1
	    ["Status"].ToString();
	
	if (astatus == "On Hold")
	    e.Result = true;
	else
	    e.Result = false;
	``
		Same as the previous step but for the third branch.

Create a condition method for the fourth If branch.	1 Confirm that the Condition property of the fourth branch is set to code condition.
	
	2 Click the triangle next to the Condition property and type the name of a method, such as IsStatusCompleted.
	
	3 Inside the newly generated IsStatusCompleted method, enter the following code:
	
	``
	string astatus =
	    onWorkflowItemChanged1_AfterProperties1
	    ["Status"].ToString();
	if (astatus == "Completed")
	    e.Result = true;
	else
	    e.Result = false;
	``
		Same as the previous step but for the fourth branch.

itself in the In Progress state. At this point, the workflow is sitting on the OnWorkflow-ItemChanged activity and is waiting for someone to edit the work order. Edit the work order by changing Status to Pending Completion. This will cause the OnWorkflowIte-mChanged activity to fire, and the corresponding If-branch will execute, sending an email to the person you specified in the Assigned To column.

Workflow History

▫ View workflow reports
The following events have occurred in this workflow.

☐	Date Occurred	Event Type	☑ User ID	Description
	3/8/2010 3:01 PM	Comment	System Account	Status changed to Pending Completion
	3/8/2010 3:01 PM	Comment	System Account	The work order has been marked as completed.
	3/8/2010 3:02 PM	Workflow Completed	System Account	Work order has been marked as complete and the workflow is now Terminating.

Figure 8.17   Your testing results in a workflow log showing the path the workflow took.

The workflow is still in progress and is again waiting for the item to be changed. Edit the work order again; this time set the status to Completed. This action will send an email to the requestor (which, in this case, is you), and the workflow will terminate. If you click on the workflow status column showing Completed, you'll be taken to the workflow history list that should be similar to figure 8.17.

8.3   *Building a state machine workflow*

The sequential workflow you built in the previous section was useful. It helped you manage a maintenance request process for students on a college campus. That workflow starts to break down quickly if the business requirements get more complicated. For example, notice how in figure 8.18 there's an extra step between the work order completion and the workflow termination. What if a business rule requires that the students confirm the work was done to their satisfaction? If so, the workflow will terminate. If not, the workflow needs to go back to the Pending Assignment status so the manager can send another worker out to finish the job correctly.

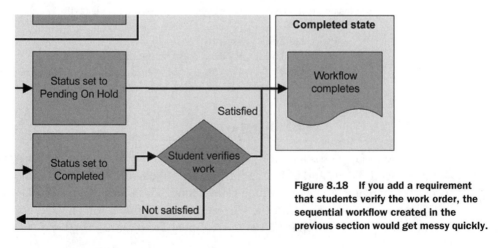

Figure 8.18   If you add a requirement that students verify the work order, the sequential workflow created in the previous section would get messy quickly.

This requirement would be difficult to meet with a sequential workflow; a state machine workflow would be more appropriate. You could hack away to make it work in a sequential workflow using more while activities or adding a good deal of complex logic that tracks it all, but taking that path will create maintainability nightmares.

Figure 8.19 shows what the diagram would look like if you were to rewrite your sequential workflow into a state machine workflow. If you recall, the sequential workflow had only two states, In Progress and Completed, with much logic crammed into the In Progress state. Figure 8.19 shows six states rather than two. Notice how the workflow can more easily go back to a previous state. It's not sequential at all. Also, if you remember from the previous example, when the work order was put on hold, the workflow terminated. A state machine workflow is allowed to reside in that state indefinitely or until the manager decides to put that work order back on the docket.

State machine workflows require more clicking to configure despite their neater diagrams. You'll find that state machine workflows require much less code because the logic is more modeled rather than coded.

Because the configuration of all the activities is nearly identical in both types of workflows, this section won't rehash the same steps to configure the activities. Rather, you'll take the high road and demonstrate how to set up and configure the states in a state machine workflow. If you're curious about configuring a certain activity, go back to the previous section and see the full set of steps.

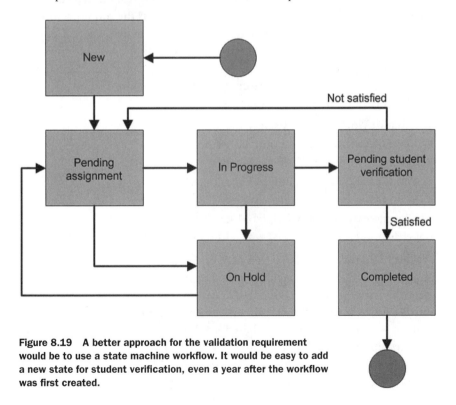

Figure 8.19 A better approach for the validation requirement would be to use a state machine workflow. It would be easy to add a new state for student verification, even a year after the workflow was first created.

To get started, create a new project using the State Machine Workflow project template. When your workflow loads, you'll see a template that looks different from the sequential workflow's template. You'll get a single box (a state) with a StateInitialization activity inside. Rename this default state to New. When you do this, you'll notice a red exclamation point near the text State Machine Workflow. Right-click that text and choose properties. Change the InitialStateName property to New. This tells the State Machine what the state of the workflow should be when it first starts.

After you've configured the New state, add five more states onto the template by dragging and dropping the state activity from the Toolbox. Use the following as state names:

- New
- PendingAssignment
- InProgress
- PendingValidation
- Completed
- OnHold

For the Completed state, drop a StateInitialization activity. Within all the other states, drop an EventDriven activity. To work, each state needs either an EventDriven activity or a StateInitialization activity. All the states besides the Completed state need to wait for an action to occur before they execute. This action is the modification of the workflow item and is handled through the EventDriven activity. The Completed state doesn't need an event to occur before it executes, because it will terminate the workflow.

After you get all the EventDriven (and StateInitialization) activities inside the states, rename them to be more descriptive:

- InitializeWorkflow (New state)
- WaitForAssignment (PendingAssignment state)
- WaitForCompletion (InProgress state)
- WaitForValidation (PendingValidation state)
- WaitForResume (OnHold state)
- CompleteWorkflow (Completed state)

With your states and EventDriven activities in place, it's time to tell the workflow how the different states interrelate. In essence, make the state machine workflow look like figure 8.19. The state machine template has a useful feature that allows you to connect the various states together with arrows. This is similar to Visio diagrams. As in figure 8.19, you draw the arrows on the template between the states. The workflow knows which state comes next based on the directions of the arrows.

To start connecting your states, hover you mouse over the New state and look for the four blue dots on the edges of the state box. Click and hold one of those blue dots and drag your cursor over to the PendingAssignment state. Hover over the

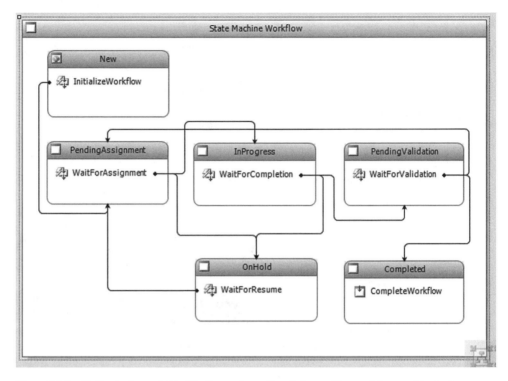

Figure 8.20 Similar to figure 8.19, this figure shows the state machine workflow as it looks in Visual Studio.

PendingAssignment state's blue dots and release the mouse. This will draw an arrow between the New state and the PendingAssignment state. Make sure the arrow is going in the right direction!

Repeat this step until all the states are connected. Your template should look similar to figure 8.19 and, more specifically, figure 8.20 when you're done.

At this point you may be thinking, "This diagram is cute, but where's my logic going to go?" All the workflow activities live inside a state. For example, if you double-click the New state, you'll be taken to a template for that state. You can now drag and drop activities into that state. Notice that the New state contains two activities (figure 8.21). The first activity, OnWorkflowActivated, is the default activity for SharePoint workflows and needs to be the first activity that fires. The next activity is a SetState activity that tells the workflow to which state to move next. You

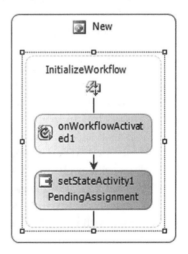

Figure 8.21 The New state does two things: it initializes the workflow and moves the workflow into the PendingAssignment state.

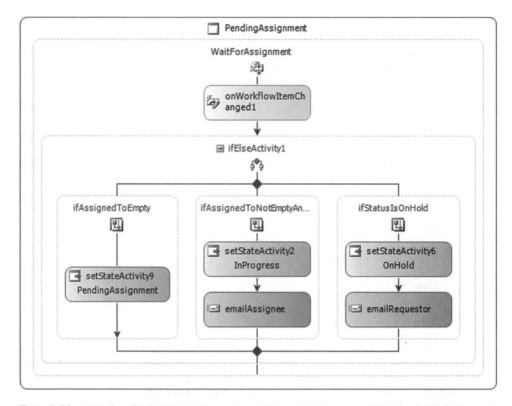

Figure 8.22   In the PendingAssignmet state, the workflow waits for a person to be assigned to the work order and the status to be updated.

can see that the New state initiates the workflow and moves the workflow to the PendingAssignment state.

To build out the Work Order example, you only need to add your activities into the various states. Take the PendingAssignment state for example (figure 8.22). Because the root activity is an EventDriven activity, the first activity must be an activity that waits for an event to fire. In this case, you're using the OnWorkflowItemChanged activity again. When the workflow is in this state, it will wait for the work order to be updated. When it is updated, a series of three if statements determine what to do. The first checks if the AssignedTo column is empty. If it is, it repeats the PendingAssignment state. Otherwise, it looks at the Status column. The second branch checks if the status is set to InProgress. If it is, the workflow moves to the InProgress state and emails the assignee. Last, if the status is set to OnHold, the workflow moves into the OnHold state.

The InProgress state (figure 8.23) behaves in a manner similar to the PendingAssignment state. The big difference is that the logic in the If branches checks for different things. The InProgress state represents the workflow waiting for the maintenance worker to finish the work order. When they finish the work order, the

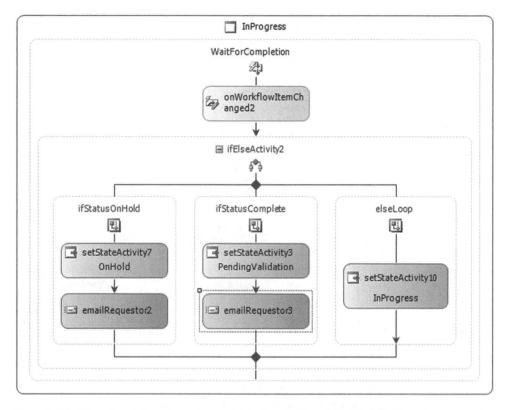

Figure 8.23 When the status column is changed to PendingCompletion, the workflow state moves to InProgress where it waits for the worker to complete the work item. If the work order is set to Completed, the workflow moves into the PendingValidation state. Otherwise, it either repeats itself or goes into the OnHold state.

individual updates the status column to Completed. This causes the OnWorkflowItemChanged event to fire again, and it is handled by the second branch, which forwards to workflow onto the PendingValidation state. Otherwise, the state repeats itself or goes into a hold.

When the work order is completed, the state goes into PendingValidation, and the requestor is emailed a request to validate that the work was completed to their satisfaction. There are several ways to accomplish this. One option is to embed a link in the email. When users click that link, they go to a page that reads a unique ID out of the query string and programmatically updates the correct work order. You could use a Yes or No column in the work order to track if the student has validated the work. The PendingValidation state would wait for that column to be updated. That's what's depicted in figure 8.24—the PendingValidation state. If the column is set to Yes, the workflow moves to the Completed state. If set to No, it moves all the way back to the PendingAssignment state.

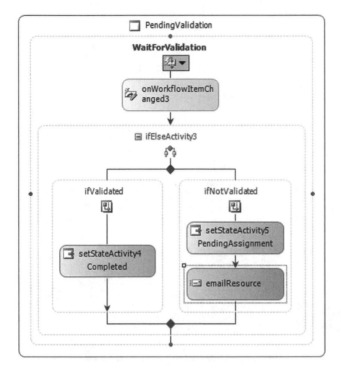

Figure 8.24   While in the PendingValidation state, the workflow waits for the student to
submit their validation that the
work has been completed. When
they do, the workflow moves to
the Completed state.

Last is the Completed state (figure 8.25). Workflow
termination is the purpose of the Completed state.
You could have put the terminate activity in the second branch in the PendingValidation state; however, your workflow would have terminated but still
show Pending Validation in the workflow status column. Because Completed is a preferable status, its
own state is a better way of reflecting this.

8.4   *Importing an SPD Workflow into Visual Studio*

Figure 8.25   The Completed state
terminates the workflow.

One of the new exciting features with Share-
Point 2010 and Visual Studio 2010 is the ability to import workflows from SharePoint
Designer (SPD) into Visual Studio. This brings considerable value to businesses because
legacy workflows created in SharePoint Designer can easily be imported and expanded.
Also, nontechnical resources can prototype workflows in SharePoint Designer and then
hand off their work to someone more technical.

It's actually easy to do this. The high-level steps include exporting the workflow
template from SharePoint Designer. When you export the workflow, it saves it in the
Site Assets library at the root of the site collection. The file has a .wsp extension. You
can download that file onto your computer and create a new Visual Studio project.

When you select the type of project, choose Import Reusable Workflow, and browse to the .wsp file you downloaded. It's that simple! Table 8.6 shows more granular steps.

Table 8.6   Exporting and importing a SharePoint Designer workflow into Visual Studio

Action	Steps	Result
Build and export a SharePoint Designer workflow.	1 Create a new reusable workflow. Add actions and conditions as you see fit. For example: 2 Save the workflow, then click Publish. 3 On the left navigation in SharePoint Designer, click Workflows and select the workflow you created. Then, in the Ribbon, click Save as Template: 	By saving the workflow as a template, the workflow will be exported as a .wsp file and sent to the Site Assets library at the root of the site collection.
Browse to the Site Assets library and download the .wsp file onto your desktop.	1 Browse to the root web in the site collection and click All Site Content. 2 Click the Site Assets document library and download the TestImportToVS WSP file: 	With the .wsp file on your desktop, you can now import in into Visual Studio.
Create a new Visual Studio project using the new Import Reusable Workflow template.	1 Create a new project and use the Import Reusable Workflow project template. 2 Enter the URL of a Site Collection. Click Next, and then browse out to the .wsp file you downloaded earlier. Click Finish.	The result is a new project with all the activities imported form SharePoint Designer. Even the Info-Path forms are imported (figure 8.26).

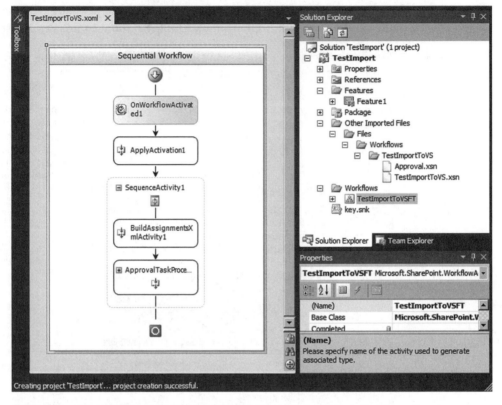

Figure 8.26   When importing from SharePoint Designer, you'll notice that all of the actions are recreated as activities, and all your custom InfoPath forms are carried over!

8.5   Summary

In many regards, this chapter is the most exciting chapter of the book. This is true for those developers who are new to SharePoint, because it can easily be seen that Visual Studio workflows for SharePoint are powerful, fast, and easy to create. Visual Studio 2010 has made the life of a SharePoint developer so much easier than the previous versions. All the packaging and deployment struggles are now over. You don't need to know as much under-the-hood information.

This leaves the developer solely focused on the workflows they're trying to develop. A developer can build sequential workflows and state machine workflows for Share-Point. Sequential workflows are similar to SharePoint Designer workflows in that they always flow forward. You can use looping techniques to overcome this, but the limitation remains that these workflows act in sequence. A new step always comes after the previous step.

On the other hand, state machine workflows are powerful. State machine workflows can go any direction you wish, even backwards. How you model the State Machine will dictate the flow of work. How you program the logic will dictate when the workflow should terminate—it's the ultimate in workflow flexibility. State machine workflows will accommodate the most complicated workflow needs.

If you're comfortable with sequential workflows, there is one great advantage that shouldn't be overlooked—the fact that you can import a SharePoint Designer workflow into Visual Studio. There is power, too, in this feature because your nontechnical people can pass the baton to more technical people when the limits of SharePoint Designer are reached. This provides a return on investment based on a more effective utilization of your resources.

If you liked working in Visual Studio in this chapter, stay tuned! Each of the four remaining chapters contains Visual Studio workflow techniques. Read on to learn about forms, tasks, custom activities, and events!

Forms in
Visual Studio workflows

This chapter covers

- Adding .NET code to an InfoPath form
- Programmatically retrieving form data
- Using InfoPath and ASP.NET forms in workflows

This chapter deals with forms that run *inside* a workflow including association, initiation, and modification forms.

Initiation forms gather information directly before the workflow starts. With association and modification forms, users enter information into the workflow. The difference between the two is that an association form is presented to users when the workflow is added to the list, library, or site, and modification forms are presented to users during the workflow's execution.

Initiation forms come in handy when you need to gather data from the user before the workflow starts, as with an expense report. When you initiate a workflow, you might not know who needs to approve the expense report. An initiation form could capture from the submitter the identification of their manager, and the workflow could then ensure that the proper individual receives the approval request.

The association form is also useful with expense reports. Rather than have employees specify their managers every time they upload an expense report, you could use an association form so that employees enter the information only once—when the custom workflow is first added to the library.

With a modification form, you can change the behavior of the workflow after it has started whereas the other two forms present themselves before the workflow starts. Here's an example of an effective workflow modification. A workflow assigns a task, and the assignee wants to reassign the task to someone else. The modification form comes into play through a link on the workflow status page. The link shows up only after you enable modification on that workflow. The modification starts after the users click the modification link on the status page and they are redirected to the modification form, where they enter information. After the form is submitted, the modification executes. It's important to remember that modifications can occur only when your workflow says they can.

Whichever form you decide your workflow requires, you'll need to consider several implementation approaches. All three types of forms can be built in either InfoPath or ASP.NET. InfoPath's strength is its intuitive form designer surface, but its weakness in this scenario is that there are more hoops to jump through to deploy the form in the workflow. ASP.NET forms are straightforward to deploy but not to develop.

The steps to implement each form with each tool are the primary focus of this chapter. In addition, this chapter explains how to add .NET code to an InfoPath form and how to programmatically retrieve data. You'll go through a series of examples that add custom forms into workflows in both SharePoint Designer and Visual Studio. For Visual Studio workflows, we look at both InfoPath forms and ASP.NET workflow forms.

9.1   *Adding .NET code to an InfoPath form*

In section 7.5, you set up two new pieces of data in an expense report form and mapped that data into columns on the form itself. One piece of data contained the expense type, and the other contained the total dollar amount of all the expenses in this report. Currently, the total dollar amount field isn't automatically calculated. To calculate this number, you need to add to your form the code that sums the expenses. You want the code to fire whenever someone changes the Amount field in any of the expenses in the repeating table. That code will then cycle through all the Amount fields in the table and calculate the total amount. This is a generic example, but having .NET code in a form often comes in handy.

Before you can add this code to the form, you need to make sure you have Visual Studio Tools for Applications installed on your workstation. If you don't have it installed, you can rerun the Office 2010 setup and choose to add new features. Under the Info-Path folder, select Visual Studio Tools for Applications, then Run from My Computer (figure 9.1). Click Continue, which will then install Visual Studio on your computer.

With Visual Studio ready to go, it's time to add the code that will execute when the Amount field is changed. First, open your InfoPath form. For the expense report form

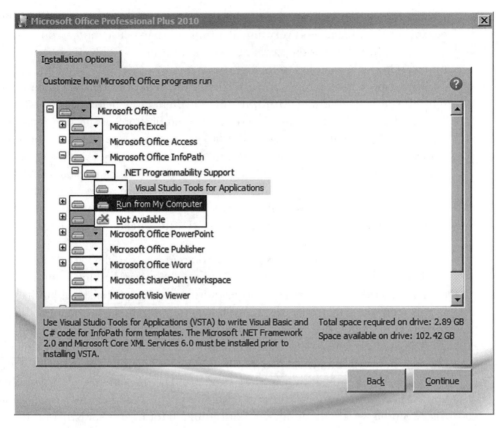

Figure 9.1   Visual Studio Tools for Applications is required to add .NET code behind to any InfoPath form. To install this application, run the Office setup, choose Add Features, and select Run from My Computer under the Visual Studio Tools for Applications dropdown.

created in chapter 7, navigate to the Library Settings of the Expense Reports library, and under Advanced Settings, click to edit the form template. To get started, first click the Amount field. Then, on the Ribbon under the Developer tab, click the Changed Event button. This will open Visual Studio and a new project that is linked to your form template will be automatically generated (figure 9.2). Inside the project, you'll notice a single code file titled FormCode.cs. Within this code file are two methods, InternalStartup and Amount_Changed. Because you selected to respond to the Amount field's Changed event, you'll see the InternalStartup method has an event that will fire when changes occur. When a change occurs, it is handled by the Amount_Changed method.

When working in an InfoPath form's .NET code, it's helpful to know a couple of things. First, the InfoPath form and its code are linked together so all you have to do is build the project and then, from within InfoPath, republish to get the code changes back into SharePoint. Another useful feature is that you have your expected debugging experience available. Hit F5 and the InfoPath client will appear with the form. If you

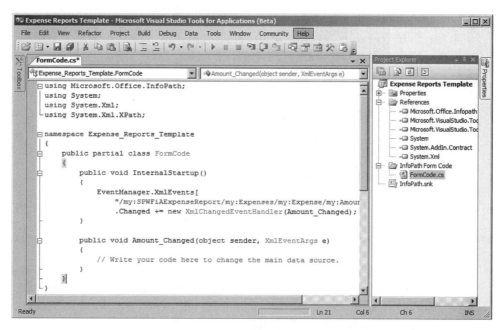

Figure 9.2   When the code-behind is first added to an InfoPath form, a new Visual Studio project is automatically created.

have break points set, you can walk through your code. Keep in mind that, when debugging, you are not going to have a web context, so if you're trying to run code that behaves differently based on who's running it, unit testing and debugging will be trickier.

Setting your preferred programming language

By default, all new Visual Studio projects created out of InfoPath are set to use Visual Basic as the programming language. This can easily be set to use C# instead. In the Developer tab in the Ribbon, the first button is Language. Language provides a form template code language dropdown that you should update accordingly. If the dropdown is disabled, you have already created a project and it can't be changed. If you are not worried about losing code, click the Remove Code button to orphan that project. Then you can change the language and start over by setting up a new project.

Next, you need to add code into the method that will crawl all the expenses in the form and total the amounts, as shown in listing 9.1. Copy the listing and replace the Write your code here… comment in the Amount_Changed method.

Listing 9.1   Amount Changed Event Handler code

```
XPathNavigator formData = this.CreateNavigator();

XPathNavigator expenseGroup = formData
    .SelectSingleNode("/my:SPWFiAExpenseReport/my:Expenses",
```

❶ Selects only the Expenses XML data

```
    NamespaceManager);

XPathNodeIterator expenses = expenseGroup.SelectDescendants(
    "Expense",
    expenseGroup.NamespaceURI,
    false);

double total = 0;
foreach (XPathNavigator expense in expenses)
{
    string value = expense.SelectSingleNode(
        "my:Amount", NamespaceManager).Value;

    double amount = double.Parse(value);
    total += amount;
}
formData.SelectSingleNode(
    "/my:SPWFiAExpenseReport/my:TotalAmount", NamespaceManager)
    .SetValue(total.ToString());
```

Loads
Expenses into
❷ **a collection**

**Iterates through
each expense and**
❸ **sum expenses**

❹ **Updates TotalAmount
with new total**

The first thing that happens in this code is that an XPathNavigator is created to help you dig around in the XML data that contains all the values entered into the form. You then select only the Expenses data from the form. To do this, you call the ❶ SelectSingleNode method on formData, which requires the XML path to the data element you want (along with the namespace). It is important to reiterate that when you create your forms in InfoPath, make sure to give the fields descriptive and meaningful names. The XML structure maps directly to the field names as seen in the path that is specified in the SelectSingleNode method.

Now that you have your Expenses (repeating table's data), you need a collection object so you can iterate through each expense. To get this collection, you call ❷ SelectDescendants on the expenseGroup object and you pass in the element name in the XML that you want back, which, in this case, is the Expense node. Next, you iterate through each expense and pull out the amount of each expense ❸. You, then, add that amount to a running total and, after you've gone through all the expenses, that total amount is ❹ saved back into the TotalAmount field.

TotalAmount field's data type

If you get an error when you publish, check the TotalAmount field's data type in the Expense Report library. It should be Double, and not Text (the default).

Now that your code is neat and tidy, you should make sure it works as expected. Build the project to ensure there are no errors and, if there are none, hit F5 to launch the debugger. Unit-test the expense report form and ensure that it is totaling the expenses correctly and saving the total back into the TotalAmount field. When you're certain it's behaving correctly, publish into SharePoint.

Sandboxed solutions must be enabled

When you publish, you may get an error saying that sandboxed solutions are not enabled (figure 9.3). To enable sandboxed solutions, navigate to your server's Central Administration site. Click System Settings and then click Manage services on server. Ensure that the Microsoft SharePoint Foundation Sandboxed Code Service is started on all your web front ends.

Figure 9.3   InfoPath forms with .NET code are packaged as a sandboxed solution. By default, sandboxed solutions are not enabled on the farm, so you must enable them.

Sandboxed solutions versus administrator-approved templates

A step in the publishing wizard gives you the option to publish as an Administrator-approved template. If you select form library or content type and your form has .NET code in it, by default that code runs in what is called a sandboxed solution. Sandboxed solutions are a new concept in SharePoint 2010. In SharePoint 2007, all browser-enabled form templates needed to be uploaded into Forms Server through SharePoint Central Administration. With 2010, a site collection administrator can upload their form templates into the site collection's own solution gallery. The difference between these two deployment options is mainly scope and security related. A form deployed into a sandbox obviously is viewable only within that site collection, whereas an Administrator-approved template (central admin) is usable across the entire farm. In addition, Administrator-approved templates can be set to have full trust, so the code in those forms can do things like cross domains (get and set data in separate SharePoint farms) and use things like SQL data.

9.2   *Programmatically retrieving form data from within a workflow*

In the last section, you saw how to programmatically read data out of a form from within the form's own code-behind. What happens when an external system, like a workflow, needs to interact with that data? A common business requirement is to have a workflow react to the submission of a form and then have that workflow retrieve data stored in the form. After it has a handle on the data, it can do something with it, like ship it off to a separate line of business application or external process or send email notifications.

To meet this business requirement, you first create a .NET proxy class for the InfoPath form from the form's XML schema definition file. This class will be strongly typed, so it will be much easier to code against the form data because you will have

IntelliSense in the form fields and their values. If you remember, this is unlike working in the code-behind of the form where you had to leverage XPath. Undoubtedly, you will like this proxy approach because the code will be much cleaner and easier to understand. You can use this proxy class to both read and write data in and out of the form. Note that this can't be done while the user is editing the form. The proxy class can be leveraged before or after user interaction, while XPath must be used during the interaction.

Therefore, to get started, let's build a new sequential workflow called ExpenseReportWorkflow with Visual Studio 2010. This workflow will sit on top of the form and will fire each time a new expense report is entered into the system. You will add your proxy class into this new workflow project, and the workflow will have a generic code activity that will use the proxy to pull out the form data. Follow the steps in table 9.1 to set up the sequential workflow project shell and the code activity.

Table 9.1   Setting up a sequential workflow with a code activity

Action	Steps	Result
Create a new sequential Visual Studio workflow project with a name of ExpenseReportWorkflow.	1 Enter the URL to your SharePoint site, and deploy as a farm solution. Then, click Next. 2 Name the workflow Expense Report Workflow, choose the List Workflow template, and then click Next. 3 Click Yes to automatically associate your new workflow with a SharePoint list. In the library or list dropdown, select your expense reports form library to add the new workflow, and then click Finish.	The project will be created with a workflow file called Workflow1.
In the workflow designer surface, add a Code Activity below the OnWorkflowActivated1 activity that was placed on the surface by default.	1 After the Code Activity has been placed on the surface, edit its properties and name it RetrieveFormData. 2 Right-click the Code Activity and select Generate Handlers.	When you finish these steps, your new project's workflow designer surface will look something like figure 9.4.

Now that you've started the workflow project, you need to generate a proxy class from your InfoPath expense report template. To generate the proxy, you're going to run an XSD command from the Visual Studio Tools command prompt, and you'll point the command at your template's XML schema definition file. Every InfoPath form is a .cab file that has several files packaged into a single file. Your schema definition file lives within this .cab. To save all these subfiles, click the Export Source Files button under the Publish tab in the File menu in InfoPath. Browse to a place on your hard drive to save the files in a desired directory. Figure 9.5 shows the seven files that are exported.

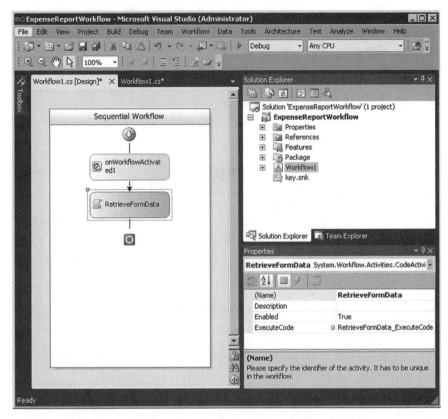

Figure 9.4   This sequential workflow responds to the submission of new expense reports to the system.

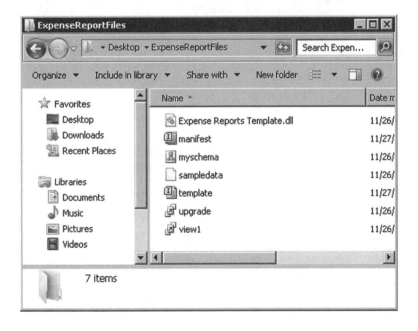

Figure 9.5
Every InfoPath
form is a .cab that
contains several
files. You can ex-
port these files
from the Publish
tab in the File
menu in the Info-
Path client.

The file of interest is myschema.xsd, which contains your form's XML schema. This schema file will instruct the XSD command on which classes, properties, and fields to automatically provision for you when it generates and spits out your proxy class. There will be a class created for every group of fields in the InfoPath form. For example, your proxy file will contain three classes: one for the root; one called Expenses, which has a collection of all the expenses; and another called Expense, which contains all the data in each expense. Follow the steps in table 9.2 to generate this proxy class.

Table 9.2   Generating a proxy class of an InfoPath Form

Action	Steps	Result
Run a command to create a new file named myschema.cs.	With Visual Studio command prompt, run the following command against the exported files: `xsd myschema.xsd /c /l:cs` **NOTE:** If you get an error that is similar to "Error: The process cannot access the file c:\export\ myschema.xsd because it is being used by another process," you have to close the InfoPath form first. When the form is open, it has a lock on the schema file. Close InfoPath and rerun the command.	This command will spit out a new file named myschema.cs in the same directory as the exported files. This code file contains the proxy class you can use to code against the expense report data.

Add the myschema.cs file into the Visual Studio project.	1 Right-click the project name, point to Add, and then click Add Existing Item. Browse out and find myschema.cs and click Add.
	
	2 Rename the code file to something more compelling than myschema.cs, like SPWFiAExpenseReport.cs. It's helpful to keep the file name the same as the root class name.
	
	Fields:
	
	    SPWFiAExpenseReport
	      Expenses
	        Expense
	          Date*
	          Amount*
	          Descriptoin*
	      ExpenseType*
	      TotalAmount
	
	NOTE: Renaming the myschema.cs file name to SPWFiAExpenseReport.cs is a personal preference only. If you want to rename the class name itself, please be aware that it's a two-step process. The generated class name comes out of the root XML element name in the InfoPath form. You must change this field name first and then rerun the XSD command to generate a new proxy class. The figure above contains the fields in the example expense report form. Notice that the root data element is named SPWFiAExpenseReport. The proxy class will have the same name as this element. First, change it in the form and, then, rerun the XSD to update the class name to your liking.
		The proxy class will be added to the Visual Studio project, and renamed SPWFiAExpenseReport.cs (from myschema.cs).

Table 9.2 Generating a proxy class of an InfoPath Form *(continued)*

Action	Steps	Result
Add a namespace to SPWFiAExpenseReport.cs.	**1** Open the code file. Above the class name, and under the using statement at the top, add a namespace. Directly below the using System.Xml.Serialization statement at the top of the file add "namespace ExpenseReportWorkflow.Workflow1 {" **2** At the last line of the file, add a close bracket, }. Now your proxy class is contained in the namespace that your workflow code is running in.	The SPWFiAExpenseReport class by default doesn't have a namespace. With a newly added namespace, you'll be able to reference this class from other classes in the project.

Now that you have the proxy class added to your Visual Studio project, let's instantiate that class and start working with the form's data. Listing 9.2 contains code for updating the code activity's method. Right-click on the RetrieveFormData code activity and choose View Code. Replace the autogenerated RetrieveFormData_ExecuteCode method with the method in listing 9.2 and add two using statements for System.Xml and System.Xml.Serialization.

Listing 9.2 Retrieving form data through a strongly typed proxy class

```
private void RetrieveFormData_ExecuteCode(object sender, EventArgs e)
{
    SPFile file = onWorkflowActivated1.WorkflowProperties.Item.File;

    XmlTextReader reader = new XmlTextReader(file.OpenBinaryStream());

    XmlSerializer serializer = new XmlSerializer(
        typeof(SPWFiAExpenseReport));

    SPWFiAExpenseReport fields = (SPWFiAExpenseReport)serializer
        .Deserialize(reader);

    double total = 0;
    foreach (Expense expense in fields.Expenses)
    {
        total += expense.Amount;
    }

    file.Item["Total Again"] = total;
    file.Item.Update();
}
```

Loads file's data into XML reader ❷

Deserializes XML into proxy instance ❸

Sums each expense ❹ (much cleaner!)

Assigns the value ❺ back to the item

Loads InfoPath form through SPFile object ❶

Listing 9.2 starts by instantiating an SPFile object ❶. The OnWorkflowActivated property has an instance of the form's list item (SPListItem), and a list item in SharePoint can have an attachment. This attachment is required in Form Libraries. The File property for SPListItem contains the SPFile object (the attachment), which also happens to be your InfoPath XML form data file.

You then open a binary stream on that SPFile object ❷ and load the stream into an XmlTextReader. Afterwards, your proxy class gets instantiated ❸ and is assigned to a deserialized version of that stream cast into your proxy class type. With this, your proxy class object contains all the properties and collections of data that are present within your InfoPath form. That data is mapped to the XML schema that is mapped to the fields in the form.

Just as in your code-behind example, you're going to iterate through all the expenses in the expense report ❹, and total all the expense amount field values. As with the code-behind example, you're going to take that value and ❺ assign it to a column in the form's list item, but this time the column is called Total Again. This is a second plausible way to map columns but it usually is not preferred because the other approach doesn't require custom code. It demonstrates the proxy concept nicely.

The last thing to do is build, deploy, and unit test your workflow. Build the project and ensure there are no errors. If there are none, deploy the project by right-clicking the project name and selecting Deploy. This will package your workflow and deploy it into the list you specified in the beginning of this section.

Now, either create a new expense report or edit an existing one. Before you start your custom workflow on an expense report, create a new column titled Total Again on the form library because your code will write to this column. After this column has been added, start the custom expense report workflow you deployed (figure 9.6).

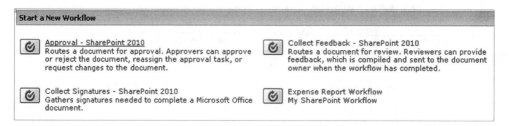

Figure 9.6   The expense report workflow is automatically packaged and published to your form library when you deploy it from Visual Studio.

The workflow should complete quickly. Notice that a new column called Expense Report Workflow has been added, and the Total Again column has also been populated correctly (figure 9.7). The code activity successfully instantiated the proxy class to the form data, and crawled and totaled all the expense amounts in the form.

Figure 9.7   After you run the custom workflow, the workflow status should read Completed and the Total Again column should show the total of all the expense reports.

9.3 InfoPath forms in Visual Studio workflow

As mentioned before, you can build forms for a Visual Studio workflow in either ASP.NET or InfoPath. This section will cover how to add InfoPath forms into your Visual Studio workflows. Specifically, this section will cover association, initiation, and modification forms. The example you're going to work with involves a workflow that manages the support needs of a site collection. If you have thousands of users working in a site collection, it may be helpful to have a workflow that can manage their help requests such as helping them to add or configure a web part or set up a document library. The workflow will manage the help requests through each level of support. The first stage may be the IT help desk and, if they can't resolve the issue, the ticket can be elevated to the site collection administrator. The third level can then be the technical architect.

9.3.1 Building a custom association form

The first InfoPath form you want to add is an association form that captures the support personnel for each support tier. When this support workflow is added to a list, this form prompts the user to specify SharePoint groups containing people who are responsible for supporting each level.

The goal for the project in this section is to wire up your association form and deploy your workflow. In later sections, you'll cover how to use initiation and modification forms. For the present, let's start simple and focus on this association form. Figure 9.8 shows what this form looks like.

Prerequisite for the example

All the examples built through the end of this chapter are built on top of an issues list. Create a new Issues list named Support Requests and you'll be good to go.

As shown in figure 9.8, use a blank form template when creating the form itself.

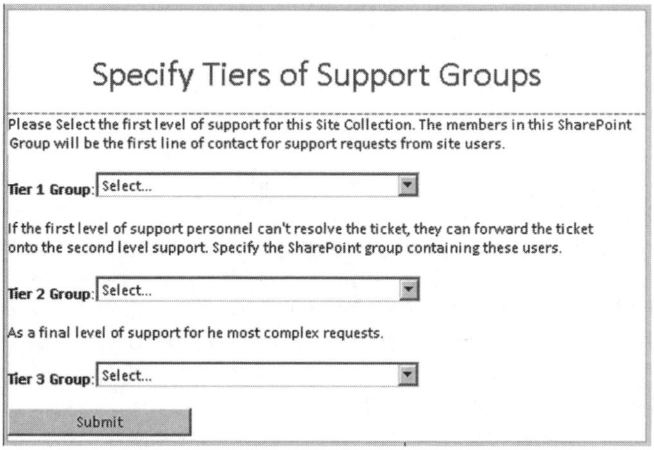

Figure 9.8 This sample association form built in InfoPath will capture from the user the SharePoint groups of users who will make up the three tiers of support in the system.

It is important to note how to configure the submit button on this form. The drop-down boxes and verbiage are not complicated, but the Submit button involves a few steps. Follow the steps in table 9.3 to configure a Submit button for any InfoPath form used in a workflow.

Table 9.3   Configuring a Submit button to submit to the SharePoint Host

Action	Steps	Result
Add the button on the designer surface.	1 Right-click the button, and choose Button Properties. 2 From the Action dropdown list on the General tab, select Submit 3 Click Submit Options. 4 Check Allow users to submit this form. 5 Under the Send form data to a single destination dropdown, choose Hosting Environment.	A new button will show on the form, allowing users to submit the form.
Add a new data connection for the button to use.	1 On the Submit Options popup, below the "Send form data to a single destination" dropdown, click the Add button to add a new data connection. 2 A new dialog defaults to Main submit. Leave the defaults and click Finish and, then, click OK twice. 3 Publish the form to a network location and leave the Access Path blank in the publishing wizard (figure 9.9).	The button is configured with a data connection and will now submit the form data appropriately.

InfoPath deployment caveats

There are two other tricks you should know when creating your InfoPath form for the Visual Studio workflow. First, make sure the form's security level when you publish is set at least to Domain. If you have it set to automatically detect the level, it may already be set to Domain. You can set this in Form Options under Security and Trust. Domain is needed to interact with SharePoint data. Full trust would be needed to access your personal computer's hard drive, for example.

(continued)

Secondly, the form that you add into the Visual Studio workflow needs to be the published version of the form. Before you add the form into your Visual Studio project, make sure to publish it. You'll want to use the Publish to Network Location feature. When you publish to a network location, make sure to leave the Access Path blank. Your workflow will know the URL to access the form from Forms Server but will not if you specify a network location or URL.

Figure 9.9 shows what your form should look like in the last step of the publishing wizard.

Now that you have your InfoPath form settled, let's create a new Visual Studio sequential workflow for your support process. In Visual Studio 2010, create a new project from the SharePoint sequential workflow template. Name the project SiteCollectionSupportWorkflow and the workflow Site Collection Support workflow. You'll be prompted to create a list workflow or a site workflow. Leave the type set to list workflow because you want to bind your workflow to a list that contains your support requests. On the last screen in the wizard, uncheck the checkbox asking you to bind the workflow to a list. You want to do the binding yourself to test your association form. Essentially, if you leave this checkbox checked, you're associating the workflow at that time, and you won't see your association form later.

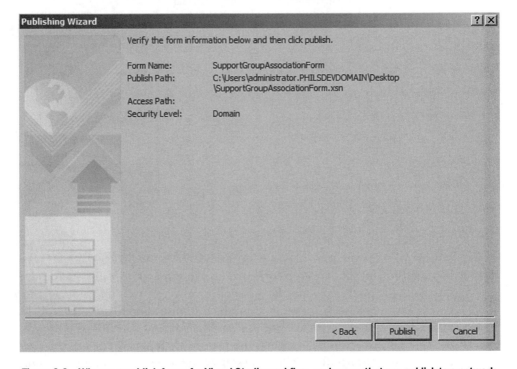

Figure 9.9   When you publish forms for Visual Studio workflow, make sure that you publish to a network location, that your Access Path is blank, and that your security level is set to Domain or higher.

When a new Visual Studio workflow project is created, a feature definition is automatically created that deploys that workflow into SharePoint. You need to get your Info-Path form into that feature definition and instruct the workflow to use that form rather than the default blank form. The first step is to add the InfoPath form to the workflow. Then, you can set its deployment type property to ElementFile. After the form is set to ElementFile, the feature definition will automatically know to include it in the feature. Follow the steps in table 9.4 to add the form into the feature.

Table 9.4   Adding a custom association form into a Visual Studio workflow

Action	Steps	Result
Add the form inside the workflow itself, and update its DeploymentType property to include it in the feature.	**1** Right-click on Workflow1, point to Add, and then click Add Existing Item. **2** Browse out to your Published Info-Path form (figure 9.9) and add it. **3** After it is added, right-click on the Info-Path form and choose Properties. **4** Change the DeploymentType property to ElementFile. **NOTE:** When you build and deploy your project, your InfoPath form will be placed in the Features directory under 12\Template\Features\[Feature Name]\[Workflow Name]\[Form Name].xsn.	

With your feature definition properly packaging up your form, you now need to instruct your feature to deploy it to Forms Server. InfoPath association forms (as well as initiation and modification forms) must be deployed globally in Forms Server to work. At this point, you may be wondering why you wouldn't upload the form to Forms Server manually, through Central Administration. The trouble is that those manually uploaded forms are not *workflow enabled,* and your forms obviously need to be. To enable the forms, you need the feature to deploy the form into Forms Sever through an event handler. Follow the steps in table 9.5 to set up this event handler.

Table 9.5 Adding a custom association form into a Visual Studio workflow

Action	Steps	Result

Instruct the feature to deploy the association form upon the feature's activation.	**1** Open Feature1.feature, click Manifest, and then click Edit Options.
	
	2 Add the ReceiverAssembly and ReceiverClass attributes within the Feature element:
	
	`ReceiverAssembly=`
	`    "Microsoft.Office.Workflow.Feature,`
	`     Version=14.0.0.0, Culture=neutral,`
	`     PublicKeyToken=71e9bce111e9429c"`
	`ReceiverClass="Microsoft.Office.Workflow.Feature.`
	`    WorkflowFeatureReceiver`
	
	NOTE: Keep all on one line with no spaces or tabs!
	
	3 Add the RegisterForms property element in the `Properties` element (again, keep on one line):
	`<Property Key="RegisterForms"`
	`Value="Workflow1\*.xsn" />`
		When these steps are completed, your feature XML should look something like figure 9.10.

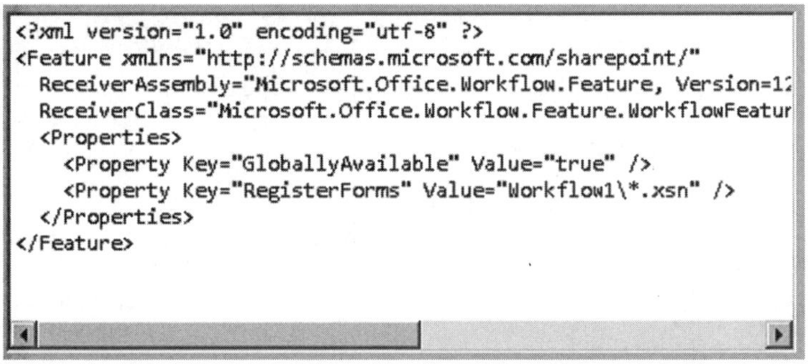

```
<?xml version="1.0" encoding="utf-8" ?>
<Feature xmlns="http://schemas.microsoft.com/sharepoint/"
  ReceiverAssembly="Microsoft.Office.Workflow.Feature, Version=1
  ReceiverClass="Microsoft.Office.Workflow.Feature.WorkflowFeatur
  <Properties>
    <Property Key="GloballyAvailable" Value="true" />
    <Property Key="RegisterForms" Value="Workflow1\*.xsn" />
  </Properties>
</Feature>
```

Figure 9.10 When you've customized the feature file, your feature XML should be similar to this.

Before you move on, let's test that your form was successfully deployed to Forms Server. It's important to test now because you're going to need the form's unique ID (URN), which you can easily get when it's in Forms Server. Right-click on the project and choose Deploy. Wait a bit and, when it has successfully deployed, navigate to the Central Admin to see if the template was deployed. Under General Application Settings, click Manage Form Templates under the InfoPath Forms Services heading. Note that the form was successfully added, and the Workflow Enabled column is set to Yes.

The last step in this process is to instruct the workflow to use your custom association form when the workflow is first added to a list. This is done by modifying the workflow's Elements.xml file. There are two main things you want to configure in this XML file: the AssociationUrl attribute of the workflow and a piece of metadata called Association_FormURN. The AssociationUrl attribute is set to an ASPX page in the Layouts directory in SharePoint. This ASPX page has an InfoPath Form viewer web part that renders your InfoPath form. The web part looks at the Association_FormURN metadata to figure out what form to render in Forms Server. You'll need to stick your form's URN in this meta property. Follow the steps in table 9.6 to configure this Elements.xml file.

Table 9.6   Adding a custom association form into a Visual Studio Workflow

Action	Steps	Result
Configure Workflow1's Elements.xml file.	1 Inside the Workflow element, right after CodeBesideAssembly, add `AssociationUrl="_layouts/CstWrkflIP.aspx"` 2 Inside the MetaData element, add an Association_FormURN element with an open and close tag. 3 Within the Association_FormURN element, add your custom form's URN. You can get this URN from within Forms Services, Manage Form Templates and by clicking View Properties on the form. You should see a property called Form ID.	When completed, your Elements.XML file should look something like listing 9.3.

Listing 9.3   The Elements.xml file of Workflow1 after adding an association form

```
<Elements xmlns="http://schemas.microsoft.com/sharepoint/">
  <Workflow
     Name="Site Collection Support Workflow"
     Description="My SharePoint Workflow"
     Id="719253c3-78d7-41b3-a0a8-bfa228b8588a"
     CodeBesideClass="SiteCollectionSupportWorkflow.Workflow1.Workflow1"
     CodeBesideAssembly="$assemblyname$"
     AssociationUrl="_layouts/CstWrkflIP.aspx">            Hosts InfoPath
     <Categories/>                                         viewer web part
     <MetaData>
       <Association_FormURN>urn:schemas-microsoft-
             com:office:infopath:SupportGroupAssocationForm:-
             myXSD-2009-12- 12T17-59-13
       </Association_FormURN>                              Loads form from
       <AssociationCategories>List</AssociationCategories>   Forms Server
       <StatusPageUrl>_layouts/WrkStat.aspx</StatusPageUrl>
     </MetaData>
  </Workflow>
</Elements>
```

Let's test your workflow and custom association form. Build and deploy the project again to push your latest changes. Then, find a SharePoint list and add your Site Collection Support workflow. You'll notice that, when you add the workflow to the list, your association form loads to provide the user options for the groups that represent each tier of support (figure 9.11).

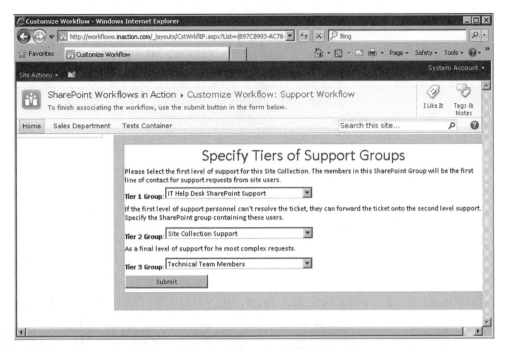

Figure 9.11 Here's your association form in the browser. The form loads whenever you add the Support workflow onto a list.

9.3.2 Building a custom initiation form

Initiation forms are added into a Visual Studio workflow in almost the same way that association forms are added. The previous section walked you through this process in great detail. Because the plumbing for both association forms and initiation forms is similar, we're not going to rehash that same process in this section. Rather, you will learn how to add an initiation form into the project that was set up in the previous section. Before you start, create an InfoPath initiation form using figure 9.12 as a guide (table 9.7).

Table 9.7 Building a custom initiation form

Action	Steps	Result
Add the form into the project, and deploy it to Forms Server.	1 In the Visual Studio project, right-click Workflow1 and choose Add Existing Item.	Workflow Enabled
	2 Browse to and select the published version of the initiation form.	Yes
	3 After the file is added, right-click the file, choose Properties, and change the Deployment Type property to ElementFile.	Yes
	4 Build and deploy the project. This will deploy the form into Forms Server.	Yes
	NOTE: All forms in Forms Server must be marked as Workflow Enabled (Yes) to be viable in the workflow.	Yes

Table 9.7 Building a custom initiation form *(continued)*

Action	Steps	Result
Copy Form's unique ID.	1 Navigate into Manage Form Templates within Central Administration under InfoPath Forms Services. 2 Find the initiation form that was deployed. 3 Click on the form and choose View Properties and copy the Form ID (URN). You will need this URN a bit later.	You'll need the form's unique ID in your clip board for the next action.
Back in the workflow, edit the Elements.xml file.	1 In the Workflow element, add an InstantiationUrl attribute and set it to _layouts/IniWrkfllP.aspx. 2 Inside the MetaData element, add an Instantiation_FormURN element. 3 Within the Instantiation_FormURN element, paste in the URN from the previous action.	After you paste in the URN from the initiation form that was deployed into Forms Server, you can build and deploy your project. If you go back into a list where the workflow is installed and you start a workflow on an item in that list, you should see your custom initiation form (figure 9.12).

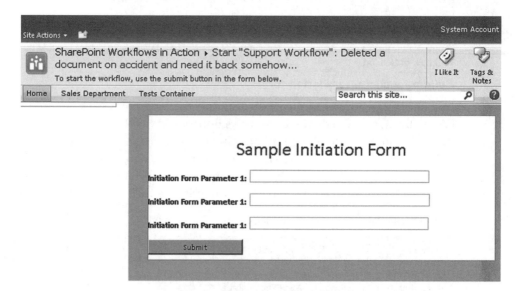

Figure 9.12   Initiation forms are built in a manner similar to association forms. Rather than display when the workflow is added to the list, initiation forms present themselves when the workflow starts.

Autostarting workflows won't show the initiation form

If your workflow is set to automatically start when a new item is added, the initiation form will not load when the new item is added. The initiation form will show only when the workflow is manually started.

9.3.3   *Working with the association or initiation form data*

Now that your association and initiation forms are integrated into a custom workflow, what does the workflow do with the data in those forms? It is important to know how to retrieve the form data out of the form in the workflow. Essentially, the OnWorkflowActivated activity has a property called WorkflowProperties. Within WorkflowProperties, there are two more properties that store your association and initiation data, AssociationData and InitiationData. These properties are strings that contain your form's XML data. You cast this string into a .NET class that is built from the form's schema definition file. Going back to the association form, build a proxy class from the form's schema and from the workflow take the AssociationData and cast it into an object your workflow can work with. Follow the steps in table 9.8 to do this.

Table 9.8   Programmatically retrieving InfoPath Form Data

Action	Steps	Result
Add the form's proxy class into your Visual Studio project.	1 Open the form in InfoPath Designer, and under File click Publish and then Export Source Files. 2 Open the Visual Studio 2010 command prompt and browse to the directory to which you exported the source files. 3 Run the following command on the schema definition file to generate your proxy class: 4 `xsd myschema.xsd /c /l:cs`. 5 Add the generated myschema.cs file into your Visual Studio project and rename the file to its corresponding class name.	A new class will be generated off the form's XSD schema file and added to the Visual Studio project.

Add a namespace into the proxy class and two using statements to the workflow's code-behind.	1 By default, the class is not in a namespace. Wrap the class in the same namespace in which your workflow is running. This will allow you to create an instance of this class in your workflow.
	2 In your workflow's code-behind, add the following using statements at the top:
	
	`using System.Xml.Serialization;`
	`using System.Xml;`
		The proxy class will now be in the same namespace as the workflow, and the necessary using statements will allow the project to build successfully.

Add code into the OnWorkflowActivated activity that will serialize the form's data into the proxy class.	Back in your workflow's designer surface, right-click on the OnWorkflowActivated activity and choose Generate Handlers. This will generate an event handler and method. Inside this method, add the code from listing 9.4. **NOTE:** Replace SupportGroups and associated fields with your association form's class name and fields.	When the workflow first starts, an event will fire and serialize the Form's data into the proxy class.

Listing 9.4   Deserializing your association form's data into an object

```
XmlSerializer serializer = new XmlSerializer(typeof(SupportGroups));

XmlTextReader reader = new XmlTextReader(new System.IO.StringReader(
        onWorkflowActivated1.WorkflowProperties.AssociationData));

SupportGroups associationFormData =
    (SupportGroups)serializer.Deserialize(reader);

string tier1 = associationFormData.Tier1Group;
string tier2 = associationFormData.Tier2Group;
string tier3 = associationFormData.Tier3Group;
string currentTier = tier1;
```

Reads in AssociationData string into reader ❷

Casts XML into strongly typed object ❸

Creates serializer object off schema class ❶

Starts programming against association data ❹

First, listing 9.4 creates an XmlSerializer off your proxy class ❶. In this case, the SupportGroups class was built upon the association form's schema definition file. Next, you read the association data that the user entered into an XmlTextReader ❷. This XmlTextReader will hold the data entered by the user in a format that is consistent with the association form's schema definition. After you have this XML, you can cast it into a new instance of your proxy class ❸. With this object, you can start coding against the data that was entered in the form ❹.

This wraps up the discussion on initiation and association forms. Remember that both those form types always appear to the user before the workflow starts. Now, it's time to discuss a form type that presents itself after the workflow starts, modification forms.

9.3.4   *Configuring activities for workflow modifications*

Modifications in workflows give your end users the ability to alter their workflow's behavior after the workflow starts. This is commonly done when someone wants to reassign a task. This section will extend the Support workflow that was built earlier in this chapter to provide a way for users to escalate a support ticket. Essentially, they will be able to modify the workflow and specify a different group of SharePoint users who will be responsible to complete the support request.

Before you build and deploy your modification form, you need to tell your workflow that modifications are allowed. A modification link shows up on a workflow's status page. When a user clicks this link, they are taken to a modification form and, after they submit that form, your workflow can react to the submission and the data the users had entered. The trick is to get this link to appear on the workflow status pages because it is not there by default. You must specifically allow modifications for it to show. Figure 9.13 shows this link's placement on the workflow status page. Note that the link uses configurable text.

There are two main workflow modification activities used to enable this functionality, EnableWorkflowModification and OnWorkflowModified. You can use the EnableWorkflowModification activity to enable modifications and, in effect, display the link on the

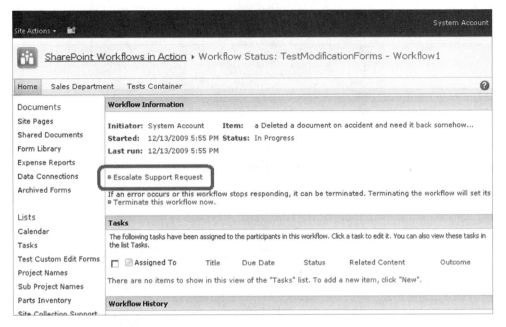

Figure 9.13 Workflow modifications are initiated from the workflow status page with a link that can present a configurable text to the user. The link displays only when modifications are specifically allowed on this workflow.

workflow status page. When users click that link, they are taken to the modification form and when that forms is submitted, the workflow framework fires a WorkflowModified event to which an OnWorkflowModified activity reacts.

As mentioned, you can specify when a workflow can and cannot be modified. Typically, the EnableWorkflowModification activity is deployed inside an EventHandlingScope activity. You can use the EventHandlingScope activity to manage when a modification can take place. While the workflow is executing inside the EventHandlingScope activity, and the EnableWorkflowModification activity is also inside it, modifications will be enabled. As soon as the workflow passes out of the EventHandlingScope activity, modifications will no longer be available.

Notice in figure 9.14 that the EventHandlingScope activity has multiple views. The OnWorkflowModifed activity is placed inside the Event Handlers view and can react to any workflow modifications that take place in the scope of the EventHandlingScope activity.

You can toggle between views by right clicking the activity, and then selecting the view you want to edit. Within that view you can start dropping activities. Notice that besides reacting with generic event handlers, you can react to exceptions (faults) as well as cancelations. Now it's time to configure these activities. Follow these steps to add this functionality into your support workflow.

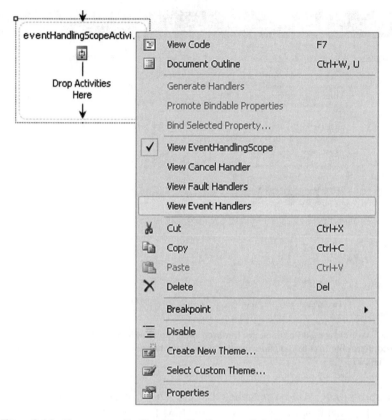

Figure 9.14   You can use the EventHandlingScope activity to manage when a workflow modification can and cannot take place.

Table 9.9   Configuring EventHandlingScope and EnableWorkflowModification activities

Action	Steps	Result
Add the two activities onto the Workflow designer surface.	1 Directly below the OnWork-flowActivated activity, add a EventHandlingScope activity 2 Inside the EventHandling-Scope activity, add a Sequence activity. 3 Inside the Sequence activity, add an EnableWorkflowModifi-cation activity.	
Notice the red exclamation point, signaling that you need to assign a correlation token. Assign a token to the enableWorkflowModification1 activity.	Set the correlation token to Modi-ficationToken. Click the plus sign next to the token and set the OwnerActivityName property to your workflow name. In this case, it is Workflow1.	The red exclamation point on the activity will disappear.

Table 9.9 Configuring EventHandlingScope and EnableWorkflowModification activities *(continued)*

Action	Steps	Result
The EnableWorkflowModification activity needs a way to pass data between the form and the workflow. In the activity's properties, click the ellipses on the ContextData property and Bind to a new member. Leave the defaults and click OK.		The ContextData property will now be bound to a field.
Every workflow modification needs a unique ID. Assign a unique GUID to the ModificationID property of the EnableWorkflowModification activity.	1 Use the GUID generator under Tools, Create GUID (registry format) to copy a new GUID. 2 Paste the GUID into the ModificationId property. **NOTE:** Make sure to remove the braces in the GUID generated from the GUID generator	

Now you add business logic into this workflow to make it lively. Let's add a while loop activity and an OnWorkflowChanged activity to wait for the support request to be completed. If the request is completed, the workflow execution is finished. Follow the steps in table 9.10 to configure the while and OnWorkflowChanged activities that the workflow will use to wait for the request to be completed.

Table 9.10 Add activities to make the workflow wait for the request to be completed

Action	Steps	Result
Add a while and OnWorkflowItemChanged activities.	1 Below the EnableWorkflowModification activity, add a while activity. 2 Inside the while activity, add an OnWorkflowItemChanged activity.	
Set the correlation token.	Set the correlation token of the OnWorkflowItemChanged activity to the same token as the OnWorkflowActivated activity. The default would be workflowToken.	The red exclamation point on the OnWorkflowItemChanged activity will disappear.

Table 9.10   Add activities to make the workflow wait for the request to be completed *(continued)*

Action	Steps	Result
Add code into the while activity.	**NOTE:** You still have to deal with the red exclamation point on the while activity. See the next action. **1** Right-click the while activity and choose Properties. Change the Condition property to be a Code Condition. **2** Click the plus sign next to the Condition property, and type the name of a method to execute for this while loop, like WhileRequestIsNotComplete. **3** This will kick you into the code editor. Enter the code from listing 9.5 into the WhileRequest-IsNotComplete method.	The red exclamation point on the while activity will disappear.

Listing 9.5   WhileRequestIsNotComplete method

```
string status = onWorkflowActivated1.WorkflowProperties.
    Item["Status"].ToString();

if (status == "Resolved")
    e.Result = false;
else
    e.Result = true;
```

❷ **Exits while loop if yes**

❸ **Continues looping if no**

❶ **Checks if support request is compete**

This code first retrieves the value from the Status column ❶ into a standard issues list item. If the request is resolved, the while loop stops looping ❷, and the workflow finishes. If the request is not complete, the while loop keeps looping ❸ and waiting for it to be completed. After this code is entered, you should be finished with the body of your EventHandlingScope activity. Figure 9.15 shows what your workflow should look like at this point.

When everything looks good, it's time to configure the modification event handler and set up the OnWorkflowModified activity. To do this, add an EventDriven activity into the Event Handlers view of the EventHandlingScope activity. With your OnWorkflowModified activity inside this EventDriven activity, each time the workflow is modified in this scope, this activity will fire. Follow the steps in table 9.11 for the configuration.

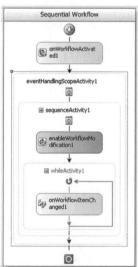

Figure 9.15   When the EnableWorkflowModification activity is inside an EventHandlingScope activity, workflow modifications will be allowed only while the workflow is executing in the EventHandlingScope activity.

Table 9.11 Configuring the modification event handler

Action	Steps	Result
Add the EventDriven and OnWorkflowModified activities.	1 Right-click the EventHandlingScope activity and choose View Event Handlers. 2 Add an EventDriven activity into the EventHandlers activity that was automatically added inside the EventHandlingScope activity. 3 Add the OnWorkflowModified activity inside the EventDriven activity.	
Set the correlation token of the OnWorkflowModified activity to be the same token as the EnableWorkflowModification activity.	Set the correlation token to ModificationToken.	The red exclamation point on the OnWorkflowModified activity disappears.
Configure three of the properties on the OnWorkflowModified activity.	1 Bind the ContextData property of the OnWorkflowModified activity to be the same ContextData member that the EnableWorkflowModification activity is using. This member was created in the third action in table 9.9. This will allow the workflow to pass and receive data between the forms. 2 Similarly, bind the ModificationId property of the OnWorkflowModified activity to give it the same GUID that the EnableWorkflowModification activity is using. 3 Bind the User property of the OnWorkflowModified activity to a new member. This property contains the username of the person who made the modification. 4 Drop a LogToHistoryList activity below the OnWorkflowModified activity and then set the HistoryDescription property of the activity to Modification Success!	The OnWorkflowModified activity is complete. At this point, your Event Handlers view of the EventHandlingScope activity should look something like figure 9.16.

Table 9.11   Configuring the modification event handler *(continued)*

Action	Steps	Result
	NOTE: You'll use the LogTo-HistoryList activity to log the workflow's progress so that you know the modification plumbing is working properly. To take this example a step further, you could add code to the OnWorkflowModified activity that updates the current-Tier field and perhaps emails the group members of the next tier, notifying them that a support request requires their attention.	

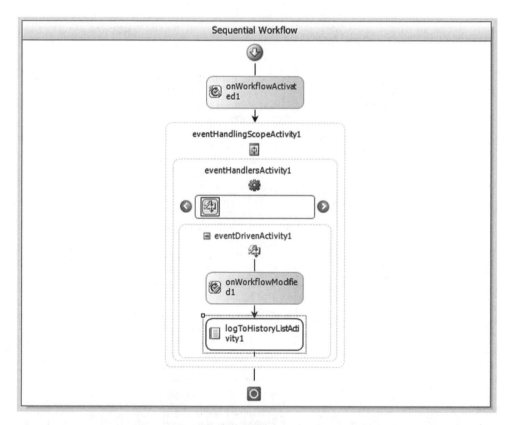

Figure 9.16   By placing the OnWorkflowModified activity inside the Event Handlers view of the EventHandlingScope activity, you create a situation in which the OnWorkflowModified activity will respond to any workflow modifications made during the execution of the EventHandlingScope activity.

With these activities and code in place, you're ready to start configuring your modification forms. The next section will walk you through integrating an InfoPath modification form.

9.3.5 *Building a custom modification form*

Now that you have the foundation of your modification-enabled workflow in place, it's time to add your modification form into the mix. An InfoPath modification form is the first in the batter's box. At a high level, the following steps are required to integrate an InfoPath modification form:

1 Create the form.
2 Set up the context data that the workflow and the form use to communicate with each other.
3 Edit the workflow's elements.xml file to tell the workflow which form to use.

Let's start with the first step, which is setting up the form itself.

The InfoPath form you'll be using in the section will be an extension of the Support request system you set up earlier. You need a form that a user can use to modify the workflow, and in doing so, escalate the support request to the next level of support. Users would do this if they didn't feel they had the expertise to answer the requestor's question or problem. Figure 9.17 shows the sample form this demonstration will be using.

This form has two pieces of data in it, the current level of support (CurrentOwner-Group), and the level of support that comes next (NextTierGroup). If you remember, your workflow's association form allowed users to specify SharePoint groups that

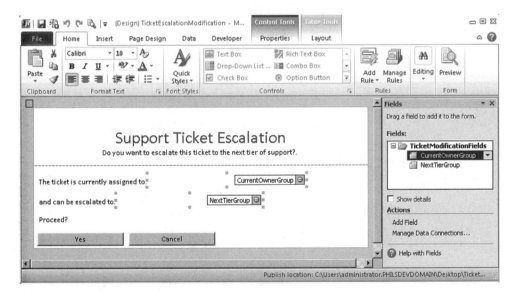

Figure 9.17   This InfoPath form will be used in your workflow modification to escalate a support ticket from one level of support to another.

contain users who were responsible to answer support tickets for each tier of support. You want this modification form to let the user escalate the ticket from one group and level to another. Your workflow code will pass these two pieces of data into the form when it loads, and users will confirm that they want to escalate the ticket. If they do, your workflow code will reassign the support ticket by flagging an owner column on the list item.

Before you can start configuring your workflow's .xml file to tell it to use this form, you need to set up your context data. As mentioned, the workflow can pass data back and forth with the form through the ContextData property of the EnableWorkflow-Modification and OnWorkflowModified activities. At this point, this property is set to an empty string. It needs to be set to a string that contains the form's XML schema definition as well as any preset data you want to pass to the form. With this setup, your workflow will pass the CurrentOwnerGroup and NextTierGroup values into your Info-Path form.

First, instantiate a proxy class off your form's XML schema definition. To get this class, you need to use the XSD command again. Follow the steps in table 9.12 to build your form's proxy class and add the class into your Visual Studio project.

Table 9.12 Adding the form's proxy class into the Visual Studio project

Action	Steps	Result
Generate the form's proxy class of its schema definition file.	1 Start in your InfoPath form, and under File > Publish, choose Export Source Files. Export the source files to a directory you can access with command prompt. 2 Open the Visual Studio command prompt and navigate to the published directory. Run this command: `xsd myschema.xsd /c /l:cs` 3 This command will write a new file called myschema.cs. Add this file into your Visual Studio project with the workflow you set up in the previous section.	Your Visual Studio project will have a new class that is a proxy to the form's data.
Name the class file name and provide a namespace for the class.	1 Rename the file to the class name (or, more specifically, the name of the root element in the InfoPath form data). In this case, rename the file to TicketModificationFields.cs. 2 Wrap the TicketModificationFields class with the same namespace as that in which your workflow is running. By default, TicketModification-Fields will not be in a namespace, and it'll be easier to instantiate it if it is.	The class name will be unique (rather than the generic myschema.xsd) and will be in the same namespace as Workflow1.

Table 9.12   Adding the form's proxy class into the Visual Studio project *(continued)*

Action	Steps	Result
Add code to the enableWorkflowModification1 activity.	1 Back on your workflow designer surface, right-click the EnableWorkflow-Modification activity and click Generate Handlers. 2 Add the code in listing 9.6 into this method. 3 Add a using statement for the System.IO namespace.	A new method is created. You want to use this enableWorkflowModification1_MethodInvoking method to instantiate your TicketModificationFields class and get your data ready for your form to consume

New fields required for listing 9.6

In section 9.3.3, you created four string fields in the onWorkflowActivated1_Invoked method: tier1, tier2, tier3, and currentTier. These fields were local to this method. Listing 9.6 references these fields, so they will now need to be declared outside the method and made available to the entire class.

Listing 9.6   EnableWorkflowModification1_MethodInvoking

```
TicketModificationFields data = new TicketModificationFields();

data.CurrentOwnerGroup = currentTier;
    data.NextTierGroup = tier2;

using (StringWriter writer = new StringWriter())
{
    XmlSerializer s = new XmlSerializer(
        typeof(TicketModificationFields));
    s.Serialize(writer, data);

    this.enableWorkflowModification1_ContextData1 = writer.ToString();
}
```

❷ Determines support group for escalation

❶ Instantiates form's proxy class

❸ Serializes data into StringWriter

❹ Assigns ContextData to output string

First, this code instantiates your proxy class built upon the form's XML schema definition ❶. You then set a couple of values in that class that will be passed into the Info-Path form ❷. The form needs to know the current tier and the next tier to which the ticket can be escalated. Next, serialize this data into a StringWriter ❸ that can set its string value to the InfoPath modification form's ContextData property ❹.

enableWorkflowModification1_MethodInvoking only fires once

This method sets the values that will show in the modification form. Because this code fires only once, the current tier will be tier 1, and the next will be tier 2. Another EnableWorkflowModification activity with a different correlation token will be needed to update the modification form with new values after the first modification occurs.

(continued)

If a second EnableWorkflowModification activity is not used, the modification form will have the same field values, when, in fact, they ought to have been incremented (current = tier 2 and next = tier 3). This second and, possibly, third EnableWorkflow-Modification activities are not difficult to set up, but unnecessarily elongate the scope of this example.

With the ContextData under your belt, you now can focus on the last part of this InfoPath journey, which is to tell your workflow which form to use when the modification link is clicked. All this is done in the workflow's Elements.xml file. You first need to get your form into the project and feature. To do this, add the Published form inside the workflow container as you did before. When it is inside, right-click the form and set the DeploymentType property of the form to ElementFile. Afterwards, your Visual Studio solution explorer should look something like figure 9.18.

With your modification form inside the workflow, it's finally time to tell your workflow to use this form. Follow the steps in table 9.13 to edit the Elements.xml file.

Build and deploy the project again, which will ship off the latest Elements.xml updates. As a reminder, you should be using an out-of-the-box issues list named Support Requests for testing.

Figure 9.18   Add the modification form into the workflow and change its DeploymentType to ElementFile to package it in the feature.

Table 9.13   Editing the feature's Elements.xml file to tell the workflow to use the modification form

Action	Steps	Result
Add a new ModificationUrl attribute and deploy the Visual Studio Project.	1 In the Workflow element, add a new ModificationUrl attribute: `ModificationUrl=" layouts/ModWrkflIP.aspx"` 2 Deploy the Visual Studio project by right-clicking the project and choosing Deploy.	This will deploy your new form into Forms Server because of the plumbing you set up in section 9.2 for your association form.
Within the MetaData element, add a Modification_[UNIQUE GUID]_FormURN element.	1 In the MetaData element, add a child element called `<Modification_[UNIQUE GUID] FormURN></Modification_[UNIQUE GUID]_FormURN>`. Replace [UNIQUE_GUID] with the ModificationId GUID that your EnableWorkflowModification and OnWorkflowModified activities are using.	A new child element will be added to the MetaData element.

Table 9.13   Editing the feature's Elements.xml file to tell the workflow to use the modification form *(continued)*

Action	Steps	Result
	2 If you haven't done so already, publish your modification InfoPath form into Forms Server and then grab the form's URN from within Forms Server (via View Properties) and paste it into this element.	This element will tell the workflow which form in Forms Server is acting as your modification form.
Add a Modification_GUID_Name element.	1 Similarly, create another element called \<Modification_GUID_Name>. 2 Inside this Name element, type a name for your modification. This name is what the title of the URL will be on the workflow status page. For example, type Escalate Support Request.	A new child element will be added to the MetaData element. This element will tell the workflow the name of the modification. This name shows on the Workflow Status page.

Note the dependency on the Status column (Issue Status is the display name). Add the workflow to the list and specify some values in the association form. Afterwards, create a new item in the list (with Status set to Active) and start the workflow on that item. After you start it, the workflow will be In Progress waiting for the Issue Status column to be set to Resolved. While it waits, a modification is enabled. Click on In Progress and that will take you to the workflow status page, where you can start a modification. Click the Escalate Support Request modification link, and your form should appear with the values sent from the workflow. After you click Yes or Submit, the OnWorkflowModifed activity will fire and, because there is no code currently in that activity, the workflow will log Modification Success! (figure 9.19) into the history log through the LogToHistoryListActivity place directly after the OnWorkflowModified activity.

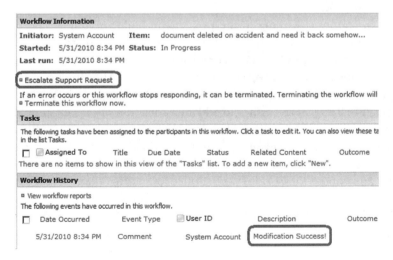

Figure 9.19
After you click the Yes button on your modification form, the onWorkflowModified1 activity will fire followed by the logToHistoryList1 activity, which logs the success of the modification.

To take this example a step further, in the OnWorkflowModifed activity, you could include code that changes the currentTier field to the next tier if the user selects the Yes button in the form. If the user cancels, then do nothing and the while loop will keep the workflow looping until the request is resolved. If Yes is chosen and the request is escalated, you could then send an email to the users in that tier's group notifying them that a request is awaiting their attention. To make the example even more complete, you could assign a task to that tier, which, when marked completed, changes the Issue Status to Resolved, ending the workflow. Refer to chapter 10 to learn more about tasks in Visual Studio workflows.

9.4 *ASP.NET forms in Visual Studio workflows*

After our discussion on InfoPath association and initiation forms, you'll find ASP.NET forms refreshing. That's because it's much easier to deploy an ASP.NET Form into a Visual Studio workflow. Although ASP.NET Forms are a bit trickier to develop, they are much easier to deploy. Part of the reason is this—you add a new ASP.NET Form into a workflow by right-clicking the workflow and choosing Add > New Item and then select the form type you want to add. After you add it, the form will be automatically packaged into the feature and the package, and all that's left will be to deploy the project. Then, when you associate your workflow to a list or initiate a workflow on an item, you'll get your new custom ASP.NET Form! That takes only seconds to do! Before you get too excited, you'll notice when you see your form in the browser that it's blank. Deployment was easy; now it's time to put your developer hat on to build some controls on that form and start passing data between the form and the workflow.

The example you'll be creating in this section is a generic initiation form. Because association and initiation forms are created in an almost identical way, it makes sense to walk through only one of the two. During the walkthrough, differences for association forms will be called out, so even if you're building an association form, this walkthrough will be helpful.

Rather than continue working in the project you built for your Support Request workflow in the previous section, let's start with a new project. Create a new sequential workflow project called TestASPNETWorkflowForms. Create a list workflow and bind it to a list of your choice with the project provisioning wizard. After the project has been created, right-click on Workflow1 and choose Add > New Item. The new item dialog will appear (figure 9.20). Select either to add an association or an initiation form.

After you have the form added, you'll notice that you're taken to the ASP.NET HTML view of the form (figure 9.21). This autogenerated form already has a button that's wired up and ready to go. If you go to the form's code-behind (right-click the form in the Solution Explorer and choose View Code) you'll notice four autogenerated methods of particular interest. The first is the Page_Load method. You can use this method to set default values for the fields on your form. Second is the GetInitiationData (or conversely, GetAssociationData) method. Your workflow calls this method to retrieve the values that the user entered into the form. In this method, you only need to return a string

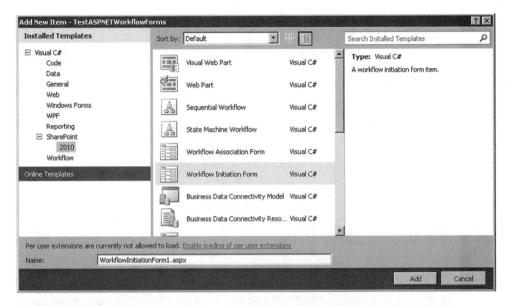

Figure 9.20   ASP.NET Forms are easy to integrate into a Visual Studio workflow. Right-click the workflow and add a new item. Afterward, the ASP.NET form will be automatically packaged and deployable through the workflow feature.

that contains a serialized class with the form data stored in it. Then, on the workflow side of things, you can deserialize this class and the workflow can do something with the data. The third and fourth methods of interest are the StartWorkflow_Click and Cancel_Click. These methods submit or cancel the form, respectively.

There's little to worry about with these because they've been filled out for you. Typically you won't even need to alter these methods but, depending on your business logic, you may want or need to.

Going back to your ASP.NET HTML view, you add ASP.NET controls onto this form for user interaction. Inside the PlaceHolderMain content placeholder, add a few text boxes. You will use these text boxes to allow the user to enter information. You will later take this information and pass it into your workflow. Figure 9.21 shows what your ASP.NET code may look like when it's complete.

```
<asp:Content ID="Main" ContentPlaceHolderID="PlaceHolderMain" runat="server">
    Please enter the first initialization parameter: 
    <asp:TextBox ID="InitParameter1" runat="server"></asp:TextBox><br />
    Please enter the second initialization parameter: 
    <asp:TextBox ID="InitParameter2" runat="server"></asp:TextBox><br /><br />
    <asp:Button ID="StartWorkflow" runat="server"
        OnClick="StartWorkflow_Click" Text="Start Workflow" />
          
    <asp:Button ID="Cancel" runat="server" OnClick="Cancel_Click" Text="Cancel" />
</asp:Content>
```

Figure 9.21   You can add ASP.NET controls on the form and, in the code–behind, you pull out these values and send them back to the workflow through the GetInitiationData method.

Now that you have your form the way you want it, you need to ship the data entered by the user back to the workflow. To do this, you'll return a string containing the data returned through the GetInitiationData method (or GetAssociationData). Be sure to ship back only the string that represents a serialized class that both the form and the workflow can instantiate and serialize or deserialize. Right-click Workflow1 and choose Add > New Item. Select a class file and name the class InitiationFormParameters. Make the class public and add two public strings, one for each parameter in the initiation form.

```
public class InitiationFormParameters
{
    public string InitiationParameter1;
    public string InitiationParameter2;
}
```

Back in the code-behind of the ASP.NET Form, find the GetInitiationData method. Add the code in listing 9.7 into this method and add two using statements for System.Xml and System.IO.

Listing 9.7   GetInitiationData method

```
string initdata = string.Empty;

InitiationFormParameters data = new InitiationFormParameters();
data.InitiationParameter1 = InitParameter1.Text;
data.InitiationParameter2 = InitParameter2.Text;

using (StringWriter writer = new StringWriter())
{
    XmlSerializer s = new XmlSerializer(
        typeof(InitiationFormParameters));
    s.Serialize(writer, data);

    initdata = writer.ToString();
}
return initdata;
```

① Creates class off form data

② Serializes class values into string

③ Returns string

This code first **①** creates an instance of your class and assigns its properties to the values stored in the form that the user provided. Afterwards, you **②** serialize that class into a string with a StringWriter and then **③** return that string.

Your workflow calls this GetInitiationData method and loads the string into a property of the OnWorkflowActivated activity called InitializationData (or AssociationData). In the event handler of the OnWorkflowActivity activity, you can deserialize the string stored in the InitializationData property into a class your workflow can use. To do this, on the workflow designer surface, right-click on the OnWorkflowActivated activity and choose Generate Handlers. Replace the code found in listing 9.8 with the onWorkflowActivated1_Invoked method. Also, add using statements for System.Xml.Serialization and System.Xml.

Listing 9.8   onWorkflowActivated1_Invoked method

```
string param1;
string param2;

private void onWorkflowActivated1_Invoked(object sender,
    ExternalDataEventArgs e)
{
    XmlSerializer serializer = new
    XmlSerializer(typeof(InitiationFormParameters));

    XmlTextReader reader = new XmlTextReader(new System.IO.StringReader(
        onWorkflowActivated1.WorkflowProperties.InitiationData));

    InitiationFormParameters initiationFormData =
        (InitiationFormParameters)serializer.Deserialize(reader);

    param1 = initiationFormData.InitiationParameter1;
    param2 = initiationFormData.InitiationParameter2;
}
```

Lists global workflow variables ❶

Reads InitiationData string into XmlTextReader ❷

Deserializes XML into class object ❸

The goal of this code is to retrieve the data that the user entered in the initiation (or association) form. Your workflow can then perform some action on that data. The first thing you want to do is ❶ read the string out of the InitiationData property (or AssociationData) into an XmlTextReader. Then, ❷ deserialize that XML into a new object that is the same type as the one into which the string was serialized (in this case, the InitiationFormParameters object). After you have your object, you can start ❸ assigning some global variables or take other actions.

With this last bit of code in, you need to do one last step to make sure everything is working. Let's add a LogToHistoryListActivity activity below the OnWorkflowActivated activity. You can use this history logger to render your form values on the workflow status page. After the LogToHistoryListActivity activity is added, right-click on it and choose Generate handlers. In the generated method, add the following line of code to write out your form values:

```
logToHistoryListActivity1.HistoryDescription =
    "Param1: " + param1 + " Param2: " + param2;
```

After this activity logs your form parameters, you can begin testing. Build the project and then deploy it. If you haven't already associated the workflow to a list, do so now. Otherwise, start the workflow on an item in the list. When you start the workflow, you should see your custom ASP.NET initiation form (figure 9.22).

After you enter some values and submit the form, you should see a Completed status. Click the status column and this will take you to the workflow status page. At the bottom, you should see the workflow history, with the parameters you entered into the listed initiation form (figure 9.23).

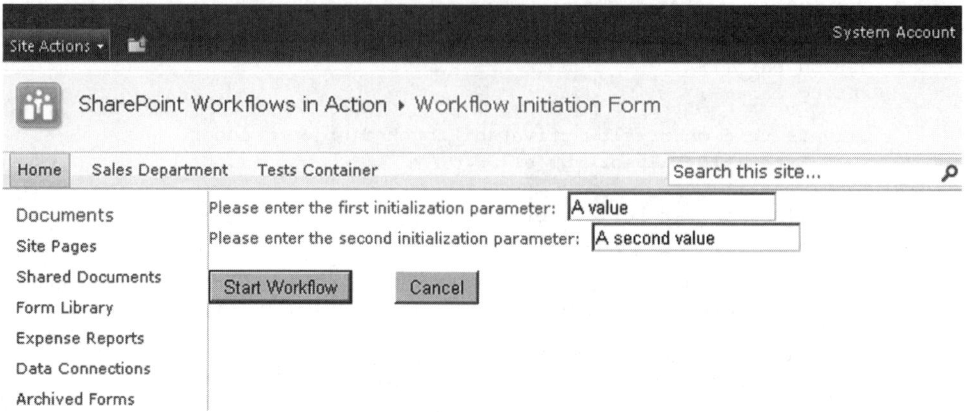

Figure 9.22   Your initiation form will prompt the user for pertinent information when the workflow starts.

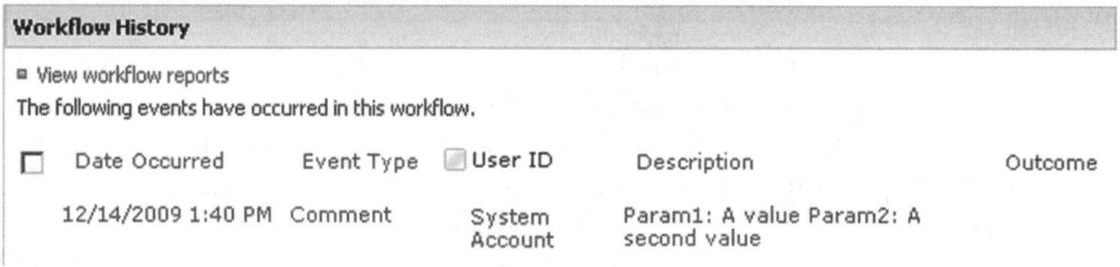

Figure 9.23   You can tell that the code ran correctly because the values entered in the form were written to the workflow history on the workflow status page.

9.5   *Summary*

It is important to know how to work with the data stored in an InfoPath form. For instance, data can be mapped to columns in the library, and you can add .NET code to alter the form's behavior. After a form is submitted, you can use a workflow to programmatically retrieve data from the form. These development techniques are a good foundation for workflow forms such as custom initiation and association.

Workflow forms are a powerful way to enable your end users to provide information to their workflows and edit their workflow's behavior. There are three main types of workflow forms: workflow initiation forms, association forms, and modification forms.

Association forms present themselves when a workflow is first bound to a list, a library, or a site. You can use this form to provide settings for all workflows of the given type that run on that list, library, or site. Initiation forms, on the other hand, display directly before a workflow executes. By default, this form is blank, but you can easily customize it through either InfoPath in SharePoint Designer or Visual Studio or with ASP.NET in Visual Studio. If you go with InfoPath, the Form Template is added to the feature and deployed into Forms Server. You also have to tell the workflow to use your form in the workflow's Elements.xml file by specifying the form's unique URN ID. ASP.NET forms require much less plumbing. Just right-click the workflow, choose Add

> New Item, and select an Association Form! It's easier to add and deploy with ASP.NET but harder to work with if you're not proficient in HTML or ASP.NET programming.

Association and initiation forms allow the user to provide data to the workflow before the workflow starts. Modification forms, on the other hand, allow the user to provide data to the workflow after it has started. This gives you the ability to alter the behavior of the workflow and provide new data into the workflow during its execution. Often, you do so when reassigning a task or approval to another individual. This modification is accomplished through two main activities in a Visual Studio workflow, the EnableWorkflowModification activity and the OnWorkflowModifed activity. With the EnableWorkflowModification activity, you can create a scope in the workflow where modifications are allowed and appropriate. This gives you control when users can and cannot modify the workflow. Then, if the WorkflowModified event is raised in that scope, the OnWorkflowModified activity will fire and execute your change logic.

You may at this point be wondering about task edit forms. If so, check out the next chapter, Task Processing in Visual Studio Workflows. In that chapter, you cover these forms in detail, with many other notable task management-related concepts that will add value to your workflows.

Workflows
and task processes

This chapter covers

- Using task-related workflow activities
- Building custom task edit forms

In chapter 4, you worked with task processing capabilities for SharePoint Designer workflows. Visual Studio provides similar task processing capabilities for its workflows. Task-related activities for Visual Studio workflows can create tasks, delete tasks, and complete tasks. There are also event activities that your workflows can use to react to human input such as task editing and deletion. By putting these activities to use, you can create and assign tasks to users and have the workflow go idle until the task is completed.

Visual Studio also supports full customizations of task edit forms with custom InfoPath forms. These forms can easily be integrated into your Visual Studio workflows to support complex form requirements or to make the form more intuitive for your end users. When the task's assignee edits the task, by default, he sees the out-of-the-box task edit form and this form may be inadequate. For example, the out-of-the-box form contains many fields that you may not require end users to edit. This extra data may be confusing to users, and building a custom InfoPath form may be preferable.

10.1 *Using task-related activities*

In addition to workflows created in SharePoint Designer, Visual Studio workflows offer a similar task processing opportunity. Several SharePoint activities for Visual Studio help manage tasks in workflows. You can use these activities in your Visual Studio workflows to create, delete, and update tasks. Table 10.1 shows the complete listing of task-related activities. In this chapter, rather than covering all the activities in table 10.1, we'll cover the most commonly used activities such as those that create and delete tasks and react to events like task modification and deletion.

Table 10.1　Out-of-the-box task-related activities for Visual Studio

Activity	Purpose
CompleteTask activity	Marks a task as completed
CreateTask activity	Creates a default task
CreateTaskWithContentType activity	Create a task off a content type
DeleteTask activity	Deletes a task
OnTaskChanged activity	Responds to a task's change
OnTaskCreated activity	Responds to a task's creation
OnTaskDeleted activity	Responds to a task's deletion
RollbackTask activity	Rolls back a task to its last accepted state
UpdateAllTasks activity	Updates all incomplete tasks associated with the workflow
UpdateTask activity	Updates a task's fields through its TaskProperties property

Now that you have a picture of all the available task activities, let's build an example that puts them to use. The example you'll go through will be the same Capital Expenditure Request workflow that you built in SharePoint Designer but, this time, you'll build it in Visual Studio. This will help you compare the two workflow tools. There's no need to create a new requests list; you'll add a second workflow to the list you used in section 4.2. To get started, create a new Visual Studio sequential workflow project titled CapitalExpenditureRequests. In the project creation wizard, enter the URL to the site containing your capital expenditure request list, and create a new List workflow with the name Expenditure Requests Approval—VS. Last, associate the new workflow to the capital expenditure request list.

If you remember, in the SharePoint Designer requests example you had two actions that audited whether the workflow item was changed or deleted. In either case, you wanted the workflow to stop processing. To set up this same functionality in

Chapter 4 example dependency

Note that the example in this chapter builds upon section 4.2. That section walks you through building a Capital Expenditure Request workflow with SharePoint Designer. If you do not wish to go back to chapter 4, create a new custom list called Capital Expenditure Request. Add two new columns to the list, Request Description as a multiline text field and Dollar Amount as a currency type. With this generic list in place you'll be all caught up!

your Visual Studio workflow, you can use an EventHandlingScope activity paired with the OnTaskDeleted and OnWorkflowItemChanged activities. The EventHandling-Scope activity allows you to react to events that fire inside that activity's scope. You'll put the core of your workflow's business logic inside this activity, so each time a task is deleted, for example, your EventHandlingScope activity will capture the event and execute the code. Follow the steps in table 10.2 to configure these events.

Table 10.2   Stopping the workflow when the task is deleted or the workflow item is changed

Action	Steps	Result
Set up the EventHandling-Scope and two EventDriven activities.	1 Drop the EventHandlingScope activity onto the workflow Designer surface. 2 Navigate to the View Event Handlers view of the EventHandlingScope activity by clicking the activity name and, on the dropdown, click the View Event Handlers link. 3 Drop two EventDriven activities inside the Event-Handlers activity that is automatically added for you.	
Configure the OnWorkflowItemChanged and SetState activities in the first EventDriven activity.	1 Drop an OnWorkflowItemChanged activity and set the correlation token property of the activity to workflowToken. 2 Below the OnWorkflowItemChanged activity, add a SetState activity and set the correlation token of this activity to workflowToken. Rename the activity to setCanceledState1. **NOTE:** You can use this activity to set custom work-flow states rather than the default In Progress and Completed. 3 Right-click the setCanceledState1 activity and choose Generate Handlers. You'll fill out the code for this activity later.	The OnWorkflowItemChanged activity is the first activity inside the EventDriven activity. This tells the EventDriven activity to wait for the workflow item to change and, if it does, you terminate the workflow.
Configure the DeleteTask activity so you won't have any orphaned tasks.	1 Drop the DeleteTask activity below the SetState activity, and set the token to a new token such as TaskToken.	The DeleteTask activity now sits below the SetState activity. With this activity in place, your workflow deletes any orphaned tasks when the workflow terminates.

Table 10.2 Stopping the workflow when the task is deleted or the workflow item is changed *(continued)*

Action	Steps	Result

	2 After you set the token to a new token, you'll need to set the OwnerActivityName below the correlation token to Workflow1 by clicking the plus sign next to the CorrelationToken property.
	
	3 Set the TaskId property of the activity to inform the DeleteTask property which task to delete. Set the property to a new field named TaskId by binding to a new member.
	
	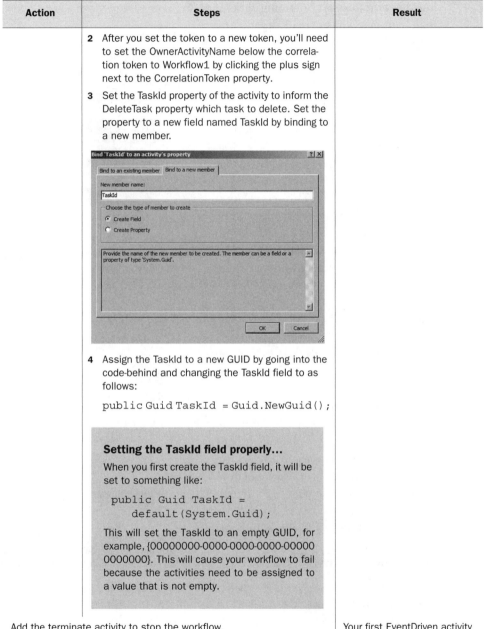
	
	4 Assign the TaskId to a new GUID by going into the code-behind and changing the TaskId field to as follows:
	
	`public Guid TaskId = Guid.NewGuid();`
	
	Setting the TaskId field properly...
	When you first create the TaskId field, it will be set to something like:
	
	`public Guid TaskId =`
	`    default(System.Guid);`
	
	This will set the TaskId to an empty GUID, for example, {00000000-0000-0000-0000-000000000000}. This will cause your workflow to fail because the activities need to be assigned to a value that is not empty.	

Add the terminate activity to stop the workflow.		Your first EventDriven activity looks like figure 10.1.

Now that your workflow is listening for the request to be updated and canceling the workflow and deleting tasks if that happens, you're ready to do the same if the task itself is deleted. If the workflow is waiting for the submission of a task and that task is deleted, you want to ensure your workflow doesn't end up in an orphaned state. In the second EventDriven activity, add a new OnTaskDeleted.

Add and configure the SetState and terminate activities as you did for the first EventDriven activity. The correlation token for the SetState activity should be workflowToken as before. There's no point in adding the DeleteTask activity because, by this point, it will have been deleted. Afterwards, your second Event-Driven activity should look like figure 10.2.

Now that the changed and deleted events are wired up, it's time to add the main business logic into your workflow. As with the SharePoint Designer example, you want a task to be created when the workflow is first started. After the task has been created, you want to wait for the approver to approve or reject the request. After the approval or rejection, you set the workflow's status to the corresponding approval. Let's start with the creation of the task, and the wait for its approval. Follow the steps in table 10.3 to configure this part of the workflow.

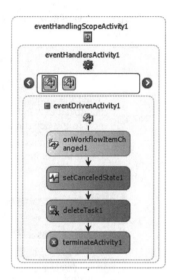

Figure 10.1   The OnWorkflowItemChanged activity fires whenever the workflow item is changed while the workflow is waiting for request approval.

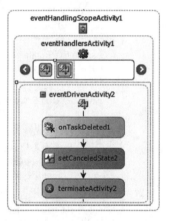

Figure 10.2   Similarly to the OnWorkflowItem-Changed activity, the OnTaskDeleted activity fires if the task is deleted before it has been approved.

TaskId Property and CorrelationToken of the OnTaskDeleted activity

Make sure that the TaskId property of the OnTaskDeleted activity is set to the same field as the DeleteTask activity was set to earlier. All these activities in the capital expenditure request workflow are working off the same task, and their TaskId properties should all be the same. Note as well that the correlation token should be set to TaskToken because that was the token used earlier for the DeleteTask activity.

Table 10.3 Configuring the workflow to create a new task and wait for its approval

Action	Steps	Result
Drop a sequence and CreateTask activities inside the EventHandling-Scope activity.	1 Navigate back to the View EventHandlingScope view of the EventHandlingScope activity. 2 Drop a sequence activity inside the EventHandling-Scope activity. 3 Drop a CreateTask activity inside the sequence activity.	The main area of the EventHandlingScope activity is configured to have a sequence and a CreateTask activity.
Configure the CreateTask activity.	1 Set the correlation token to the same token that was used in the DeleteTask and OnTaskDeleted activities. In this case, set it to TaskToken. **NOTE:** You should see TaskToken in the dropdown of pre-existing token options because TaskToken was defined earlier. If you don't see the TaskToken dropdown option, manually type TaskToken again and set the owner to Workflow1. It is *very important* to then go back to the EventDriven activities and toggle the correlation token dropdown values of the DeleteTask and OnTaskDeleted activities because now there will be two TaskToken options in their correlation token dropdowns. All three activities (Create, Delete, and On Delete) need to share the same token. Ensure that you never have two tokens in the dropdown that share the same name. They have the same name but not the same ID and are treated as different tokens and, if the three activities don't share the same token, the workflow will fail on start. 2 Set the TaskId property of the activity to the same ID that was used in the DeleteTask and OnTaskDeleted activities. 3 Bind the TaskProperties property to a new member called TaskProperties. You can use this field to set values of the task like Title, Assigned To, Due Date, and so on. 4 Right-click the CreateTask activity and choose Generate Handlers. Inside the createTask1_MethodInvoking method, enter the following code to set a few of the task's properties before it's created (listing 10.1)	The CreateTask activity is now configured to create the same task that the DeleteTask activity deletes if the workflow item is changed.

Listing 10.1 createTask1_MethodInvoking

```
private void createTask1_MethodInvoking(object sender, EventArgs e)
{
    TaskProperties.Title =
      onWorkflowActivated1.WorkflowProperties.Item.Title;
    TaskProperties.Description =
      onWorkflowActivated1.WorkflowProperties.
      Item["Request Description"].ToString();
    TaskProperties.AssignedTo = "philsdevdomain\\pwicklund";
}
```

Table 10.3   Configuring the workflow to create a new task and wait for its approval *(continued)*

Action	Steps	Result
Add a while activity below the CreateTask activity, making the workflow keep looping until the task is completed.	1 Below the CreateTask activity, drop in a while activity. 2 Change the Condition property of this activity to Code Condition. 3 Click the plus sign next to the Condition property, and enter a condition method name of WhileTaskNotComplete. This will kick you over to the code view of the workflow. 4 Replace the autogenerated WhileTaskNotComplete method with the one in listing 10.2.	The while activity is below the CreateTask activity. It is configured to keep looping until the taskComplete field is set to True.

Listing 10.2   WhileTaskNotComplete

```
bool taskComplete = false;
private void WhileTaskNotComplete(object sender, ConditionalEventArgs e)
{
  if (taskComplete)
    e.Result = false; // similar to while(0)
  else
    e.Result = true;  // similar to while(1)
}
```

Table 10.3   Configuring the workflow to create a new task and wait for its approval *(continued)*

Action	Steps	Result
Add an OnTaskChanged activity inside the While activity.	1 On the designer view of the workflow, drop the OnTaskChanged activity inside the While activity. 2 This activity will execute each time your task is updated, and the while loop will check if the task has been completed or not. If it has completed, the while loop will finish looping. 3 Set the correlation token to TaskToken, and set the TaskId property to the previously created TaskId field. 4 Similarly to binding the TaskId property, bind the Before-Properties and AfterProperties properties to new members called BeforeProperties and AfterProperties, respectively. 5 Right-click the OnTaskChanged activity, and click Generate Handlers. 6 Replace the generated onTaskChanged1_Invoked method with the code in listing 10.3.	The OnTaskChanged activity is inside the while activity. It is configured to wait for the task created in the previous action to be updated. When it is updated, it checks to see if the Status column is set to something other than Not Started.

Listing 10.3   onTaskChanged1_Invoked

```
private Guid statusColumnId =
  new Guid("{c15b34c3-ce7d-490a-b133-3f4de8801b76}");
private string status = "";
private void onTaskChanged1_Invoked(object sender, ExternalDataEventArgs e)
```

```
{
  status = AfterProperties.ExtendedProperties [statusColumnId].ToString();
  if (status == "Not Started")
    taskComplete = false;
  else
    taskComplete = true;
}
```

How the ExtendedProperties property works

The TaskProperties property contains many of the task's common fields such as Title, DueDate, and Description. For a few default columns like Status and any custom columns, ExtendedProperties must be used. ExtendedProperties is a hash that contains the rest of the default columns such as Status, as well as any custom columns you may have added to the list yourself, or through a content type. The interesting thing about this is that the default columns are entered in the hash through a unique ID, their GUID, whereas custom columns are entered with their column name.

Figure 10.3 shows how to get the field ID with PowerShell if you want to retrieve a default column from the extended properties hash.

With these steps in place, your while activity will stop looping when the Status column is changed to something other than Not Started. Now you add an IfElse activity to determine what to set the workflow's status to. If the status in the task is set to Approved, set the workflow status to Approved. If the status in the task is set to Deferred, set the workflow's status to Deferred, and so on.

NOTE By default, the Approved and Rejected statuses are not in the status column.

In the tasks list, edit the Status column and enter the statuses shown in figure 10.4.

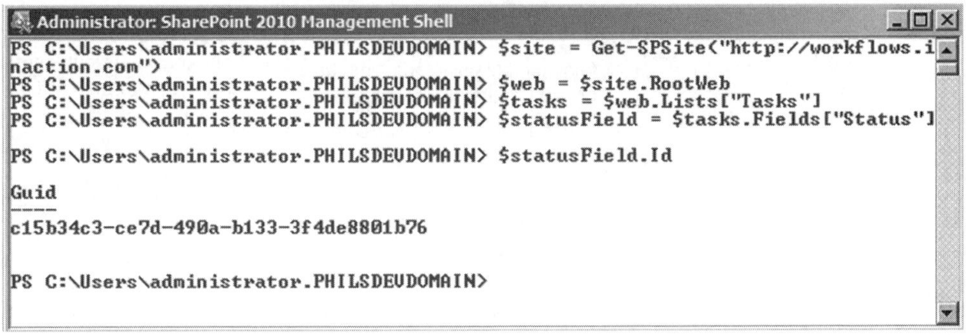

Figure 10.3 The default ExtendedProperties can be retrieved from the hash through their unique ID. You can use PowerShell to get this ID.

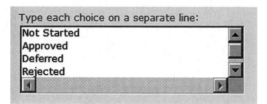

Figure 10.4   By default, a task doesn't have your statuses in the Status column, and you'll need to modify the column to include your statuses.

Table 10.4   Configuring an IfElse activity to determine whether the status is Approved or
             Deferred

Action	Steps	Result
Add an IfElse activity with three branches.	1 Drop the IfElse activity below the EventHandlingScope activity. 2 Right-click the IfElse activity and click Add Branch to add a third branch into the activity.	A new IfElse activity is below the EventHandlingScope activity.

Add a code condition to the first branch to determine if the status was Approved. If it was approved, set the state of the workflow to be Approved.	1 For the first branch, edit the Condition property and specify Code Condition.
	
	2 Click the plus sign and type the condition method as `IsApproved`.
	
	3 In the `IsApproved` method that was generated , enter the following code:
	
	`if (status == "Approved")`
	`    e.Result = true;`
	`else`
	`    e.Result = false;`
	
	4 Add a SetState activity into the first branch and rename it to setApprovedState.
		The first branch in the IfElse activity checks to see if the status is set to Approved. If so, the first branch executes; otherwise, it moves on to the second branch.

Add a code condition to the second branch to determine if the status was Deferred. If it was deferred, set the state of the workflow to be Deferred.	1 For the second branch, edit the Condition property and specify Code Condition.
	
	2 Click the plus sign and type the condition method as IsDeferred.
	
	3 In the generated IsDeferred method, enter the following code:
	
	`If (status == "Deferred")`
	`    e.Result = true;`
	`else`
	`    e.Result = false;`
	
	4 Add a SetState activity into the second branch and rename it to setDeferredState.
		The second branch in the IfElse activity checks to see if the status is set to Deferred. If so, the second branch executes; otherwise, it moves on to the third branch.

Table 10.4 Configuring an IfElse activity to determine whether the status is Approved or Deferred *(continued)*

Action	Steps	Result
Add a SetState activity into the third branch and rename it to setRejectedState. **NOTE:** If the first branch returns False and the second branch returns false, the activities in the third branch will execute		ifElseBranchActivity3 setRejectedState
Give each of the three SetState activities a correlation token of workflowToken. Right-click each and choose Generate Handlers.		The red exclamation point on each of the Set State activities disappears, and each has a method that can be used to set the state.

At this point, your workflow is nearly complete. All that's left is to fill out the handlers for the five SetState activities. Before you do that, confirm that your workflow Designer surface looks something like figure 10.5.

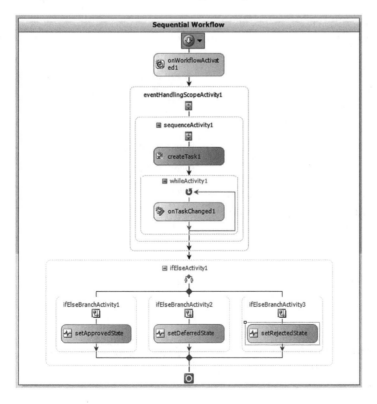

Figure 10.5 Your workflow Designer surface should look like this after you have all the activities configured.

```
<MetaData>
  <AssociationCategories>List</AssociationCategories>
  <StatusPageUrl>_layouts/WrkStat.aspx</StatusPageUrl>
  <ExtendedStatusColumnValues>
    <StatusColumnValue>Approved</StatusColumnValue>
    <StatusColumnValue>Rejected</StatusColumnValue>
    <StatusColumnValue>Deferred</StatusColumnValue>
    <StatusColumnValue>Canceled</StatusColumnValue>
  </ExtendedStatusColumnValues>
</MetaData>
```

Figure 10.6 Custom workflow statuses need to be defined in the workflow's Elements.xml file.

To be more consistent with the SharePoint Designer workflow we created in the last section, we would need to add a few sendEmail activities to send out the notifications. That activity is covered in chapter 8 where we introduced Visual Studio workflows, so we'll skip it here.

The first step to setting up your custom workflow statuses is to define those statuses in the workflow's Elements.xml file. Any custom statuses need to be defined in this XML file, inside the MetaData element. The statuses live inside the child element called ExtendedStatusColumnValues, with each status inside a StatusColumnValue tag. Open the Workflow1's Elements.xml file and define your extended status values as shown in figure 10.6.

Each SetState activity has a property called State. This corresponds to an integer value that determines the state to which to set the workflow status. There are 15 states by default, so you can set this property to a number from 1 to 15, and you'll set your workflow's status to one of those out-of-the-box states. Table 10.5 shows the object model's current values for these states.

To set the workflow to one of your custom states, you need to set it to 16 or higher. For example, if you set it to 16, you'd set the workflow's status to Approved. If you set it to 19, the workflow's status would be Canceled. Rather than hard-coding a value in the State property, it's better to do this through code. Through code, you can use the SPWorkflowStatus.Max property. This will protect you if Microsoft ever changes the state Max from 15, to say 16, which would throw your status values off and might even break your workflow. To do this, configure your SetState handlers similarly to those in listing 10.4.

State (SPWorkflowStatus enum)	Value
Completed	5
ErrorOccurred	3
ErrorOccurredRetrying	7
FailedOnStart	1
FailedOnStartRetrying	6
InProgress	2
Max	15
NotStarted	0
StoppedByUser	4
ViewQueryOverflow	8

Table 10.5 Ten workflow states are defined in the SPWorkflowStatus enum, with a Max value set to 15.

Listing 10.4 Handlers for the SetState activities

```
enum CustomStates                          ◁─┐  Refactors status
{                                            ❶  integer into enum
    Approved = 0,
    Rejected,
    Deferred,
    Canceled
};

private void setCanceledState_MethodInvoking(object sender, EventArgs e)
{
    ((SetState)sender).State = (Int32)SPWorkflowStatus.Max +        ◁─┐
        (Int32)CustomStates.Canceled;               Adds Max value to
}                                                      custom status  ❷

private void setApprovedState_MethodInvoking(object sender, EventArgs e)
{
    ((SetState)sender).State = (Int32)SPWorkflowStatus.Max +
        (Int32)CustomStates.Approved;
}

private void setDeferredState_MethodInvoking(object sender, EventArgs e)
{
    ((SetState)sender).State = (Int32)SPWorkflowStatus.Max +
        (Int32)CustomStates.Deferred;
}

private void setRejectedState_MethodInvoking(object sender, EventArgs e)
{
    ((SetState)sender).State = (Int32)SPWorkflowStatus.Max +
        (Int32)CustomStates.Rejected;
}
```

As you can see, you're using an enum ❶ to set your custom state integers. Then, in each handler, you're adding the Max value to your enum's integer value ❷, calculating the state to which to set the workflow status.

After you have this code entered, build your project and deploy into SharePoint. Next, create a new expenditure request and run this new workflow on that request. You should notice the workflow sitting in the In Progress state, and a new task created in the tasks list. Edit the Status column on that task by changing it to a state other than Not Started. Then on the Capital Expenditure Request list, the Visual Studio workflow's status column should correspond to the status that was selected in the task (figure 10.7).

☐	📎	Title	Dollar Amount	Expenditure Request Approval	Expenditure Requests Approval - VS
		New office location	$100,000.00	Deferred	Deferred

➕ Add new item

Figure 10.7 After the task is deferred, the workflow's status column is updated just as in the SharePoint Designer workflow.

10.2   *Custom task edit forms*

The core of your Capital Expenditure Request workflow is complete, but one problem still exists. The task edit form that the approver uses is not intuitive. The only thing they're supposed to edit is the Status column, and there are nine columns showing on that form. It would be easy for the approver to lose track of what they're supposed to do.

Forms Server dependency

This section requires the SharePoint Server edition of SharePoint. SharePoint Foundation does not allow for the deployment of InfoPath forms into Forms Server.

The solution involves creating a custom InfoPath task edit form. This custom form will have the request's title and description and three buttons: a button to approve, defer, and reject the form. That's it! This custom InfoPath form (figure 10.8) is more intuitive for handling expenditure requests.

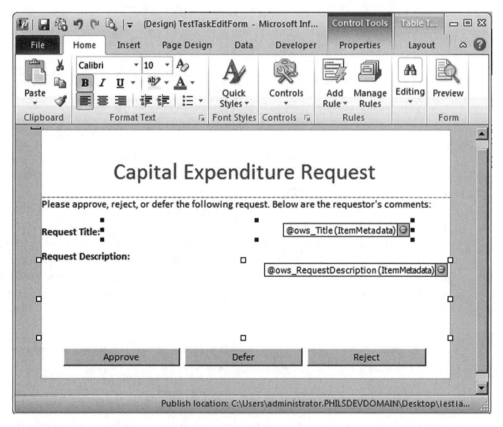

Figure 10.8   Custom InfoPath task edit forms are useful when you need an intuitive and customized form for your workflow.

At this point, you may be thinking, "Why not customize the out of the box form as was described in chapter 8?" Although this is an option, most workflows are reusable in that they can be deployed across larger scopes than one list. Rather than customize the out-of-the-box task edit form time and time again, you'll build it once and your workflow will deploy that custom InfoPath form on your behalf.

Before jumping into the Visual Studio project, you need to do a few special things to make this InfoPath form work. Notice in figure 10.8 two main requirements of the form: first, to show the capital expenditure request's title and description to the approver, and, second, to show three buttons, one for each acceptable status.

Because at design time, InfoPath does not know what task list you are associating the form with, you can't added SharePoint data directly to the form. SharePoint automatically sends the list item data to the InfoPath form on form load. All you need to do is tell the InfoPath form what data to grab. To do this, you need to set up a secondary data source pointing to a XML file titled ItemsMetadata.xml, which references the schema that SharePoint is passing. Follow the steps in table 10.6 to set this up.

Table 10.6   Configuring a secondary data source pointing to your task data

Action	Steps	Result

Create an ItemsMeta-data.xml file that references the schema that SharePoint is passing.	1 Open Notepad, and enter the following XML:
	
	``
	<z:row xmlns:z="#RowsetSchema"
	    ows_Title=""
	    ows_Body="" />
	``
	
	NOTE: The internal name of the Description field is `ows_Body`. The fields with ItemMeta-data.xml should all represent their respective internal names, not their display names.
	
	2 Save the file as ItemMetadata.xml.
	
	NOTE: The filename and the XML are case sensitive!
		A new file called Items-Metadata.xml is created. This file contains the XML schema for your task list data.

Configure the secondary data source for the task edit form in InfoPath.	1 In the task edit form in InfoPath designer under the Ribbon's Data tab, click Data Connections. 2 Click Add to add a new data connection, leave Create a new connection to: Receive data, and then click Next. 3 Choose XML Document, select the Item-Metadata.xml file on the file system where you saved it, and then click Next. 4 Select to include the file as a resource, click Next, and then click Finish. **NOTE:** When you click Next, you will see a warning saying that connections to XML files are not allowed in web browser forms. SharePoint treats this item metadata file as *special* and this warning does not apply.	Your task edit form is configured with a secondary data source to your Share-Point data through the ItemsMetadata.xml file.

With your secondary data source now created, you can add controls to the form that read data out of this source. Add two new controls to the form, one titled Title and the other titled Description. For the title text box, right-click and choose Change Binding. Select ItemMetadata from the data source dropdown and select the ows_Title field. Do the same for the Description text box, except select the ows_Body field. With these two text boxes in place, when your form loads, it will pull the title and description out of the task list item and place it in these fields. This will help approvers know whether they should approve the request or not. Last, configure the three buttons. Then, you'll be ready to publish. Follow the steps in table 10.7 to configure the submit buttons.

Table 10.7   Configuring the Approve, Defer, and Reject submit buttons

Action	Steps	Result
First, set up a data field to store the approval status. Your workflow will look at this field to determine if the request was approved or not.	1 Under the Data tab, click Show Fields. 2 In the Main data source, add a new field called ApprovalStatus and leave the data type set to text.	A new data field is configured to store the information stating which of the three buttons was clicked.
Drop three button controls on the form and change the Label property of each button to Approve, Defer, and Reject, respectively.		Three buttons appear on the form with unique names (similar to figure 10.8).
Configure the Approve button to set the ApprovalStatus field, submit the form, and close the form.	1 Click the Approve button and, under the Home tab, click Manage rules. Click the New dropdown and choose Action. Title the action Approve. 2 Under the Run these actions dropdown, select Set a field's value. Select the ApprovalStatus field and set it to Approved. 3 Under the Run these actions dropdown, add a second action, Submit Data, to submit the form. A dialog will appear. Click Add to add a new Data Connection and choose to submit to the hosting environment. Title the data connection Submit. 4 Add a third action under the Run these actions dropdown. This time, choose the close the form action.	The approval button is now configured to set the ApprovalStatus field and submit and close the form.

Table 10.7   Configuring the Approve, Defer, and Reject submit buttons *(continued)*

Action	Steps	Result
Repeat the previous action for the Defer and Reject buttons, except, this time, set the ApprovalStatus to Deferred and Rejected, respectively. **NOTE:** You won't need to create a new Data Connection. Use the connection created for the Approve button.	Now all three buttons are configured to set the ApprovalStatus field and submit and close the form.

You are ready to publish your form. Save the form and publish it to a network location. Ensure that the security level is set to Domain when you publish.

Now let's integrate this published form into your Visual Studio workflow. For a more detailed walkthrough please refer to section 9.3. Follow the steps in table 10.8 to tell the workflow to use your custom task edit form rather than the one out of the box.

Table 10.8   Configuring your workflow to use your custom task edit form rather than the default, out of the box form

Action	Steps	Result
Add the task edit form into the Visual Studio project.	**1** In the Capital Expenditure Request workflow, right-click the Workflow1 workflow and choose Add Existing Item. Select the published version of the task edit form you created. **2** After the form has been loaded into the project, right-click the form. choose Properties, and change the DeploymentType property to ElementFile.	The earlier created task edit InfoPath form is now in the Visual Studio project.

Next edit the Feature's manifest to include an event receiver that will deploy this form into Forms Server.	Double-click the feature and, under Manifest, click Edit options. Enter the following into the Feature element as attributes:
	
	`ReceiverAssembly="Microsoft.Office.Workflow.Feature,`
	`    Version=14.0.0.0, Culture=neutral,`
	`    PublicKeyToken=71e9bce111e9429c"`
	`ReceiverClass="Microsoft.Office.Workflow.Feature.`
	`    WorkflowFeatureReceiver"`
		The feature is now set to deploy the form to Forms Server when the feature is first activated.

Register the form with the Feature.	Enter the following property into the Properties element: `<Property Key="RegisterForms" Value="Workflow1\*.xsn" />`	The feature now knows which forms need to be deployed to Forms Server.
Now that the form is deployable to Forms Server, deploy the solution and check Forms Server to ensure it worked.	**1** Right-click the project and click Deploy. **2** Navigate to SharePoint Central Administration and find the form in Forms Server. **3** View the properties on the form and note its URN.	The form's unique ID (URN) is retrieved from Forms Server.

Table 10.8   Configuring your workflow to use your custom task edit form rather than the default, out of the box form *(continued)*

Action	Steps	Result
With the form deployed, tell the workflow to use the form.	1 Open the workflow's Elements.xml file. 2 Enter the following as attributes in the Workflow element: `TaskListContentTypeId="0x01080100C9C9515DE4E240019050 74F980F93160"` **NOTE:** The above content type ID is for the out-of-the-box task content type. If you're using a custom task content type, you'll need to retrieve and use your content type's unique ID. 3 Enter the following element under the MetaData element: 4 `<Task0_FormURN></Task0_FormURN>` 5 Inside the Task0_FormURN element, paste the form's URN copied from Form Server.	The workflow's Elements.xml file looks something like figure 10.9.
Add another property setting to tell the task which form to use.	On the workflow's designer surface, double-click the CreateTask activity. In the createTask1_MethodInvoking method, add another property setting to tell the task which form to use: `TaskProperties.TaskType = 0;`	The workflow now knows which form to render when the user edits the task.

```xml
<Elements xmlns="http://schemas.microsoft.com/sharepoint/">
  <Workflow
      Name="Expenditure Requests Approval - VS"
      Description="My SharePoint Workflow"
      Id="65bdb960-e5b4-4e07-b7e5-8ac2ad5205de"
      CodeBesideClass="CapitalExpenditureRequests.Workflow1.Workflow1"
      CodeBesideAssembly="$assemblyname$"
      TaskListContentTypeId="0x01080100C9C9515DE4E24001905074F980F93160">
    <Categories/>
    <MetaData>
      <Task0_FormURN>
        urn:schemas-microsoft-com:office:infopath:CapitalRequestEditForm:-n
      </Task0_FormURN>
      <AssociationCategories>List</AssociationCategories>
      <StatusPageUrl>_layouts/WrkStat.aspx</StatusPageUrl>
      <ExtendedStatusColumnValues>
        <StatusColumnValue>Approved</StatusColumnValue>
        <StatusColumnValue>Rejected</StatusColumnValue>
        <StatusColumnValue>Deferred</StatusColumnValue>
        <StatusColumnValue>Canceled</StatusColumnValue>
      </ExtendedStatusColumnValues>
    </MetaData>
  </Workflow>
</Elements>
```

Figure 10.9   The Elements.xml file is updated with two main things, the TaskListContentTypeId and the task's form's URN.

TaskProperties.TaskType

The TaskType property lets you create multiple types of tasks, and you can associate each type of task with a different form. Notice the zero in the `Task0_FormURN` element in the workflow's Elements.xml file. The zero in the element name corresponds to the TaskType property of the task. The TaskType property is set to zero to inform the workflow to use form zero when the task is edited.

This is helpful when you're creating two tasks, one for a regular approver and one for the CEO. CEOs should see a different form when they approve requests than what the regular approver would see. In this case, the regular approver could get a task type of zero, the CEO could get a task type of one, and both could have their own FormURN in the elements file.

Before you can deploy, you need to do one last thing—update your OnTaskChanged activity. If you remember, that activity is currently looking at the Status column on the task. Now, with your custom task edit form you are no longer going to be looking at that status column but rather at the ApprovalStatus field in the InfoPath form's data when the form is submitted. Go into the event handler of the OnTaskChanged activity and ensure the code is referencing the ApprovalStatus column such as in listing 10.5.

Listing 10.5 onTaskChanged1_Invoked

```
private string status = "";
private void onTaskChanged1_Invoked(object sender, ExternalDataEventArgs
    e)
{
  status = AfterProperties.ExtendedProperties
    ["ApprovalStatus"].ToString();
}
```

It's important to note that, with a custom task edit form, your task cannot be modified if it is not submitted. This means you no longer need the while activity. Before, someone could easily edit the task's Title column, for example, and never change the Status column on which your workflow was dependent. Feel free to move the OnTaskChanged activity out of the while activity and directly after the CreateTask activity. Later, you can delete the while activity altogether.

You're finally ready to test. Build and deploy the Visual Studio solution. Then, create a new Capital Expenditure Request, and start the workflow on that request. Click the task that is created and you should see your custom InfoPath task edit form (figure 10.10). In the form, you'll notice the title and description of the expenditure request and, after you click one of the three approval buttons, the workflow will complete and its status will be updated.

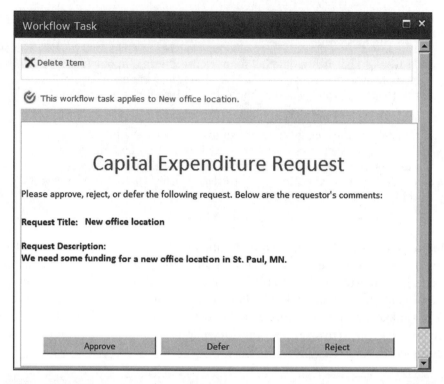

Figure 10.10   The new custom task edit form has a more concise and easier to use interface for your end users.

10.3   *Summary*

When building Visual Studio workflows that need to perform task processing, you'll find a host of task-related activities you can use. Activities such as the CreateTask and OnTaskChanged activities allow you to create a new task and wait for that task to be completed. Other tasks such as the DeleteTask and OnTaskDeleted are commonly used as well.

The task edit forms of Visual Studio workflows can be more complex than Share-Point Designer workflows. In SharePoint Designer, you could merely add or remove fields from the task edit form. In Visual Studio, you can design an InfoPath form that your workflow can use to meet even the most complicated form and task management requirements. These InfoPath task edit forms can be integrated and deployed through your Visual Studio project.

Custom workflow activities and conditions

This chapter covers

- Building custom leaf activities
- Building custom composite activities
- Publishing activities to SharePoint Designer
- Coding custom conditions for SharePoint Designer

In the most fundamental sense, activities are object-oriented classes. In object-oriented programming, you would never have one class that does everything. Instead, you would have many classes that combine to make up an application. This approach applies to workflows and activities as well. You would never want a large, complex Visual Studio workflow to have, for example, 10,000 lines of code in its code view. It's a better practice to extract discrete pieces of code into custom activities that are managed outside the workflow's template. The workflow template should be used to model the workflow's activities, and pictorially show the flow of work. The vast majority of the custom code should be managed outside the template in custom activities.

Using custom activities you'll greatly improve the readability and maintainability of your workflows. From the readability perspective, consider the code activity. If you remember, a code activity is used to add code into a workflow template. This activity is often abused. For example, if you have a code activity containing 500 lines of code, you're defeating the value of the workflow template. You can't see pictorially what that activity is doing. If you took the logic out of that activity and extracted it into several custom activities, you'd not only gain readability benefits by seeing those activities modeled on the template, but the code would also be more maintainable.

You can build two types of custom activities: leaf activities and composite activities. Although composite activities are akin to branches with many leaves (child activities), leaf activities can only contain functionality that is specific to them. A composite activity contains many leaf activities and is, in some sense, a mini-workflow within the parent workflow template. Examples of leaf activities include Delay, CreateTask, and SetState. Examples of composites include while, IfElse, and sequence.

Activities can be packaged and published into SharePoint Designer and used in Visual Studio workflows. Deploying to SharePoint Designer involves creating an ACTIONS file and deploying it to the file system. SharePoint Designer will download that file when it remotely connects to your SharePoint site, and the file will tell Share-Point Designer which custom actions to load and make available to the user.

Custom conditions can also be published into SharePoint Designer. Conditions are used to determine if a block of actions should execute or not. To create a condition, you need a .NET class and a method that returns a Boolean. You then point to your method in the same ACTIONS file, and SharePoint Designer treats the method as a custom condition for use in SharePoint Designer workflows.

11.1 *Building custom leaf activities*

Building custom leaf activities is relatively easy. The procedure involves creating a class and extending the base `Activity` class. You then override the `Execute` method and start coding! To add your activity to the workflow, build the project and the activity will appear in the toolbox. Beyond this, you can incorporate a few other techniques to make your custom activity more robust. This includes creating custom properties that will be loaded in the properties interface. With these properties, you can also write custom validation and specify defaults settings. You can even theme your activity by changing the background color of the activity when it is dropped on the workflow template.

11.1.1 *Custom activity fundamentals*

Before you get into anything advanced, let's build a generic custom leaf activity. To do this, you're going to create a new project and a new class that extends the base `Activity` class. You're then going to override the `Execute` method and build and drop your activity onto a workflow template. Follow the steps in table 11.1.

Setting the stage for your example

This subsection is intentionally generic to keep things simple. You're going to create an activity named CreateSubSites, which you'll extend in later sections to provision subsites from a workflow. This is a simple example of how a custom activity can be beneficial because subsites can be reusable across many workflows.

Table 11.1 Building a custom leaf activity and using it in a workflow

Action	Steps	Result
Create a new workflow project.	1 Create a new sequential workflow project. 2 Name the project CustomActivities and associate the workflow with as a Site Workflow. **What is the name of the workflow?** CustomActivities - Workflow1 **What type of reusable workflow temp** ○ List Workflow ◉ Site Workflow	A new Visual Studio project is created and bound to a SharePoint site.

Create a new class and extend the base Activity class.	1 Right-click the project, and choose Add, Class...
	2 Name the class CreateSubSite.
	3 In the class's code file, add the following using statements at the top:
	`using System.Workflow.ComponentModel;`
	`using Microsoft.SharePoint;`
	4 Make the CreateSubSite class public and extend it to the Activity base class:
	`public class CreateSubSite: Activity`
		Your project has a new class that extends Activity.

Override the Execute method.	1 Within the class, override the protected Execute method. 2 Change the return value to be ActivityExecutionStatus.Closed.	The class has a single method, and afterward the code in its entirety looks similar to listing 11.1.

Listing 11.1 CreateSubSite activity class file contents

```
using System;
using System.Collections.Generic;
using System.Linq;
using System.Text;
using System.Workflow.ComponentModel;
using Microsoft.SharePoint;

namespace CustomActivities
{
```

```
public class CreateSubSite: Activity
{
    protected override ActivityExecutionStatus Execute(
        ActivityExecutionContext executionContext)
    {
        return ActivityExecutionStatus.Closed;
    }
}
}
```

Table 11.1   Building a custom leaf activity and using it in a workflow (continued)

Action	Steps	Result
Drag and drop the custom activity onto Workflow1's Designer surface.	**1** Build the project. **2** Double-click Workflow1 and notice your custom activity in the toolbox: *Toolbox panel:* Toolbox — CustomActivities Components — Pointer — CreateSubSite — Windows Workflow v3.0 — Windows Workflow v3.5 — SharePoint Workflow **3** Drag and drop the custom activity onto the workflow template.	**Sequential Workflow** onWorkflowActivated1 createSubSite1

Pretty easy, isn't it? Now, before you can move onto the next section, note the following. You need to understand the return value of the Execute method and, because Execute isn't the only method you can override, you need to look at the other available methods and what they can be used for.

The ActivityExecutionStatus is the return type on the Execute method because the runtime needs to know the status of the activity after execute is called. Table 11.2 shows a list of possible statuses and when they are useful.

Table 11.2   ActivityExecutionstatus enumeration options

Status	Description
Canceling	Canceling will tell the runtime that something in the activity is causing it to cancel what it was trying to do.
Closed	Closed is what is used under normal conditions. This tells the runtime the activity has executed successfully and the runtime can move to the next activity.
Compensating	Compensating tells the runtime that the activity is cancelling and is trying to roll back its changes.

Table 11.2　ActivityExecutionstatus enumeration options *(continued)*

Status	Description
Executing	Executing tells the workflow that the activity is still executing. This is most commonly used in composite activities, where a parent activity has child activities that are still executing.
Faulting	Faulting tells the runtime that an exception or error has occurred while the activity was executing.
Initialized	Initialized tells the runtime that the activity has initialized but has not yet executed. This is typically not used by developers.

11.1.2　*Adding dependency properties and validation*

By adding custom properties into your activities, you're giving the person building the workflow the ability to specify values at design time. Additionally, with custom properties, activities will be able to pass values back and forth among each other at runtime. For your CreateSubSite activity, you want to add properties for the SiteName, SiteUrl, SiteTemplate, and the workflow context. After your properties are added, the person building the workflow will be able to specify values in the property editor (figure 11.1).

You should consider two types of properties: standard .NET properties, and the dependency properties. Standard .NET properties work nicely if you merely want to make a property available in the property pane (figure 11.1) so that the person building the workflow can specify a value at design time. Dependency properties come into play if the value isn't known until runtime. For instance, you may want to have the output of one activity pass a value into

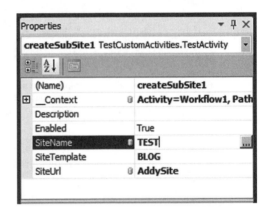

Figure 11.1　You can add properties into your activity to allow the user who's building the workflow to set values in the property menu at design time.

the input of another activity. That value won't be known to the receiving activity until runtime. In this case, dependency properties are needed.

Figure 11.2 shows how dependency properties show up underneath the activity in the property binding dialog. You can then bind the property of one activity to a property of another.

Dependency properties store their values in a hash controlled by the workflow runtime rather than local variables, as with most .NET property values. Because a .NET property could be bound to any variable anywhere, this dependency makes them less reusable. Dependency properties, on the other hand, are not dependent

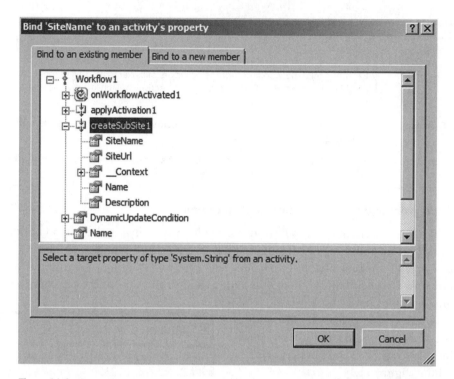

Figure 11.2   Dependency properties are needed when you won't know the value until runtime. For example, you want to set the value of a property to the value of a property in a separate activity. Only dependency properties show up in the bind dialog under the corresponding activity.

because they always reference the same hash. Dependency properties are more often than not the better type to use, and all the properties you build in this section will be dependency properties.

Dependency properties are coded similarly to standard .NET properties, with a few small exceptions. Notice a sample dependency property in listing 11.2.

Listing 11.2   Sample dependency property

```
public static DependencyProperty SiteUrlProperty =
    System.Workflow.ComponentModel.DependencyProperty.
    Register("SiteUrl", typeof(string), typeof(TestActivity));

[Description("Enter a relative URL for the new site")]
[Browsable(true)]
[DesignerSerializationVisibility(DesignerSerializationVisibility.Visible)]
public string SiteUrl
{
    get
    {
        return ((string)(base.GetValue(TestActivity.SiteUrlProperty)));
    }
    set
    {
```

❶ Registers property with runtime hash

❷ Uses a standard .NET property

❸ References property in get/set

```
        base.SetValue(TestActivity.SiteUrlProperty, value);
    }
}
```

The first thing you'll notice is that your dependency property, SiteUrlProperty, is registered with the workflow runtime's hash through the DependencyProperty's Register method ❶. In addition, notice the standard .NET property titled SiteUrl ❷, but its getter and setter ❸ are referencing the SiteUrlProperty dependency property above rather than a generic string object, for example.

Now, getting back to your custom CreateSubSite activity, you want to add four custom dependency properties that will help in the provisioning of the subsite. First, you add two simple string properties for the site's name and URL. Then, you need a property to specify which site template to use (for example, blog, wiki, or team site). Last, you need a property that will contain the workflow's context. The workflow context will have valuable information like the context SPSite and SPWeb objects. This will enable you to avoid hard-coding any URLs, and your activity can be entirely generic. To add these properties, enter the code found in listing 11.3 inside the CreateSubSite class, above the Execute method.

Two more using statements needed

After you enter the code in listing 11.3, add a using statement to System.Component-Model and Microsoft.SharePoint.WorkflowActions so it would build successfully.

Listing 11.3   SiteName, SiteUrl, SiteTemplate, and Context dependency properties

```
public enum SiteTemplates
{
    BLOG,
    MPS,
    STS,
    WIKI
};
public static DependencyProperty SiteNameProperty =
    System.Workflow.ComponentModel.DependencyProperty.Register(
    "SiteName", typeof(string), typeof(CreateSubSite));

public static DependencyProperty SiteUrlProperty =
    System.Workflow.ComponentModel.DependencyProperty.Register(
    "SiteUrl", typeof(string), typeof(CreateSubSite));

public static DependencyProperty SiteTemplateProperty =
    System.Workflow.ComponentModel.DependencyProperty.Register
    ("SiteTemplate", typeof(SiteTemplates), typeof(CreateSubSite));

public static DependencyProperty __ContextProperty =
    System.Workflow.ComponentModel.DependencyProperty.Register(
    "__Context", typeof(WorkflowContext), typeof(CreateSubSite));

[Description("Enter a name for the new site")]
[Browsable(true)]
```

```csharp
[DesignerSerializationVisibility(DesignerSerializationVisibility.Visible)]
public string SiteName
{
    get
    {
        return ((string)(base.GetValue(CreateSubSite.SiteNameProperty)));
    }
    set
    {
        base.SetValue(CreateSubSite.SiteNameProperty, value);
    }
}

[Description("Enter a relative URL for the new site")]
[Browsable(true)]
[DesignerSerializationVisibility(DesignerSerializationVisibility.Visible)]
public string SiteUrl
{
    get
    {
        return ((string)(base.GetValue(CreateSubSite.SiteUrlProperty)));
    }
    set
    {
        base.SetValue(CreateSubSite.SiteUrlProperty, value);
    }
}

[Description("Specify the site template that will be used.")]
[Browsable(true)]
[DesignerSerializationVisibility(DesignerSerializationVisibility.Visible)]
public SiteTemplates SiteTemplate
{
    get
    {
        return ((SiteTemplates)(base.GetValue(
            CreateSubSite.SiteTemplateProperty)));
    }
    set
    {
        base.SetValue(CreateSubSite.SiteTemplateProperty, value);
    }
}

[Browsable(true)]
[DesignerSerializationVisibility(DesignerSerializationVisibility.Visible)]
public WorkflowContext __Context
{
    get
    {
        return ((WorkflowContext)(base.GetValue(
            CreateSubSite.__ContextProperty)));
    }
    set
    {
        base.SetValue(CreateSubSite.__ContextProperty, value);
    }
}
```

Property naming rules can't be broken

The name of the context property is preceded by two underscores, _ _Context. You may be thinking this is a bit odd, but it is necessary because later in this chapter you're going to publish this activity to SharePoint Designer. SharePoint Designer looks for a few properties with specific names, and __Context happens to be one of them. When Designer sees this property, it saves the WorkflowContext in that property.

You may also notice how all the static dependency properties have *Property* at the end of the name. This is a requirement. Also notice the first parameter in the `Register` method. This is the key in the runtime property hash. This key must be the property name, for example, *SiteUrl*.

Failure to comply with these naming rules will result in runtime errors!

When you have entered the listing into your activity, build the project again. Afterward, go back to Workflow1 and click on the CreateSubSite activity. Notice that your four properties show up in the property menu (figure 11.3). Feel free to specify a site name and URL and pick your favorite template.

Now you may be wondering what you're supposed to do with the __Context property. This property must be a dependency property because you won't know the value of the property until runtime. You get the WorkflowContext from the output of the ApplyActivation activity. Follow the steps in table 11.3 to configure the ApplyActivation activity to set your context.

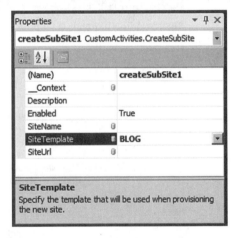

Figure 11.3   After you build, properties will show up in the property menu of the activity.

Table 11.3   Configuring the ApplyActivation activity to set the WorkflowContext property

Action	Steps	Result
Configure the ApplyActivation activity.	1 Drag and drop the ApplyActivation activity between the onWorkflowActivated1 and the createSubSite1 activities. 2 Bind the __Context property of the ApplyActivation activity to a new member field called workflowContext. 3 On the CreateSubSite activity, bind the __Context property to the workflowContext field.	

After completing these steps, the CreateSubSite activity will have a WorkflowContext object at runtime. If you didn't first use the ApplyActivation activity, the __Context property would have been null. You may have noticed on the ApplyActivation activity that there was another underscore property titled __WorkflowProperties. Another one of those tokens that SharePoint Designer looks for is _ _WorkflowProperties. The __Context and __WorkflowProperties have similar objects like SPSite and SPWeb. You could've used the workflowProperties object that the OnWorkflowActivated activity initializes. If you ever need a WorkflowContext object rather than a WorkflowProperties object, you know how to configure the ApplyActivation activity to initialize that WorkflowContext property.

Before moving onto the next section, let's add code into our `CreateSubSite` class. With our properties in place, we can add the code that will provision the subsite. Enter the code found in listing 11.4 inside the `Execute` method.

Listing 11.4   Site provisioning code within the Execute method

```
SPSecurity.RunWithElevatedPrivileges(delegate()                ← ❶ Elevates user to
    {                                                              service account
        using (SPSite site = new SPSite(__Context.Site.ID))
        {
            using (SPWeb web = site.AllWebs[__Context.Web.ID])  ← ❷ Gets site
            {                                                          and web
                if (web.Webs.Names.Contains(SiteUrl))          ←       from context
                    throw new UrlAlreadyInUseException();
                else                                           ← ❸ Confirms URL
                {                                                    is unique
                    web.Webs.Add(                              ← ❹ Provisions
                        SiteUrl,                                    the subsite
                        SiteName,
                        "desc.",
                        1033,
                        SiteTemplate.ToString(),
                        false,
                        false);
                }
            }
        }
    });
return ActivityExecutionStatus.Closed;
```

In the `Execute` method, the user's privileges must first be elevated to that of the service account ❶. This is because you can't guarantee that the user will have the rights necessary to create subsites in SharePoint. Thereafter, you need to get the SPSite and SPWeb objects from your context ❷. The SPWeb object will be the parent site to the subsite that is to be created. Before you create the subsite, confirm that the URL is unique ❸. You can't have two sites with the same URL. It would be proper to use a FaultHandlingActivity to handle a uniquely named exception like the UrlAlreadyInUseException shown in this listing (figure 11.4). With this route, you can put the burden on

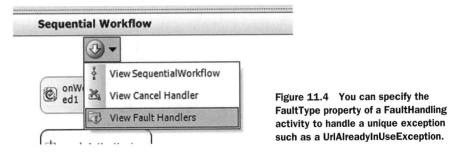

Figure 11.4 You can specify the FaultType property of a FaultHandling activity to handle a unique exception such as a UrlAlreadyInUseException.

the workflow to know how to handle the exception. After you confirm the URL is available, the site is provisioned ❹.

It's easy to create a custom exception. Create a new class and use the following code as an example of how to create a custom exception:

```
public class UrlAlreadyInUseException : Exception
{
    public UrlAlreadyInUseException()
    {
    }
}
```

11.1.3 *Property validation*

At this point, wouldn't it be handy to add some validation to your newly created properties? Take the SiteUrl property, for example. The URL is a sensitive property because, with incorrect entry, the Add method on the Webs collection will throw an exception, for example, if you enter special characters in the URL or if you don't make the URL relative but put in a full URL such as http://intranet/someurl. When you call the web.Webs.Add method in listing 11.4, the URL must be relative and must not contain any forward slashes or special characters. Let's enhance your activity with a custom validator that will raise a compile time error if the URL is given a value that does not meet your requirements.

To create a custom validator, you need to create a new class that extends ActivityValidator. The ActivityValidator class has a method called Validate that you'll then need to override. It's within this method that you can put whatever code you want to determine if the property was configured properly. The return type on the method is ValidationErrorCollection, a collection of ValidationError objects. You can fill this collection with ValidationErrors, and Visual Studio will show those errors in the error screen when you build the project and the build fails (figure 11.5).

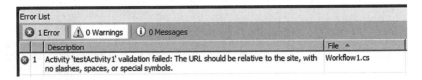

Figure 11.5 By creating a custom validator, you can render compile time errors when properties are set incorrectly.

The `Validate` method is programmed as you want. If you want to validate five properties, you may write code that validates all five in the one `Validate` method. On the other hand, you could write five separate validators. Your choice. Use the steps in table 11.4 to create a validator for your CreateSubSite activity.

Table 11.4   Creating a custom activity validator

Action	Steps	Result

Create a new class called UrlValidator.	1 Right-click the project, choose Add, Class... and name the class UrlValidator.
	
	2 At the top of the class add the following using statements:
	
	`using System.Workflow.ComponentModel.Compiler;`
	`using System.Text.RegularExpressions;`
	
	3 Make the class public and extend ActivityValidator:
	
	`public class UrlValidator: ActivityValidator`
	
	4 Override the `Validate` method.
		After you override the `Validate` method, the class in its entirety will look similar to listing 11.5.

Listing 11.5   UrlValidator class shell

```
using System;
using System.Collections.Generic;
using System.Linq;
using System.Text;
using System.Workflow.ComponentModel.Compiler;
using System.Text.RegularExpressions;

namespace CustomActivities
{
    public class UrlValidator: ActivityValidator
    {
        public override ValidationErrorCollection Validate(
            ValidationManager manager, object obj)
        {
            return base.Validate(manager, obj);
        }
    }
}
```

Table 11.4   Creating a custom activity validator (continued)

Action	Steps	Result
Enter the code found in listing 11.6 into the Validate method.		The `Validate` method will contain the code found in listing 11.6.

Listing 11.6   Validate method code

```
CreateSubSite createSubSite = obj as CreateSubSite;
ValidationErrorCollection errCol = new ValidationErrorCollection();

if (createSubSite != null)                          ← ❶  Ensures activity and URL are not null
```

```
{
    string url = createSubSite.SiteUrl;
    if (url != null && url.Trim() != string.Empty)
    {
        Regex noSpecialChars = new Regex(@"\W");
        if (noSpecialChars.IsMatch(url))
        {
            errCol.Add(new ValidationError(
                "The URL should be relative to the site, " +
                "with no slashes, spaces, or special symbols.", 0001));
        }
    }
    if (url == string.Empty)
    {
        errCol.Add(new ValidationError(
            "The SiteUrl property cannot be null", 0002));
    }
    if (createSubSite.SiteName == string.Empty)
    {
        errCol.Add(new ValidationError(
            "The SiteName property cannot be null", 0003));
    }
}
return errCol;
```

2 Checks URL for special characters

3 Adds error message into collection

4 Confirms neither the URL nor Name is empty

The Validate code first gets a reference to the CreateSubSite activity. The properties can be pulled out of this object. Next, you check to ensure that the activity isn't null **1** and, if not, you run a regular expression against the URL, checking to see if any special characters are present **2**. If any special characters are found, an error message is added to the collection **3**. Next, you confirm that both the SiteUrl and SiteName properties have a value **4**. Because the SiteTemplate is an enumeration and the Context is built at runtime, it isn't necessary to validate those properties.

Table 11.4 Creating a custom activity validator (continued)

Action	Steps	Result
Add an Activity-Validation attribute onto the CreateSubSite class.	1 In the CreateSubSite activity, add the following attribute onto the class: `[ActivityValidator(typeof(UrlValidator))]` 2 Add a using statement for System.Workflow.Component-Model.Compiler	The activity is now instructed to run the UrlValidator Validate method when properties change and when the project is built.
Build the project and test the validator.	1 Build the project 2 On Workflow1, change the SiteUrl property to /blog.	You see a red exclamation point next to the activity (figure 11.6) and, after you build you, you'll receive a build error.

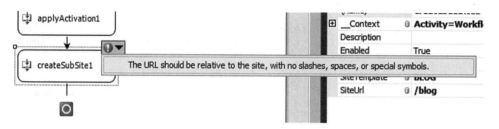

Figure 11.6   In addition to compile time errors, users will get red exclamation points next to the activity when a property is set incorrectly.

You finished adding valuable custom properties and property validation into your custom activity. Nevertheless, your activity is not aesthetically pleasing, and you're not setting any default values to your properties. The next section will walk you through customizing the toolbox item as well as setting default values to your parameters when the user drops the activity onto the workflow template.

11.1.4 *Activity toolbox items*

By creating a class that extends ActivityToolboxItem you can easily customize the activity's appearance in the toolbox. You can also assign default values to your custom properties when the user drops the activity onto the workflow's template. This is simple and requires only a few lines of code.

The ActivityToolboxItem you build in this section is simple, but when you get to composite activities, this class becomes much more involved. Follow the steps in table 11.5 to add a custom ActivityToolboxItem to your custom activity.

Table 11.5   Adding a custom ToolboxItem to the createSubSite activity

Action	Steps	Result
All proper toolbox items should have a custom icon. Add a 16 × 16 pixel icon as a project resource that will be referenced in code later.	1 Right-click the project, choose Properties, and then select the Resource tab. 2 Click the blue link to create a new resource file. 3 Under the Add Resource menu item, select Add Existing Item, browse out, and select the STSICON.GIF file under c:\Program Files\ Common Files\Microsoft Shared\Web Server Extensions\14\TEMPLATE\IMAGES. **NOTE:** Ensure you select the GIF file version and not other files using the same name, for example STSICON.ico.	Application Images ▾ Add Resource Build Build Events Debug Resources Reference Paths STSICON
Create a new class file for the custom ActivityTool-boxItem.	1 Right-click the project and choose Add, Class... and name the class CreateSubSite-ToolboxItem.	The ActivityToolboxItem class is completed.

Table 11.5 Adding a custom ToolboxItem to the createSubSite activity *(continued)*

Action	Steps	Result

	2 Add the using statements to the top of the class for the following namespaces:
	
	`System.Workflow.ComponentModel.Design;`
	`System.Runtime.Serialization;`
	`System.ComponentModel;`
	`System.ComponentModel.Design;`
	
	3 Replace the class with the code found in listing 11.7.
	
	4 Add the following class attribute above the class name next to the validator attribute you added earlier:
	
	`[ToolboxItem(typeof(CreateSubSiteToolboxItem))]`	

Listing 11.7 CreateSubSiteToolboxItem class

```
[Serializable]                                                          ← Declares
internal class CreateSubSiteToolboxItem : ActivityToolboxItem            the class as
{                                                                    ❶   serializable
    public CreateSubSiteToolboxItem(Type type)
        : base(type)
    {
    }

    private CreateSubSiteToolboxItem(SerializationInfo serializeinfo,
        StreamingContext context)
    {                                                               ❷   Specifies toolbox
        this.Deserialize(serializeinfo, context);               ←       metadata
        this.Description = "Creates sub site below context web.";
        this.Company = "SP WFs in Action";
        this.DisplayName = "Create Sub Site";
        this.Bitmap = new System.Drawing.Bitmap(
            CustomActivities.Properties.Resources.STSICON);
    }                                                               ❸   Specifies
                                                                        default
    protected override IComponent[] CreateComponentsCore(       ←       properties
        IDesignerHost host)
    {
        CreateSubSite css = new CreateSubSite();
        css.SiteName = "Contoso Team Site";                     ❹   Returns custom
                                                                        activity
        return new IComponent[]                                 ←
        {
            css
        };
    }
}
```

Notice that the first thing your code does is mark the class as serializable ❶. Two required constructors follow. In the second constructor, you deserialize the class and assign the item's metadata values such as description, company, and an icon ❷. The following overridden method allows you to specify default values to your properties ❸. It's not required to override this method, but it can be helpful when you want preset values. This method becomes more important when you get into composite activity because you'll be programmatically adding child activities into the activity. Right now, you're only returning the activity itself ❹, with no child activities.

At this point, you can build your project and test the toolbox item. The first thing you'll notice when you get to the toolbox is that neither your item metadata nor icon is showing. On the plus side, if you go ahead and drop the activity onto the workflow template, the SiteName property will have been set to Contoso Team Site. What's going on? Why is the code only half working? Visual Studio looks at activities it finds within the current project differently than the activities that are manually added into the toolbox. Therefore, you need to browse out and add your custom activity to the toolbox manually. This is one reason why many people keep their workflows and their activities in separate projects. Follow the last step in table 11.5 to manually add your activity to the toolbox.

Table 11.5 Adding a custom ToolboxItem to the createSubSite activity *(continued)*

Action	Steps	Result

Add the Create-SubSite activity manually into the toolbox.	1 Right-click inside the toolbox and select Choose Items.
	
	2 Click the Browse button and browse out to the CustomActivities.dll assembly in the Bin\Debug directory of your project.
	
	3 Click OK and take another look at the toolbox!
		SharePoint Workflow
		  Pointer
		  ApplyActivation
		  CompleteTask
		  Create Sub Site
		  CreateTask
		  CreateTaskWithⱭ **Create Sub Site**
		  DeleteTask Version 1.0.0.0 from SP WFs In Action
		  EnableWorkflowN .NET Component
		  InitializeWorkflow Creates sub site below context web.

With your toolbox item showing custom metadata and an icon, you can spruce up the activity once it gets onto the workflow template. You can change the background color of the activity and provide a custom icon to render.

11.1.5 Theming your activity

By theming your activities, you can customize the background colors, font types, font colors, and icons. Obviously, it's not the most critical technique but it certainly adds spice and uniqueness to your home-grown activities. This is done with the combination of two classes, ActivityDesigner and ActivityDesignerTheme. In addition, using a consistent theme across sites will lend familiarity, which can help users feel more comfortable when working with new workflows.

When you create a custom ActivityDesigner class you can do several things to your activities. For example, you can change the size of the activity or change the placement of the text in the activity itself. Even better, you can add custom verbs into your activity. When you right-click the activity, you get a menu that includes the Properties button. Other familiar verbs are Generate Handlers, Copy, and Disable. You can add custom verbs into this menu with an event handler attached to the verb to run custom code.

ActivityDesigner is needed for themes, and not the ActivityDesignerTheme class, because an activity can have a *Design* attribute pointing to the ActivityDesigner. Then, the ActivityDesigner has an *ActivityDesignerTheme* attribute pointing to your custom theme. If all you want to do is theme your activity, the ActivityDesigner class will be empty. Inside the ActivityDesignerTheme class's constructor, set all your properties such as BorderStyle, BackgroundStyle, and ForeColor. Follow the steps in table 11.6 to configure your activity's custom theme.

Table 11.6 Creating a custom ActivityDesigner and ActivityDesignerTheme for the Create Sub Site activity

Action	Steps	Result

Create a new class file for the ActivityDesigner.	1 Right-click the project, and choose Add, Class... and name the class CreateSubSiteActivityDesigner.
	2 Add using statements for the following namespaces:
	`System.Workflow.ComponentModel.Design`
	`System.Drawing`
	3 Make the class public and extend the ActivityDesigner class:
	`public class`
	`CreateSubSiteActivityDesigner:`
	`ActivityDesigner`
		A new class file called CreateSubSiteActivityDesinger.cs is created with appropriate using statements added and a public class extended from Activity Designer.

Create a second class either in the same file or a new file for the ActivityDesignerTheme.	1 Under the first class, add a second public class called CreateSubSiteActivityDesignerTheme, which extends the class ActivityDesignerTheme.
	2 Create a public constructor that takes a WorkflowTheme as a parameter and sets to color properties:
	`public`
	`CreateSubSiteActivityDesignerTheme(`
	`    WorkflowTheme theme)`
	`    : base(theme)`
	`{`
	`    this.BackColorStart =`
	`        Color.Orange;`
	`    this.BackColorEnd =`
	`        Color.OrangeRed;`
	`    this.BackgroundStyle =`
	`        System.Drawing.Drawing2D.`
	`        LinearGradientMode.Horizontal;`
	`}`
		A second public class that extends ActivityDesignerTheme is added in the same cs file.

Table 11.6   Creating a custom ActivityDesigner and ActivityDesignerTheme for the Create Sub Site activity *(continued)*

Action	Steps	Result

Add the ActivityDesignerTheme attribute onto the CreateSubSite-ActivityDesigner class.	Above the CreateSubSiteActivityDesigner class, add the following attribute:
	
	`[ActivityDesignerTheme(typeof(`
	`CreateSubSiteActivityDesignerTheme))]`
		The ActivityDesignerTheme attribute will be placed on the ActivityDesigner class.

Add an ActivityDesigner attribute onto the custom activity and test the theme.	1 Navigate to the CreateSubSite activity and add the following attribute onto the class:
	
	`[Designer(typeof(`
	`CreateSubSiteActivityDesigner))]`
	
	2 Build the project and navigate back to the workflow template. Notice how the activity's background is now orange.
	
	NOTE: Visual Studio likes to cache the display properties of these actions. To clear the cache, close Visual Studio, remove the DLL from the GAC (c:\windows\system32\assembly, if necessary), and relaunch Visual Studio.	

The final step is to update the activity's icon so that is the same icon you configured in the toolbox in the previous section. Add a ToolboxBitmap attribute to the activity's class to configure the icon.	1 If your icon is a .gif file, it needs to be a .png instead. Save the icon as a .png and add it as a resource like you did for the ToolboxItem.
	
	2 Change the build action of the .png to an Embedded Resource through the properties of the .png.
	
	3 Add the ToolboxBitmap attribute to the CreateSubSite class, build the project, and navigate back to the workflow template to see if the icon renders:
	
	`[ToolboxBitmap(typeof(CreateSubSite),`
	`    "Resources.STSICON.png")]`
	
	NOTE: When you add a file as a resource, it places it in a folder called Resources. Because CreateSubSite is at the root namespace of the project, you can use your activity in the typeof; otherwise, you'll need to specify a different class that is at the root Many people create an empty class at the root namespace called ResourceFinder for this purpose.
		
		When you're finished, your CreateSubSiteActivityDesign.cs file will look similar to listing 11.8.

Listing 11.8   CreateSubSiteActivityDesigner.cs in its entirety

```
using System;
using System.Collections.Generic;
using System.Linq;
using System.Text;
using System.Workflow.ComponentModel.Design;
using System.Drawing;

namespace CustomActivities
```

```
{
    [ActivityDesignerTheme(typeof(CreateSubSiteActivityDesignerTheme))]
    public class CreateSubSiteActivityDesigner : ActivityDesigner
    {
    }

    public class CreateSubSiteActivityDesignerTheme : ActivityDesignerTheme
    {
        public CreateSubSiteActivityDesignerTheme(WorkflowTheme theme)
            : base(theme)
        {
            this.BackColorStart = Color.Orange;
            this.BackColorEnd = Color.OrangeRed;
            this.BackgroundStyle = System.Drawing.Drawing2D.
                LinearGradientMode.Horizontal;
        }
    }
}
```

Now that you've conquered leaf activities, it's time to take things to the next level. Composite activities allow you to create activities that contain child activities. Most of the information covered in this leaf activities section is foundational to composites and, with it under your belt, you're ready to tackle something more advanced.

11.2 *Building custom composite activities*

Composite activities are most helpful when you want to create reusable groups of activities. For instance, you may have five or six activities all working together, and you want a parent activity that can package those child activities, making them reusable in other workflows. This is the first and most common use for composite activities.

A second use is for creating control flow activities. Activities that control the flow of work are called control flow composite activities. This includes activities that are iterative, such as the while activity, and those that are not iterative, such as the IfElse and parallel activities. You could create a custom composite that served a similar purpose as a for loop (rather than while loop). The subject of creating custom control flow activities is a bit beyond the scope of this book. A book focused solely on Windows Workflow Foundation techniques may be a good option for researching these more advanced techniques. Rather, let's focus on composites that are more common, such as parent and child composites for reuse purposes.

Composite activities extend the CompositeActivity class. The while, IfElse, sequence, and parallel activities all extend CompositeActivity. When you want to create a custom composite, you have the option of extending CompositeActivity directly or to extend a composite activity such as the sequence activity to serve as your base. The latter is the most common approach.

As figure 11.7 shows, when you extend a sequential activity, you're left with an activity that looks identical to the sequence activity on the activity's Designer surface. It, then, becomes a simple process of dragging and dropping your child activities inside the custom sequential activity and, thereafter, building and reusing that activity in as many workflows as you wish.

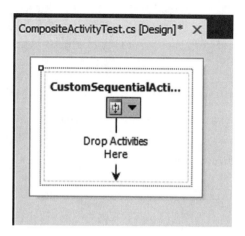

Figure 11.7   You can create a composite activity
that extends another composite activity. As in this
case, you can extend a sequence activity for quick
access to dropping child activities in that execute
sequence.

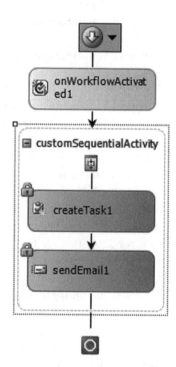

Dependency properties also play a role in composite activities. Notice how in figure 11.8 all child activities inside the custom sequential composite activity display padlock icons. This is informing you that you cannot edit those activities. Rather, you must edit the composite activity that is packaging those child activities. In regards to properties, what if those locked child activities have properties that need to be set? You can *promote* those properties to the parent composite activity, and they will show up in the composite's property window. You can only promote dependency properties, not the standard .NET properties.

With the introduction out of the way, let's go ahead and build a custom composite activity. Your composite activity is going to be a wrapper for the CreateSubSite activity you built in the previous section. In addition to creating a subsite, it will also email the site collection administrator notifying them that the site was provisioned. Follow the steps in table 11.7 to create this composite activity.

And that's it folks! It's easy to see that building reusable composite activities is not difficult. Listing 11.9 shows the CreateSitePlusNotify activity code in its entirety for your reference.

Figure 11.8   When you drop a
composite activity onto a workflow
template, the child activities will be
locked, and you won't be able to edit
them or their properties.

Table 11.7   Creating a custom composite activity that contains child activities

Action	Steps	Result

Within the CustomActivities project, create a new class that extends the sequence activity.	1 Right-click the project, and select New, Class… and name the class CreateSitePlusNotify.
	
	2 Add a using statement to each of the following namespaces:
	`System.Workflow.Activities`
	`System.Workflow.ComponentModel`
	`System.ComponentModel`
	
	3 Make the class public and have it extend the SequenceActivity base:
	`public class`
	`CreateSitePlusNotify:`
	`    SequenceActivity`
	
	4 Build the project and the icon of the activity file should change such that it looks like the icon for CreateSubSite.cs. After it does, double-click the activity to open the activity's template:
	
	☐ ⊞ 🖿 Resources
	⊞ 📄 Workflow1
	    📄 CreateSitePlusNotify.cs
	    📄 CreateSubSite.cs
	    📄 CreateSubSiteActivityDesigner.cs
	
	NOTE: You may have to close and reopen Visual Studio to get the icon to update.	

Configure the ApplyActivation activity.	1 Drag and drop the ApplyActivation activity onto CreateSitePlusNotify's template. 2 Bind the __Context property of the ApplyActivation activity to a new member field called workflowContext.	
Configure the CreateSubSite activity.	1 Below the ApplyActivation activity, drop the CreateSubSite activity. 2 Provide a SiteName and SiteTemplate for the activity.	

Table 11.7   Creating a custom composite activity that contains child activities *(continued)*

Action	Steps	Result
Bind the SiteUrl to a new Dependency Property.	1 Click on the "..." ellipsis inside the SiteUrl property. 2 Bind the property to a new member (property, NOT field) named SiteUrl. **NOTE:** By binding to a new property, you promote the property and make it available on the parent's property editor.	Enabled True SiteName Contoso Team Site SiteTemplate STS ⊞ SiteUrl Activity=CreateSitePlusN

Configure the sendEmail activity.	1 Drop a sendEmail activity under the CreateSubSite property.
	
	2 Edit the correlation token property of the activity to name the token something like CreateToken and, under the plus symbol next to the correlation token properly, specify the owner as CreateSubSitePlusNotify:
	
	CC
	⊟ CorrelationToken CreateToken
	   OwnerActivityName CreateSitePlusNotify
	   Description
	   Enabled True
	
	3 Enter text into the Body and Subject properties and promote the To property to a new dependency property named SCAdminEmail, similarly to your methodology in the previous action.
		A sendEmail activity will be configured and the To property will be promoted to the parent composite activity.

Because you created the activity off the Add > New Item > Class template, rather than the Activity template, you need to do a few things that otherwise would have been done for you. Add a constructor to the activity and two attributes to the InitializeComponent method.	1 Right-click the CreateSitePlusNotify activity and choose View code. Notice how a method named InitializeComponent was created for you with all the child activities configured.
	
	2 Add the following attributes to the InitializeComponent method:
	
	`[System.Diagnostics.`
	`    DebuggerNonUserCode]`
	`[System.CodeDom.Compiler.`
	`    GeneratedCode("","")]`
	
	NOTE: You're not supposed to directly edit this system-generated InitializeComponent method!
	
	3 Add a constructor to the activity:
	
	`public CreateSitePlusNotify()`
	`{`
	`    InitializeComponent();`
	`}`
		A constructor is added to the activity and two attributes are added to the InitializeComponent method.

Table 11.7 Creating a custom composite activity that contains child activities *(continued)*

Action	Steps	Result
Build the project and drop the CreateSitePlusNotify activity onto Workflow1's template.		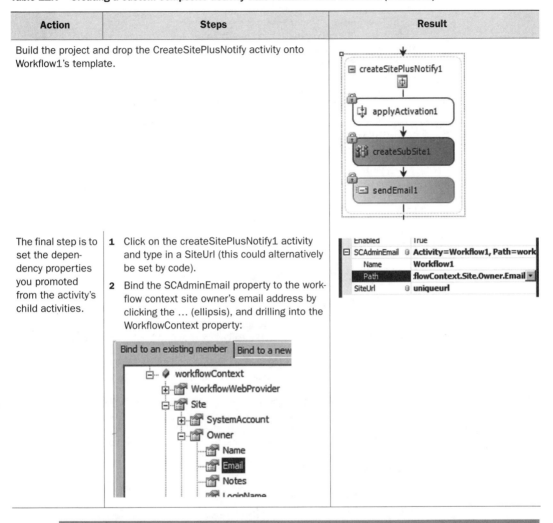
The final step is to set the dependency properties you promoted from the activity's child activities.	**1** Click on the createSitePlusNotify1 activity and type in a SiteUrl (this could alternatively be set by code). **2** Bind the SCAdminEmail property to the workflow context site owner's email address by clicking the … (ellipsis), and drilling into the WorkflowContext property:	

Listing 11.9 CreateSitePlusNotify activity code

```
using System;
using System.Collections.Generic;
using System.Linq;
using System.Text;
using System.Workflow.Activities;
using System.Workflow.ComponentModel;
using System.ComponentModel;

namespace CustomActivities
{
    public class CreateSitePlusNotify : SequenceActivity
    {
        private Microsoft.SharePoint.WorkflowActions.
            ApplyActivation applyActivation1;
```

```
private CreateSubSite createSubSite1;
public Microsoft.SharePoint.WorkflowActions.
    WorkflowContext workflowContext = new
    Microsoft.SharePoint.WorkflowActions.WorkflowContext();
private Microsoft.SharePoint.WorkflowActions.SendEmail sendEmail1;
public static System.Workflow.ComponentModel.DependencyProperty
    SiteUrlProperty = DependencyProperty.Register(
        "SiteUrl", typeof(System.String),
        typeof(CustomActivities.CreateSitePlusNotify));

public static System.Workflow.ComponentModel.DependencyProperty
    SCAdminEmailProperty = DependencyProperty.Register(
        "SCAdminEmail", typeof(System.String),
        typeof(CustomActivities.CreateSitePlusNotify));

public CreateSitePlusNotify()
{
    InitializeComponent();
}

private void InitializeComponent()
{
    this.CanModifyActivities = true;
    System.Workflow.Runtime.CorrelationToken correlationtoken1 =
        new System.Workflow.Runtime.CorrelationToken();
    System.Workflow.ComponentModel.ActivityBind activitybind1 =
        new System.Workflow.ComponentModel.ActivityBind();
    System.Workflow.ComponentModel.ActivityBind activitybind2 =
        new System.Workflow.ComponentModel.ActivityBind();
    System.Workflow.ComponentModel.ActivityBind activitybind3 =
        new System.Workflow.ComponentModel.ActivityBind();
    this.sendEmail1 =
        new Microsoft.SharePoint.WorkflowActions.SendEmail();
    this.createSubSite1 = new CustomActivities.CreateSubSite();
    this.applyActivation1 =
        new Microsoft.SharePoint.WorkflowActions.ApplyActivation();
    //
    // sendEmail1
    //
    this.sendEmail1.BCC = null;
    this.sendEmail1.Body = "Body";
    this.sendEmail1.CC = null;
    correlationtoken1.Name = "CreateToken";
    correlationtoken1.OwnerActivityName = "CreateSitePlusNotify";
    this.sendEmail1.CorrelationToken = correlationtoken1;
    this.sendEmail1.From = null;
    this.sendEmail1.Headers = null;
    this.sendEmail1.IncludeStatus = false;
    this.sendEmail1.Name = "sendEmail1";
    this.sendEmail1.Subject = "Subject";
    activitybind1.Name = "CreateSitePlusNotify";
    activitybind1.Path = "SCAdminEmail";
    this.sendEmail1.SetBinding(
        Microsoft.SharePoint.WorkflowActions.SendEmail.ToProperty,
        ((System.Workflow.ComponentModel.ActivityBind)
            (activitybind1)));
    //
```

```
// createSubSite1
//
this.createSubSite1.@__Context = null;
this.createSubSite1.Name = "createSubSite1";
this.createSubSite1.SiteName = "Contoso Team Site";
this.createSubSite1.SiteTemplate =
    CustomActivities.CreateSubSite.SiteTemplates.STS;
activitybind2.Name = "CreateSitePlusNotify";
activitybind2.Path = "SiteUrl";
this.createSubSite1.SetBinding(
    CustomActivities.CreateSubSite.SiteUrlProperty,
    ((System.Workflow.ComponentModel.ActivityBind)
        (activitybind2)));
//
// applyActivation1
//
activitybind3.Name = "CreateSitePlusNotify";
activitybind3.Path = "workflowContext";
this.applyActivation1.@__WorkflowProperties = null;
this.applyActivation1.Name = "applyActivation1";
this.applyActivation1.SetBinding(
    Microsoft.SharePoint.WorkflowActions.
        ApplyActivation.@__ContextProperty,
    ((System.Workflow.ComponentModel.ActivityBind)
        (activitybind3)));
//
// CreateSitePlusNotify
//
this.Activities.Add(this.applyActivation1);
this.Activities.Add(this.createSubSite1);
this.Activities.Add(this.sendEmail1);
this.Name = "CreateSitePlusNotify";
this.CanModifyActivities = false;
}

[System.ComponentModel.DesignerSerializationVisibilityAttribute(
    DesignerSerializationVisibility.Visible)]
[System.ComponentModel.BrowsableAttribute(true)]
[System.ComponentModel.CategoryAttribute("Misc")]
public string SiteUrl
{
    get
    {
        return ((string)(base.GetValue(CustomActivities.
            CreateSitePlusNotify.SiteUrlProperty)));
    }
    set
    {
        base.SetValue(CustomActivities.
            CreateSitePlusNotify.SiteUrlProperty, value);
    }
}

[System.ComponentModel.DesignerSerializationVisibilityAttribute(
    DesignerSerializationVisibility.Visible)]
[System.ComponentModel.BrowsableAttribute(true)]
[System.ComponentModel.CategoryAttribute("Misc")]
```

```
public string SCAdminEmail
{
    get
    {
        return ((string)(base.GetValue(CustomActivities.
            CreateSitePlusNotify.SCAdminEmailProperty)));
    }
    set
    {
        base.SetValue(CustomActivities.
            CreateSitePlusNotify.SCAdminEmailProperty, value);
    }
}
}
}
```

11.3 Publishing activities to SharePoint Designer

No doubt, many people building SharePoint Workflows won't be programmers and will use tools like SharePoint Designer instead. The trouble is they often will still need to meet complex business requirements that typically can be met only with Visual Studio workflows. How does someone narrow the chasm between SharePoint Designer and Visual Studio? Publishing your custom activities into SharePoint Designer as custom actions is the easiest way to do this.

When SharePoint Designer connects to a SharePoint site, it first goes to the server and pulls down files on the server with an ACTIONS extension. It's within this file, or files, that SharePoint Designer knows what actions and conditions it should make available to its users when they're developing workflows. All you (the programmers) have to do is create your own ACTIONS file to get your custom activities deployed to SharePoint Designer. The final task is to mark your activity as safe in the web.config of the web application. Follow the steps in table 11.8 to deploy your custom CreateSub-Site activity into SharePoint Designer.

Table 11.8 Publishing the CreateSubSite activity to SharePoint Designer

Action	Steps	Result
Add a mapped folder in the CustomActivities project.	1 Right-click the project, and choose Add > SharePoint Mapped Folder… 2 Select the Workflow folder under TEMPLATE > 1033: 	A folder is added to the project and mapped to the SharePoint file system. Any files in the folder are automatically deployed to SharePoint.

Table 11.8   Publishing the CreateSubSite activity to SharePoint Designer *(continued)*

Action	Steps	Result

Create a new XML file in the new Workflow folder in the project.	**1** Right-click the workflow folder and choose Add > New Item.
	2 Under the Data tab, select XML file and name the file CustomActivities.ACTIONS and then click Add.
		⊞ 📦 Package
		⊞ 📁 Resources
		⊟ 📁 Workflow
		       📄 CustomActivities.ACTIONS
		⊞ 📊 Workflow1
		     📄 CreateSitePlusNotify.cs
		     📄 CreateSubSite.cs

Enter listing 11.10 into the ACTIONS file.

NOTE: Make sure you enter your own PublicKeyToken in the Assembly section. The easiest way to get your token is by browsing to C:\Windows\system32\assembly, finding your assembly, right-clicking, and choosing properties and then copying your token out of the properties window.

The ACTIONS file is populated with the needed XML that tells SharePoint Designer to load your custom action.

Action	Steps	Result
Add an authorized type in your web application's web.config file.	**1** Open your web.config file (usually under c:\inetpub\wwwroot\wss\virtual directories\[your web app]) **2** Find the authorizedTypes section within System.Workflow.ComponentModel.WorkflowCompiler. **3** Add a new authorized type: `<authorizedType Assembly="CustomActivities, Version=1.0.0.0, Culture=neutral, PublicKeyToken=60cb170cc12e2631" Namespace="CustomActivities" TypeName="*" Authorized="True" />` **NOTE:** Make sure you enter your own PublicKeyToken as you did for the ACTIONS file!	An authorized type is added into the web.config telling SharePoint that you trust your assembly and namespace.

Listing 11.10   CustomActivities.ACTIONS

```xml
<?xml version="1.0" encoding="utf-8"?>
<WorkflowInfo Language="en-us">
  <Actions Sequential="then" Parallel="and">
    <Action Name="Create Sub Site"
        ClassName="CustomActivities.CreateSubSite"
        Assembly="CustomActivities, Version=1.0.0.0, Culture=neutral,
            PublicKeyToken=929a2d1b8d7f5b6c"
        AppliesTo="all"
        Category="Custom Actions">
      <RuleDesigner Sentence="Create sub-site named %1
            with the URL of %2 and using the %3 site template.">
        <FieldBind Field="SiteName" Text="name" Id="1" />
        <FieldBind Field="SiteUrl" Text="url" Id="2" />
        <FieldBind Field="SiteTemplate" DesignerType="Dropdown"
            Text="template" Id="3">
          <Option Name="Blog" Value="BLOG"/>
          <Option Name="Meeting Workspace" Value="MPS"/>
          <Option Name="Team Site" Value="STS"/>
          <Option Name="Wiki" Value="WIKI"/>
```

❶ Assembly reference
❷ Category in Actions dropdown in SPD
❸ User specified field values
❹ User specified field values
❺ User specified field values

```
        </FieldBind>                          ➏ Values mapped back
      </RuleDesigner>                            to dependency              ➐ Workflow-
      <Parameters>                      ◄──┘     parameters                   Context
        <Parameter Name="__Context"                                  ◄──┘     token
            Type="Microsoft.SharePoint.WorkflowActions.WorkflowContext,
            Microsoft.SharePoint.WorkflowActions" Direction="In"/>
        <Parameter Name="SiteTemplate" Type="System.Enum, mscorlib"
            Direction="In" />
        <Parameter Name="SiteName" Type="System.String, mscorlib"
            Direction="In" />
        <Parameter Name="SiteUrl" Type="System.String, mscorlib"
            Direction="In" />
      </Parameters>
    </Action>
  </Actions>
</WorkflowInfo>
```

You'll notice in this listing that an action has three main elements: an assembly reference, a RuleDesigner, and Properties. The attributes on the Action element make up the assembly reference that tells SharePoint Designer what assembly your custom activities is contained in ➊. Notice how it's referencing your CustomActivities assembly and default namespace. Also notice the PublickKeyToken setting in the assembly reference. Make sure to specify your own token here. Another interesting attribute is the Category attribute ➋. This attribute tells SharePoint Designer in which category of actions to put your custom activity (figure 11.9). The next main category of elements in this ACTIONS file is the RuleDesigner element. The RuleDesigner element has a Sentence attri-bute ➌

that renders to the user. You can use this sentence to gather information from the user. Within the sentence, you can add tags in the format of percent/id (for example, %1). This tag is mapped to the field with ID equal to 1. Take SiteName, for example ➍. The Site-Name field has a text attribute set to *name* which will be rendered as a blue link and, when users click the link, they'll be prompted to specify a value for the site's name. That value is mapped to one of the parameters in the Parameters element ➏. Those parameters are, in turn, mapped to dependency properties in the .NET activity. This is how values specified by the SharePoint Designer user are passed into the .NET activity.

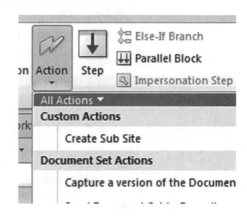

Figure 11.9   When you deploy your custom activity into SharePoint Designer, you can specify a category name to place your activity in, such as Custom Actions.

There are a couple more points that we need to hit quickly. Notice how the Site-Template field has a DesignerType attribute ➎. You can use this designer type to con-trol how you want the user to specify the value. In the case of SiteTemplate, it's rendered with a dropdown populated by hardcoded options. Refer to table 11.9 for DesignerType settings.

Table 11.9   DesignerType options

Option	Purpose
Boolean	Dropdown shown with true and false as options
ChooseDoclibItem	Document library selector
ChooseListItem	List item selector
CreateListItem	Default pop-up
Date	Date/Time selector
Dropdown	Dropdown box with Option elements to populate dropdown
Email	Advanced Email control pop up
FieldNames	Dropdown with options for all the fields in the current list or library
Float	Text box allowing for numbers with decimals
Hyperlink	URL browser pop-up allowing to you browse to a local or remote UR
Integer	Text box allowing for only integer numbers
ListNames	Dropdown showing options for all the lists in the current web
Operator	Dropdown showing operator options, for example, <, >, !, =, and so on. Operators must be statically defined as Option elements.
ParameterNames	Dropdown showing a list of all variables defined in the workflow
Person	Person or group selector
SinglePerson	Person or group selector, but you can only select one person or group
Stringbuilder	Advanced text box
Survey	Default pop-up
Text	Default pop-up
TextArea	Default pop-up
UpdateListItem	Default pop-up
writablefieldNames	Dropdown showing either fields in the current list or the list of document libraries that are editable by the running user

Lastly, remember the _ _*Context* dependency property you created for your CreateSub-Site activity? You gave it an odd name because SharePoint Designer looks for a dependency property with that name and is smart enough to take the workflow's WorkflowContext object and assign it to the __*Context* parameter ❼. Other options for this are found in table 11.10.

Table 11.10 Parameter tokens

Token	Purpose
__ActivationProperties	SPWorkflowActivationProperties: used to get workflow information such as when the workflow started.
__ListId	String: gets the list name the workflow is running on.
__ListItem	Integer: gets the ID of the list item the workflow is running on.
__Context	WorkflowContext: gets helpful objects such as SPSite and SPWeb.

With your ACTIONS file in place, you're ready to publish your activity. Build and deploy the project. This will update the assembly and publish your ACTIONS file into the Workflows folder on the server. Open SharePoint Designer and connect to a site. Create a new workflow (any type) and SharePoint Designer will then look at your custom ACTIONS file to determine what actions to make available to you. You should notice your custom action in the Custom Actions category. Figure 11.10 shows what your action looks like after it has been added to the workflow template, and the parameters have been specified.

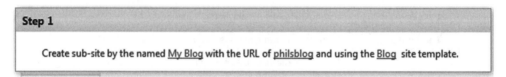

Figure 11.10   The sentence in the ACTIONS file was rendered with all the fields and parameters editable by the user.

11.4 *Building custom conditions for SharePoint Designer*

You've finished building a custom action for SharePoint Designer, but what about custom conditions? Building custom conditions for SharePoint Designer can introduce power into your SharePoint Designer workflows. For instance, you could write a custom condition that checks an external data source or system before executing on a block of activities. The best part is that it's easy to do! All you have to do is write a .NET method that returns a Boolean and make that method available in SharePoint Designer as a condition by adding an element in an ACTIONS file.

To build on your CreateSubSite example, you're going to write a custom condition that you can use to check for URL availability. It's convenient that you can create a subsite from a SharePoint Designer workflow, but how will you know that the URL you've specified is available? A subsite might already exist that's using that URL. Your custom activity will take the proposed URL as a parameter and confirm that a site is not using that URL. If not, the condition will return True; otherwise, it will return False. Follow the steps in table 11.11 to create and publish your condition to SharePoint Designer.

Table 11.11 Creating a custom condition and deploying it into SharePoint Designer

Action	Steps	Result

Create a new class file named SubSiteExists-Condition.	**1** Add a new class into the CustomActivities project named SubSiteExistsCondition.cs.
	2 Make the class public and add using statements for the following namespaces:
	`Microsoft.SharePoint.WorkflowActions;`
	3 Create a public static method named SubSiteExists with the following code:
	<pre>public static bool SubSiteExists(
	    WorkflowContext context, string listId,
	    int itemId, string url)
	{
	    if (context.Web.Webs.Names.Contains(url))
	        return true;
	    else
	        return false;
	}</pre>
		A new class is created with a single method that returns True or False. SharePoint Designer uses this Boolean return type to determine the outcome of the condition.

The first thing you'll see in the SubSiteExists method are three parameters you didn't think you would need. The first three parameters are required parameters. The fourth is optional but needed for your example. You check to see if the current site has a subsite with a URL (Name) that is the same as the URL passed into the method in the fourth parameter. If so, return True. If no, return False. Next, all you need to do is add a few elements into our ACTIONS file and you'll be set to go!

Table 11.11 Creating a custom condition and deploying it into SharePoint Designer *(continued)*

Action	Steps	Result
Add a Conditions element into the ACTIONS file.	**1** Above the Actions element, add the Conditions element found in listing 11.11. **2** Again, update the PublicKeyToken to reflect your token.	In addition to your custom action, the ACTIONS file will also be publishing a custom condition pointing to the SubSiteExists method.

Listing 11.11 Conditions Element

```
<Conditions>
  <Condition Name="If Sub Site Exists"
             FunctionName="SubSiteExists"                          ❶ Specifies
             ClassName="CustomActivities.SubSiteExistsCondition"      method name
             Assembly="CustomActivities, Version=1.0.0.0, Culture=neutral,
               PublicKeyToken=60cb170cc12e2631"
             AppliesTo="all"                                  Uses token instead of ❷
             Category="Custom Conditions">                       parameter name
    <RuleDesigner Sentence="Sub Site exists with a relative url of %1">
      <FieldBind Id="1" Field="_1_" Text="url" DesignerType="TextArea" />
```

```
      </RuleDesigner>
      <Parameters>
        <Parameter Name="_1_" Type="System.String, mscorlib" Direction="In"/>
      </Parameters>
    </Condition>
</Conditions>
```

The XML for Conditions is nearly identical to the XML for Actions. There are only a few small differences. First, in addition to declaring the assembly and namespace, you also must declare the method name that will execute your condition ❶. Second, notice how you're no longer referencing the field name or what you'd expect to see, the URL ❷. Rather, you're using a _1_ token to tell the Designer to pass the string into the first optional parameter. Even though URL is the fourth parameter in the method, it is still the first optional parameter. Additional parameters would follow a similar pattern to _2_, _3_, and so on.

That should be the last step. Build and deploy your project and create a new workflow in SharePoint Designer (or edit existing). You'll need to close and reopen the connection to get the latest ACTIONS file. When you finish, add the If Sub Site exists condition and add an Else branch to it. Inside the If branch, add a Logger to log that the URL has already been taken. In the Else branch, add a Create sub-site action along with a Logger to log that the site was created successfully. When you're finished, your template should look something like figure 11.11. Publish and test your workflow.

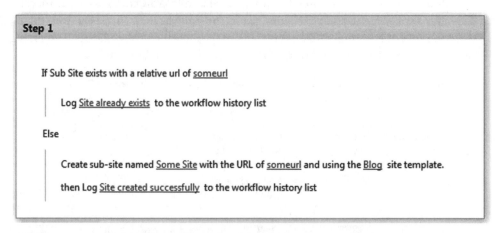

Figure 11.11   Custom conditions can also be deployed into SharePoint Designer. This condition checks to see if a URL has already been taken by another subsite.

11.5 *Summary*

Knowing how to build custom activities is a fundamental skill for any workflow developer, even SharePoint workflow developers. By building custom activities, you can gain the benefits of improved code maintainability and reuse. You'll have a better maintained solution because you're less likely to have a workflow template with 2,000+ lines of nasty looking code. Rather, you have your code split into the various activities (classes) instead of one big template (class). You'll have a better reuse of code as well because now you can start dropping your custom activities onto other workflows rather than recreating them from scratch each time.

As far as the types of activities go, you have the simplest activities called leaf activities and more complex activities called composite activities. Examples of leaf activities are CreateTask, Delay, SetState, and OnWorkflowItemChanged. These activities do one thing, and they do it well. Composite activities, on the other hand, are activities that contain child activities. Some examples are the while, IfElse, sequence, and parallel activities. These activities are excellent for packaging larger chunks of reusable business processes that other workflows can use.

Both types of activities can be published into SharePoint Designer to help add more robust functionality for workflows created from that tool. This is done by publishing an ACTIONS file into the file system on each server in the farm. When SharePoint Designer connects to a site, it first downloads this ACTIONS file so it knows what actions to make available to the user building the workflow. Custom conditions also can be deployed into SharePoint Designer. A custom condition is a public static method that returns a Boolean. Add the condition into the ACTIONS file and point it to your method, and you're rolling.

A bag of
workflow developer tricks

This chapter covers
- Handling faults and debugging workflows
- Versioning workflows
- Using workflow event receivers
- Receiving external events with pluggable services
- Working with the workflow object model

Everything in the first 11 chapters of this book was fundamental to a SharePoint workflow developer. We discussed out-of-the-box SharePoint workflows, other non-developer techniques with SharePoint Designer and Office Visio, workflows with Visual Studio, and custom forms. With chapter 12, you round out the SharePoint developers skills with a few key techniques.

These techniques include how to debug and handle faults in your workflows, version workflows, set up event receivers, send and receive external events, and work with the SharePoint workflow object model. Debugging and exception handling are an obvious must, but versioning is not well understood. If you don't properly version your workflows, idle workflow instances might break when they resume execution.

Why study event receivers in a workflow book? Event receivers can save you time if they fit the business requirements. Event receivers are typically easier and faster to create for smaller, one-time processing than their workflow counterparts and a few new events for workflows.

Sending and receiving events to and from external sources is often a must for larger business processes. This is handled through a new feature in SharePoint 2010 called pluggable workflow services. With the use of two activities and a new class called SPWorkflowDataExchangeService, you can easily communicate with your organization's line of business applications.

Finally, every developer should take a peek at the workflow object model found in the Microsoft.SharePoint.Workflow namespace. You never know when you may need to programmatically start or stop a workflow or perhaps retrieve a workflow's tasks or history.

12.1 Fault handling and debugging workflows

If you don't properly handle exceptions in the workflow and an error occurs, you'll get the dreaded Error Occurred string in the workflow status, without a clue as to what went wrong. You're left with debugging your workflow and, if you don't know how to debug, you're up a creek.

Let's start with what's easy—debugging. You debug your workflows almost the same way as any other .NET application you build. Within your workflow's code view, right-click on the line of code where you want to start debugging and choose Breakpoint > Insert Breakpoint (figure 12.1). Also note that you can debug the activities on the templates. To do this, right-click the activity you want to debug and select Breakpoint > Insert Breakpoint again.

The next thing to do is attach the Visual Studio debugger to the w3wp.exe SharePoint process (figure 12.2). In Visual Studio, click the Debug menu dropdown and select Attach to Process. Scroll down and select the w3wp process and click Attach. If there are multiple w3wp processes, select all that show up. If you don't see the process, navigate to the SharePoint site to start the process, then go back to the process list and click the Refresh button. Also ensure that Show processes in all sessions is checked. After you attach, you can start your workflow, and Visual Studio will automatically step into the debugger when the line of code or activity hits.

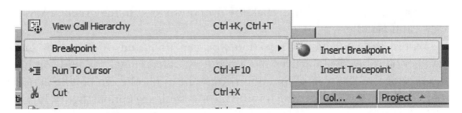

Figure 12.1   You debug a workflow in almost the same way you debug any .NET program. Add a breakpoint and attach the debugger to the SharePoint process.

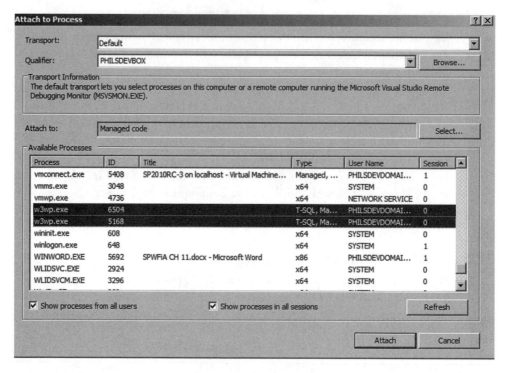

Figure 12.2   You must attach to the w3wp SharePoint process to debug your SharePoint workflows.

Handling exceptions is a bit different than your standard .NET application. When you're in a workflow template, there's no obvious place to add a Try/Catch block. Many developers never handle exceptions and spend a good deal of time debugging and trying to figure out where the error occurred. The better approach is to use the FaultHandler activity at the root of your workflow (green arrow) as well as all your composite activities (sequence, parallel, IfElse, and so on).

Within the FaultHandler activity, you can insert activities that handle the error in an appropriate way. With SharePoint, it's popular to log the error, location, and stack trace into the workflow's history list. This makes determining the error and location easier.

At the least, every workflow should have a Fault Handler set up at the root of the workflow template. To do this, click the dropdown next to the green arrow and select View Fault Handlers.

Within the fault handlers section, you can drag and drop one or more Fault-Handler activities. Each activity has a property called FaultType, and you need to set this property to the type of exception you want to handle. To handle all exceptions, set it to System.Exception, which is the most generic exception (figure 12.3). Alternatively, you could set it to a custom exception to handle errors that are specific to your workflow. This is the best approach; it makes debugging easier because you'll know when and why your custom exceptions are being raised.

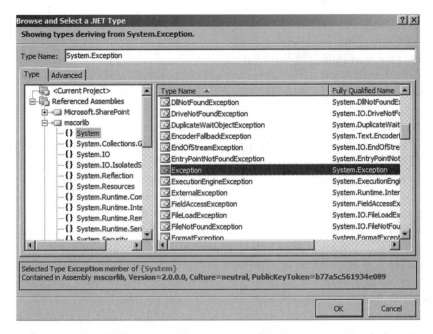

Figure 12.3 When you add a fault handler, you need to specify the exception to be handled.

After you have specified the exception to be handled, you should add actions to react to the error appropriately. It's helpful to use the Log to History List activity to log a more descriptive error and the stack trace to help with debugging (figure 12.4).

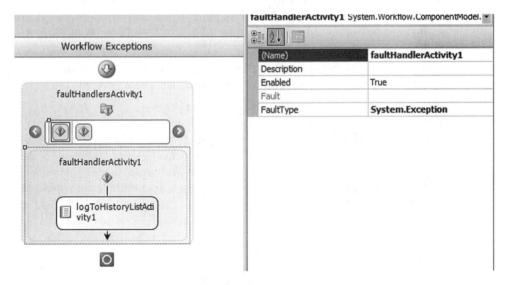

Figure 12.4 After you specify the exception to be handled, log an informative error description and, possibly, the stack trace to help with debugging. You can do this by dropping the Log to History List activity within the fault handler.

12.2 Versioning workflows

You built this compelling Visual Studio workflow and deployed it into production. But, after a few months, the business requests a small change to the workflow. You go back into the workflow code, add a few activities to fulfill the request, and redeploy the workflow into production. To your shock, all the workflows start breaking! You're frantic because you're certain you adequately unit-tested the changes and can't figure out what might be going wrong. You didn't version your workflow.

Workflow versioning is an important technique. When a workflow goes idle, the state of the workflow is saved into the database. This saving of a workflow's state is called hydration. When the workflow resumes, the state is dehydrated out of the database, and the workflow starts processing again. Versioning is important because, if you change the assembly while the workflow is hydrated (saved in the database), there's no guarantee that, when the workflow is dehydrated, it will match the construct of the new assembly. If it doesn't match the construct upon deserialization, the workflow will break. Changes like adding or removing activities and changing property values may necessitate a new workflow version. The best practice is to create a new version every time rather than deploying the assembly and crossing your fingers.

Think of a new workflow version as a new workflow. The basic technique is to make your assembly increment the version number with each build (rather than leaving it at 1.0.0.0 forever). Then, for each upgrade, you create a new feature for that version of the workflow, pointing to the new assembly. You add the new assembly into the global assembly cache (GAC) alongside the old assembly. Last, you specify that the old version cannot start new instances of the workflow and then you add the new workflow onto the list. This way, the old version of the assembly never changes, so there's no risk of hydrated workflows breaking when they are dehydrated. You deploy another version of the assembly and add the new workflow to the list and disable previous versions. You don't want to remove the previous versions because that will orphan those running instances. For the full set of procedures, follow the steps in table 12.1 to create a new version for an existing workflow.

Old version overwritten

If you don't create a new version and merely upgrade the solution, all running instances of the workflow will be deleted. The old version of the workflow will be removed, and the new version will be added with zero running instances. Don't upgrade without creating a new version unless you're entirely sure you don't need to retain the running instances.

Table 12.1   Creating a new version for an existing workflow

Action	Steps	Result

Create version 1.0.0.0 in your workflow's elements file.	1 In the Elements.xml file of your workflow, replace $assemblyname$ in CodeBesideAssembly with the following:
	
	`[assembly name], Version=1.0.0.0,`
	`Culture=neutral, PublicKeyToken=[token]`
		Your workflow's feature is now specifically referencing the 1.0.0.0 version of your assembly.

Table 12.1   Creating a new version for an existing workflow *(continued)*

Action	Steps	Result
	2 Replace [assembly name] with your assembly name. 3 Replace [token] with your public key token. You can do this by finding your assembly in the GAC (c:\windows\assembly) and right-clicking it, choosing Properties, and copying the token. 4 Change the name of the workflow in the Elements file to reference the new version. **NOTE:** This ensures that the user working with the workflow knows what version it is. It has no technical implications. For example: **Workflow** Select a workflow to add to this document library. If the workflow template you want does not appear, contact your administrator to get it added to your site collection or workspace. Select a workflow template: Workflow1 - Version 1.0.0.0 Workflow1 - Version 2.0.0.0 Collect Feedback - SharePoint 20- Collect Signatures - SharePoint 2 5 Add a copy of version 1.0.0.0 to solution package by double-clicking on the Package and, under the Advanced tab, add an existing assembly and browse to your 1.0.0.0 assembly version: Additional Assemblies: Source ▼ Deployment Target Location Add bin\Version 1.0.0.0\TestWFVersions.dll GlobalAssemblyCache Version 1.0.0.0\TestWFVersions. Edit... Delete **NOTE:** Notice how the Location and Source of the assembly are in a path under Version 1.0.0.0. When the package is created, the 1.0.0.0 version is put in its own path. It cannot be in the same path as the current version because they both have the same name.	
With version 1.0.0.0 established, you can now simulate the need to create version 2.0.0.0. Change the version of the assembly to 2.0.0.0.	1 Under the Properties folder in the solution, open the AssemblyInfo.cs file. 2 Scroll to the bottom of the file and change the two versions to 2.0.0.0.	The current version of the workflow's assembly is now 2.0.0.0.
Update the workflow's Elements.xml file to reference both the version 1.0.0.0 workflow and now the new 2.0.0.0 version.	1 Under the workflow, open the Elements.xml file. 2 Copy the Workflow element in its entirety and paste it directly after the </workflow> tag. 3 Change the name and the version (in the CodeBesideAssembly) of the second workflow to reference version 2.0.0.0. 4 Change the ID in the 2.0.0.0 version to a new GUID. You can create a new GUID by using the Create GUID tool under the tools menu. 5 Build and deploy the solution.	The workflow's feature now enables two workflows. The main difference is that one is referencing the 1.0.0.0 assembly, and the other is referencing the 2.0.0.0 assembly.

Table 12.1   Creating a new version for an existing workflow *(continued)*

Action	Steps	Result
Activate version 2.0.0.0.	1 Within the root site in the site collection, click Site Actions and, then, click Site Settings. 2 Click Site Collection Features. 3 Deactivate and reactivate your workflow's feature.	The 2.0.0.0 workflow is able to associate with lists or sites.
With version 2.0.0.0 deployed and activated, you now need to prevent any new instances of version 1.0.0.0 from being created.	1 Navigate to the workflow settings page of the list or site you're working on. 2 Click Remove a workflow. 3 Change version 1.0.0.0 to not allow new instances and click OK (figure 12.5).	The 1.0.0.0 version can no longer be started, but running instances dehydrate without error.

Workflows

Specify workflows to remove from this document library. You can optionally let currently running workflows finish.

Workflow	Instances	Allow	No New Instances	Remove
Workflow1 Version 1.0.0.0	0	○	◉	○
Workflow1 Version 2.0.0.0	0	◉	○	○

| OK | Cancel |

Figure 12.5   By deploying a 2.0.0.0 version of the workflow, all running instances of 1.0.0.0 will dehydrate without error when they resume execution. Users can no longer start new instances of version 1.0.0.0.

12.3   *Building workflow event receivers*

You can't have a SharePoint workflow book without a discussion of event receivers. You might immediately think you need a workflow when, in fact, an event receiver will do. The main difference between the two is that a workflow is typically long running whereas an event receiver is immediate. Why would you want an event receiver? What if all you want to do is execute a piece of code when a document is deleted. For example, you want with code to archive that document when a user deletes it. This example shows how useful an event receiver can be because a deleting event can trigger your custom code. You could do this with a Visual Studio workflow that has one only activity in it, but that's a lot of overhead for something that an event receiver does with much less effort. Table 12.2 shows more comparisons between workflows and event receivers.

Table 12.2   Comparing event receivers and workflows

Event receivers	Workflows
Immediate execution	Long running
Lives and dies (no state)	Maintains state

Table 12.2 Comparing event receivers and workflows *(continued)*

Event receivers	Workflows
.NET code only	.NET or SharePoint Designer
No human interaction	Typically involves human interaction
Before or after events	Only after events
Executes on sites, features, lists, and list items	Executes on sites, items, and content types.

You can't say one is better than the other. It depends entirely on your business requirements. In addition, when documents are deleted, there are many other events you can respond to. The events fall into six categories, as shown in table 12.3. Each category has a few of the more common events shown in the second column, but note that there are many more events available.

Table 12.3 Event receiver categories

Event category	Common events
List events	Adding or added a new list, field Updating or updated a field
List item events	Adding or added a new list item or document Document checking or checked in or out Adding or added an attachment Deleting or deleted an item or document
List email events	A list received an email
Web events	Deleting or deleted a site collection or site Creating or created a new site collection or site
Feature events	Feature activating or activated, deactivating or deactivated
List workflow events	A workflow is starting or started, postponed, or completed

You'll notice two things in this table. First, there are many events that you can have custom code respond to, and second most events have a before and after (adding or added) event associated with it. As shown in figure 12.6, *before events* happened *before* the change is committed to the SharePoint content database. This is helpful when you want to cancel a change before it is saved. The event receiver for when a site is being deleted is a good example. Before the site is deleted, you could do some additional processing such as backing it up.

To demonstrate how to build an event receiver, you're going to use the workflow events as an example. (After all, this is a book about workflows.) Table 12.3 shows that there are four events under the list workflow events category. You can respond to when a workflow is starting, started, postponed, and completed. To keep the example simple, let's write an event receiver that creates an announcement when a new calendar event is created.

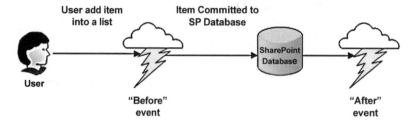

Figure 12.6   Events typically have a before and an after event corresponding to when the event happens in relation to when the source is committed to the database.

Start by creating a new project in Visual Studio 2010. You'll notice under the Share-Point tab that there's a new project template called Event Receiver (figure 12.7). You can use this template to create any of the previously mentioned event receivers.

After you create the project, you'll get a dialog menu asking you to specify the URL of the site where you want to deploy and unit-test your event receiver and if you want to choose a full-trust (farm) or sandboxed solution. Specify the URL and, then, the farm solution because our code example requires full trust. Click Next and you'll be prompted to specify the type of event receiver you want to create (figure 12.8). The dropdown will contain the event types for each of the six categories except the feature events category. Feature events are created by right-clicking the feature in the project after it's created. For the announcement example, select the List Workflow Events category.

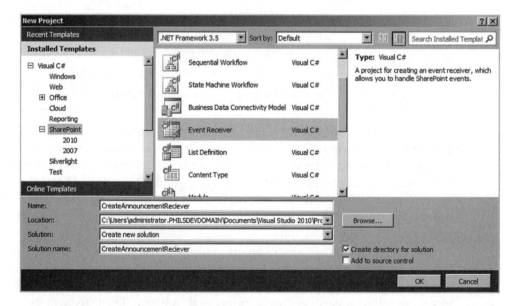

Figure 12.7   Visual Studio 2010 now has a new project template you can use to easily create new event receivers.

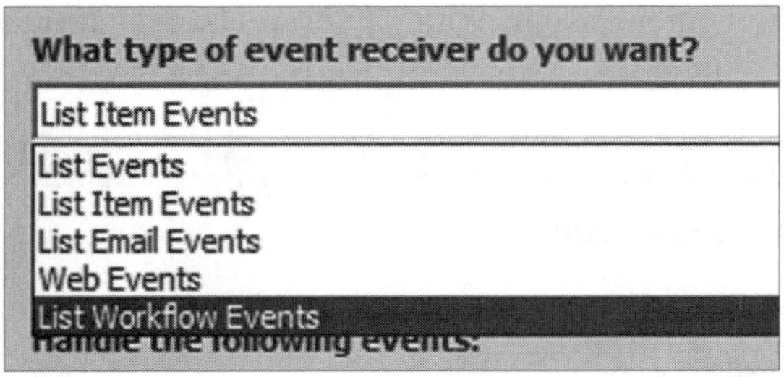

Figure 12.8 There are six main event categories. Five are shown.

After you select the event category, specify the event source. This tells the feature that you're going to create events you want to respond to. Notice in figure 12.9 that you can handle events from announcements, document libraries, and many other list and library options. Select the Calendar source.

Next, you specify which workflow event you want to handle. Specify the A workflow has started event. Now, your code will execute each time a workflow is started on a calendar (figure 12.10).

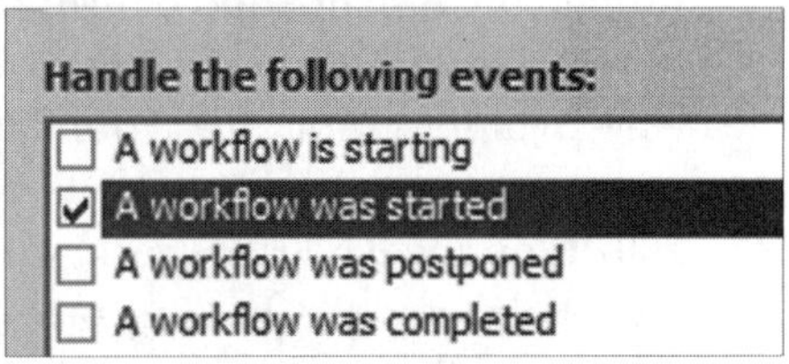

After you create the project, you'll be sent to a method named `Workflow-Started`. This is where you can add your code to create the announcement. Enter the code in listing 12.1 to create the announcement.

First, this code block looks at the activation properties to determine which calendar the event came from ❶. Remember that your source was Calendar, which means any calendar on the site will raise this event when a workflow is started. If you have more than one calendar on the site, you'll want to determine which calendar the event came from.

Next, you elevate the running user's privileges to the service account ❷. You're not sure if the running user has contribute rights on the announcements list, so you elevate his permissions to be

Figure 12.9 You'll need to specify the event source that will raise the event and call your event receiver.

Figure 12.10 After you choose the event source, you need to specify the event you want to respond to. In this case you want to execute your code when a workflow has started.

safe. Next, you create the announcement, assign a title value, and commit the announce-ment to the database ❸.

Listing 12.1 Event receiver that creates an announcement

```
if (properties.ActivationProperties.List.Title == "Main Calendar")
{
    string siteurl = properties.ActivationProperties.Site.Url;

    SPSecurity.RunWithElevatedPrivileges(delegate()
    {
        using (SPSite site = new SPSite(siteurl))
        {
            using (SPWeb web = site.RootWeb)
            {
                SPListItem item = web.Lists["Announcements"].Items.Add();
                item["Title"] = "The workflow has started!";
                item.Update();
            }
        }
    });
}
```

Confirms the calendar ❶

Elevates permissions ❷

Creates announcement ❸

With this code in place, you deploy the solution. Right-click the project name in Visual Studio, and click Deploy. This will deploy the feature and assembly on your *before.* Next, create a new calendar entry and start a workflow on that event. As a result, a new announcement will show up in the announcements list on that site.

12.4 *Pluggable workflow services*

Pluggable workflow services is one of the most highly anticipated new workflow fea-tures for SharePoint 2010. This is because SharePoint 2007 workflows lacked the abil-ity to communicate with the outside world. The most basic scenario is a workflow that needs to go idle and wait for a message from a separate system, like a line of business applications such as customer relationship management (CRM). Another desired technique was for interworkflow communication, when one workflow needs to send a message to another workflow. A third scenario would be a long running process. If you had a calculation or a service call that took thirty minutes to execute, there would be no sense in keeping the workflow instance in memory. It would be better to hydrate the instance and dehydrate it when the process is finished.

All three of those examples were not easily accomplished in SharePoint 2007. Now, Windows Workflow Foundation on the .NET 3.5 Framework has the ability to meet these needs through Workflow Communication Services. Since SharePoint 2007 is on the 3.5 Framework, you'd think it wouldn't have been a problem. Because SharePoint was the hosting provider, there was no class that was provided to easily get at workflow instances and raise events into those instances that the workflow was listening for. This changes in SharePoint 2010, with the introduction of a new class, SPWorkflowExternalDataExchangeService.

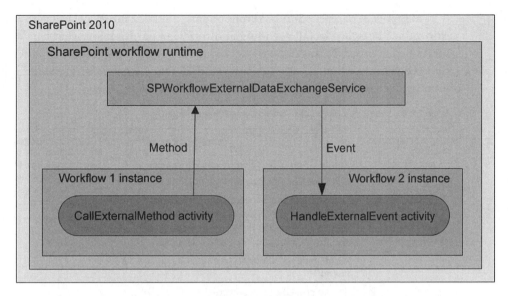

Figure 12.11 Windows Communication Services has become friendly with SharePoint workflows. Using the SharePoint workflow external data exchange service, your workflows can send and receive messages from other workflows or .NET applications.

Just as in Workflow Communication Services, in SharePoint 2010 workflows, you can create a local service that your workflows can use to communicate with each other. Using the CallExternalMethod activity and the HandleExternalEvent activity, Share-Point workflows and .NET applications can send and receive messages to each other (figure 12.11).

Before we get into how to set up a local service that uses the SharePoint external data exchange services, let's talk briefly about the example. The example you're going to build will be a glorified Hello World! example. A workflow is going to say Hello Event Handler! to an event receiver on an announcements list by creating a new announcement. Then, an event receiver is going to say Hello Workflow! back to the workflow.

To accomplish this, the workflow will call into a local service. The local service then creates an announcement in an announcements list. Then, an event receiver responds to the new announcement by raising an event through the local service that the workflow is listening for. This example will demonstrate how a SharePoint workflow can communicate with a .NET application. Follow the steps in table 12.4 to build the Hello World! pluggable workflow service.

Table 12.4 Creating a pluggable workflow service

Action	Steps	Result
Create a new Visual Studio 2010 project.	**1** Open Visual Studio 2010 and create a new sequential work-flow project titled PluggableWorkflowServices and click OK. **2** Type the URL of the site you'll use to debug, click Next, select a Site Workflow, and click Finish.	You have a new Visual Studio project with a Site workflow.

A local service is composed of two components, a service interface and a service class. The service interface lets the sending and receiving parties know what type of data to send to each other. This is done by declaring a method the sender calls and an event the receiver listens for. To tap into the external data exchange services, the interface must be declared with an ExternalDataExchange attribute.

Table 12.4   Creating a pluggable workflow service (continued)

Action	Steps	Result

Create a new class to use for our local service and add our interface.	1 Create a new class titled HelloWorldService.cs.
	2 Add the following using statements to the class file:
	`using System.Workflow.Activities;`
	`using Microsoft.SharePoint;`
	`using Microsoft.SharePoint.Workflow;`
	`using System.Workflow.Runtime;`
	3 Above the HelloWorldService class, add the following interface:
	`[ExternalDataExchange]`
	`public interface IHelloWorldService`
	`{`
	`    event EventHandler<HelloWorldEventArgs>`
	`        HelloWorkflow;`
	`    void HelloHost(string message);`
	`}`
	The HelloHost method is called by the workflow via the CallExternalMethod activity, in the example, which creates the announcement. The event receiver then executes and invokes the HelloWorkflow event that the workflow is listening for through the HandleExternalEvent activity.
		A new file named HelloWorldService.cs that contains your local service interface is created.

Extend the HelloWorldService class, and add the HelloHost method and the event defined in the interface.	1 Make the HelloWorldService class extend Microsoft. SharePoint.Workflow.SPWorkflowExternalDataExchangeService. 2 Make the HelloWorldService class implement the IHelloWorldService interface. 3 Add listing 12.2 into the HelloWorldService class.	The HelloWorldService class is extended and implements the interface you built in the previous step.

Listing 12.2   HelloHost local service method

```
public event EventHandler<HelloWorldEventArgs> HelloWorkflow;        ◁── Declares
public void HelloHost(string message)                    ◁──┐          ❶ the event
{                                                            │
    SPWeb web = this.CurrentWorkflow.ParentWeb;    ❷  Defines the
    SPList list = web.Lists["Announcements"];          method
    SPListItem item = list.Items.Add();        ◁── ❸ Adds a new announcement
    item["Title"] = message;
    item["Instance"] = WorkflowEnvironment.WorkflowInstanceId.ToString();
    item.Update();
}
```

In the `HelloHost` method you want to create two things, the event handler ❶ and the method ❷ that is defined in the interface. Within the method, you're creating the new announcement ❸ and passing the workflow's instance ID into the Instance column within the announcement. This is how the event receiver will know to which workflow to send a message.

After you add listing 12.1 and the code found in the second and third actions, you may notice that the compiler cannot find the class for HelloWorldEventArgs. This class you have yet to define, but it will allow your event receiver to send a custom message to your workflow.

Table 12.4 Creating a pluggable workflow service *(continued)*

Action	Steps	Result

Add the code that will allow passing a custom set of event arguments.	Add the following code below the HelloWorldService class:
	
	`[Serializable]`
	`public class HelloWorldEventArgs :`
	`ExternalDataEventArgs`
	`{`
	`    public HelloWorldEventArgs(Guid id) :`
	`base(id) { }`
	`    public string Answer;`
	`}`
		Your local service will now be set up to pass a custom set of event arguments.

Notice that your custom arguments take two values, a GUID that will store the workflow instance ID and the Answer, which is the message the event receiver will pass to the workflow. This message will eventually be logged into the workflow's History List.

There's one more thing you must do before your local service is complete and you can build the workflow and the event receiver. You need to add three more methods to satisfy interface requirements in SPExternalDataExchangeService.

Table 12.4 Creating a pluggable workflow service *(continued)*

Action	Steps	Result
Add listing 12.3 within the HelloWorldService class.		The HelloWorldService class now satisfies all interface requirements.

Listing 12.3 SPExternalExchangeService interface methods

```
public override void CallEventHandler(Type type, string eventName,
   object[] parameters, SPWorkflow workflow, string identity,
   System.Workflow.Runtime.IPendingWork handler, object item)
{
   switch (eventName)              ⟵❶ Switches event type        Creates ❷
   {                                                              args with
      case "HelloWorkflow":                                     instance ID
         var args = new HelloWorldEventArgs(workflow.InstanceId);  ⟵
```

```
            args.Answer = parameters[0].ToString();
            this.HelloWorkflow(null, args);
            break;
        }
    }
}

public override void CreateSubscription(
    MessageEventSubscription subscription)
{ throw new NotImplementedException(); }

public override void DeleteSubscription(Guid subscriptionId)
{ throw new NotImplementedException(); }
```

The CallEventHandler method is called each time an event is requested in the local service. First, you check to see which event is being requested ❶. If it's your HelloWorkflow event, you create a new HelloWorldEventArgs instance and pass in the workflow's instance ID ❷. This will let the event know which workflow to invoke the event with. Next, you pass in the message string ❸ from the event receiver and, last, invoke the event ❹.

With the local service now complete, you can start building the workflow and the event receiver that interfaces with this service. Continue the steps in table 12.4 to build the workflow and the event receiver.

Table 12.4   Creating a pluggable workflow service *(continued)*

Action	Steps	Result
Configure the CallExternal-Method activity.	1 Within Workflow1, add the CallExternalMethod activity. 2 In the properties of the activity, click the ellipsis next to the InterfaceType property, specify the IHelloWorldService interface, and click OK: 3 Change the MethodName property to HelloHost. 4 Change the message property to Hello Event Handler!	The CallExternal-Method activity is configured to call the HelloHost method through the local service.
Configure the HandleExternal-Event activity.	1 Add the HandleExternalMethod activity below the CallExternalEvent activity. 2 Within the properties of the activity, click the ellipsis next to the InterfaceType property, specify the IHelloWorldService interface, and click OK. 3 Change the EventName property to be HelloWorkflow. **NOTE:** This is the only event the workflow will listen for. The event receiver must invoke this event to communicate with the workflow. 4 Bind the e property to a new field handleArgs by clicking the ellipses and choosing Field in the Bind to New Member tab and clicking OK.	The HandleExternal-Event activity is now set up to listen and wait for the HelloWorkflow event.

Table 12.4   Creating a pluggable workflow service *(continued)*

Action	Steps	Result
	5 Go to the code view of the workflow and take the = new ... off the end of the handleArgs property so it looks like this: **1** ```public HelloWorldEventArgs handleArgs;```	
Configure a Log to History List activity.	**1** Below the HandleExternalEvent activity, add a LogToHistoryList activity. **2** Right-click the LogToHistoryList activity and choose Generate Handlers. **3** Within the activity's MethodInvoking method, add the following line of code to write the event receiver's message to the history: ```logToHistoryListActivity1.HistoryDescription = handleArgs.Answer;```	After the HelloWorkflow event is raised, the workflow is configured to log the message sent from the event receiver to the workflow history list.
Add an Instance column to an announcements list.	**1** Find or create the announcements list on the site on which you're unit-testing and, under List Settings, click Create Column. **2** Type a name of Instance, choose a Single Line of Text column type, and click OK.	The HelloHost method saves a GUID into the Instance column in the announcements list, which is configured with that column.
Add a new Event Receiver to the project.	**1** Right-click the project, choose Add > New Item, and select the Event Receiver item. **2** Give the receiver the name of AnnouncementsReceiver and click Add. **3** Choose List Item Events, Announcements, An item was added and click Finish: **What type of event receiver do you want?** List Item Events **What item should be the event source?** Announcements **Handle the following events:** ☐ A file is being moved ☑ An item was added ☐ An item was updated **4** Add listing 12.4 in the ItemAdded method of the receiver.	The event receiver is configured to fire when an announcement is created and to invoke the HelloWorkflow event on the workflow instance found in the Instance column.

Listing 12.4   ItemAdded event receiver method

```
if (properties.ListTitle == "Announcements")
{
    Guid instance = new Guid(properties.ListItem["Instance"].ToString());   <─┐
    string answer = "Hello Workflow!";
                                                    Grabs workflow instance ID ❶
```

```
SPWorkflowExternalDataExchangeService.RaiseEvent(
    properties.Web, instance, typeof(IHelloWorldService),
        "HelloWorkflow", new object[] { answer });
}
```

Invokes
HelloWorkflow
❷ event

This listing first grabs the workflow's instance ID out of the Instance column and sets it to a GUID ❶. This GUID is passed as a parameter into the RaiseEvent method ❷, which is how the RaiseEvent method knows to which workflow to send the message. Other parameters of interest are the SharePoint site where the workflow is running, the event to invoke (HelloWorld event), and your message to the workflow, Hello Workflow! That last parameter is an object array so you can load that up with any serializeable object you think the workflow needs.

Before you test, register your local service with the SharePoint workflow runtime. You do that by adding an entry into the web.config. Follow this last step to register your service.

Table 12.4 Creating a pluggable workflow service (*continued*)

Action	Steps	Result

Register the HelloWorldService with the SharePoint workflow runtime.	**1** Open your web application's web.config under c:\inetpub\wwwroot\wss\virtual directories\ (plus the appropriate web application's unique folder name)
	
	2 Find the <WorkflowServices> element.
	
	3 Add the following WorkflowService in the WorkflowServices element (all on one line and note that you'll need to change the PublicKeyToken to your assembly's token):
	
	`<WorkflowService`
	`Assembly="PluggableWorkflowServices,`
	`Version=1.0.0.0, Culture=neutral,`
	`PublicKeyToken=c1c16502a94a0846"`
	`Class="PluggableWorkflowServices.`
	`HelloWorldService">`
	`</WorkflowService>`
	
	NOTE: If you find yourself getting an error "The workflow failed to start due to an internal error" when you try to start a workflow, you probably didn't perform the last correctly or the DLL isn't found in the GAC.
		The local service is registered with the SharePoint workflow runtime.

You're *finally* ready to test. Build and deploy your project. Navigate to your SharePoint site and, under View Site Content, click Site Workflows. Start your pluggable workflow. (It should be named PluggableWorkflowServices-Workflow1.) Navigate to the Announcements list and you should see a new announcement titled Hello Event Handler!, as shown in figure 12.12.

Go back to Site Workflow and click the Completed status of the workflow titled PluggableWorkflowServices-Workflow1. You should see the event receiver's response Hello Workflow! (figure 12.13).

SharePoint 2010 Workflows in Action ▸ Announcements ▸ All items ▾

Use this list to track upcoming events, status updates or other team news.

I Like It

Home			Search this site...	

Libraries	☐	📎	Title	Instance
Site Pages			Hello Event Handler! ▨ NEW	7fddd034-d0e6-4bfa-a9b6-065eec8f46b9
Shared Documents				

➕ Add new announcement

Figure 12.12 The workflow wrote to an announcements list, and an event receiver on that will respond by calling back into the hydrated workflow instance.

Workflow Information

Initiator: System Account
Started: 4/10/2010 11:57 PM   **Status:** Completed
Last run: 4/10/2010 11:57 PM

Tasks

The following tasks have been assigned to the participants in this workflow. Click a task to edit it. You can also view these tasks in the list Tasks.

☐	☐ Assigned To	Title	Due Date	Status	Related Content	Outcome

There are no items to show in this view of the "Tasks" list. To add a new item, click "New".

Workflow History

The following events have occurred in this workflow.

☐	Date Occurred	Event Type	☐ User ID	Description	Outcome
	4/10/2010 11:57 PM	Comment	System Account	Hello Workflow!	

Figure 12.13 The event receiver has called back into the hydrated workflow instance, and the workflow logged the string message received from the event receiver.

12.5 *SharePoint workflow object model*

The SharePoint workflow object model falls within the Microsoft.SharePoint.Workflow namespace. You can leverage this object model to programmatically work with your workflows. You can start and stop a workflow, check a workflow's status or history, or retrieve a list of tasks associated with a workflow. This section will provide an introduction into the workflow object model and some common uses. Reference the complete SDK on www.msdn.microsoft.com. The namespace has many classes, but the following are the top two:

- *SPWorkflow*—This class represents a workflow instance on an item or site. It can be used to see who started the workflow (Author property) and get the state of the workflow (InternalState property).

- *SPWorkflowManager*—This is the class with many helper methods that you can use with workflows. The most useful methods include the following:
  - *GetItemActiveWorkflows*
  - *GetItemWorkflows*
  - *GetWorkflowTasks*
  - *RemoveWorkflowFromListItem*
  - *StartWorkflow*

Although these classes are most useful, they work in concert with a host of other classes in the same namespace. Table 12.5 shows a list of classes and their SKD descriptions.

Table 12.5   Microsoft.SharePoint.Workflow main classes and SDK definitions

Main classes	SDK Definitions
SPWorkflow	A workflow instance that has run or is currently running on an item or site.
SPWorkflowActivationProperties	Represents the initial properties of the workflow instance as it starts, such as the user who added the workflow and the list and item to which the workflow was added.
SPWorkflowAssociation	Represents the association of a workflow template with a specific list, content type, or site that contains members that return custom information about that workflow's association with the specific list or content type.
SPWorkflowAssociationCollection	Represents the workflow associations on a SharePoint list or site.
SPWorkflowCollection	A collection of the workflow instances that have run or are currently running on a list item or site.
SPWorkflowFilter	Represents the filter criteria to apply to a workflow or workflow task collections, such as to whom the workflow is assigned and the workflow state.
SPWorkflowManager	Contains members that enable you to centrally control the workflow templates and instances across a site collection.
SPWorkflowModification	Represents a workflow modification.
SPWorkflowModificationCollection	Represents the collection of workflow modifications that are currently in scope for the workflow instance.
SPWorkflowTask	Represents a single workflow task for a given workflow instance.
SPWorkflowTaskCollection	Represents a collection of the workflow tasks for a workflow instance.
SPWorkflowTaskProperties	Represents the properties of a workflow task.
SPWorkflowTemplate	Represents a workflow template currently deployed on the SharePoint site and contains members you can use to get or set information about the template, such as the instantiation data and the history and task lists for the template.
SPWorklowTemplateCollection	The collection of workflow templates currently deployed on a site.

Now that you have a high level understanding of classes, let's take a look at a few common uses of the workflow object model. The following code snippets are five common examples.

The first snippet shows starting a workflow programmatically:

```
foreach (SPWorkflowAssociation association in
    splistitem.ParentList.WorkflowAssociations)
{
    if (association.AllowManual)
    {
        splistitem.Web.Site.WorkflowManager.StartWorkflow(
            splistitem, association, association.AssociationData, true);
    }
}
```

The code in this snippet first gets all the workflows associated with the list. This could easily be a content type or a site for site workflows. The SPWorkflowAssociation object contains properties such as the workflow's start options. Next, the statement checks if manual starts are allowed through the UI. If so, it starts the workflow through the workflow manager's `StartWorkflow` method.

The second snippet shows how to stop a workflow programmatically:

```
SPWorkflow workflow = splistitem.Workflows[1];
web.Site.WorkflowManager.RemoveWorkflowFromListItem(workflow);
```

Stopping a workflow is simple. Use the workflow manager and call the `RemoveWorkflowFromListItem` method and pass the workflow you want to terminate. The workflow manager is again useful to retrieve the list of active workflows on an item, as seen in the following snippet:

```
SPWorkflowCollection runningWFs =
    web.Site.WorkflowManager.GetItemActiveWorkflows(splistitem);

Console.WriteLine("Names of Running Workflows:");

foreach (SPWorkflow workflow in runningWFs)
{
    Console.WriteLine(workflow.ParentAssociation.Name);
}
```

The workflow manager's `GetItemActiveWorkflows` method retrieves a collection of workflows representing all the running workflows on that item. The workflow collection on the item would contain all the workflows, regardless of whether they are currently running or not. Some may have completed or faulted. You can optionally use GetItemWorkflows and pass in an SPWorkflowFilter parameter that specifies an SPWorkflowState object. By using the filter and the state, you could retrieve only orphaned workflows, for example.

With an active workflow, you may want to get the workflow's tasks. The following snippet shows how to do this:

```
SPWorkflow workflow = splistitem.Workflows[1];

Console.WriteLine("Titles of Workflow's Tasks:");
foreach (SPWorkflowTask task in workflow.Tasks)
```

```
{
    Console.WriteLine(task["Title"].ToString());
}
```

Every workflow's Tasks property is an SPWorkflowTaskCollection object. You can iterate through each workflow task to retrieve all the tasks that the workflow has created. This can optionally be done through the workflow manager's `GetWorkflowTasks` method, and you can also pass in an SPWorkflowFilter parameter again to filter the tasks. The counterpart of tasks is the workflow's history.

The following snippet shows how to retrieve a workflow's history programmatically:

```
SPWorkflow workflow = splistitem.Workflows[1];

SPList historyList = workflow.HistoryList;

SPQuery query = new SPQuery();
query.Query =
    "<OrderBy><FieldRef Name=\"ID\"/></OrderBy>" +
    "<Where><Eq><FieldRef Name=\"WorkflowInstance\"/>" +
    "<Value Type=\"Text\">{"+ workflow.InstanceId.ToString() +"}</Value>" +
    "</Eq></Where>";

SPListItemCollection historyItems = historyList.GetItems(query);
foreach (SPListItem historyItem in historyItems)
{
    Console.WriteLine(historyItem["Description"].ToString());

}
```

Every workflow has a HistoryList property that points to the SPList object in which the workflow's history is stored. That list can be queried to get the history items. The querying is done using the SPQuery object (as shown previously) or LINQ to SharePoint. Enter the CAML query and pass the workflow's instance ID to get only that workflow's history items. The history is stored in the Description column of each SPListItem that is returned.

12.6   *Summary*

Any programmer will tell you that exception handling and debugging code is important. This is no exception with Visual Studio SharePoint workflows. Fortunately, your workflows can use the HandleFault activity and can be debugged like any other .NET application, so the learning curve should be minimal. Versioning workflows is sometimes new to developers. When a workflow is persisted to disk (hydrated), subsequent changes to the workflow's assembly can cause problems. If you change the assembly while the workflow is hydrated (saved in the database), there's no guarantee that, when the workflow dehydrated, it will match the construct of the new assembly. If it doesn't, the workflow will break. Instead, a new version of the workflow must be published.

SharePoint 2010 offers new event capabilities to developers. They include new workflow event receivers and an easier ability to send and receive events with applications external to the workflow. External communication is handled through the new pluggable workflow services feature.

Under all these excellent SharePoint workflow features resides a workflow object model that a developer may sometimes want to use. Using the SPWorkflowManager object, for example, you can programmatically start and stop a workflow. You can also do other tasks such as retrieve the running workflows on a document or, perhaps, look up the tasks and history associated with a workflow instance.

This chapter isn't the end of what you can read on workflows. As mentioned in chapter 1, SharePoint workflows are built on Windows Workflow Foundation. This book discusses the most critical areas for SharePoint workflow developers, but there's a whole world underneath the SharePoint surface. In that sense, this book is only the beginning.

index

RELATED MANNING TITLES

Silverlight 4 in Action
Silverlight 4, ViewModel Pattern,
and WCF RIA Services
by Pete Brown

    ISBN:978-1-935182-37-5
    800 pages, $49.99
    September 2010

Azure in Action
by Chris Hay and Brian H. Prince

    ISBN: 978-1-935182-48-1
    488 pages, $44.99
    October 2011

jQuery in Action, Second Edition
by Bear Bibeault and Yehuda Katz

    ISBN: 978-1-935182-32-0
    488 pages, $44.99
    June 2010

The Cloud at Your Service
The when, how, and why
of enterprise cloud computing
by Jothy Rosenberg and Arthur Mateos

    ISBN: 978-1-935182-52-8
    272 pages, $29.99
    November 2010

For ordering information go to www.manning.com